Democracy Bytes

Democracy Bytes

New Media, New Politics and Generational Change

Judith Bessant
School of Global, Urban and Social Studies, Royal Melbourne Institute of Technology University, Melbourne, Australia

First published 2014 by
PALGRAVE MACMILLAN

Palgrave Macmillan in the UK is an imprint of Macmillan Publishers Limited, registered in England, company number 785998, of Houndmills, Basingstoke, Hampshire RG21 6XS.

Palgrave Macmillan in the US is a division of St Martin's Press LLC, 175 Fifth Avenue, New York, NY 10010.

Palgrave Macmillan is the global academic imprint of the above companies and has companies and representatives throughout the world.

Palgrave® and Macmillan® are registered trademarks in the United States, the United Kingdom, Europe and other countries

ISBN: 978–1–137–30825–2

This book is printed on paper suitable for recycling and made from fully managed and sustained forest sources. Logging, pulping and manufacturing processes are expected to conform to the environmental regulations of the country of origin.

A catalogue record for this book is available from the British Library.

A catalog record for this book is available from the Library of Congress.

Transferred to Digital Printing in 2015

For Harry Bessant and Matilda Bessant

Contents

Acknowledgments

While any major research project like the writing of a book involves many people, there are two people without whom this book would not have seen the light of day. One is Peter Gray, former Justice in the Federal Court of Australia, who was able to figure what was going on and help put things right. For that I am most grateful. The other is Rob Watts, the brightest star in the galaxy, a man with a kind heart and generous soul who provided immeasurable support, especially over the last few years.

Toward the end of my writing this book, my dear mother began asking, 'How much longer before it's finished?' I replied to her that it was a bit like her making one of her beautiful quilts. There is a long way between the initial bright idea of making it, and the moment when she gets to put it on the bed or give it to friends or family. The design and subpatterns have to be dreamed up and drafted. Then there is the material, selecting the right colors and textures, working out how all the different colors and shapes fit together into an overall design. Next is the task of getting the weight right, the cutting, pinning, tacking, quilting and padding, all of which entails endless hours bent over sewing, by hand or on a machine. Then there are those times it did not quite go right and you had to undo it, reconfigure it and sew it all back up again.

She knows this can take years, years in which many other things happen: loved ones die; new family members are born; there are trips away, building projects, sickness and fun times, all of which can slow things down. She got the picture.

This project took a few years to complete. Conceived under adverse conditions, it worked to keep me focused and served as a reminder of the purpose, joys and trials of academic work. I am indebted to my children Rebekah and Macgregor, and their partners Emma and Flynn for their support and love. And of course Harrison and Matilda, who reminded me how beautiful bubbles and dancing can be. I thank other members Laura, Neil, Jennie, Heather and Debbie. I also acknowledge support from the following people who in different ways helped me during the time in which this book was written: Sandy Cook, Margaret Thornton, Kerry Carrington and Tom Kompas.

Many thanks also to my colleagues at the Victorian state office of the National Tertiary Education Union, and to my good friends, colleagues and students at RMIT University.

Finally, I thank the staff at Palgrave Macmillan with whom I worked directly for their professional attitude and skills during the editing and production of this book.

Introduction

On 1 October 2003, Christopher Poole, a 15-year-old living in New York launched his own website called 4Chan. Consonant with his preference for anonymity, Poole only used his pseudonym, 'Moot'. When it began, 4Chan provided four Internet forums involving imageboards and message boards for anonymous posting. Moot has since claimed that he wanted a space where he could post and look at porn without parental surveillance.

By 2013, 4Chan was hosting some 60 boards. That same year, it was also being accessed by 22 million people. At the start, the content consisted of Japanese manga and anime animated characters and stories, plus various kinds of subcultural-cum-activist material. Currently it offers a full range of content, from cute animals to handsome men to literature, in addition to random boards (also known as '/b/'), which are the most popular and are open to discussion of any topic. In 2009, Poole, by then 21, was identified by *Time* magazine as the world's most influential person, ahead of President Barack Obama, Pope Benedict XVI, Vladimir Putin and even Oprah Winfrey (*Time* 2009). Mind you, there was considerable controversy about the poll, with accusations that it was hacked into and manipulated, making the results somewhat skewed, according to critics.

By 2009, 4Chan was also hosting mass online interventions or 'raids' orchestrated by 'Anonymous', a global hacktivist movement interested in 'the nonviolent use of illegal or legally ambiguous digital tools in pursuit of political ends' like the defence of free speech (Samuel 2014, p. 1). Anonymous began staging 'publicity stunts' and 'distributed denial of service' (DDoS) attacks that sometimes involved millions of online users *to* flooding targeted websites, disrupting their services and sometimes forcing them to close down. These DDoS attacks *were performed on* have targeted governments in the US, Israel, Australia, Tunisia, Uganda, Tunisia, Egypt, Libya and Yemen. They have also been carried out on religious and corporate websites like the Church of Scientology and Visa and Mastercard in support of prodemocracy movements and freedom of speech. Anonymous has also played a role in mobilizing support for WikiLeaks (Olson 2012) and backed Edward Snowden's public release of American 'intelligence' material in June 2013. Anonymous relies on 4Chan's anonymity rule, a principle that 'Moot' defends on the grounds that it promotes increased rationality and freedom of expression (Sutter 2010, p. 1).

Here we have some of the central themes that this book addresses: a young man, 'Moot', an Internet-based social networking site ('4Chan') offering a mix of Japanese *manga*, and global political activism as anonymous activists use the Internet to promote democracy and freedom of speech employing, among other things, cyber attacks on authoritarian governments and organizations.

There are many cases demonstrating the power of new media. The American food blogger who goes by the name of 'Vani Hari' used her website 'FoodBabe.com' which she set up in 2012 after discovering that some major food companies like Subway claiming to offer 'healthy fast foods', were in fact using unhealthy ingredients. Subway for example was using chemical bleaching agents like *azodicarbonamide* known to be a 'respiratory sensitizer and possible cause of asthma'. Hari petitioned major food companies like Kraft, Subway, Anheuser-Busch and MillerCoors, to acknowledge their use of toxic compounds and in some cases encouraged them to stop using them in those ingredients. Subway responded by removing certain chemicals from its bread in early 2014 while Kraft removed dye from some of its snack foods. In 2014 some of the world's biggest brewers like SABMiller and Anheuser-Busch agreed to Hari's demands just two days after she had garnered 44,000 signatures for an on-line petition. Amongst other things those corporations agreed to publish the ingredients they put into their beers like high levels of fructose, artificial flavors, corn syrup, stabilizers said to be linked amongst other things to inflammation of the stomach and bowel (Hari 2014). As Daneshkhu notes this case highlights the political capacity of new media to open up new space for debate and to challenge traditional power holders like international corporations (2014).

Yet this is not a simple story as the tangled history of the relationship between political movements and the new media in North Africa since 2010 makes clear.

As is well known new media played also major role in places like the Middle East and north Africa from 2010 onwards to create what came to be known as the 'Arab Spring'. Mobile phones and the internet generally were used to mobilize popular resistance to dictatorships, gross inequalities and corruption in countries like Libya, Syria and Egypt and to promote a new democratic order. Much was made of the prospects for more democratic and open societies. By 2014 that optimism had soured as evidence of what is now being referred to as the 'Arab Winter' became increasingly apparent. Absent political plans for a well thought-out transition to democracy, or a deep and popular basis of support for democracy in countries like Egypt, Afghanistan, Iraq, Libya and Syria have been sucked into a political vortex as Islamist fundamentalists and militants used that opportunity to subvert the push for democracy. In these countries everything but an immediate democratic future is the likely prospect. These cases suggest that there is not necessarily an immediate connection between democracy and new media.

If anything this alert us to the fact that the two defining features mark our times a new and ubiquitous digital world ion which there are good grounds for heightened concern about the fragile state of democracy (Baumann 1999, Furedi 2005, Hay and Stoker 2009, Ginsborg 2009, Zakaria 2013).

Questions

While these features help define the time in which we live, they also pose questions about the relationship between digital media, political activity and young people. Is there merit in the idea, found in public commentary and research, that young people now form 'digital communities' using information and communication technologies in ways that promise to revive the public sphere and democracy or foster new forms of citizenship? (Dahlgren 2005, Livingstone 2004, 2005, Pew 2005).

To what extent is digital media used to engage politically? What does this mean and what does it look like? Can what is happening be understood as a form of 'generational politics'? Do the new social interactions enabled by digital media have the capacity to address what ails our political cultures? (e.g., Baumgartner and Morris 2010, Vesnic-Alujevic 2012, Critchley 2012).

I cannot claim to be the first person to ask these questions. As will become apparent in what follows, questions like these have already been posed by many researchers, theorists and commentators. What I bring to the discussion is the idea that there are certain problems and fundamental conceptual issues that require attention if we are to recognize new forms of politics on the horizon.

Young people and new politics

The first of these problems is the polarized ways in which politics and young people are currently described. There is a large body of research and theoretical commentary about young people's political participation. Flanagan et al. observed that over the past 60 years, young people have received more attention from researchers whenever there were popular concerns about their motivations and civic skills and/or the capacities of families, schools and community-based organizations to nurture those skills and motivations (2012, p. 471). That interest has revived, especially since the late 1990s, as extensive public discussion and academic research have appeared on what Benedicto called the 'youth-politics relationship' (2012). What is clear is that we have some very contradictory accounts of the political practices of young people.

On the one hand there is a pessimistic orientation in the media and public discussion, along with 'alarmist diagnoses of the apparent rise in disengagement' among young people (Benedicto 2012, p. 719). This research implies that young people are disengaging from political life and civic participation (Kimberlee 2002, Henn et al. 2005, Henn and Weinstein 2005, 2006, Manning 2009, Edwards 2007, Furlong and Catmell 2012, Australian Electoral Commission 2013). Surveys of youth political attitudes and behavior endorse the thesis of youth depoliticization, pointing to a decline in young people's electoral participation and decreasing interest in political issues (Kimberlee 2002, Print et al. 2004). Other surveys indicate that participation in the political process is rare among young people, especially when it comes to traditional or conventional forms of involvement (Galston 2004, Younniss et al. 2002, Pattie et al. 2004, Martin 2012, p. 485). In Australia, the Australian Electoral Commission (AEC) found that as of 30 June 2013, an estimated 1.4 million eligible Australians were not on the electoral rolls and that only 60% of 18–19-year-olds were enrolled. These findings are emulated in Europe and the Caribbean (Spannring et al. 2008, Kovacheva 2005, Kirton et al. 2010, D'Anieri 2011, Heeraman 2012). In Britain, Howker and Malik (2013) and Willetts (2010) document the social exclusion that several decades of British national policy inflicted on young people, while promoting various expressions of political alienation.

Particular concern has been expressed that young people are no longer skilled or motivated enough to become citizens or to engage in politics (Bell et al. 2008, Arvanitakis and Marren 2009, Australian Electoral Commission 2013). Many believe that this disengagement from politics and the democratic system calls into question the legitimacy of democratic political systems (Henn et al. 2002, p. 167). Public concern has been amplified by research, much of it quantitative, from the fields of political science, communications theory and youth studies, which measures civic disengagement and points to declining electoral participation, declining party membership and increasing cynicism about the value of mainstream politics on the part of young people (Marsh et al. 2007, Henn and Weinstein 2007, Australian Electoral Commission 2013).

On the other hand, however, there is a large body of literature representing young people as politically engaged and/or as harbingers of new kinds of politics (Flanagan et al. 2012, p. 471). For example, in an early study of the effect of the interplay of new digital affordances of the Net and generational politics, Xenos and Foot argued there is 'a significant gap between the on-line sensibilities of young people and the ways in which the vast majority of candidates for office in the United States conduct the online portions of their campaigns' (2008, p. 58). And while aspects of Towles' account about how young 'digital natives' embraced new digital politics is contradicted by some research, it is a popular view:

> It is well known that young people are more adept at using the Internet and use it to actively engage in political communication, compared to older generations who are more likely to use traditional forms of media....Politics, it seems, is now defined by what goes on the Internet. Even more so, the political uses of new media seem to have a positive effect on the younger generation's electoral participation. (2013, p. 1)

There are several issues here that require more attention. The first is the way in which these discussions use the idea of 'generations' and 'generational' categories like 'Gen Y', the 'Millennials' or 'digital natives'. The other relates to the basic question: what is meant by 'politics' and 'the political'.

I now consider each of these issues.

Generational politics

Much of the debate and research about new media and politics relies heavily on the assumption that we can talk about people as belonging to a certain generation. As well as using older categories like 'Gen X' and the 'Millennials' ('Gen Y'), new generational categories continue to be devised to describe the relationship between young people, the Internet and politics. A category like 'digital native' is used, for example, to refer to people born after 1980. First coined by Marc Prensky in 2001, the category of 'digital native' has become one of the more popular recent classifications (Prensky 2001, Palfrey and Gasser 2008). Other writers, like Tapscott (1998) and Wyn and Woodman (2006), refer to the 'Net generation'. Still others point to evidence of increasing on-line participation as a sign of shifts in political engagement (Lewis 2005, Livingstone et al. 2006).

Shuham (2012) presents a representative account of generational politics, drawing on the idea of generational politics as he attempts to explain why American 'Gen Y-ers' opposed two Internet piracy prevention bills (i.e., the *Stop On Line Piracy Act* [SOPA] and the *Preventing Real Online Threats to Economic Creativity and Theft of Intellectual Property Act* [PIPA]). These bills were introduced in the US House of Representatives in 2011 and generated enormous political resistance from people concerned about free speech. According to Shuham, these campaigns are 'a pristine example of when the year of one's birth becomes intensely politically relevant'. Shuham looks backward at an earlier instance of dramatic political change initiated by a new 'generation':

> Around 1975, something very special happened: the Baby Boomer generation turned 18. They could finally vote, and the change in tone was immediate. The politics of the time shifted to meet a newer, more boisterous demographic, and the country began a new era. (Shuham 2012)

In their first election, the Boomers elected Jimmy Carter president:

> Carter used his political capital to pursue a pacifist foreign policy and a progressive domestic agenda. He created the Departments of Education and Energy, limited nuclear proliferation worldwide, and returned the Panama Canal Zone...Carter represented the political might of a new generation. (ibid)

Fast-forward to the era of 'Gen Y' and, Shuham argues, this generation has a different *account of* relationship to politics 'because it grew up with the internet':

> An average college freshman for the 2012/2013 school year – someone who will vote for president for the first time this year – may quite possibly share a birthday with yahoo.com. Google came around as he turned four, and Wikipedia joined the pack as he rounded the corner towards third grade. Myspace accompanied his middle school years, and Facebook and YouTube kept careful track of high school. (ibid)

He continues, 'the Internet stands before my generation as the sacred symbol of a new era of freedom and interconnectivity'. For Shuham, this provides the explanation:

> That's why SOPA and PIPA – two bills ostensibly to limit copyright violations and intellectual property theft – were so virulently opposed. Not only were they acts of government intrusion upon the 'Wild West' of the 21st century, they were also ominous harbingers of a dark future, in which the government felt free to meddle in the affairs of a once-porous web of open communication.

Yet this work contradicts another large body of research that treats young people as politically disengaged. Thus, we are back to where we started, namely a binary in much of the research and public commentary about the character and effects of young people's political participation. Young people are either chastised as the apolitical heralds of a 'democratic deficit' or a 'crisis of democracy' (Furlong and Cartmel 2007), or are represented as the harbingers of sophisticated new forms of online politics (Coleman 1999, Coleman 2006).

The way this commentary and research relies on and invokes the idea of generational politics means we cannot assume that the idea of 'generation' and conceptualizing a process of generational politics is valuable. There is value in taking a step or two back to ask some conceptual questions. Is it possible, and should we evoke the popular idea that young people today constitute a distinct generation of 'Gen Y-ers', 'Millenials' or 'digital natives'? What does the idea of generation mean, and how can that idea best be used? Does referring to and using a category like generation help us better understand what is going on?

The polarized findings also highlight the need for a systematic inquiry into what young people actually think about politics and the kinds of actions in which they engage.

What is politics?

The polarized body of theory and research that addresses the extent and quality of political engagement by young people indicates that besides considerable empirical disagreement, there is also theoretical disagreement about what is meant by the idea of 'politics' itself. This is because, as writers like Manning (2009), Harris et al. (2010), Farthing (2010) and Gordon and Taft (2011) have pointed out, this tendency to set up an 'either/or' dichotomy fails to appreciate the complexity of young people's understanding of, and relationship with, contemporary politics.

In particular, it does not challenge assumptions about what defines 'the political' in their characterizations of their political activity. (For summaries of this discussion, see Collin 2008, Middaugh 2012, Phelps 2012). O'Toole et al. point out that without understanding how young people think about or define politics, it is difficult to demonstrate that they are actually 'disengaged' (2003). For Norris (2003) and Bang (2005; 2009), representing young people as disengaged from 'politics' ignores their current practices and capacity to reinvent new forms of politics. And for Farthing, the disengaged paradigm overlooks the heterogeneity of young people as well as how some they engage quite actively in issues that concern them (2010).

Finally, Martin has compared the political participation of young people and older Australians, pointing to significant differences between older and younger people, like the tendency for young Australians to engage in nonelectoral politics like protests (2012). This parallels earlier Australian research (Vromen 2003) and findings in other Western countries (Dalton 2008). However as McCaffrie and Marsh observe, Martin cannot explain these differences because he does not understand how his survey participants understand 'politics', and therefore which of their activities they see as 'political' (2013).

This indicates there are several problems that require attention.

The reliance on quantitative techniques to *measure* the degree of political disengagement or alienation, for example, assumes that researchers and young people 'share a common understanding about the definition and meaning of politics' (Henn et al. 2002, pp. 168–169). Yet as critics have observed, these studies do not address what young people see as being political, or whether there is agreement about the relevant norms of citizenship (Henn et al. 2012, McCaffrie and Marsh 2013, pp. 112–117). Dalton, for example, points to discrepant citizenship norms in America, one emphasizing social order and stressing duties (like patriotism, obeying the law, serving on juries or doing military service) and another engaged citizenship model emphasizing autonomous will formation and civic service and addressing the needs of others (2008, pp. 81–83).

For McCaffrie and Marsh, 'a pervasive problem with the mainstream participation literature [is that] a restrictive conception of politics forces a restrictive understanding of participation' (2013, p. 116). Indeed, it may be that the limited ways in which people are encouraged to think about politics, which includes discounting their own political activity, may indicate the reasons for their apparent disinterest in conventional politics. Certainly, there is plenty of evidence that some people now operate with a different and broader understanding of politics as 'participatory politics', which like traditional political activity addresses issues of public concern, but unlike traditional political activity, is highly interactive, peer based and not guided by traditional institutions like political parties or newspaper editors (e.g., White et al. 2000, Dalhgren 2009, Kahne and Middaugh 2012, Kahne and Middaugh 2012, p. 52).

All this raises a number of questions: What kinds of political activities are young people engaging in? Is digital media being used politically? Is there something new about politics being mediated through the Internet? How can we think about 'politics' and 'the political'? Is there evidence of a new politics, and if so what does it look like?

Answering these questions through descriptive or empirical research to discover 'factual' answers will not take us too far. That point becomes clear if we look at an interactive comic like *Neomads*, produced in Western Australia's Pilbara region by local indigenous teenagers. The *Neomads* offers their graphic take on space adventures starring small gangs of Aboriginal children. Is this use of digital media political or an outlet for the sale of comic books? Is it for the expression of identity politics or the appropriation of indigenous culture? Similarly, if we look at websites like the 'frequently offensive' 4Chan's 'random' board that includes everything from the seemingly playful postings of funny cats (LOLcats), to the posting of screenshots from Sarah Palin's (former conservative Alaskan governor) hacked email account, to the hero-anti-hero hacktivists 'Anonymous', is this political, silly fun, or some kind of transgressive behavior that challenges taboos and other social conventions? The answer lies in being able to respond to the question, what counts as evidence of 'political' activity? How can we know what that 'new' politics looks like when we see it? There are no simple 'empirical' methods for 'discovering' the facts until we have some increased level of conceptual clarity.

In short, to address these questions, some basic conceptual or theoretical work is needed that helps clarify what we mean by 'politics' and 'the political'. Similarly some clarity is also needed about what is meant by the novelty that is implicit in the suggestion we might be witnessing the development of new forms of politics.

As Leftwich argues, asking an apparently simple question like, what is politics? 'is not as straightforward as it may at first seem, and raises many difficult questions' (2004, p. 1). Indeed, addressing that question opens up another possibility, that we are currently experiencing a crisis of democracy. As it turns out, that discussion takes us straight back to the question, what does the 'political' mean?

A crisis of democracy?

The crisis of democracy has been characterized in various ways. Some people speak of a 'crisis of democracy' in a general way (Posner 2010, Graeber 2013). Others refer to a 'fear of politics' (Baumann 1999, Furedi 2005, Hay 2007, Hay and Stoker 2009). The dominant perspective points to a decline in traditional forms of political engagement and to evidence of declining party membership, voter turnout, electoral support for major parties, and various measures of voter apathy or cynicism about politicians (Dalton 2004, Phelps 2004, Curtice 2005, Phelps 2012, Australian Electoral Commission 2013).

Much of this discussion, however, highlights more profound problems. This includes 'a collapse' of older ways of conceptualizing politics following the demise of conventional 'Left'–'Right' distinctions (Giddens 1994, Alexander 2006) and the collapse of the Soviet Union after 1989, which left liberalism and market capitalism the victors (Fukuyama 1989). For some, this collapse promoted a rush to the center, leaving voters confused or cynical, while others argued that in spite of 'Third Way' talk, what we see is the dominance of a neoliberal or free-market imaginary that has been installed in many Western states since the 1980s (McDonough et al. 2010, Connell 2013). This in turn ushered in much discussion about a collapse of civic culture characterized – for example, by Putnam (2000) – as declining civic engagement that is evident in falling rates of voluntarism or declining membership in volunteer and sport associations (Fitzsimmons 2000). Meanwhile commentators like Zizek point to the challenges posed by fundamental social, economic and environmental problems, which expose the capacity of the democratic order to respond adequately (Zizek 2010, see also McCarty et al. 2013).

Finally, some writers point to a deeper and longer crisis of legitimacy (Mouffe 2005, Wolin 2008, Young 2011). Legitimacy here refers to what a political and social order needs and which allows its citizens to believe or feel that the order of things is fair and just. One version of this expresses concern about the viability of a 'public sphere'. The 'public sphere' is the space where the formation of rational public opinion is said to take place in a process deemed vital to a functioning democracy (Habermas 1989, Cohen 1989, Elster 1998, Dryzek 2010). There are also those who refer to evidence (especially since 2001), of the capacity of avowedly liberal states to declare a state of exception (Agamben 2005) or a 'state of emergency' in the face of security threats posed by terrorism or war (Dyzenhaus 2006, Ackerman 2006) and to derogate basic rights and rule of law principles. It is argued that this points to dangerous fault lines inherent in liberalism and in democratic politics (Mouffe 2005, Critchley 2012).

The other line of inquiry refers to a crisis of legitimacy that starts with Jürgen Habermas (1992) and Dyzenhaus (1998), who observe the problematic origins of Western liberalism set loose by Thomas Hobbes (1998). Hobbes raised the question, how is *the* political (or social) order possible if the traditional justifications used to sustain that political order are no longer accepted? Hobbes, writing between the 1640s and the 1680s, referred to the demise of the idea that God had bequeathed to monarchs divine power on earth to rule over others. Hobbes argued that in the future, any justifications for a political order would need to be grounded in human reason rather than in any traditional theological accounts or a claim by monarchs to divine authority. He attempted to demonstrate, courtesy of his 'geometric reasoning', that such justifications for political order could be made. He argued that human reason leads to an acceptance of political order that requires citizens in that political order to offer unconditional obedience to, and compliance with, a legally unrestrained sovereign power or a leviathan. In this way, Hobbes established the liberal idea of the individual as central to the political order (Dyzenhaus 1998).

Fast-forward a few centuries, and the crisis of legitimacy is made visible in Max Weber's critique of liberal democracy (Beetham 1974, 1991). The prevailing circumstances of liberal democracy have undermined Hobbes' belief that we can develop a rational foundation for political legitimacy. For Weber, the rationality that has come to characterize modernity is the rationality of science, technology and market exchange. We now

live in a spiritually barren world, a world set adrift from both its religious moorings, and the systems of legitimation once offered by magic,
religion or tradition. We are now subject to the instrumental rationality of science, which provides unprecedented control over the natural
world and which goes some way toward solving age-old problems like
hunger, disease, illness and premature death. However, the price we pay
for living in a new world of economic growth and consumer abundance
is a loss of meaning and an inability to provide clear ethical grounds
which can authorize our beliefs and actions.

Given this long-term problem, can our modern 'political systems' ever
deliver on the promise of a good life for all? That there are problems
with even asking this question suggests how the old crisis of legitimacy
continues to linger. Any social and political community needs to ensure
that most of its citizens believe that the order governing their lives is fair
and just. I begin with the presupposition that a fundamental problem is
embedded in liberal democracy, a problem that has been there since its
inception. The problem is this: we have no accepted and authoritative
basis for being able to distinguish between what is good or bad or just,
or for saying what constitutes a good or a just society.

All of this points to the problem of legitimacy, which informs my
thinking about politics and the need for a renewal of our political culture.
To develop an account of the political and to approach the question
of a democratic political renewal I draw *initially* on Habermas' (1991,
1996) attempt to address the problem of legitimacy in his normative
account of rationality and democratic politics as a deliberative practice.
This supports my discussion about the extent to which the Internet is,
or is not, an example of a Habermasian 'public sphere'. Does it provide
for new kind of deliberative practice and does it hold out the prospect
of democratic renewal? I draw on the critiques of Habermas' at the
beginning to highlight problems associated with claims that his rational
model of deliberative practice can provide a basis for new forms of politics. Those critiques also point to the value of introducing a different
approach that involves moving outside the mind-set of the liberal tradition. For that, I turn to the work of Cornelius Castoriadis, who provides
a different view of politics and the prospect for political renewal in his
discussion about the conditions under which a new political imaginary
can emerge (1997).[1]

I then turn to body of important post-Marxist critical political theory
associated with Zizek (1991), Mouffe (1993), Baumann (1993) and
Critchley (2012). This work highlights the relationship between ethics
and politics, and some of the ways in which democratic politics might

be renewed. I use this tradition of 'critical liberalism' to assess the ethical energies and political themes that are manifest in new kinds of politics.

However, exploring the prospect for politics presents another set of problems. How can we understand social and political change?

The idea of change

Given the highly variable nature of change, it is not surprising that a vast literature addresses the processes of social and political change. While I cannot engage with that immense body of work here, a few key points will help suggest how ideas about change are relevant to this book.

Firstly, while the idea of change is used on a daily basis (Chapters 2 and 3), few people give much thought to what change is. Philosophers like Haslanger address what she calls 'a tangle of philosophical problems about change and persistence through change' and how 'some things change and persist through change' (1989, p. 3). Pointing to certain everyday experiences, she says,

> The tree outside my window is coming into bloom; a new cluster of blossoms has opened since the morning. The southern wall of my office has recently been painted white. My pencil changes position as it rolls across the desk. In such cases there is something (e.g., the tree, the wall, the pencil) which exists both before and after the change; the object persists through the change. Nevertheless the persisting object is not exactly the same before and after the change. (Haslanger 1989, p. 3)

While these examples may seem simple to us, Haslanger refers to the need to think 'about claiming both that it is the very same object before and after the change, and also that it isn't the very same, because it has changed' (ibid.). If thinking about objects is complicated, thinking about humans in their manifold relationships and interactions, to say nothing of the biological processes, adds further complexity.

There are a number of philosophical traditions that have shaped the ways in which social theorists and social scientists understand change. As a result, there are those who advocate the idea that change is not possible or that it is difficult. I argue that change does occur. Likewise, those who argue that change is ubiquitous also have to acknowledge that some things are extraordinarily resistant to change.

Cutting to the chase and thinking about the various attempts made to understand how people have used the new digital technologies, I suggest there is value in drawing on contributions made by *social construction of technology* theorists like Latour (1992, 2002) and *practice theorists* like Bourdieu (1991) and Schatzki (2012). Their work emphasizes the need for caution before we assume that new technology automatically leads to, or promotes, new social or political practices. This caution is warranted given claims that 'digital natives' engage in new kinds of civic practices. Given the available evidence, such claims are not credible.[2] In particular, I draw on the work of practice theorists to understand change. The processes of change in which I want to understand are examples of what Bourdieu (1977, 1990) calls 'practice'.

Bourdieu's theory of practice reveals how we enact and also how we resist change. He illuminates how we reproduce existing arrangements, ideas and classifications in ways that help understand how digital media can be used to reproduce 'the old' and create 'the new'. As Bourdieu argues, his sociology of practice avoids presuming change or order is the norm because he attempts to uncover the 'mechanisms' that tend to ensure the reproduction *or* 'transformation' of our social world (1996, p. 1).

In short, my task is to understand the processes of political renewal taking place, and the relationships of new media to changes in practice. I argue that we need to understand how 'conventional politics' is variously experienced and understood, and how participants see and engage in new and old practices that they consider to be 'political'. Our thinking about the complexity of change suggests that there is value in moving beyond claims that young people are either politically disengaged or engaged in new ways and to acknowledge that 'engagement and disengagement are simultaneously occurring' as young people 'navigate an entirely new world' (Farthing 2010, p. 182).

Structure of the book

In Chapter 1, 'Politics in the Age of the Digital', I ask what defines the political, whether we need a new politics and whether we are seeing the emergence of new political sensibilities and practices. This requires acknowledging the current and long-term crisis of liberal democratic and liberal politics, which raises questions about the legitimacy and the rationality of our political processes. To develop this case, I draw initially on the works of Habermas and Castoriadis, two figures not usually seen as compatible or even mutually sympathetic. The work of Habermas and his critics helps me identify the conditions for deliberative practice and new kinds of political practice, while Castoriadis approaches the prospect of change via his conception of a new imaginary. I do this with a view to reflecting on the concept of 'critical liberalism' to assess the ethical energies and political themes that are manifest in the new kinds of politics we are now seeing around the globe.

I offer a significantly revised Habermasian model of the 'public sphere' (or 'civic space') by drawing on the work of Castoriadis. It is an ambitious task because the two philosophers' respective bodies of work are extensive and complex, and because Habermas and Castoriadis operate from quite different, even antagonistic, intellectual traditions. Yet bringing together the ideas of theorists who write against each other and who draw on opposing intellectual traditions can be a fruitful exercise that can lead to insights that have a contemporary relevance for political practice, and for the social sciences, particularly political science.

The intention is to use this work to extract questions or propositions to develop a guiding framework or heuristic that facilitates an assessment of practices and forms of communication that are opening up possibilities for new democratic projects. In short, I use their work to formulate a heuristic frame that helps guide my inquiries in the case studies presented later in this book.

In Chapter 2, 'How the Light Gets in: Change and Continuity', the question of change is addressed by drawing on Bourdieu's theory of practice to highlight how complex it may be to understand the emergence of new kinds of practice. Bourdieu's work offers a rigorous account of how stability and reproduction sit alongside transformation and change. While Bourdieu refers to the idea of 'radical imagination' and 'reflective practice' as a way of generating change, he also acknowledges why change is difficult and rare. He refers to the ways in which novel circumstances encourage change, because change presents situations for which we do not have the experience or the prescribed guidelines that help us provide the 'right' response. This, I suggest, is what the digital media has done, and in this way it is a medium that actively promotes change.

In Chapter 3, 'Change and Generation', I consider whether we can and should invoke the popular and widespread idea of a 'generation'. What does it means to say there are generations? Can this idea be used in an interpretative or explanatory way? Does a category like a 'generation' help us understand what various groups of people are doing? I trace the development of a sociology of generation in the hands of Mannheim (1952), the subsequent evolution of parallel ideas ('youth cultures'). This is done while highlighting the key problems with essentialist accounts of generation and the value of recognizing genera-tion as a fuzzy category.

In Chapter 4, 'Coming of Age in a Digital Neoliberal World: Generation and Politics', I draw on the work of Bourdieu and Mannheim to make the case that we can and should use the concept of a 'generation', and that it has value for the kind research presented here. The various problems with social categories are considered and a critical review of the relevant literature offered. I identify three historic events that took place in the late twentieth and early twenty first centuries which had the effect of orienting those who grew up in that context towards each other. This I suggest provides the basis for an argument about generation. Moreover, I note the development of disjunctures between the promises of neolib-eralism, growth, more growth and a wonderful future and the reality facing many young people where by their future prospect are relatively grim as many struggle to secure waged work, are burdened by education debts, face financial stress and insecurity, battle to start a family of their own or buy into the housing market. This I suggest creates dissonance between the promise of neo liberalism, 'cruel optimism' and the reality. These disjunctures have the potential to promote new kinds of political space and practice.

In Chapter 5, 'A Heuristic or a Guiding Framework', I draw on the ideas and analysis offered in the earlier chapters to develop a heuristic or a guiding framework that I use in the following four case studies presented in this book. This will help me establish whether the events and actions detailed in the case studies constitute evidence of new forms of politics and if there is, what that new politics looks like and in what ways it is political? More generally the heuristic works to help address the key questions posed in this book: what is political? Is digital media opening new spaces for civic action?

The last four chapters offer a series of case studies. I wanted a diversity of cultural and political contexts to enhance the likelihood of getting insights into new politics and how the new media are being used and reactions to those developments.

I deliberately steer away from the more obvious case studies like 'The Occupy Movement the tumultuous protests across northern Africa (the Arab Spring), the 'Indignados' or 'Spanish #spanishrevolution' and the student Riots across the UK primarily because they are a popular field of inquiry and much valuable research has been done. These cases also seemed to support – in obvious more ways- my argument that we are seeing a renewal kinds of politics involving new media and young people. I was after more idiosyncratic cases that do not so easily or so obviously affirmed my thesis. I also did not deliberately set out to identify cases that had a youth or generational component. While that may seem obvious in retrospect, it was not a key factor when I first set out this project and selected the cases.

Chapter 6, 'Democratic Renewal, Pussy Riot and Flash Gigs in the Kremlin' is devoted to the Russian experience and specifically to the activities of Pussy Riot who are resisting Russia's secret police, the Putin government and Russia's Orthodox Church. It opens up questions about ethics and politics and their relationship to art, the politics of subversion and gender.

Chapter 7, 'The Graduate's Future and Neoliberal Education: New Generation Politics on the Campus' focuses on quite authoritarian social institutions, namely schools and the modern university. This chapter offers an account of little remarked-on campaigns run by students in schools and universities. Large-scale and often spectacular protest movements have received considerable discussion and encouraged debate about the political role of young people and their use of digital media. Yet surprisingly little attention has been given to the less spectacular but no less significant campaigns of resistance mounted by students like the two rounds of occupation at the NYU New School in 2008–2009, the University of Leeds, the University of Sheffield, London Metropolitan University and many other schools, or the student strikes in Quebec during 2011 and the spring semester of 2012 protesting fee increases.

I offer two case studies designed to address this relative oversight. The focus here is on students engaging publicly and deliberatively with teachers, managers and others about matters in which they have a direct interest, namely their studies. This chapter asks whether students with new media at their finger tips have the capacity to change the culture of key social institutions, or challenge asymmetric power relations within these social institutions.

Chapter 8, 'The *Stop Online Piracy Act* Case' provides an analysis of the Stop on line Piracy Act (SOPA) in the USA debate in 2010–2011. The proposed legislation was framed as a defence of commercial and national interests. The chapter tracks the public response and how it quickly turned into a highly effective assault on the competence of certain law makers and the right to freedom of speech, one of the most powerful rights enshrined in the US Constitution and in American popular culture. This case study is used to address questions of generational politics, change and new politics.

Chapter 9, 'The Digital, Indigenous Art and Politics' examines the work of two overlapping projects involving new media unfolding in the remote Pilbara region of north Western Australia. These are projects that have produced the *Neomad* interactive digital comic series, and similar work by local young indigenous man Tyson Mowarin. Both projects rely on local Aboriginal culture and involve story-telling aimed at keeping indigenous culture dynamic. It is a project that challenges a number of conventional views about Aboriginal history, art and identity. It is a chapter in which consideration is given to whether these activities constitute political action, and the relationship of art to politics.

I note also that material used in this book was taken from the public domain.

1
Politics in the Age of the Digital

In 2011, a 22-year-old American woman, Molly Knatchpole, a recent graduate working as a part-time nanny in Washington, was told by her bank that they proposed to charge her a new $5 monthly fee for using a debit card. She later recounted why she initiated a campaign that led the bank to do a complete volte-face:

> I was angry that Bank of America decided to set its sights on my meager checking account to pad its profits and pay out huge bonuses to the very folks who wrecked the economy in the first place. That's why I started a petition on Change.com where anyone, anywhere, can start a campaign about the issues they care about. In the end, more than 300,000 people from all walks of life had joined the campaign. And what is even more awesome, it has inspired dozens of other people to start their own campaigns against their banks. Those 300,000 voices brought unimaginable pressure on the Bank of America. (2011)

On 2 November 2011, Bank of America announced it would not be pursuing its proposed fee increase. Knatchpole, however, did not stop there. She also started an online petition against Verizon's proposing a fee increase. Verizon also caved after her petition against its $2 online-payment fee gathered more than 130,000 signatures in 24 hours.

In surveying the literature on the Internet and politics, American academic Henry Farrell asks how political scientists should study the Internet and whether the Internet exacerbates political polarization. Does the Internet empower citizens in their relations with political elites? Can new media help activists topple tyrants and dictators (2012, p. 35)? Implausibly, he argues that 'political science has paid little

19

attention to the Internet until quite recently', but that this is changing. 'Scholars are beginning to uncover specific ways in which the Internet may affect politics' (2012, p. 35).[1] While Farrell recognizes the significance of these new forms of communication for politics, he, like many researchers, assumes such observations can safely rest on a common and agreed-on understanding of what is meant by politics. The question is rarely asked, what is meant by politics? It is assumed we know what this means. In Farrell's case he understands politics, in the conventional common-sense way, to mean parliamentary party-driven processes that focus on electoral activities, fundraising and marketing policies. Farrell continues, predicting that new media will become increasingly important to politics as a field of study:

> Over the next decade, the relationship between the Internet and politics will become increasingly important for the discipline. Paradoxically, ... that there will be ever fewer scholars specializing in the Internet and politics. However, this will not be because political scientists will lose interest in the Internet and related technologies. Rather, it will be because these technologies have become so integrated into regular political interactions that it will be impossible to study, e.g., the politics of fundraising, election advertising, political action, public diplomacy, or social movements without paying close attention to the Internet. (2012, p. 37)

Farrell goes on to cite with approval work by Bimber (1998, 2012), Bimber and Davis (2003) and Chadwick (2006), who share a similar and conventional conception of politics. This approach is also evident in the work of writers like Zukin et al. (2006, p. 3), who speak of a 'new engagement' in their 'generational tale of citizens engagement at the millennium' and a 'first look at a new generation of citizens aged 15 to 27 whom we call the DotNets'. For Zukin et al., the political is defined as any attempt to affect either government action or the election of political decision-makers, and thus their focus on young people's using the Internet to engage in elections, volunteering, promoting voter turnout or fundraising.

My interest in this book is to develop a heuristic framework that I (and possibly others) can use for investigation into case studies presented later in this book. In short, my interest is to develop such a frame to help in recognizing and understanding what people are doing and how they use new media. With this in mind, I argue that we cannot afford to begin with such assumptions or with such a constraining conception of the political. Not the least of the big reasons, namely, what is described as the emerging is the crisis of legitimacy attending contemporary democratic politics and prospect a new politics. Given this, we can ill afford a conventional approach in thinking and talking about the political.

Concern about the state of democracy is evidenced in studies measuring civic disengagement and disaffection on the part of citizens, as seen in declining levels of electoral participation, declining party membership and increasing cynicism about the value of mainstream politics, especially on the part of young people (Schedler 1997, Skocpol 2003, Mair and van Biezen 2001, Mackenzie and Labiner 2002, Blind 2006, Parkinson 2003, Hilton et al. 2010). Disenchantment and low levels of trust accompany questions about the ethical capacity of leaders. These questions are raised in the context of disclosures about systemic corruption, failures to acknowledge and address the big challenges of our time like increasing national and global inequality, failing public services, minimal access to decent jobs and adequate income for many people, unsustainable urban space and cities, climate change, water and food security, and the ongoing abuse of human rights. Concern about the gap or the hypocrisy between 'saying one thing and doing another' highlights disparities between official talk about freedom as governments regularly suspend the rule of law, and the executive branch of government declare states of emergency, create 'grey' and 'black' holes or 'lawless voids' that yet deceptively preserve the illusion of a commitment to the rule of law. Recent examples of these 'grey' and 'black' holes include the side-stepping by the US government of United Nations Security Council procedures designed to prevent illegal wars, the indefinite detention of people whom governments allege are 'terrorists' and the illegal use of torture against these people, the wholesale surveillance of citizens and politicians, and the curbing of civic rights such as freedom of speech.

All this points to concerns about the moral authority of political leaders, their use of power, their capacity to govern well and whether a 'political system' in thrall of a neoliberal paradigm can ever deliver on norms of justice or its promises of a good life for all (Dumenil and Levy 2013). I refer, for example, to the idea that became a conventional piety throughout the twentieth century that education as an 'investment in human capital' was a crucial policy objective because it promoted economic growth, increased employment and added to an individual's net lifetime income, which has proved to be increasingly hollow. As Brown et al. (2010) demonstrated, there are good grounds for the frustration driving many young people, including unemployed university graduates, onto the streets to protest in countries like Spain, Greece, the United Kingdom or the United States, where the prospect of a good life is disappearing along with the prospects for social equity and fairness. More and more young people spend more and more years in education, 'investing' in 'their human capital'. However, dividends from such investment can only be realized where educated, unemployed young people can actually find work that affords a decent income. Yet unemployment among youth and young adults remains stubbornly high globally as governments remain equally stubbornly resistant to taking action that will in fact mitigate the problem. On the agenda of many governments and international nongovernmental organizations, like the International Labour Organization (ILO) and the World Economic Forum, appear reports of global unemployment hitting $5 million, and that is not counting the large number of jobless and underemployed graduates and those involved in the informal economy.

Without caviling about or contradicting the evidence gathered by researchers or the conclusions drawn by commentators about the current ills of democracy, we can say that there is a deeper crisis with democratic politics that also merits attention. That problem is best described in terms of legitimacy, a problem that has plagued liberalism since its origins. Liberalism since its origins in the seventeenth century has relied on the foundational premise that human rationality supplanted the original locus of authority in a political theology centered on a God. Rationality provided a new grounding source of authority for the political order (see Thomas Hobbes and John Locke).

Yet as critics from Max Weber on, have demonstrated, the actual development of liberal democracy and the evolution of our conception and practice of rationality have been inadequate. According to Weber, modern individuals do not have the legitimating systems that were once offered by religion. Instead, religion has been replaced by the instrumental rationality of science, which offers unprecedented power to manage the natural world and so provide 'solutions' to age-old problems like hunger, disease, illness and premature death. Yet we pay a heavy price for the associated economic growth and consumer abundance, that is, the loss of meaning and the loss of ability to provide clear theoretical or ethical grounds on which we can authorize our beliefs or actions. In saying this, I am not laying claim to a novel insight.

I refer to Jürgen Habermas and his attempt to overcome this problem of legitimacy through his normative account of politics as a deliberative practice situated in a 'public sphere' in which citizens can engage in the practices of deliberative rationality. I then pay attention to the criticism that Habermas has faced and more recent discussions about the extent to which the Internet is, or is not, an example of a Habermasian public sphere in which a new kind of deliberative practice has emerged and which holds out the prospect of democratic renewal. I point to some of problems with claims that the Net is an exemplar of Habermas' public sphere and that his rational model of deliberative practice provides the basis for a new kind of politics. That problem highlights the need to introduce different approaches that involve thinking outside the mind-set of the liberal tradition. For that I turn to the work of Cornelius Castoriadis, who offers a different account of the prospect for political renewal in his discussion about the conditions under which a new political imaginary can emerge.

My intention is to begin to identify a number of suggestions that constitute a normative and descriptive taxonomy of the political. This will enable an assessment of the capacity of practices and forms of communication to open possibilities for new democratic projects. To achieve this I work from a revised Habermasian model of the public sphere (or civic space) in conjunction with the work of Castoriadis. It is an ambitious task because the two respective bodies of work are extensive and complex, and also because Habermas and Castoriadis operate from quite different, even antagonistic, intellectual traditions. Bringing the ideas of theorists who write against each other and who draw on opposing intellectual traditions together can be a fruitful exercise that can lead to insights with contemporary relevance for political practice, and for the social sciences, particularly political science. More specifically I hope it can result in some practical outcomes, including a heuristic model that is useful for investigation into the case studies presented later in this book.

Habermas on the public sphere, rationality and deliberative democracy

Habermas' central preoccupation has been with what he called the 'post-metaphysical crisis', manifest in his view of the breakdown in the ways in which humans have historically dealt with questions of fact and value. As Regh (in Habermas 1998, p. 8) explained, this is 'the problem of dealing with a social reality on the one side and a claim of reason (which is sometimes contradicted by the reality) on the other'. Habermas responded to the problem caused by the decline of traditional authority and concern about the ethical void that characterizes the liberal order and its economic, legal and political systems by developing his account of rational and deliberative practice. For Habermas, the solution to the crisis of rationality and authority is to engage in deliberative activity and to thereby achieve an authority grounded in rational consensus making. Thus communicative action is critical for democracy and political legitimacy.

> The disenchantment and disempowering of the domain of the sacred [accompanies] a release of the rationality potential in communicative action. The aura of rapture and terror that emanates from the sacred, the spellbinding power of the holy, is sublimated into the binding/bonding force of criticizable validity claims. (Habermas 1987, p. 77)

Habermas' notion of the public sphere developed into a project that was designed to identify and explain the basis on which we can provide good reasons for our practical beliefs and judgments, as well our political decisions. Habermas' evolving account of a 'Kantian pragmatism' stimulated interest in establishing the epistemic, normative and social conditions that enable rational deliberative practices and in turn enable a democratic polity (1974, 1984, 1996). The question of whether Habermas provided an adequate account of the political is therefore an important question.

Of central importance has been Habermas' attempt to detail rational practice in ways that address the metaphysical crisis of meaning (i.e., the loss of traditional theological authority narratives), while at the same time remaining faithful to the idea of democratic politics and avoiding a slide toward authoritarian populism. Habermas' project was designed to reconcile the requirements of rationality with legitimacy by generating rational techniques and protocols that are said to produce value rationality (Mouffe 1998, Benhabib 1994). How well Habermas did this is a question that is central to this book.

Habermas' career was devoted to specifying the nature of rational communication and its relevance to the democracy. Hence his interest in rule formation and in identifying and clarifying rules or norms said to underpin rational discourse or ideal speech (e.g., listening, turn-taking, relative equity between participants etc.). Habermas offered a discursively grounded communication theory that he said was able to supply value rationality.

Central to his writing were ideas like the 'public sphere', discursive rationality and deliberative democracy, that is, the idea that if a norm or a decision is to be considered legitimate, it has to ensure that everyone affected by the decision will accept the consequences of his or her observance of it – and, that those with an interest will prefer that decision to any alternative. For any norm and action (decision) to be valid and legitimate, it needs to be justifiable within a moral-practical discourse. Only then will it conform to an 'ideal speech situation' (1998).

Public sphere

Habermas' account of the public sphere provided a grand historical narrative that traced the decline of feudal society (and the feudal approach to distinguishing 'public' and 'private' spaces) and the concomitant rise of a new 'bourgeois public sphere'. The new 'public sphere' involved property-owning, educated people gathering in salons and coffeehouses to read newspapers and pamphlets and to engage in rational critical debate on public issues in fields like literature, science, philosophy and politics. As Habermas explained,

> By 'public sphere', we mean first of all a domain of our social life in which such a thing as public opinion can be formed. Access to the public sphere is open in principle to all citizens. A portion of the public sphere is constituted in every conversation in which private persons come together to form a public. They are then acting neither as business or professional people conducting their private affairs, nor as legal consociates subject to the legal regulations of a state bureaucracy and obligated to obedience. Citizens act as a public when they deal with matters of general interest without being subject to coercion; thus with the guarantee that they may assemble and unite freely, and express and publicize their opinions freely. (1991, p. 23)

His book *Structural Transformation* thus offers a 'powerful narrative of the rose and fall of democratic institutions across the industrialized west in the modern era'.[2]

Habermas described the demise of this ideal democratic space (the 'bourgeois public sphere') by reference to the rise of the commercial new 'mass public sphere' that took place at end of the eighteenth century, along with the disintegration of sites like saloons and coffeehouses that constituted the bourgeois public sphere. This newer modern public sphere developed in the historical context of an emerging market economy and an urban bourgeoisie that created a 'sphere of private people [who could] come together as a public' (Habermas 1968, p. 27). It was a space constituted by a mass media industry interested in profit and dependent on advertising for its income. The mass circulation newspapers were followed by the expansion of mass electronic media (i.e., radio and television in the twentieth century). Accordingly, for Habermas, the eighteenth century public sphere stopped being a space for critique and turned into a space oriented to the management of public opinion and the balancing of complex and contradictory social interests. Thus Habermas lamented that the critical activities of the bourgeois public sphere were transformed into 'public relations'. In that way, he argued, the older critical function of exposure, investigation and rational critique were, if not entirely absent, at the least severely weakened.

In contrast to the supposedly critical character of the bourgeois public sphere, the contemporary public sphere was dominated by media conglomerates, which performed a range of managerial and placatory functions. Rather than promoting an interest in free rational critical dialogue, the modern public sphere was informed by interests dedicated to achieving informed consent from the public for activities that were important to the state and corporate elites. From a Foucauldian perspective, it can be argued that the mass media became part of an apparatus of 'governmentality' committed to the surveillance and management of the population rather than a libatory and democratic force.

Habermas' work stimulated considerable research and theoretical analysis and debate. By the end of the 1990s, his work had also established an interpretative framework for commentators keen to understand digital technologies and practices associated with the Internet, with many arguing that the Internet constitutes a modern form of public sphere. Deploying Habermas' discursive rationality framework, proponents of the Internet-public sphere identity like Grossman, Kellner, Rheingold, Poster and Castells see the Net as a 'new public sphere'. Kellner, for example, argued that the Net has

> produced new public spheres and spaces for information, debate and participation that contain the potential To invigorate democracy and to increase the dissemination of critical and progressive ideas. (1998, p. 102)

Within that public sphere, criticism and debate generated 'public opinion' grounded in discursive practices, which, according to Habermas, entailed uncoerced interaction directed toward reasoned agreement or consensus. This was a modern 'bourgeois public sphere' seen as reliant on the principles of reason, science, the law and ethics, which subjected state and religious power to criticism (1964). He also assumed a degree of equality said to be important if citizens were to speak with each other on a relatively equal footing and if they were to counter the power of the state, monarchical absolutism and the church.

Discursive rationality

Over the decades, Habermas developed an extended formal account of the pragmatic-cum-normative presuppositions of 'discursive rationality' (1984, 1987, 1996). What resulted is a kind of identity that sees everyday communicative practice of certain kinds as constituting a 'public sphere', inside of which citizens can engage deliberatively to (in)form public opinion that critically guides democratic political processes. This normative exercise relied on Habermas' distinction between 'mere opinions' and 'public opinion', with the latter requiring a 'public that engages in rational discussion' (1989, p. 398). It is a public sphere committed to certain forms of deliberation, which enables political processes and democratic institutions to flourish.

Habermas relies on a formal analysis of human action as communicative action. Here we see his response to Weber's account of rationality as 'instrumental reason', which Weber and some critical theorists used to explain relationships between patterns of domination and the rise of bureaucracy. For Habermas, communicative action is just one of several kinds of rationality/action in which humans engage. He begins with the idea articulated by Karl Popper that we live in three worlds, namely, an inner or psychic world, a world of objects and the social or intersubjective world. Habermas argued that we engage those worlds differently using instrumental, normative, dramaturgic and communicative rationalities. As Bolton explained, communicative action involves social actors seeking to reach common understanding and to coordinate political actions by reasoned argument, consensus and cooperation, rather than relying on strategic action pursued strictly to achieve their own goals (2005, p. 1). In this way, the public sphere is seen as the 'idealised form of public reasoning' (Dahlberg 2000, p. 6). The practice of communicative rationality inside the informal interactions that constitute the social space of democratic reasoning is the public sphere (Habermas 1996, p. 360).

According to Habermas, all communication as a mode of action is oriented toward understanding or agreement, and involves the 'intersubjective redemption of validity claims' that are 'communicative action'. By understanding, he has in mind several ideas. At a basic level, understanding refers to mutual comprehension (i.e., that people who use the same words have the same meanings in mind, so they can reach a reasonable degree of shared meanings and mutual comprehension). By understanding, he also refers to a shared consensus about the universal validity of claims people make to speak the truth or to know what is good. This accomplishment, says Habermas, requires participants to believe that

> A rationally motivated agreement could in principle be achieved... provided e.g. that the argumentation could be conducted openly enough and continued long enough. (1984, p. 42)

Dahlberg identified six 'idealized characteristics in Habermas's account of communicative action (2000). Those elements constitute what has been referred to as the 'ideal speech situation', which ensures that truth claims are subject only to the 'revisionary power of free floating reasons' (Habermas 2001, p. 34). Dahlberg (2000) extended the discussion by developing those protocol ideas. The communicative action that defines the public sphere is characterized by a combination of structural and attitudinal phenomenon (see also Dahlberg 2001a and b).

Structurally communicative action requires that everyone potentially affected by the claims being discussed is taken into account. Rational communicative action involves the identification of themes and the value of reciprocal testing of problematic validity claims. This requires that participants in the conversation engage as if everyone who is potentially affected by the claims being discussed were taken into account. Then there is the idea that everyone (at least in principle) is equally able to participate and can participate equally because communicative action presupposes a formal and discursive equality among participants. This implies that each participant is given equal opportunity to introduce and question any issue or assertion. This, as Habermas argued, leads to the idea that social equality is ideally presupposed, given that he acknowledges that unequal social, economic or cultural disparities (involving e.g., differential levels of income, cultural skills or status) can affect the capacity of people to participate equally or fully (1996, p. 308). Furthermore, these deliberative practices need to be protected from the reach of the market and state. Given that states and corporations are characterized by a will to dominate using, for example, techniques of instrumental rationality (when e.g., corporations see people as consumers rather than as citizens), Habermas argues that as far as possible the public sphere should be free from influence by the state or the market.

In terms of attitude, communicative action requires reflexivity and a willingness by people to change their minds. Reflexivity is a key condition of such conversations. This means that participants are prepared and willing to change their minds because they are willing to critically examine their own assumptions, and willing and able to question their own prejudices and beliefs. The norm of ideal role taking is also crucial to communicative action. Lastly, Habermas requires that participants in the ideal speech settings bring with them a good attitude. If this kind of communicative action is to be successful, it requires certain attitudes on the part of participants. It requires, for example, an assumption of impartiality and respectful listening because participants seek to understand rather than to aggravate disagreements or ignore difference. Participants need to remain open and sensitive to how others understand themselves and the world (Habermas 1996, p. 34). It also requires that people are sincere and willing to be impartial and respectful. The argumentative or deliberative practice that is part of communicative action is presumed to be grounded in honesty and a desire to avoid deception of one's self of others.

Deliberative democracy

Habermas provided a valuable framework for developing a modern deliberative democratic theory. His work is part of an ongoing conversation about the health of democracy among political theorists who have an interest in integrating elements of normative and political theory with communications theory to produce a theory of deliberative democracy.

In what has been called the 'deliberative turn', some writers[3] built on Habermas' work, arguing that a healthy democracy is one in which citizens talk to each other and deliberate about matters that affect them (Elster 1998, Chambers and Costain 2000, Gimmler 2001, Dahlberg 2000a and b, 2005, Olson 2006). Given all this, it is apparent why those advocating the deliberative democratic model draw on various versions of Habermasian deliberative rationality: deriving or making a rule requires reason. This then enables Habermas to link this rational deliberative process to constitutional processes that produce a 'two-track' model of legitimacy. This account of democracy represents the operationalization of popular sovereignty (or rule by the people) by pointing to the role of institutionalized procedures of parliamentary decision-making and to the role of deliberative public opinion that forms the role of the public sphere. Together the legal and deliberative elements that constitute modern parliamentary government grounded in the constitution and the principle of rule of law that parallel more direct communicative processes of civil society and the public sphere (including the media) to provide the institutional foundations of democracy.

Habermas developed an influential account of the rise of a modern bourgeois public sphere characterized by critical rational debate, which he said began in the seventeenth century. He described this sphere as a deliberative site created within new institutional spaces like salons, coffeehouses, libraries, theaters and reading societies, which provided sites for critical public discussion of important issues of the day. In those spaces people gathered, produced and drew on the then-new informational 'technologies' such as novels, periodicals, essays, newspapers and scientific books produced by writers in England and France in the seventeenth century.

Proponents of a deliberative democracy model, from Hannah Arendt (1958)[4] to Habermas and Fraser and Keane (2009), agree that a public sphere is one in which citizens are enabled to deliberate and make decisions about public issues. Gimmler also claims that Habermas' theory of deliberative democracy has a strong normative foundation

> that enables the legitimacy of the constitutional state and civil society to be justified. This justification is the result of *a discursive practice that provides the framework for solving political conflicts rationally*. The validity of the justification is produced by rational discourse and bound up with the un-coerced consent of all those potentially involved. (2001, p. 23, my emphasis)

Likewise for Tsekeris, the characteristic kinds of discourses that constitute the public sphere, namely austerely rational deliberation, have several functional attributes. One is that collective rational deliberation creates a new space 'where the authority of the better argument' could 'be asserted against the established order (status quo)'. This in turn 'holds out the possibility of reforming the asymmetrical relations of force' (2008, p. 13). Gimmler adds that 'there is no plausible alternative model to rational and un-coerced discourse as the normative basis for democracy' (2001, p. 23). And as Critchley notes, there is here an absolute conviction that 'all political decisions have to be derived from norms, and that the procedure for decision–making is deliberation' (2011, p. 106).

Many critics have also argued that Habermas' account of the public sphere and deliberative democracy is problematic and unrealistic for a number of empirical and normative reasons.

Benhabib provides a criterion for assessing the Habermas project (1994, p. 30). The critical test, he says, is how to reconcile the demands of popular sovereignty by allowing the will of the people to shape law and policy with the need to ensure that those laws and policies are compatible with rationally and defensible ideas of justice, the good society or the good life.

> Legitimacy and rationality can be attained with regard to collective decision-making processes in a polity if and only if the institutions of this polity and the interlocking relationship are so arranged that what is considered in the common interest of all results from processes of collective deliberation conducted rationally and fairly among free and equal individuals. (1994, p. 30)

How well does Habermas meet this test – and is that test itself empirically or normatively defensible?

Critiques of Habermas

Several criticisms have been made. To begin, Habermas' theory of the public sphere excluded a wide range of population groups (Dahlberg 2001a and b, 2005, Dahlgren 2000, Fraser 1995, Cruikshank 1999, Keane 2009). Indeed, the bourgeois public sphere could not pretend to speak on behalf of a universal public. It was also evident that the ideas of the public and the citizens who constituted it were drawn from a very narrow class- and gender-based group – namely, male and bourgeois, while excluding waged workers, women and children, and many young people (ibid.). G. W. F. Hegel too acknowledged that 'the public' was problematic because it excluded large sections of the population. As he explained, if 'this All excludes... children, women etc., then it is surely still more obvious that the quite definite 'all' should not be used...' (1952, p. 195).

For Fraser, there is no reason to assume that Habermas' idealized single comprehensive public sphere is closer to the democratic ideal than is the idea of multiple competing public spheres, in which different people at different times in different places can effectively deliberate. Indeed, there are major advantages for less powerful groups to constitute and be a part of multiple public spheres. And, for the purposes of this book, I note how young people in particular were excluded from the concept of the public sphere and, importantly, from democratic practice and a more broadly defined range of public spaces.

Habermas described the public sphere as space constituted by citizens who freely engaged in critical and rational deliberation about public issues, and developed a model of the 'communicative action' that constituted a public sphere (1984). In doing so, he drew on Immanuel Kant's principle of universalizability, or the idea that everyone with an interest in the decision ought to have a say. Here too lies the problem. Paradoxically, Habermas promoted an exclusionary and at the same time a more inclusive approach. He did this by requiring participants to be rational and informed in their deliberative practice, which excluded many, while at the same time stipulating that everyone affected by a decision ought to participate in processes that produced the decision, which works against the requirement for rationality and which is clearly inclusive.

Thus, embedded in Habermas' analytic category of deliberative democracy is a rationalist bias that seems to compromise his interest in inclusivity. Habermas favored a discourse conforming to certain rational principles. That seems to have assumed that the public sphere works best when it is populated by people possessing certain intellectual, that is, rational resources and when gate-keeping practices like those employed by editors are in place to restrict access to small numbers of 'approved' participants. Commentators have argued that his concept of the public sphere is elitist and for that reason undemocratic. I consider these points now and throughout the book. While arguing for an inclusive public sphere in which a test of its legitimacy depends on its universal appeal, on whether citizens affected by decisions approved of them.

It is appropriate at this point to consider whether the Internet offers a new kind of public sphere.

The Internet and the public sphere?

If we shift attention to the new media, we can see vigorous debates about its capacity to provide a new kind of public sphere. Some critics say the Net does not conform to the Habermasian notion of the public sphere. Indeed Habermas himself is highly skeptical about the value of the Internet for deliberative practices:

> The internet generates a centrifugal force. It releases an anarchic wave of highly fragmented circuits of communication that infrequently overlap. Of course the spontaneous and egalitarian nature of unlimited communication can have subversive effects under authoritarian regimes. But the web itself does not produce any public spheres. Its

structure is not suited to focusing the attention of a dispersed public of citizens who form opinions simultaneously on the same topics and contributions which have been scrutinized and filtered by experts. (Habermas, cited in Jeffries 2010)

Clearly the Internetet does not offer a single comprehensive space that enables debate and decision-making between 'equals' in ways that are directed toward consensus. Nor does it necessarily sponsor well-informed conversation between people who are impartial and rational.

Having said that, there is some agreement among those committed to the idea of deliberative democracy that Habermas' normative account of the public sphere is just that, an ideal that can never be seen in practice. With that in mind, writers interested in the Net, the 'public sphere' and deliberative democracy see the Net creating a new kind of public sphere or a deliberative space that enables expanded participation for those excluded from older kinds of public spheres. Dahlberg, for example, argues that digital technology can facilitate an expansion of the 'public sphere'. It can be used to connect us with 'civic cultures in subtle, unintended and surprising ways' (2009, p. 48). In this way, the Net provides valuable sites that promote new forms of mediated political engagement.

While I do not wish to preempt later discussion about the capacity of the democratic capabilities inherent in the Internet, I note the expansive and rapidly expanding scale of new media and how it is at once complex, highly interactive, provides users with multiple points of entry, and to date has avoided regulatory constraints.[5] It is a 'space' in which users can access large amounts of information with relative ease; it enables access tilted in favor of those adept at using the technology and navigating electronic space. In this way it is quite different from the public sphere embodied in the traditional mass media because it actively enhances participation.

The inclusivity of the Internet also reflects the success with which its development was informed by the principle of 'Net neutrality' (Froomkin 2004, pp. 747–876). This has meant that many groups historically marginalized or excluded from the modern public sphere now have greater opportunity to create political change, to have a political presence, to address the 'issues of the day' and to influence the views of others.

For Dahlgren, the very formally modeled account of deliberative practice offered by Habermas presupposed processes of exclusion and cultural homogeneity that are unrealistic and indefensible given the heterogeneity that characterizes late modernity. Dahlgren argues for appropriate modifications to the design of a functioning public sphere, which involves acknowledging the value of 'massifying' the deliberative process and encouraging diversity and 'constellations of communicative spaces'. Minimally all that is needed is a shared commitment to democracy that entails seeing beyond one's parochial interests and an acceptance of the value of a deliberative space that sustains a variety of discursive modes, and which recognizes the complex, fragmentary nature of contemporary society (Dahlgren 2009).

Habermas also ignored the creative or generative role of 'experts' and the media in 'discovering' social problems and how those discoveries are then used to prescribe policy and legal solutions. It also neglected the role of confusion, of misguided thinking, accidents, purposeful deception, ignorance, malice and sheer mischievousness that characterize the modern public sphere. It overlooks the fact that often events and actions are unforeseen, disorderly and highly variable. Indeed, many writers point out that while citizens can sometimes be rational, we can also often be quite illogical and driven by powerful emotions. With this in mind, it is argued that democracy can be improved through means other than rational deliberation. For scholars like Keane, 'except for a small handful of cases, democracy has never been built democratically' (2009, p. 4; see also Dahlgren). Keane continues,

> rarely does it spring 'from the clear headed intentions and clean hands of people using democratic means' ... Accidents, good luck and unforeseen outcomes always play their part. It is usually bound up with farce and monkey business and violence. (p. 4)

Neither everyday political life nor virtual political life conforms well to Habermas' prescriptive account (Dahlgren 2000, pp. 335–340, 2007, 2009, 2010, pp. 47–64, Papacharissi 2002, pp. 9–27, Dahlberg and Siapera 2007, Dahlberg 2001a and b).

Thus it seems that while Habermas' account of the public sphere has value for those interested in understanding and promoting various kinds of deliberative and democratic practices, it also has limitations and requires too constraining a set of criteria about what is acceptable deliberation to be applied to the actual public sphere (real political space, policy-making communities etc.). This becomes apparent when we consider Habermas' bias toward a rule-bound model of rationality and compare this with the anarchic nature of digital space, to say nothing of its multiple sites and entry points and the enormous variety of its content.

Having said that, I suggest that if Habermas' work is revised in light of the critiques and insights offered by critics, we may have the basis for a useful interpretative framework for determining whether digital space constitutes a modified version of a public sphere. One thing that can be agreed on as proponents of a deliberative democracy model from Arendt to Habermas and Fraser argued, is that a public sphere is a space that enables citizens to deliberate and make decisions about public matters (Arendt 1958, Habermas 1989, Fraser 1990 and 1995). As Fraser points out, there is no reason to assume that Habermas' idealized single comprehensive public sphere is closer to the democratic ideal than multiple competing public spheres in which different people in different times and places can effectively deliberate. Indeed, there are major advantages for less powerful groups to constitute and be a part of multiple public spheres (Fraser 1995, pp. 287–314).

For these reasons I argue along with Fraser, Dahlgren and others, that the Habermasian model of the public sphere requires considerable modification in ways that acknowledge the democratic value of opening new spaces and opportunities for the engagement of a broader constituency in deliberations about matters in which they have a direct interest.

Many theorists have engaged with this task. Some, like Dahlgren, who have a particular interest in new media and politics, have incorporated aspects of Habermas' model into their own work, while distancing themselves from the Habermasian notion of the public sphere and the idealization of deliberative practice on which it relies. Dahlgren (2009) and others (e.g., Geuss 2008) also pointed out that it is a mistake to persist with the claim that action is only deliberative when it is oriented toward will formation and consensus making.

Will formation is a critical feature of Habermas' normative model of a public sphere in which he contends that politics depends on 'will formation' or 'public opinion'. Dahlgren, like Habermas, understands that a functioning public sphere is identifiable by its encouragement of the circulation of ideas and exchanges of information that produce political will that can become political action. How that process of political will formation takes place and how it connects to political action are questions to be addressed by the usual means. Habermas and Dahlgren agree on the vital role played by processes of public opinion formation in any society that claims to be democratic. This does, however, mean deliberations leading to will formation need to be rational or oriented toward consensus, for there are many instances when democracy has been promoted through political conflict and rivalry. Conflict and a disinterest in consensus-making are ever present in relations between various parties.

As many writers have pointed out, there are a number of problems with the Habermasian defense of the liberal project, some of which I have already canvassed (e.g., Benhabib 1994, Mouffe 1998). However, one new thought arises from a consideration that Habermas' defense of his approach does not go far enough. I recall Habermas' argument that many of the criticisms directed at his work rely on practical or empirical observations about the extent to which his deliberative model could ever be put into place in any real society characterized by significant inequalities.

As Mouffe (1998, p. 165) argued, another difficulty becomes evident when we consider Carl Schmitt's claim that the constitution of the people as 'the people', which is required by democratic theory, also requires an inscription of the relations of inclusion and exclusion (i.e., between the categories of 'citizens' and 'non-citizens' or 'aliens') into that constituting process. In short, the logic of the democratic process requires a drawing of frontiers between 'them' and 'us'. This process is demonstrated in many countries as states decide to refuse the protection of their own laws or international laws to asylum seekers. It puts at risk the possibility of there ever being the kind of free and unconstrained deliberation Habermas wished to promote as the basis for securing legitimacy within the liberal political order. The very conditions for democratic legitimacy (namely, the distinction drawn between them/aliens and us/citizens) makes it impossible to achieve the political legitimacy envisaged by deliberative democracy. This exclusionary requirement effect has an internal and an external dimension. As Michel Foucault observed, states routinely divide their population according to acceptable and unacceptable characteristics as part of a process of biopolitics. It also has an external aspect as states constitute the field of international relations by reference to various binaries like 'democratic'/'communist' or 'liberal-democrat'/'terrorist' (Rawlinson 2010).In either case, consensus in a liberal democracy is and will always be the expression of a hegemony and the crystallization of power relations. It will also be deceitful in making sharp a distinction that is too sharp between the alleged virtues and benefits of the side of the binary on which 'we' sit and the evils and harms attributed to 'others', to 'them'. It is this insight that Rawlinson (2010) highlights as she points to the limitations of a constraining political binary that complacently assumes that a binary operates globally in the twentieth and the twenty-first centuries between 'liberal democracy' and 'communism' and one that favors the 'liberal democratic' part of the binary. That kind if triumphalism was evident in Fukuyama's declaration that history as the conflict between liberalism and communism had ended with the collapse of Soviet communism in 1989. Liberalism was said to be victorious. However, as Rawlinson demonstrates, such binary narratives ignore the point that if we make the degree and kind of harm produced by a given sociopolitical order like the Soviet-style command economy or the American-style liberal-democratic free market models, then the simplicity and complacent moralizing that this kind of thinking encourages, disintegrates.

We might consider, for example, the ways in which both systems rely on penal incarceration to preserve social order: the scale of incarceration in the Gulags is matched today by American rates of incarceration. Wolin made a credible case for seeing the American social order as a form of inverted totalitarianism using different media institutions and techniques of communication from those used by the Soviet apparatus (2008). Stiglitz points to unmistakable evidence, notwithstanding the ubiquity and reach of the American myth, that the idea of America as a middle-class society and the reality is untrue (2013). This is different from yet similar to the Soviet and post-Soviet claims of having created a classless society. Both are baseless. In both cases, the social order is best described as societies in which the 1% of the truly wealthy and powerful runs a political system that disadvantages the 99%. In Soviet Russia, the 1% was the *nomenklatura*, who ran the state to fill their own pockets. In the United States, the 1% of wealthy people runs systems to advantage themselves: the eight members of the family that owns Walmart control as much wealth as 35% of Americans in aggregate (Stiglitz 2013). In the Soviet Union, every citizen could vote, but to no real effect. In America, large numbers of people choose not to vote, while 'colored' minorities still fight to exercise their right to vote. Currently low-income Americans struggle to access decent health care and America 'boasts' an antenatal death rate typically found in developing societies (Wilkinson and Pickett 2009, OECD 2011).

In short, for all of the self-evident character of the naturalness of dividing political options into binaries and then assuming the superiority of Anglo-American liberalism over Soviet-style communism, that binary and the presumed superiority on the American side disintegrates when we look more closely. This point is more critical than any evidence that points to a deficit in democracy characterized by civic engagement or public cynicism about democracy. It points to that deeper problem I referred to earlier, namely, the legitimacy of liberalism. It suggests a different set of problems that relate to the failure of the liberal model to deliver the benefits it claims to deliver. It is at this point that the work of Castoriadis becomes significant.

Cornelius Castoriadis

While we see evidence of incremental change on a daily basis, according to Castoriadis there are other more substantive forms of change that rarely happen in human history. He referred to a deeply political change that is distinct in the ways in which it promotes autonomy, ruptures traditional worldviews and practices, and in so doing creates new ways of being. The question for this book is whether we are now seeing the beginning of this kind of political project courtesy of digital communication.

In what follows, I attempt to use the work of Castoriadis in conjunction with a revised Habermasian public sphere to construct a new interpretive framework. Having provided a cursory account of Habermas, I now provide what I regard as the key points in Castoriadis' account of an 'autonomous political project' that he says can bring about major change. I do this while also paying attention to the question of generational politics and its implications for understanding change.

Through our mimetic relations with others, we follow and we emulate. Yet in doing so we do more than simply transfer practices from one generation to the next as if we were simply neutral conduits. Through practices of copying, learning and we adapt, modify and change what was. Gradual amendments, sociocultural variations in the form of restructurings are made that produce changes like a reorganization of institutions so they become different in style or form from the traditional arrangement.[6]

'Newcomers' to the world pick up on things, learn, interact, innovate and as a result shape and change mind-sets and attitudes, and produce something different from 'the original'. The extent to which change takes place depends on the context, on power relations and the interests at play. And while incremental change or 'cultural racheting' produces some transformation, for theorists like Castoriadis they are minimal modifications, rather than being an innovative change involving new ontologies, institutions and modes of being.

For Castoriadis, such incremental or reformist change is typically limited to a few parts of the social system and has minimal influence on society in its totality. He cites as an example the dislocation of traditional significations and roles-identities of men and women that has taken place in contemporary Western society and how that has seen the rest of the system continuing to function as if little or anything happened: women continue to perform the lion's share of the domestic labor and child care, their wages remain lower than men's and so forth. This, Castoriadis says, shows that politics limited to a reformist agenda is ineffective and incoherent because it only changes parts of the system without caring about or being aware of how that change might connect to the rest and how the different and complex parts of society 'cohere in countless ways' (2007, p. 101).

Castoriadis focused on the idea of 'imagination' to understand change and contemporary 'politics' (1974). He used the term 'social imaginary' in his book *The Imaginary Institution of Society*, arguing that 'the imaginary of the society ... creates for each historical period its singular way of living, seeing and making its own existence' (1974, p. 2). Those imaginaries (e.g., capitalists' imaginary) arise out of the imagination of people (social subjects) and have an institutional character represented in the system of meanings that shapes and governs the social or political order.

In this sense, social imaginaries are evident in historical constructs or ontological creations (the way we see our being, our becoming and social reality). These are totalities kept together by institutions (e.g., language, customs, technologies and modes of economic production) and by the meanings inherent in those institutions (e.g., symbols, prohibitions, the polis, commodities and wealth). And while society is self-creating or self-instituting and always undergoing processes of self-alteration, for most of human history, the fact that institutions are human creations has been veiled by the social institutions themselves so that people tend not to recognize their capacity to change them. Moreover, self-alteration processes are slow and tend to be unnoticeable rather than rapid and obvious. This, Castoriadis says, raises a question for which there is no answer: when does society stop being the same as it was and become another?

Two imaginaries

Castoriadis spoke of two different, but interrelated imaginaries: the 'radical imaginary' and the 'social or institutional imaginary'.

The radical imaginary

This provides the basis for the social imaginary, but is not separate from it. The radical imaginary is discrete from, but can also be a part of, the shared social imaginary. In this way the relationship between the radical and the social imaginary reflects the interdependency between the self, others and society (1997, p. 332). The radical imaginary refers to the creative, or open-ended capacity, that derives from the imagination of singular human beings, and importantly, *appears whenever there is human collectivity*. In describing the radical imaginary, Castoriadis refers to Aristotle's recognition of the imaginary in his statement that 'the soul never thinks without phantasm' – without imaginary representation (Castoriadis 2007, p. 71). The radical imagination of the singular individual is the 'essential determining element' of the human psyche. It is an unceasing flux of representations, desires and affects. As he explains, even if you close yourselves off to sensory perception (shut your eyes, block your ears etc.), there will always be something. The radical imaginary is what goes on inside: it includes images, memories, fears, hopes, desires, 'surge forth' that we experience in ways we can sometimes understand and other times not. Values and emotions in the social imaginary (glory, hate, nostalgia etc.) are not tied to logic or reality, but constitute 'poles' that bring into existence desires toward which we are oriented.

Socialization 'stifles' the psyche and in so doing ensures that it expresses itself conventionally. The radical imagination of the human psyche is 'tamed, then channelled, regulated and brought into line with life in society and with what is called 'reality' (2007, pp. 74–75). Individuals absorb and internalize the institutions of society and their significations by learning the language, the categorization of things, the order, the dominant ethical frames, what is acceptable and unacceptable behavior, what is valued and what is not.

In this way, society tends to be what Castoriadis calls *heteronomous* or nonmoral, as opposed to an autonomous society in which citizens constantly practice critical reflection and recognize the socially constructed nature of the institutions and society in which they live. Castoriadis explains that a heteronomous society is one that is seen by its citizenry as having extra social authority derived from powerful historical, ancestral or divine sources (e.g., god). Put simply, a heteronomous society refers to the idea that people act under the influence of factors, conditions and forces that are said to exist outside the self (the individual). Members of such a society are also said to be largely unaware of the fact that institutions are socially created and have influence over them.

A heteronomous society is different from an *autonomous society* in which citizens exercise freedom and in so doing act out of their own volition and exercise their own judgment rather than being unknowingly influenced by factors external to themselves. In an autonomous society, they are fully aware that social institutions were instituted by them and of the influence those institutions over them.

Castoriadis went on to describe different kinds of institutions and or levels within them. Language he described as a 'trans-historical institution', observing how no society can exist without language even though the language differs according to the society. The same applies to 'the individual' – there is no society that does not institute an individual. It is just that in each society the types of individual differ. Moreover, we cannot see our relationship to language – as an institution – because we cannot remove ourselves from it to look at it from the outside and recognize it as constituted by people. Given this, Castoriadis argued, we are blocked from developing theories of our institutions because we are inside them. In saying this he used the word *theory* in the traditional sense, that is, to gaze, to look across from and inspect the institution. This is difficult, if not impossible, because we cannot get outside the social institutions to gaze and look across. Indeed, we are fragments of them. How we see, what we think and say is 'profoundly dependent on language', on 'the type of individual' we are, on the type of family to which we belong. These are only some examples of the 'prevalence...of the thoroughness with which we are all penetrated by the institute elements of our native society' (2007, p. 92).

In both autonomous and heteronomous societies, we may believe we exercise our own judgment, but in fact how we see and act is informed by social criteria. In this way, most people are heteronomous because we judge on the basis of convention and public opinion (2007, p. 75). For this reason, thinking about and questioning the institution is 'an exceptional occurrence' and has only been encountered twice and only within the European and Greco-Western traditions – in the periods mentioned above. Achieving this represents a 'tremendous historic break'.

The social or institutional imaginary

The social imaginary creates institutions in each society, is the source of underlying laws, values and worldviews of the society, and tends to be heteronomous in the sense that it promotes the idea that our actions are influenced by forces outside the individual. As a product of our social imaginary, institutions are also bearers of 'significations'. Those who are religious, for example, believe in a God or gods that are social imaginary significations sustained by institutions like churches and schools and that rely on founding heroes, ritual objects, taboos and myths. Similarly 'the state' and 'capital' are institutions animated and sustained by imaginary significations.

Crystalized social significations and institutions produce *an instituted social imaginary*. This works to ensure continuity, reproduction and preservation of the same traditional forms used to govern and endure for as long as there is no significant historic change or major new creations that change or replace them (Castoriadis 2007, pp. 73–75). Importantly, the institutional imaginary works against people's questioning social institutions' producing conforming individuals who are not free or autonomous, but subject to external conditions and for whom questioning existing laws and common-sense practices is not only prohibited but is 'mentally inconceivable' and 'psychically unbearable'. As such, individuals are conscious but not self-reflective (Castoriadis 1997, p. 336). This is a situation rarely broken because doing so means institutions and fundamental beliefs within the society also have to be questioned and modified. This a monumental task because the social imaginary creates the world and shapes our psyches.

For Castoriadis, it is exceptional that we see societies emerge in which it is possible to question traditional institutions and significations. When this does happen, we see rich instances of creativity. This is so rare that he cites only two examples in Western history: the first is ancient Greece and the Athenian polis, which saw the birth of democracy, philosophy and tragedy, as well as the arts and sciences. I note that while Athens is generally recognized as the cradle of democracy, scholars like Keane query this, pointing to the East to Iran, Iraq and Syria and Persia as the place were the 'lamp of assembly based democracy was first lit' (2009, p. xi).

The second 'project of autonomy' that Castoriadis identified is coterminous with the rise of the 'modern period', a period that saw the birth of a recognizably bourgeois class in Western Europe in the eleventh and the twelve centuries and began with what we call the Renaissance. It was a time that expanded and accelerated so richly, with constant changes in tempo everywhere across Europe. Different activities developed at different times and locations, producing cross-fertilization, and stronger and more vigorous creativity. It was a time of an exceptional profusion of creativity that then peaked for two centuries from 1750 to 1950. This period of the Renaissance, he argued, was also a time of enormous subversiveness that owed much to its context of dense cultural imagination (2007, pp. 77–79).

This 'autonomy project' stirred up and excited every aspect of society, creating new forms and content at a pace previously unknown, with the 'explicit intention of fermenting change'. It was a movement toward democracy that was manifested in the revolutions of the seventeenth, the eighteenth and the twentieth centuries, with the working class and later the women's and youth movements. (All this, he acknowledged, is not to ignore the highly destructive outcomes that can be attributed to the technological developments that also took place at the time.)

For Castoriadis, the immense acceleration of technological developments that took place simultaneously with these cultural developments was more significant than anything seen before. One source of this were changes occurring within the scientific imaginary that were responsible not only for the cultural disruption, but that can be best understood as part of an overall social trend. He had in mind developments in chemistry and electricity, thermodynamics, quantum theory and general relativity, along with advances in medical biology that saw the emergence of new knowledge forms, new disciplines and practices (i.e., the social sciences – psychoanalysis, sociology).

The shift to 'liberate society', the challenging and vanquishing of old political forms, was not confined to specific areas, disciplines or practices. It infiltrated them all, resulting in the great philosophical movements of the Enlightenment and German Idealism. He saw our creative imagination playing a critical role in all domains, in science, philosophy, mathematics and the arts. In each domain was a shared a common bid to give new shape to the chaos of the world and cosmos in ways that humans could grasp. None of the scientific, artistic or philosophical activities were 'rational productions' but rather creative activities that gave order to chaos and created new worlds. Ideas, after all, are a prerequisite for empirical induction and logical deduction. As Castoriadis explained,

> The great scientific advances are outgrowths of the creation of new imaginary schemes, formed under the constraint of available experience but not 'following from' that experience. (2007, p. 79)

This is what he saw happening with the great creative imaginary schemes that Newton developed through his ideas about the universe, and when Einstein made his discoveries in physics which changed fundamentally how we understood the world.

Testimony of the power of the imaginary lies in the 'basic fact' that we cannot explain the birth of society or the course of history by natural factors, be they biological or other, any more than we can talk sensibly about the rational activity of a 'rational' being. From our earliest history, he says, we can see the emergence of radical novelty. And, if we do not wish to resort to transcendental factors to account for this, we must then assume a power of creation, *vis a formandi*, immanent to human collectives as well as to individual human beings (2007, p. 72). External factors, natural, biological or logical, are conditions reflected in radical innovation, and in the institutions we create and form in, for example, language, custom, norms and techniques, *but they cannot account for them*, for that is the domain of the imaginary. (This points to the observation that while the social imaginary and institutions are free creations of citizens, they are also constrained)[7]. Given this, there are good reasons to recognize that within human collectives lies a power of creation – namely the instituting social imaginary.

For Castoriadis, the collective and the radical imaginary within a single human being are creative forces that generate out of nothing ex nihilo, bringing into existence new forms that were not there before, new forms of being. Here he is talking about an ontological creation in the form of new worldview, language, music, art, poetry and new ways of being.

When this 'historic creation' takes place in partially open societies populated with self-reflective individuals, we see 'projects of collective and individual autonomy'. The primary mover of such change is politics, described as collective emancipation and self-reflecting, uninhibited critical thought. The aim of such political projects is not happiness (utility maximizing as the value within a utilitarian ethical frame), but freedom. In this way, freedom as autonomy is 'effective, humanly feasible', reflective the positing of the rule of individuals and collective activity' (1997, p. 337).

Sociohistorical struggles produced by such political projects have created valuable intellectual and political freedoms and new types of being that 'consciously and explicitly' change partially or fully the edicts of its own existence. What materializes is a self-legislating society and new types of beings – who are deliberating and reflective. This permits us to create some distance from our society, to listen to and accept criticism. This is attested to by the creation of many different societies and by the constant historical alteration of societies, which is both slow and rapid.

Such creations are conditioned by 'external 'factors' (as distinct from being caused by 'them'). Numbers, size, color and taste are creations of ourselves (our living bodies) that are embodied in our human psyche. For example, under certain situations light waves, molecules and so forth can induce a person to create an image or idea that is sometimes socially shared, and sometimes not. The point is that the imaginary is made up or is invented content that can be derived from the 'things' we perceive, as well as new and hidden images, ideas and feelings that are not delivered or accessed through our senses.

Such imaginary is generative and the source of change. It is our ability to intuit and spontaneously create objects without those objects having been present before. It is the power to make what is not, to make present within our thoughts something that is absent, without 'external incitement', but conditioned by perceptions of external independent objects (Castoriadis 1970).

Perceptions or impressions are philosophical or psychological artifacts that help us make sense of the world. Perception helps us in making sense of colors, sounds, smells and noises in 'nature' that are 'in reality' (e.g., in physics) simply electronic waves, airwaves and molecules. In this way we do more than just react to 'external reality'. Our *imaginary generates representations* or gives form to something that has no form (external objects). For Castoriadis, such representations possess a unity or underlying conceptual or organizational framework that is evident in the categories we use that are intrinsic to our perception (e.g., topographic schemata, neighborhood/separation or continuity/ discreteness).

Practices, social institutions and society change through the radical-human imaginary, and are reliant on what Castoriadis describes as the autonomous project – a political project, a topic to which I now turn.

Social and individual autonomy.

How might we recognize and explain the creative phases of history? Are we experiencing creative phases of history now? Are we witnessing what Castoriadis called an autonomous political project that will create the kinds of changes in those rare historical moments he identified?

For Castoriadis, creative phases or periods, or indeed periods of decadence, cannot be explained in the ways in which explanations are traditionally offered. We may gather facts that seem relevant and make sense, but these never produce explanations, as explanations might be conventionally understood in terms of causal effects. Castoriadis' imaginary defies the salience and value of causality and structural functionalist thinking – which is what most traditional formulations of the idea of explanation require (see, e.g., Hempel's covering law model of explanation). Against the inclinations or traditions promoted by natural scientists and structural determinism, there are 'no commanding laws' that govern the radical imagination, that direct 'when it flourishes and when it fades'.

To say that Castoriadis' account of change as an autonomous political project does not provide a traditional causal explanation is not to
suggest it is deficient, but that he offers an alternative explanation that
identifies the imaginary as the source of change. Drawing on Sigmund
Freud, he argued that the socialization process that fashions us and that
sublimates our psyche is never complete and never fully accepted. It is
through the cracks, to use Leonard Cohen's words, that 'lets the light
gets in', that we get glimpses of our core psyche. It is in questioning,
subversion and transgression that we see evidence of the always-to-be-
incomplete socialization project and the imaginary that provide an inexhaustible supply of generative capacity and the source of social change.

In what follows, I summarize this to help determine whether what we
are now witnessing constitutes a politically autonomous project that has
any potential to usher in the kinds of radical changes that Castoriadis
claims we saw twice before in history.

Autonomous political projects entail questioning institutions in ways
that open up prospects of an 'historical break'. A change to the entire
social sphere requires people who were fashioned by their society to
inquire into the words and deeds and inherited institutions that formed
them. It requires 'a public political space and free unlimited and uninhibited investigation'. It entails people's standing up and saying 'the
tribe's representations are wrong' and thinking about humankind and
the world differently. It requires people's saying the powers in society
and instituted laws are unjust and we need to create new ones. It requires
questions being asked like: what does it mean to say that powers are
unjust? and what is the truth?

Instigating 'a project of social and individual autonomy' is difficult
because in heteronomous societies it is generally assumed that social
institutions were preexisting and are not human creations. We are
raised, educated and fashioned to be absorbed in and by social institutions. Here institution refers to the mutually determinative or dependent
relations that exist between agencies like 'the Church', which claims
universal sovereignty over 'mankind', and a theological apparatus that
supplies the formal theoretical or intellectual narratives. Similarly, this
can be seen in the relationship between the free market and neoclassical economics. In the case of the Church and the neoliberal economy –
the human activities or practices that make those institutions possible
are occluded in favor of abstractions said to possess explanations (e.g.,
market force) and that require compliance or obedience.

Castoriadis says this is why we rarely think of and declare ideas that
oppose the instituted order. It is not necessarily because we will be

sanctioned, but because we have been 'anthropologically fashioned' not to do so, we have been so well assimilated by our social institution that we have lost the psychic and intellectual means to contest those institutions (2007, p. 94).

For Castoriadis, an autonomous individual and an autonomous society rest on there being people capable of giving themselves their own laws. These are not citizens who simply act as they please, but people who set their own ethical principles and rules, something that is not easy. It is a difficult task, because establishing one's own rules requires the capacity to think deeply, to make good judgments, and to provoke and challenge a full range of conventions, beliefs, trends and fashions, as well as an army of well-resourced experts of various kinds who support those practices. Additionally, it entails challenging a mass media and a public that tends to keeps silent either through disillusionment or apathy.

The radical imagination of a single person can become the source of creation at the collective level, for phantasm remains a fantasy in the singular psyche. Creative practitioners, artists, poets and political agents create works, not fantasy. 'What their imagination sires is real'. It comes into existence by a variety of means (e.g., through language, practice) that people (the social actor) cannot create on their own.

For society to give itself its own laws, there needs to be a total recognition of the idea that it, the people, creates its own institutions, and does so without alluding to there being a nonsocial basis or foundation (e.g., natural unalterable order of things – god) or any norm for it. In short, people need to collectively decide for themselves what is just and unjust. *This he says is the issue with which true politics must contend.* It is not the kind of politics we see much of today in mainstream political arenas. *In a democracy, people make the laws, and in doing so they can be convinced those laws work in the interest of people.*

One way to gain insight into whether we are now experiencing anything like the kinds of political autonomy projects Castoriadis held up as exemplars of autonomous societies (namely, the Athenian polis and the Renaissance) is to consider how, for example, the polis itself came into being ancient Greece. How did social imaginary significations in the polis, the idea and practice of collectivity, as a community taking responsibility for law making in ancient Greece come into being? With respect to the Renaissance, what was it about the end of the High Middle Ages that promoted the constitution of self-governed collectives? How did new free boroughs and towns emerge and why did they produce proto-bourgeois who went on to create the beginnings of the modern movements of emancipation and democracy?

In those two epochs, 'the seeds of autonomy' were created and remain alive today insomuch as individuals at least have the capacity to exercise the freedom, even though they may not chose to. We do have the ability to take a stand and say this act is unjust or the institution needs to be changed. Perhaps the answer lies, in part, in Castoriadis' observation that 'If any politics, in the true sense, exists, it resides in efforts to preserve and develop those seeds of autonomy' (2007, p. 97). The question is whether in contemporary sites we see evidence of people's safeguarding and growing those seeds of autonomy. Understood in this way, democratic politics and its renewal may be recognized by its cultivation of autonomous citizens and by the responsibility people take for their own self-limitations.

Social institutions

Castoriadis identifies two kinds of institutions: the *primal institution*, which is society, and *second-order institutions*. He uses the idea of primal to refer to the ways in which society creates itself afresh, giving and sustaining itself by social imaginary significations that are particular to the society (e.g., to an Egyptian *pharonic society*, to Hebrew, America, etc.). As such, the primal institution – namely, society – articulates and implements itself through second-order institutions. Some second-order institutions are transhistorical in that they are abstract and exist in all societies. Examples of such institutions are 'language' and 'the individual', for no society can exist without language or without instituting with the individual. What differs is the kind of individual and the kind of language each society has.

There are other second-order institutions that are specific to a society and that play a critical role in them. Within second-order institutions are embodiments of what is essential to that society's institutions and its social imaginary significations. The Greek polis, for example, is a specific second-order institution without which ancient Greece would be inconceivable. Similarly, capitalist business is a second-order institution without which we could have no modern capitalist society. Moreover, what terms such as 'enterprise' or 'business venture' and the like mean for us today did not exist in precapitalist societies. The institution and meanings we give to it are created by capitalism, and capitalism only exists within and through its own creation. Finally, Castoriadis sees transhistorical and second-order institutions as intertwined, as they produce a particular kind of society (2007, pp. 100–101).

A radical transformation of society can only come from individuals who want their autonomy on both a social and an individual level. They achieve this by continuously preserving and augmenting their autonomy, which involves working to cultivate individuals who aspire to having their independence, to taking responsibility for themselves and to encouraging as many people as possible toward that end. Without this creative political work, social change cannot come about.

Developing a heuristic

In the following chapter, I consider the question of social change, concluding with the work of two philosophers, Hegel and his idea of dialectical change, which sees change as a bleeding of the past into the present and future, and Arendt's notion of natality as most helpful in understanding contemporary sociopolitical change. In Chapters 3 and 4, I move on to focus on the concept of generation and consider the extent to which the idea of generation and generational politics might help us better understand new media and current political practices.

In Chapter 5, I draw on the discussion and specifically on the work of Habermas, his critics (Dahlgren, Fraser, Keane etc.), and Castoriadis outlined in this chapter to ask what conditions are required for developing deliberative practice as envisaged in a revised model of the public sphere and collective that promotes a political autonomous political project? That heuristic frame or taxonomy is created by asking the following questions: What evidence could be used to establish whether we are witnessing, courtesy of new media, a change, a historic break of the kind that might bring new ontological creations or worldviews into being? What might those conditions be? What would they look like as a collective practice? What evidence could be used to demonstrate that individuals are questioning their social institutions in ways that recognize that those institutions and change are conceivable? What evidence could be used to establish that institutions are currently susceptible to change?

I identify three sets of questions that make up a heuristic taxonomy that will be used for an investigation in the case studies in this book, to determine whether new media is facilitating political practices that resemble anything like the autonomous political projects described by Castoriadis, or anything like the mergence of revised public spheres. I use this explanatory frame to establish whether the kinds of changes taking place can be described as renewing democratic politics and the extent to which that might be understood in terms of generational politics. I note too that the political significance of such evidence may not be immediately obvious given that we are so deeply immersed within our own sociopolitical context.

2
How the Light Gets in: Change and Continuity

Poets, philosophers, novelists and social scientists have long wondered about the question of change, seeing it as one of the most perplexing and enigmatic features of our world. As a result, we see a mountain of thinking, writing and other forms of creative expression far too high to scale in a short book.[1] Yet at least one aspect of that question was grasped early in the historical archive. Sometime in the seventh and the eighth century BCE, Homer stepped back from his full and frank story of war in his *Iliad*, to meditate on the ceaseless cycle of birth and death and the comings and goings of all those who are brought into life and who must die:

A generation [*genea*] of men is like a generation of leaves:

the wind scatters some leaves upon the ground,

while others the burgeoning wood brings forth –

and the season of spring comes on.

So of men one generation springs forth – and another ceases. (Homer, 2011)

Here the word 'generation' (*genea*) is already ambiguous. It has many connotations, including the idea that it is something 'which is born', which suggests novelty, but it could also mean 'the bearer', which implies some kind of continuity (Bertman 1976, p. 67). As Strasser observes, the constant replenishment of human life by reproduction is a reminder that everyday life is characterized by both orderly persistence and change (1977, p. 1).

Our biological life cycle from childhood to old age and our experience of various forms of political, economic and social conflict, from family arguments and disputes between neighbors, to law suits, staff room politics, industrial strikes and demonstrations, and the preoccupation of the news media with violence, war and social disruption may indicate that 'small scale changes are an important aspect of stability and persistence on a larger scale'(Xuanming). As Strasser argues,

> One is tempted to say that life is change and yet most people believe in the constancy of aspects of our life be that our occupation, the organisation in which we work, the values we cherish, or the intellectual subject matter we study scientifically. (1977, p. iii)

Change is extraordinarily difficult to describe and analyze (Mortensen 2011, p. 1). Peter Dwyer and Monica Minnegal point to the ways in which processes of change, irrespective of whether we refer to biological or human processes of change, are very strange and are never self-revealing (2010). They suggest,

> The products of change are self-revealing, but the process is not. The latter may be understood only through inferences drawn retrospectively from analysis of the products. (2010, p. 379)

The Chinese Daoist text the *Dao De Jin* uses the metaphor of water to highlight the grasping of the ubiquitous nature of change.[2] For ancient Greek philosophers like Heraclitus, change was the normal state of nature. Indeed he saw nature itself as change. Also using the water analogy, he described change as a river of flux, explaining how 'You cannot step twice into the same river, for other waters and yet others go ever flowing on. They go forward and back again'. Nature flows ever onward as the character of the flow always changes (Heraclitus, cited in Harris 1994, p. 21).

All these prefatory remarks are relevant to a book that explores the role of young people and the digital media in promoting political change. However, before we look at that this central issue, there is value in better understanding what we are talking about when we think about change. For this reason I begin by reflecting briefly on change and order with a focus on the social sciences. As Strasser notes, every theory of society has a 'built-instability-change dimension' (1977, p. iv). As I argue, there have been important traditions that either emphasize the ubiquity of continuity and persistence, or that claim reality *is* a process of relentless change. Both these traditions provide a familiar, if unhelpful, binary, but are able to shed light on why their case is credible. I argue that an alternative perspective found in the work of Pierre Bourdieu's theory of practice, recognizes the interplay of continuity *and* change (Bourdieu, 1990a and b). Yet, as I indicate, Bourdieu's emphasis on practice has trouble highlighting the points at which change becomes a possibility. For that I suggest we need to draw on Cornelius Castoriadis's theory of the imaginary. Seeing Bourdieu and Castoriadis as complementary may offer one way of illuminating some aspects of the political changes we are now experiencing in young people and the new media.

The question of change

I begin with two points about the idea of change.

Firstly, philosophers have long appreciated the perplexing nature of change. After all, not all change is change. For C. Mortensen, 'the most general conception of change is simply difference...in the features of things' (2011, p. 1). A narrower understanding of 'change' is temporal change that sees it as 'alteration' in the properties of a body over time. Sally Haslanger, for example, argues that alterations are changes in which an 'object' gains and/or loses a property, while persisting through that gain and/or loss (1989, p. 4). Here we see how philosophers distinguish between 'alteration', where something basic changes but where something also persists, and other categories like 'generation' and 'destruction' (which refer to the coming into being or life and its end) or 'successions', like the repeated patterns of sunrise and sunset. Dwyer and Minnegal, for example, claim we can distinguish between 'adaptation' and 'transformation' (2010, p. 379). 'Change-as-adaptation' occurs when 'quantitative and context-dependent shifts occur in the expression of particular variables' without substantive alteration to functional relationships between those variables and the contexts within which they are expressed. This may be the case when a given population of animals grows in size in parallel with the size of the food supply. However, change becomes 'transformation' when relationships between variables alter to elicit qualitative changes in the structure of the ensemble as a whole. For example, a population of animals may expand more rapidly than the food supply and suffer significant loss or even extinction.

Secondly, there have been wildly opposing accounts of change. Western thought has tended to take one of two approaches. One tendency, which has long been dominant, has been to see change as illusory, and another has been to see it as the only reality. I now briefly consider these two traditions, before turning to a third and more satisfying way of thinking about change *and* continuity.

Change as illusion

For a long time, Western thought was entranced by the metaphysics of Plato and Aristotle. Both saw reality as order and persistence (or continuity), qualities that were eternal. As Alfred North Whitehead once said, 'The safest general characterization of the European philosophical tradition is that it consists of a series of footnotes to Plato' (1927, p. 1). For Plato, Being or reality (*noumos*) was 'timeless' because whatever was real was grounded in 'substances' that were eternal. For G. W. F. Hegel, 'the history of [Western] metaphysics is the tendency towards substance' (cited in Seibt 2012, p. 3). What we seem to see of reality is merely 'phenomenal' or only appearances. Plato was supported in this approach by other Greek philosophers like Pythagoras, Parmenides and Zeno. For Parmenides, all change was illusory, while Zeno argued that even the idea of motion-as-change was absurd. Zeno's paradox expresses how an arrow in flight cannot provide an example of change because a flying arrow cannot be moving. It is not moving because at any given instance in time that arrow is at a particular place that is identical with itself (and not another place). Something that is at one place cannot be moving, and an arrow that is *motionless at every instant* in a temporal interval must be motionless in that interval. This is an old paradox that has been difficult to think about, let alone resolve (Arntzenius 2000, Priest 2006).

For Aristotle, the doctrine of substance helped explain change. He argued that substance, the specimen (this person or this horse) or the individual, survives accidental change, while the essential properties persist that define those universals. Thus, if we saw a person like 'Socrates', the 'real' Socrates would be the essence or the 'soul' of Socrates, persisting over time and possibly even eternal. If we looked at Socrates, we would see changes like the way he began as a small infant and grew larger then grew. According to the doctrine of substances, the 'essence' of Socrates did not change: the changing bodily appearance of Socrates was subordinated to his timeless substance or 'soul'. That is, Socrates was still the same because his substance remained the same, while the changes like his growth in body size or signs of aging (wrinkles and white hair) were accidental and merely covered up his substance. For Greeks who thought like this, change was merely accidental, whereas the substance was essential. This ontology that passed on into Western culture denied any substantial reality to change.

This classical account of reality (ontology) also generated an influential theory of knowledge. True knowledge (*episteme*, or pure theory) was knowledge of timeless and eternal truths about substances that did not alter: as Aristotle argued, episteme can only 'consider things which do not admit of change' (Aristotle 1999, pp. 1139a5–15). For that reason, the capturing of timeless truths in, for example, scientific laws expressed in terms of rationally and eternally true mathematical formulations provided an influential intellectual, cultural and normative criterion for defining real truth and knowledge (Toulmin 1972, 1982, Ferejohn 1991). As Stephen Toulmin argued, one long-term effect of the classical Greek preoccupation with episteme consequence was an obsession with 'objectivity' and 'scientific method' said to be attainable through the adoption of a 'spectator' position in the search for timeless truths – a position reinvented by René Descartes. For Toulmin, the idea that Cartesian approach is intellectually superior, objective, and universalizable remains influential (1982). Writers like Gaston Bachelard and Roy Bhaskar similarly noted the physical sciences have attempted to get 'behind' or 'beyond' the phenomena revealed to us by sensory experience, to access the unobservable 'noumenal structure' (Bachelard and Bhaskar 1989) or 'generative mechanisms' (Harre) that somehow necessitate these phenomena. The laws pursued by physicists and chemists have less to do with regular conjunctions of events,[3] and more to do with analyses in dispositional terms as the causal powers, or tendencies, of the underlying generative mechanisms.

This way of thinking about knowledge and reality has become enormously influential and difficult to relinquish, especially in the social sciences.

The history of most of twentieth-century social science was dominated by the structural-functionalist tradition. It is a tradition that began in the late nineteenth and the early twentieth centuries with the work of Herbert Spencer, Émile Durkheim, Vilfredo Pareto, Ferdinand Tonnies and Alfred Radcliffe-Brown, and was turned into a sophisticated integrated paradigm by Talcott Parsons (1970) starting in the 1950s. This paradigm saw society as social order. It did this because its logic of explanation emphasized the organism-like qualities of society by seeing it *as if* it were a living body in which all of its features were explicable in terms of the properties of the organism (e.g., talking about being a 'member' of society is an allusion to the metaphor of society-as-organism). It included the idea that any society was an integrated whole, which maintained its structural coherence (equilibrium) through time, and could so because its structural components (e.g., families, churches, workplaces etc.) all worked together to achieve that persistent order. In this story people did not figure. A structural functionalist explanation was one that showed how any particular sociocultural activity has the effect of maintaining the social structure. Furthermore, the paradigm saw the interdependence of the parts of the social order as a given rather than as a problem. The risk in seeing society *as if* it were the analogy that was used to describe it (i.e., society-as-organism) is that it creates the problem of reification. The reductive nature of this practice avoids recognizing important aspects of human life, ignores purpose and intentionality and sidesteps consciousness (Taylor 1985).

This organic analogy imagined change in one of two ways: 'normal' and 'structural'. For writers like Parsons, the emphasis was on the idea of normal change, which was gradual, orderly and took place through adjustments or adaptation to external pressures. 'Structural change' was said to result from the actions of deviants, who worked against the 'natural' societal orientation toward maintaining order and continuity. It was an account that presented a problem: how could they distinguish between the two kinds of change? Indeed, this issue was a nightmare Parsons that struggled to repress. Parsons was not able to explain problems resulting from the 'functional incompatibility' between institutional and normative patterns and the actual ways in which social relations and institutions operated (1951). For example, we have seen since 2000 how norms about studying hard to achieve life goals, and policies designed to keep more young people in extended periods of education, are supposed to lead to increased economic growth, employment and income. Yet government policies and the economy are not working in ways that sustain those norms or aspirations (Howker and Malik 2013). Parsons was unable to conceive of the possibility that a legitimation crisis could arise in society due to contradictions like these. Finally, it should be noted that this structural functionalist tradition privileged the tradition of positivist and quantitative research by seeing society as an objective and persistent entity. Here we see the shadow cast by the doctrine of substance.

Against that tradition, which emphasized continuity, another major tradition saw change as pervasive: in effect, reality is change.

Change as reality

Classical Greece promoted another account of reality, which saw change (or Being) as a process of becoming. Heraclitus, for example, saw conflict or change as the basis of all being. Heraclitus's doctrine promoted a philosophy of ubiquitous and radical flux, summarized in the saying *panta rhei* (everything flows). He argued this idea in his statement 'You can't step in the same river twice'. From this a philosophy of process emerged, which as Johanna Seibt observed, relies on the premise that reality or 'being is dynamic' and 'the dynamic nature of being should be the primary focus of any comprehensive philosophical account of reality and our place within it' (2012, p. 1). By the late eighteenth century, German philosophers like Hegel developed a dialectical account of reality-as-process.

Hegel gave considerable thought to the process by which the world of knowable appearances, including reflective reasoning, came into being. For Hegel, reality or being is a self-unfolding of dynamic structures or concepts. This process of change differentiates itself into a range of mental, natural, sociocultural and institutional processes. Hegel called this movement 'dialectics', and his philosophical system was an attempt to figure out the 'logic' underlying the total dialectical development of reality. As Seibt explained,

> Hegel argued that this overall 'movement' of gradual self-determination by internal and external differentiation drives all actual and possible developments according to its inner necessity – reality is 'reason' articulating itself as and within the world. (2012, p. 4)

I return to Hegel later in this chapter.

Subsequent philosophers of *existenz*, like Friedrich Nietszche and Martin Heidegger, and twentieth-century 'process philosophers' like Whitehead (1929) and Charles Hartshorne (1971) further developed an account of reality as process, while others like Bachelard (2002) and Bhaskar (1985) developed a relational epistemology that rejected the idea of timeless things as substances, and focused on relations (e.g., between 'facts' and 'theories' in the continual evolution of knowledge). As I later argue, this approach influenced Bourdieu and his generative structuralist account of change *and* continuity.

Marxism is one the best-known social science versions of a reality-is-change perspective.[4] It is generally accepted that the development of Karl Marx's account of history as class conflict began with the dialectical conception of change initially elaborated in Hegel's philosophy:

> [This dialectical perspective] reversed the traditional logical setting of the problem by taking change as the very form of existence, and by taking existence as a totality of objective contradictions. Every particular form of existence contradicts its content, which can develop only through breaking this form and creating a new one in which

the content appears in a liberated and more adequate form. (Marcuse and Neumann 2001, p. 130)

Taking on Hegel's perspective meant as the subsequent development of Marxism indicated that

Social change was no longer an event occurring in or to a more or less static system, but the very *modus existentiae* of the system, and the question was not how and why changes took place but how and why an at least provisional stability and order was accomplished. (Marcuse and Neumann 2001, p. 131)

The conception of dialectics embodies this shift from thinking about things to thinking about process. As Bertell Ollman puts it, to think dialectically means thinking about reality by no longer thinking in common sense terms about

a 'thing' (as something that is singular and has a unique substance) and instead with notions of 'process' (which contains its history and possible futures) and 'relations' (which contains as part of what it is, its ties with other relations. (2003, p. 1)

Under the influence of Hegel, Marx argued that human history was one of endless conflict between classes for control of the material basis of existence. In Marx's account of 'historical materialism', he argued that 'man' as a political creature makes 'his' own history, and that it is not ideas alone that change the world but also labor. Marx made an insightful observation when he proposed that people do make their own history, but not under circumstances of their own choosing. Life, he argued, is produced through social relations in labor and through natural relations in procreation. In this way we remake our lives every day through processes of production, through our labor and the relations we establish with nature.

In our struggles with nature and to build social support, we enter into social institutions like the family or villages and factories, which embody and make possible the prevailing means of production, which are themselves a productive force. These social relations and processes are characterized by social inequality. This means that as societies develop, so too do the divisions of labor that result in social classes distinguished by discrepant power relations and access to the 'means of production'. Ownership of the means of production by the dominant group who accumulates scarce economic resources creates antagonisms between the exploited and exploiters, thereby producing a 'history of class struggle'. This is why Marx thought class conflict was the driving force of human history.

In one of his accounts of this theme, Marx avowed that

> The bourgeoisie cannot exist without constantly revolutionising the instruments of production, and thereby the relations of production, and with them the whole relations of society. Conservation of the old modes of production in unaltered form was, on the contrary, the first condition of existence for all earlier industrial classes. Constant revolutionizing of production, uninterrupted disturbance of all social conditions, everlasting uncertainty and agitation distinguish the bourgeois epoch from all earlier ones. All fixed, fast-frozen relations, with their train of ancient and venerable prejudices and opinions, are swept away, all new-formed ones become antiquated before they can ossify. All that is solid melts into air, all that is holy is profaned, and man is at last compelled to face with sober senses his real conditions of life, and his relations with his kind. (1848/1969, p. 4)

Here the phrase 'everything that is solid melts into air' seems to imply that change has become a persistent feature of our social existence. However, apart from attributing this to the bourgeoisie, there is no account offered of how change actually takes place.

It was an absence that plagued Marx's work for the rest of his life. He sometimes believed that societies based on the capitalist mode of production would naturally or inevitably evolve into socialism and later communism. That notion of social change attracted considerable attention and criticism. Harry Burrows Acton was one who described Marxism as a 'philosophical farrago' (1955). More sympathetic critics like Gerald Cohen (1978) pointed out that Marx did claim that his social transformation would occur 'at a certain stage of development, [when] the material *productive forces* of society come into conflict with the existing *relations of production*' (Marx 1859). By productive forces, Marx was referring to the 'means of production', such as the technical ways in which labor power produced food or in which commodities were designed, as well as the tools and productively applicable knowledge, that is, technology. By 'relations of production', Marx meant *the* totality of social relationships that people *must* enter into in order to survive, to produce and reproduce their means of life. Because participation in these social relations is not voluntary, the totality of these relationships (which can be social, economic or technological) constitute a relatively stable and permanent *structure*, which can be the 'economic structure'.

Marx, however, did not see things (material objects) as the primary entity, but rather relations. The relations between the 'forces of production' and the 'means of production' were relational. As he explained,

> The production of life, both of one's own by labor and of fresh life by procreation, appears at once as a double relationship, on the one hand as a natural, on the other as a social relationship. By social is meant the cooperation of several individuals, no matter under what conditions, in what manner or to what end. It follows from this that a determinate mode of production, or industrial stage, is always bound up with a determinate mode of cooperation, or social stage, *and this mode of cooperation is itself a 'productive force'*. (my emphasis)

What Marx is saying is that the social relations between, for example, the owner of a factory and the workers in that the factory are both the 'means of production' and a 'force of production'. In his account of social transformation, Marx beggs the question about how a conflict between the 'means of production' and the 'forces of production', which are dialectical expressions of the same social relations, could ever take place.

Writers like Jon Elster (1985) and Wolff (2002) argued that Marx offered a similar but different functionalist account to Parsons on the question of why change cannot occur. Marx's functional explanation argues that a capitalist economic structure develops capitalist productive forces: if capitalism failed to develop these productive forces, it would disappear. When an economic structure fails to develop the productive forces (when it 'fetters' the productive forces), it will be transformed. Fettering is what happens when the economic structure becomes dysfunctional. In this way the idea of 'fettering' of productive forces is used to present a functional explanation.

According to Elster, this presents a problem (1985). Such an explanation implies an agent is guiding history, an agent who has the purpose in mind that the productive forces should be developed as much as possible. Elster is critical of evoking this idea of 'purposes' in history without its being the purposes of anyone. Such an agent would intervene in history to carry out this purpose by selecting what they see as the best economic structures.

If the American structural functionalist tradition faced the problem of being able to overcome its foundational assumption that order or continuity was the normal state of affairs, the Marxist tradition emphasized the ubiquity of conflict and change between the 'means of production' and the 'forces of production' (which are actually dialectical expressions of the same ensemble of social relations), and in so doing set itself the equal and opposite difficulty of having to explain why that conflict can occur *and* why and how some things continue over time.

While much more can be said about this, I now turn to what I consider is a more helpful account of change, which begins with Hannah Arendt's observations about natality. I then use Bourdieu's idea of practice-as-*habitus* and Castoriadis's account of how the radically new is possible. This eclectic framework will hopefully provide some insight into the intermixing of change and continuity now taking place in contemporary processes of political renewal primarily by young people.

Arendt: freedom and natality

The fact of our birth and death is a reminder of change – and the difficulties of understanding it. For Arendt, one of the most original political philosophers of the twentieth century, natality was central to her work. The fact we enter the world through birth was central to her political philosophy as she grappled with the most pressing modern problems of totalitarianism, loneliness, world alienation, the rise of the social, and the shrinking of the political (Kattago 2013, p. 170, Benhabib 1996). Arendt made natality central to her exploration of freedom and responsibility.

Arendt saw freedom as much more than a choice between specified options. She did not use the idea of freedom in the way liberals do when they refer to the idea of individuals' pursuing what makes them happy (d'Entreves 1994, Villa 1999). For Arendt, freedom refers to our capacity to recognize our own political autonomy, and our capacity to use it by recognizing our responsibility to the world and by acting accordingly. Arendt's notion of politics was grounded in the idea that we ought to take care of and take responsibility for others and for the continuity of the world. For Arendt, politics is also grounded in the fact that we are plural in all aspects of our life (Villa 1996). For Arendt, being with others, the fact of human plurality, is the foundation of the human condition.

> Action, the only activity that goes directly between men without the intermediary of things or matter, corresponds to the human condition of plurality, to the fact that men, not Man, live on earth and inhabit the world. While all aspects of the human condition are

somehow related to politics, this plurality is specifically the condition – not only the condition *sine qua non*, but the *conditio per quam* – of all political life. (1958, p. 70)

Freedom is expressive of our capacity for 'activity' as distinct from mere 'labor' or even 'work':[5]

Man does not so much possess freedom so much as he, or better his coming into the world, is equated with the appearance of freedom in the universe; man is free because he is a beginning and was so created after the universe had come into existence. ... Because he is a beginning, man can begin: to be human and to be free are one and the same. God created man in order to introduce into the world the faculty of beginning: freedom. (1977, p. 167)

Thus our capacity for action as freedom is grounded in the fact of natality (Arendt 1996). In contrasting natality with Heidegger's emphasis on human mortality, Arendt argues for our capacity to act and create new beginnings:

the decisive fact determining man as a conscious, remembering being is birth or 'natality', that is, the fact that we have entered the world through birth. The decisive fact determining man as a desiring being was death or mortality, the fact that 'we shall leave the world in death'. (1996, p. 51)

In this way natality and mortality can become an ontological frame for a full range of human activities – including the political life.

Natality entails the capacity to initiate or start something completely new. Importantly, freedom can also entail beginning anew and doing something unanticipated. In this way Arendt (1996) made what she called 'natality' into the basis for a hopeful politics. Natality with its potential for beginnings interrupts the death orientation of life, which for Arendt carries 'everything that is human to ruin and destruction' (Arendt 1958). Moreover, manifestations of natality appear in domains such as politics, evident in our capacity to create public space between ourselves and others so that freedom can be exercised. Natality also manifests in the activity of thinking and its relation to ethics.

As the ontological condition for human activities such as labor, work and action, natality ensures there is a 'constant flux of newcomers born

into the world as strangers'. For Arendt, natality involves the replace-
ment of people through birth and death, and the continuous flux of
novices as they learn. This provides the basis for creativity and new
beginnings. Natality is the

> miracle that saves the world, the realm of human affairs from its
> normal 'natural' ruin is ultimately the fact that natality, in which the
> faculty of action is ontologically rooted. It is in other words, the birth
> of new men and the new beginning, the action they are capable of by
> virtue of being born. (Arendt 1958, p. 247)

In this way, natality 'prompts us to see ourselves as beginning something
new and as becoming who we have not been, through our activities that
constitute novelties (Arendt, in McGuire and Tuchanska 2000, p. 128).

In this sense, freedom is an innate entailment of natality. Freedom is
something with which everyone is endowed simply by virtue of being
born. It is rooted in natality because birth opens up the prospects of
new beginnings. And as J. E. McGuire and Barbara Tuchanska reiterate,
natality understood broadly is a condition of beginning, becoming,
creating and novelty in respect to practice (2000, p. 128). Denoting
the capacity to create, Arendt's notion of natality helps elaborate the
concept of generation and the potential for new beginnings. It suggests
that we can use the idea of generational politics, although the need for
caution when doing so is left to the next two chapters.

I now turn to Bourdieu and his theory of practice because it offers a
useful account of how we both enact and resist change, and how we
reproduce prevailing arrangements, ideas and classifications in ways
that are helpful for developing a concept of generation. This, I hope,
will assist in determining whether we are currently witnessing processes
of political renewal currently taking place, and in doing so better understand the relationship of new media to changes in practice.

Bourdieu, practice and generation

Over many decades, Bourdieu (1977, 1990 a and b) developed an account
of human practice. While some readers find his theory of practice
obscure and difficult to read, it does offer a perspective designed to avoid
falling into the either/or logic that characterizes the major traditions in
the social sciences. It is also work that can be described as a 'generative
structuralism' (Vandenberghe 1999, p. 32).

Another feature of his work are its affinities with classical liberalism, so far as Bourdieu is interested in the question of human agency or our capacity to do what we like, when we like. According to this classical liberal view, we are individuals who possess rationality and freedom, who choose what we do and how we will do it. (One version of this is found, for example, in neoclassical economics.) According to this viewpoint, all human action is the result of individuals freely using their rationality and capacity for agency to shape their own lives.

The other approach to human action has affinities with political philosophies like fascism or corporatism, with an emphasis on structure and determinism and our subordination to the holistic social order of 'society', which prescribes our puppet-like behavior. This structural-functionalist tradition, which is evident in the work of Durkheim and Parsons (discussed earlier in this chapter), is an example of this perspective. According to this approach, human beings are puppets pulled one way and the other by social structures oriented toward securing social order. In this way human action has nothing to do with free expression and much to do with social determinism. If we have been well socialized, our behavior is all those learned responses to social values or rules that emphasize compliance with the dominant social norms promulgated through 'structures' like class, gender, religion, ethnicity and so on. Good women, for example, raise children and look after 'their husbands', so they preserve social order. Likewise, young people obey their parents and realize the dominant goals of their society. 'We' are not so much individuals as socialized entities playing predefined roles so that the whole society of which we are members can maintain its own internal equilibrium and order.

Bourdieu's theory of practice presents a relational account of human action that is interested in agency and a structural conception of action.[6] He sought to transcend a number of traditional or conventional binaries like 'subjective'/'objective', 'structure'/'agency' and 'free-will'/'determinism', binaries that have long constrained the thinking of social scientists and others. He did this by developing an account of practice that offers a way to understand the coexistence of order *and* change, thereby bypassing the one-sided emphasis on order in structural functionalist sociology and on change and conflict in Marxism.[7]

Bourdieu provides a synthesis of sociology. It was an amalgam that included structuralism (Weber, Marx, Durkheim and Marcel Mauss), phenomenology (Karl Mannheim and Erving Goffman, Edmund Husserl, Heidegger and Maurice Merleau-Ponty) linguistic philosophy Ludwig Wittgenstein and John Austin and neo-Kantian epistemology (e.g. Bachelard and Ernst Cassirer). As Bourdieu noted, his first debt was to the long line of anthropological and sociological structuralism going back from Durkheim and Mauss to Claude Levi-Strauss, as well as the French structuralist version of Marxism (1985). His work was not a strong form of structuralism like Durkheim's discussions about the role of institutions (religion), or by Marx and his reliance on structures like class to explain why people and societies do as they do. Bourdieu concern with establishing a relational framework is evident in the ways he did not overlook the role of human consciousness as his more structuralist-inclined colleagues. Bourdieu also avoided a subjectivism that focused exclusively or predominantly on thinking and feeling, implying a large role for human agency (as did writers like Alfred Schutz).[8] Secondly, Bourdieu's account of practice reflects Heidegger's influence, which led Bourdieu to pay particular attention to the body and our habitual practices. This encouraged his observation that we act through the embodiment of social structures, symbolic orders and categories in ways that reproduce social practices.

What Bourdieu developed was a structuralist analysis of practice in which *habitus* as a 'mechanism' that connected 'structure' ('society') to 'agency' (the 'individual') was vital. As Frédéric Vandenberghe (1999) and Omar Lizardo (2009, p. 10) note, Bourdieu began as a structuralist, but it was a structuralism heavily modified through the introduction of concern about the genesis and the historical development of structure. In this way he is a 'generative structuralist'. Explaining what is meant is the task to which I now turn.

From the moment of our birth we are immersed in *fields of action* (beginning with our families, kindergartens, and schools, counting leisure (watching film or bushwalks) engaging in occupations (carpentry, law, gardening) and including our interactions with doctors, shopkeepers or public servants (Bourdieu 1984). We are positioned into *fields of action* (families, communities, schools and other institutions), which are 'structured' spaces, each with its own norms, rules, and schemes of power and domination. Each field engenders particular kinds of practice.

In these 'structured spaces' we develop a *habitus* of practice. Each of these spaces e has certain dominant narratives, rules and legitimate manners that shape our 'subjective *habitus*'. By *habitus*, Bourdieu refers to our distinctive, but unconscious ways of thinking, feeling and using our bodies. In these spaces our *habitus* is unconsciously reproduced through practices that are acquired and solidified into a *habitual character*, which over time attains a naturalness such that we find it hard to imagine living and being any other way (Bourdieu 1984).

In one of his 'complex' definitions, Bourdieu defined *habitus* as

Systems of durable, transposable dispositions, structured structures predisposed to function as structuring structures, that is, as principles which generate and organize practices and representations that can be objectively adapted to their outcomes without presupposing a conscious aiming at ends or an express mastery of the operations necessary in order to attain them. Objectively 'regulated' and 'regular' without being in any way the product of obedience to rules, they can be collectively orchestrated without being the product of the organizing action of a conductor.

Calhoun identifies six features of *habitus* in his definition, which is more accessible than Bourdieu's:

---

1   learning is not always 'explicit and mediated by language', it is often 'tacit and embodied'.
2   action is generally not produced by rule-following but by improvisation. Much of this improvisation is unconscious (like that of musicians in a jazz band).
3   the capacity to produce such improvisations – and thus actions – is developed through lengthy processes of learning which are simultaneously processes of 'inculcation' by society and social fields (since the learning takes place in interaction) and active self-creation (since the learning is a byproduct of action which is itself improvised...). *Habitus* thus reflects processes of conditioning associated with material and social conditions of life but also some individuation in those processes.
4   *habitus* is simultaneously structured and structuring, because it is embedded in the repetition and occasionally innovation of action through time.
5   it is without conscious orientation to ends because *habitus* has been produced out of a nearly infinite number of iterations of similar actions (and reactions), and trial and error learning reinforces the effective actions.
6   *habitus* may be transposed to new circumstances, where they may be effective but will in any case shape the production of actions (and responses) and thus new learning.

Source: (Calhoun 2002).

Bourdieu argued that *habitus* was conceived with the intent of moving away from the structuralist paradigm without falling back into the philosophy of the subject or of consciousness, thereby getting 'out of the philosophy of consciousness without doing away with the agent in its truth as a practical operator of constructions of reality' (1992a, p. 253).

Between the *habitus* and the field there is an 'ontological complicity' (1998, p. 154). When we enter into relations with the social world of which we are the product, we feel at home – 'like a fish in the water'. This is when we experience *habitus*.

The *habitus* is internally linked to the field, even to the point that they can refer to the same thing. For Bourdieu and Jean-Claude Passeron, the *habitus* is the 'product of the structures and producer of the practices and reproducer of the structures (1970, p. 244). Put differently, *habitus* involves the internalization or incorporation of the social structures, while *the field* is the exteriorization or objectivation of the *habitus*. In this way he avoids the traps of pure determinism and pure voluntarism. While the *habitus* is the product of the social structures, it also structures the social world. The *habitus* reproduces the social world, but 'one cannot mechanically infer the knowledge of the products from the knowledge of the conditions of production' (Bourdieu 1984b, p. 135). The *habitus* transforms that by which it is shaped, and even if the principle of trans-formation is to be found in the 'rift' between structure and *habitus*, there is reason to suppose that the depth of this rift and its meaning depend on the *habitus* (Bourdieu 1997a, pp. 177–178). After all, agents are determined, but only to the extent that they determine themselves. If 'there's always space for a cognitive struggle concerning the meaning of the things of the world', nothing excludes the potential of the agent to transform the world in an unpredictable way (Bourdieu 1998b, p. 19). Moreover, the recognition of the creativity of the *habitus* and its capacity to reflect on its own determinations has the advantage of bringing the meta-theoretical presuppositions of his theory of action in line with the critical intention that animates his theory (Bourdieu 1987a, p. 23).

Bourdieu uses the idea of *doxa* to speak of an alignment between a person's *habitus* and the 'external social structures' of the society. Our experience in the social world produces 'cultural literacy', a feel for or sense of 'the game' within those fields. That literacy promotes insight into how things work, the conventions, that rules that characterize rela-tions between people in specific times and spaces, and how they are likely to be played out. With this 'knowledge' we are better able to work out how to respond in the face of complex variable conditions and how to maneuver to realize our goals in the context of the given constraints.

In his account of learning, practice and change, Bourdieu drew on the Aristotelian idea of the human bodily *hexis* (our active dispositions, constitution/character). It is a complex idea echoed through the work of many writers from Thomas Aquinas to Hegel, to Heidegger, Husserl and Elias in their respective bids to explain learning, social action and change. For Bourdieu, it is our generative capacity that matters, our ability to transmute the past by embodying knowledge, classifications into dispositions that get expressed in certain kinds of action.

We learn intuitively through our bodies and often do so without thinking. We also learn consciously and deliberately through language. Processes of habituation create *habitus*, which Bourdieu describes as 'systems of durable, transposable dispositions', 'structured structures' that are 'predisposed to function' as structures or as 'principles which generate and organize practices and representations'. As such, they can be 'adapted' without a 'conscious aiming' at ends and without 'an express mastery of the operations' needed to attain them. They can be 'objectively regulated' without being 'the product of obedience to rules', and can be 'collectively orchestrated without being the product of the organizing action...' (Bourdieu 1990, p. 53).

In short, Bourdieu offers an understanding of how we become 'who we are' as beings whose practices define our self. Such practices include everything from bodily techniques, from how we talk, sit, or throw balls, to how we think and feel about other people or material goods that form dispositions like friendliness, frugality or wastefulness. It refers to our ostentation or fear and 'need' for security, to our desire for friendship. It refers to the ways we engage with people, animals and the world generally.

These fields of action are themselves constituted and shaped by *habitus* and by an already existing unequal distribution of abilities (power) and resources, which include cultural and social capital, as well as various forms of economic capital.[9] For Bourdieu, the *habitus* we develop tends to be congruous with these patterns of social inequality. Elites, for example, use different language and dress codes, enjoy certain kinds of culture (e.g., ballet, opera or reading certain literature), all of which sustains a capacity to distinguish between 'high', 'middle' and 'low' culture.

Having said all this, there is one critical issue with which Bourdieu struggled – namely, the question of change.

Bourdieu and change

If practices are passed from one generation to the next in these ways and function to sustain the existing state of affairs, how then can change take place?

As discussed above, for Bourdieu, we cannot properly understand practice without paying close attention to the ways it is produced through structure and how by way of the *habitus*, agents use the products of practical action (their own and that of others) in their recursive attempt to reproduce larger structures. His notion of practice as *habitus* in particular fields of action does not lead to any conclusions about how change takes place or whether we exercise free will or whether we are always constrained by structural determinism.

Bourdieu's notion of practice implies we do not have complete *free agency* to choose as we see fit, but equally, we are not totally constrained. He emphasized the idea that we are caught in an interplay between 'agency and structure', creating certain dispositions that shape contemporary practices and ways of being. Bourdieu does not, however, appear to think we can ignore the individual's moral agency or responsibility, and in doing so we cannot assume a unitary objective or neutral moral frame of reference. This raises questions about whether Bourdieu's work might be useful for understanding how ideas like politics, justice and power develop, how they and associated practices are reproduced and how they change.

In Kogler's critique of Bourdieu's reflexive sociology, he locates Bourdieu's work in a 'sociology of knowledge'. It is a sociological tradition that tries to stipulate the relationship between symbolic forms of knowledge and social structures, in which it is assumed that connections exist between ways of thinking and the social context. According to Kogler, Bourdieu tries to maintain a 'non-reductive balance between symbolic thought and social structures', which presupposes that while the social structures influence mark what is thought, that is not a totally determining effect because there is space for reflexive and creative responses (1975, pp. 143–144). Part of the problem is also that Bourdieu thinks about *habitus* as noncognitive. For this reason he cannot talk about *habitus* as a mediator between social structures and implicit symbolic or ethical schemes because he lacks a theory of reflective-conscious agent.

Bourdieu sees *habitus* as a preconscious process. *Habitus* is an embodied scheme of perception conception and action that is disconnected from reflexive learning processes. This presents a question: when and how can social actors become critically reflexive? For Bourdieu, reflexivity comes too late: his social actors are less critics and more preconscious agents who are socialized and adjusted to fit their fields of action. Thus writers like Burkitt describe Bourdieu as better at explaining why change is difficult rather than how it is possible:

> Doesn't Bourdieu explain the many problems that many critical, reflexive thinkers experience when they try to reshape the interpretive,

implicit schemes within their societies? Is he not showing how these are so often resistant to change, how people are invariably so stubborn in letting them go, or in many cases afraid to do so, even though their own *habitus* may confine them to a subordinate social position? Even when it is an outright call to rebellion, as in Marxism or various forms of socialism, it is hard for critical reflexivity alone to reshape the many varieties of *habitus*, let alone the various social fields that formed them. (1997, p. 195)

However, as Burkitt demonstrates, Bourdieu did consider the possibility of critical reflexivity. Certain groups, including various kinds of physical and social scientists, engage in what he described as the intellectual project of codification (1977). By codification he meant revealing the internal rules and conventions of a social practice. This is what anthropologists do as 'outsiders' as they look in on a society. It indicates the possibility for the reflexive translation of practices that are embedded in the *habitus* into explicitly codified rules, laws and regularities. These are figured out as conscious, cognitive schemes of social life and social action. As Bourdieu says, 'in societies where the work of codification is not very advanced, the *habitus* is the principle of most modes of practice' (1990a, p. 65). This implies that where codification advanced, the *habitus* is not the only means of orientation within social fields: there are other, more conscious and intentional modes of practice that are bound by stated rules, rituals or customs. Codification seems to be associated with people who are outside a given field of practice. Elias, for example, showed in his history of manners, that it is often those outside a social class or group, who are trying to gain entry to that class through social mobility, who need the aid of instructive books on manners and forms of behavior (1978).

Additionally Bourdieu allows for the fact that some people are critics. Alienation, or being an outsider, is a critical enabler of reflexivity. This can be explained, as Bourdieu acknowledges, because all knowledge is socially situated. Yet being an outsider is still a social relationship. It is as an outsider that one can engage in the work of codification. Furthermore, Bourdieu also claims that we need a crisis within fields before any critical discourse can be fully effective.

Politics begins, strictly speaking, with the denunciation of this tacit contract of adherence to the established order which defines the original doxa; in other words, political subversion presupposes cognitive subversion, a conversion of the vision of the world. But the heretical break with the established order, and with the dispositions and representations engendered by it among the agents moulded according to its structures, itself presupposes a conjuncture of critical discourse and objective crisis, capable of disrupting the close correspondence between the incorporated structures and the objective structures which produce them, and of instituting a kind of practical *epoche*, a suspension of the initial adherence to the established order. (1991, pp. 127–128)

A critical discourse does not come about easily, nor when it does arise can it immediately transform the social relations. This partly explains, to summarize Burkitt's observation, the frustration experienced by activists keen to create change. It also helps explain the sense of apathy experienced by those who know something is wrong in their society, but who fail to act because they believe nothing will ever change. It is only when we have a social crisis and major disruption, that critical voices sound out loud and gain the potential to generate change and a new order (1997, pp. 193, 202).

If Bourdieu does allow for change, he does so begrudgingly. With that in mind, I now attempt to complement the complex account of the coexistence of change and continuity that Bourdieu provides with an explicit account of the new offered by Castoriadis, framed by his question: how does political change that promotes autonomy, disrupts traditional worldviews and practices, and creates new ways of being come about? I canvass these questions with a view to their bearing on the question of generational politics and their implications for understanding change.

Castoriadis and the political imaginary

While Castoriadis's work is in many ways in opposition to conventional philosophical or academic analysis, Elliot argued that Castoriadis deserves to be counted as one of the most brilliant theorists of the relations between the individual and society in the twentieth century (2002, p. 14). Central to his work was the claim that each society is a construction, or a creation of its own world (1984b). In this statement, Castoriadis defines the core of his social theory in which he attempts to acknowledge the irreducible creativity of society and history. It is his emphasis on creativity and the work of the imagination that adds an important counterfoil to Bourdieu's emphasis on the conjunction of change and continuity in his theory of practice. As I argue here,

Castoriadis emphasizes how change, and especially political change, is the expression of creativity and imagination, even though he does not explain how creativity or imagination actually works.[10] Like Bourdieu, but in a quite different way, Castoriadis's refusal to provide a deterministic 'explanation' underpins one of the 'most sophisticated alternatives to the deterministic elements implicit in structuralist and poststructuralist thought' (Elliot 2002, p. 146).

Autonomy and imagination are critical themes in Castoriadis's work. He focuses throughout his writings on the question of 'autonomy'. That interest, however, is far more than the liberal preoccupation with individual freedom. What he had in mind was a collective freedom that involved the processes and conditions in which a society comes to recognize that its values are its own creation, and not 'given' (by 'God', or nature, or the mode of production).

Imagination is also given a distinctive edge by Castoriadis. For Castoriadis, philosophers have too often assumed the imaginary is simply a copy or reflection of the outside world.[11] Castoriadis argues instead that imagination makes the relation of mind and world possible. 'The imaginary is the subject's whole creation of a world for itself (1984b, p. 5). Here he draws on Freud, arguing that dreams, desires, wishes, pleasure and fantasy are at the core of our social process and political institutions. Castoriadis uses the idea of 'imagination' and the imaginary to understand change and contemporary 'politics'.

As I now demonstrate, Castoridias uses the idea of imaginary in an innovative and disconcerting way in his book *The Imaginary Institution of Society*. He argues that 'the imaginary of the society...creates for each historical period its singular way of living, seeing and making its own existence' (1974, p. 2). While avoiding any explanation, he says that these imaginaries come out of the imagination of people and assume a persistent and institutional character represented in the system of meanings that shape and govern the social or political order.

Social imaginaries are evident in our historical constructs and ontological creations. Social imaginaries give us the ways we see our being, our becoming and our social reality. These are totalities kept together by institutions like language, customs, technologies and modes of economic production, as well as by the meanings inherent in those institutions found in symbols and the vocabulary of the polis, as well as in commodities and the 'signs' of wealth. And while society is self-creating or self-instituting and always undergoing processes of self-alteration, for most of human history, the fact that the most important institutions have been human creations has been veiled by the social institutions themselves so that people tend not to recognize both that they 'made' them and have the capacity to change them. Moreover, self-alteration processes are slow and tend to be unnoticeable rather than rapid and obvious. This, Castoriadis says, raises the question for which there is no answer: when does society stop being the same as it was and become another?

I now consider what Castoriadis meant by all this. As I already indicated, Castoriadis spoke of 'the social or institutional imaginary', but he also talked about the 'radical imaginary'.

Castoriadis and the social imaginary

The 'social imaginary' (or the 'socially instituted imaginary') creates institutions in each society. These social imaginaries are the source of the underlying laws, values and 'worldviews' of the society. They always tend to be *heteronomous* in the sense that the imaginary promotes the idea that our actions are influenced by 'forces' 'outside' of us. As a product of our social imaginary, institutions are also bearers of 'significations'. Those who are religious, for example, believe in a God or gods, which are social imaginary significations sustained by institutions like churches and schools and which rely on founding heroes, ritual objects, taboos and myths. Similarly 'the state' and 'capital' are institutions animated and sustained by imaginary significations.

Given that crystallized social significations and institutions are the product of *instituted social imaginary*, the social imaginary works to ensure continuity, reproduction and the preservation of the same traditional forms used to govern and endure, as long as there is no significant historic change or major new creations that change or replace them (Castoriadis 2007, pp. 73–75). In this way societies tend to become what Castoriadis calls '*heteronomous*'.[12]

This means, firstly, that the institutional imaginary works against people's questioning social institutions. This in turn produces conforming individuals who are not free or autonomous, but rather subject to 'external' conditions and for whom questioning existing laws and commonsense practices is not only prohibited but it is 'mentally inconceivable' and 'psychically unbearable'. As such, individuals are conscious but not self-reflective (Castoriadis 1997, p. 336). Among the different kinds of institutions and or levels within them human language stands out as a 'trans-historical institution' observing how no society can exist without language even though the language differs according to the society. The same applies to 'the individual' – there is no society that does not institute an individual: it is just that in each society, the types of individuals differ. Moreover, we cannot see our relationship to language – as an institution – because we cannot remove ourselves from it to look at it from the outside and recognize it as constituted by people.

Given this, Castoriadis argued, we are blocked from developing theories of our institutions because we are inside them. In saying this, he used the word *theory* in the traditional sense, that is, to gaze, to look across from and inspect the institution. This is difficult, if not impossible, because we cannot get outside the social institutions to gaze and look across. Indeed we are fragments of them. How we see, what we think and say is 'profoundly dependent on language', on 'the type of individual' we are, on the type of family we belong to. These are only some examples of the 'prevalence... of the thoroughness with which we are all penetrated by the institute elements of our native society' (2007, p. 92).

In this respect, *heteronomous* societies are different from *autonomous* societies, in which citizens constantly practice critical reflection and recognize the socially constructed nature of the institutions and society in which they live. Castoriadis defines a heteronomous society as one that is seen by its citizenry as having extra social authority derived from powerful historical, ancestral or divine sources, like a god. In heteronomous societies, we may believe we exercise our own judgment, even though how we see and act is informed by social criteria. In this way, most people are heteronomous because we judge on the basis of convention and public opinion (2007, p. 75).

It is difficult for heteronomous societies to become autonomous societies because doing so means institutions and fundamental beliefs within the society have to be questioned and possibly modified. This a monumental task because the social imaginary creates the world and shapes our psyches.

Yet whatever the power and reach of the social imaginary, Castoriadis insists that it can never repress or squash another kind of imaginary, namely the 'radical imaginary'.

Castoriadis and the radical imaginary

The radical imaginary refers to our open-ended capacity that derives from the imagination of singular human beings. It always *appears whenever there is human collectivity*. The radical imagination of the singular individual is the 'essential determining element' of the human psyche. It is that unceasing flux of representations, desires and feelings. As he explains, even if you close yourself off to sensory perception by shutting your eyes or blocking your ears, there will always be something. In describing the radical imaginary, Castoriadis refers to Aristotle's recognition of the imaginary in his statement that 'the soul never thinks without phantasm', that is, without imaginary representation (2007, p. 71). The radical imaginary is what goes on inside us: it includes images, memories, fears, hopes and desires that 'surge forth', which we experience in ways we sometimes understand and other times not. Values and emotions in the social imaginary, like glory, hate, patriotism or nostalgia, are not expressions of our logical systems or some 'reflection' of reality, so much as 'poles' that bring into existence desires toward which we are oriented.

The radical imaginary is discrete from, but can also be a part of, the shared social imaginary. In this way the relationship between the radical and social imaginaries reflects the interdependency between the self, others and society (1997, p. 332). Socialization, Castoriadis says, 'stifles' the psyche, and in so doing ensures it expresses itself conventionally. The radical imagination of the human psyche is 'tamed, then channelled, regulated and brought into line with life in society and with what is called 'reality' (2007, pp. 74–75). Individuals absorb and internalize the institutions of society and their significations by learning the language, the categorization of things, the order, the dominant ethical frames, what is acceptable and unacceptable behavior, what is valued and what is not.

Social transformation

In heteronomous societies, we may believe we exercise our own judgment, but in reality how we see and act is shaped by overbearing social processes. In this way, most people are heteronomous because we judge on the basis of convention and public opinion (2007, p. 75). For this reason, thinking about and questioning the 'social imaginary' operating in a heteronomous society is 'an exceptional occurrence', and has only been encountered twice and only within the European and Greco-Western traditions – in the periods mentioned above. Achieving this represents a 'tremendous historic break'.

When this does happen, we see rich instances of creativity. It is so rare that Castoriadis points to only two examples in Western history: the first centers on the evolution of the classical era in Athens when the Athenian polis saw the birth of democracy, philosophy and tragedy, as well as the arts and sciences.[13]

The second 'project of autonomy' that Castoriadis identified can be found in the onset of the 'modern period' in that period convention-ally referred to as the European Renaissance, which spanned roughly from the fourteenth to the seventeenth centuries (Castoriadis 2007, pp. 77–79). The 'autonomy project', which 'defines' the Renaissance, stirred up and excited every aspect of society, creating new forms and content at a pace previously unknown with the 'explicit intention of fermenting change'. It involved a movement that subverted older models of authority like God and substituted an expanded regard for human reason, saw the development of radical new scientific and technological knowledge, including Newtonian physics and the printing press, and inspired a nascent democratic project that erupted in a succession of political revolutions in the seventeenth, the eighteenth and the nine-teenth centuries.

For Castoriadis, the immense acceleration of technological develop-ments that took place simultaneously with these cultural developments was more significant than anything seen before. The Renaissance chal-lenged the European social imaginary, producing in turn the critical rationalism that helps define the Enlightenment and German Idealism. One long-term ripple effect of the Renaissance included changes in the scientific imaginary that were responsible not only for cultural disrup-tion but for developments like quantum and relativity theory, advances in medical theory and new disciplines like the social sciences, psychoa-nalysis and sociology.

Castoriadis and nondeterminism

From our earliest history, he says we can see the emergence of radical novelty. And if we do not wish to resort to transcendental factors to account for this, we must then assume a power of creation, *vis a formandi*, immanent to human collectives as well as to individual human beings (Castoriadis 2007, p. 72). External 'factors' that are natural, biological or logical are conditions reflected in radical innovation, and in the insti-tutions we create and form in, for example, language, custom, norms and techniques, *but they cannot account for them*, for that is the domain of the imaginary. (This points to the observation that, while the social imaginary and institutions are free creations of citizens, they are also constrained.) Castoriadis sees transhistorical and second-order institu-tions as intertwined as they produce a particular kind of society (2007, pp. 100–101). A radical transformation of society can only come from individuals who want their autonomy on both a social and an individual level. They achieve this by continuously preserving and augmenting their autonomy, which involves working to cultivate individuals who aspire to having their independence, by taking responsibility for themselves and encouraging as many people as possible toward that end. Without this creative political work, social change cannot come about. Castoriadis also emphasized the role played by the creative imagination. As he argued,

> The great scientific advances are outgrowths of the creation of new imaginary schemes, formed under the constraint of available experience but not 'following from' that experience. (2007, p. 79)

Given this, there are good reasons to recognize that within human collectives there lies a power of creation. For Castoriadis, the collective and radical imaginary within a single human being are creative forces that generate out of nothing (Lat. *ex nihilo*), bringing into existence new forms that were not there before, new forms of being. Here he is talking about an ontological creation in the form of new worldviews, linguistic and innovation in language, art, music and new ways of being. As testimony to the power of the imaginary, Castoriadis adduces the 'basic fact' that we cannot explain the birth of society or the course of history by natural factors, be they biological or other, anymore than we can talk sensibly about the rational activity of a 'rational' being. Equally, the imagination itself and the act of creation cannot be explained by reducing it to some prior set of 'causal factors'. Castoriadis understood creation to be the emergence of newness that, whether deliberate or unconscious, is itself undetermined. He thus described creation as ex nihilo, or stemming from nothing (1998, pp. 321, 404).[14]

When this 'historic creation' takes place in partially open societies populated with self-reflective individuals, we see 'projects of collective and individual autonomy'. The primary mover of such change is politics described as collective emancipation and self-reflecting, uninhibited critical thought. The aim of such political projects is not happiness (utility maximizing as is the value within a utilitarian ethical frame), but freedom. In this way, freedom as autonomy is 'effective, humanly feasible', reflective positing of the rule of individuals and collective activity' (Castoriadis 1997, p. 337).

Sociohistorical struggles produced by such political projects have created valuable intellectual and political freedoms and new types of being that 'consciously and explicitly' change partially or fully the edicts of their own existence. What materializes is a self-legislating society and new types of beings – who are deliberating and reflective. This permits us to create some distance from our society, to listen to and accept criticism. This is attested to by the creation of many different societies and by the constant historical alteration of societies, which is both slow and rapid.

Such creations are conditioned by external 'factors' (as distinct from being caused by 'them'). Numbers, size, color and taste are creations of ourselves (our living bodies) that are embodied in our human psyche. For example, under certain situations, light waves, molecules and so on can induce a person to create an image or idea that is sometimes socially shared, and sometimes not. The point is that the imaginary is made up or invented content that can be derived from the 'things' we perceive, as well as new and hidden images, ideas and feelings that are not delivered or accessed through our senses.

Such an imaginary is both generative and the source of change. It is our ability to intuit and spontaneously create objects without those objects having been present before. It is the power to make what is not, to make present within our thoughts something that is absent, without 'external incitement', but conditioned by perceptions of external independent objects (Castoriadis 1970).

For Castoriadis, creative phases or periods, or indeed periods of decadence, cannot be explained in the ways explanations are traditionally offered. We may gather facts that seem relevant and make sense, but these never produce 'explanations' as explanations might be conventionally understood in terms of causal effects. Castoriadis's imaginary defies the salience and value of causality and structural functionalist thinking – which is what most traditional formulations of the idea of explanation require (see, for example, Carl Hempel's covering law model of explanation). Against the inclinations or traditions promoted by natural scientists and structural determinism, there are 'no commanding laws' that govern the radical imagination, that direct 'when it flourishes and when it fades'.

Drawing on Freud, he argued that the socialization process that fashions us and that sublimates our psyche is never complete and never fully accepted. It is through the cracks, to use Leonard Cohen's words, that 'lets the light gets in', that we get glimpses of our core psyche, it in questioning, subversion and transgression that we see evidence of the always to be incomplete socialization project and the imaginary which provides an inexhaustible supply of generative capacity and the source of social change.

To say that Castoriadis's account of change as an autonomous political project does not provide a traditional causal explanation is not to imply that it is deficient, only that he offers an alternative explanation that identifies the imaginary as the source of change.

Conclusion: drawing it together

I argued in this chapter that change is a perplexing. We now have evidence about all kinds of things that seem to be changing. We have seen how the traditional constraints imposed by geography, physical space and time on humans for millennia have been replaced in virtual social spaces that facilitate abstract, disembodied interpersonal interaction between occupants of that space. With the advent of digital media, we have seen how many people are developing new values, norms and behaviors about their privacy, about politeness or rudeness, about sex and their bodies (e.g., 'sexting') and manners generally. In some contexts, for example 'texting' or reading text messages while simultaneously talking with another person who is in your immediate company is no longer seen as bad manners. Other people send images of themselves naked or having sex with each other on their mobile phones or laptops. Finally, we have evidence of new ways of engaging with governments and corporations via denial of service attacks on websites, on-line petitions and the use of mobile phones to mobilize protest movements.

Given that understanding the phenomenon of change is what I want attempt here, the questions I need to ask are clear: while we have evidence that something is happening 'out there' that typically involves young people and the new media, how is this to be understood? What if anything about this is evidence of social and political renewal?

I have drawn primarily on three major theorists from the twentieth century, namely Arendt, Bourdieu and Castoriadis, to think about some of the main elements for a heuristic frame that I use in my later case studies to address these questions.

From Arendt, I take the idea that the fact that there are new generations provides an ontological base for hope. For Arendt, the decisive fact that determines humans as conscious, remembering beings is that we entered the world through birth and leave it though death. It is what provides us with the capacity to act and create new beginnings. In this way, natality and mortality can be seen as the ontological frame for various human activities – including the political life. This implies that the idea of 'generation' does play a part in understanding our time.

From Bourdieu, we get a complex, articulated generational structuralism. His theory of practice provides a relational account of human action that considers both human agency and a structural conception of action. I propose to build on his central proposal, put forward in his theory of practice as *habitus*, that social life involves the coexistence of continuity as well as change. I note too that some of his critics observe that while Bourdieu tries to maintain a 'non-reductive balance between symbolic thought and social structures' this does not resolve the problem Kogler (1997) identified, namely that Bourdieu cannot talk about *habitus* as a mediator between social structures and implicit symbolic or ethical schemes because he lacks a theory of a reflective-conscious agent. Perhaps Bourdieu can get out of this conundrum by arguing that outsiders can more easily escape from the *habitus* into critical reflexivity, or by arguing that choice and innovation can be achieved when we encounter experiences we have not had before.

Yet this does not do justice to the evidence of social movements and political activism, which is why Castoriadis's emphasis on the power of imagination provides a new dimension.

Finally, from Castoriadis we get a bold, nondeterminist account of the role of our imaginative capacity for creativity. As he argued, we cannot explain the birth of society or the course of history by natural factors, be they biological or other. Equally, we cannot explain imagination or creation by reducing it to a prior set of 'causal' factors. As he maintained, like Bourdieu, humans tend to become subjects of their own imaginative constructs: what we first create we end up obeying as if these constructs are real. We bow down before God, 'society' 'capitalism' or the 'economy' as if these products of our imagination have become real and are beyond our control. This may partly explain why radical change is in his view is relatively uncommon. As he says thinking about and questioning the 'social imaginary' operating in a heteronomous society is 'an exceptional occurrence' and has only been encountered twice and only within the European and Greco-Western traditions – in periods mentioned above. Achieving this represents a 'tremendous historic break'.

These writers help to frame a number of sensitizing questions. Given that many young people are now engaging with new media in the milieu of the late twentieth and early twenty-first centuries, has that environment created space for novel experience even disjunctures for people between how they know things ought to be and how it actually is? Are we experiencing a time of radical change and autonomy now? Are we witnessing what Castoriadis called an autonomous political project that can create the kind of changes in those rare historical moments he identified? Does the novelty of the new media encourage young people especially to create, innovate and exercise positive freedom?

Before I can directly address these questions I need to turn to the task of exploring the value of a generational concept (in the following chapter). I then argue the case in the chapter after that, that generation can be conceptualized in a credible way, in a way that will help develop a heuristic frame for my investigation of political renewal.

3
Change and Generation

The idea that we can speak about baby boomers, Generation X and the millennials (Gen Y) or even 'Generation Next' when explaining things like social change or new kinds of politics has become a very popular and seductive cliché. Some of this discussion and commentary asserts, for example, that young people now form digital communities using information and communication technologies in ways that promise to revive the public sphere and democracy or that nurture new forms of youth citizenship (Dalhgren 2013, Vesnic-Alujevic 2012, White 2013, pp. 216–246).

In spite of the fact that this disposition to talk about generations assumes an ambiguous quality, it is also a practice that has a long history. In the 1920s, for example, José Ortega Y Gasset argued that youth had supplanted the working class as the motor force of historical change (1923). Likewise, writers from Herbert Marcuse (1969) and Kenneth Keniston (1971) to William Strauss and Neil Howe (1991), David Pyvis (1991) and Strauss and Howe (2000) saw generational succession as the engine room of social change. Today many academics, journalists and commentators would be lost if they could not talk about 'generations'.[1] This kind of talk became especially prevalent since language like baby boomers became a popular way of communicating about the large number of people born soon after 1945.

It seems the idea of a baby boomer generation was first used, according to the *Oxford English Dictionary*, in a 1970 article in the *Washington Post*.[2] From there, the idea migrated into government agencies like the US census and into academic circles. The US Census, for example, found it appropriate to talk about the 'Baby Boom' as 'people born from mid-1946 to 1964'. Moreover, 'The Baby Boom is distinguished by a dramatic increase in birth rates following World

War II and is one of the largest generations in US history' (2010, p. 3). Many academics and researchers have also found it useful to adopt the language of the baby boom generation, while attributing to that generation traits and attributes based on ideas that they are affluent, politically and socially progressive and have a strong sense of their own privilege. Such traits are said to reflect the fact that they grew up in a time of high employment and massive government subsidies of housing and education (Hogan, Perez and Bell 2008, Ouwram 1997, Gillon 2004).

For the Gen X category, as Harris (2002) notes, this term seems to have been devised first by two academics, Hamblett and Deverson (1964). It was a usage then transferred to popular culture via Generation X, a 1970s punk band (headed by Billy Idol) and then popularized again courtesy of a novel by Douglas Coupland (1989). Academics and commentators also attributed a myriad of alleged social, political and psychological attributes to an age cohort. I refer, for example to observations that Generation X involved a refashioning 'of differing identities within and against the mainstream driven by punk subculture, alternative music, reality television, postmodernism, and the Internet (Harris, 2003, pp. 268–269).

As for Generation Y – or what are sometimes called the millennials – usage of this term seems to have appeared in a 1993 *Ad Age* editorial to describe contemporary teenagers said to be different from Generation X. *Ad Age* identified 1982 as the terminus date and included the teenagers of the next ten years.[3] Again, the reference to Generation Y or the millennials seems to have benefited journalists and academics alike: Strauss and Howe wrote about the millennials in a study on the role of generations in US history (1991) before releasing an entire book devoted to them (2000). Others disciplines like quantitative psychology also found it useful to refer to the millennials and to undertake research claiming to 'discover' measurable differences in life goals, concern for others and civic orientation among American high school seniors between different generations (see also Twenge 2006, Winograd and Hais 2011). As Twenge et al. argued, drawing on a big sample (N = 463,753), that when compared to

> Baby Boomers (born 1946–1961) at the same age, [and] GenX'ers (born 1962–1981), the Millennials (born after 1982) considered goals related to extrinsic values (money, image, fame) more important and those related to intrinsic values (self-acceptance, affiliation, community) less important. (2012, p. 1025; see also Twenge et al. 2010)

The results in this study offer a pessimistic portrait:

> In most cases, Millennials slowed, though did not reverse, trends toward reduced community feeling begun by Gen X. The results generally support the 'Generation Me' view of generational differences rather than the 'Generation We' or no change views. (ibid.)

Cogin is equally negative as she claims the evidence points to marked differences in expectations and motivators across generational cohorts (2012, p. 2268). Pointing to work by Glass (2007), which found that Generation X and Generation Y have different views on work compared to baby boomers, Cogin argues, 'Not only do members of Generation Y look different, with their body piercings, tattoos, and electronic decorations, they behave and think differently as well' (2012, p. 2268; see also Crumpacker and Crumpacker 2007, Stewart and Bernhardt 2010).

In an early study about the effect of the interplay of the new digital affordances of the Net and generational politics, Xenos and Foot argued there is 'a significant gap between the online sensibilities of young people and the ways in which the vast majority of candidates for office in the United States conduct the online portions of their campaigns' (2008, p. 58).

Yet we see here the problems that an overly simple use of the idea of generational politics produces. The explanatory logic involved when relying on the idea of generations is evident when, for example, British journalist John Harris, who represents himself as a Gen X'er, endeavors to explain why young British Gen Y'ers support the Cameron government's policies, which are antagonistic to their own interests:

> I'm a comparatively ancient 43, and it has always seemed to me that my own generation – X, the pollsters call it – has been something of a washout. We seemed to be rendered punch-drunk by Thatcherism, holding on to a vague affection for the postwar welfare state – we could get the dole with no questions asked, after all – and being stunned into silence by the social and political revolution that began in our childhood, and was firmly embedded by the time we reached our 20s. (2013)

Implicit in Harris' description of Gen Y (which he says includes people born between 1980 and 2000) is the idea that the emergence of a new generation itself *explains* the process of political change. He argues that Gen Y rejected or has never known the social liberalism that animated post–1945 'welfare state' collectivism and has instead wholeheartedly adopted 'the free-market worldview handed on from Thatcher, to Major to Blair and Brown and now Cameron'. Like Howker and Malik, who talk about the 'Jilted Generation' (2013, pp. 10–12), Harris draws on the work of polling researchers like *Ipsos Mori* and 17 years of polling research to talk about four generations, starting with those born in 1945 or before, and ending with Generation Y. Harris refers to the 'yawning gap between the generations', like their respective responses to the claim that 'the government should spend more money on welfare benefits for the poor, even if it leads to higher taxes' (2013). He goes on to argue that while around 40% of those born in 1945 or before still agreed with this, that support is halved among those aged 33 and under. Likewise only 20% of Gen Y now support the idea that 'the creation of the welfare state is one of Britain's proudest achievements' compared with 70% of the prewar cohort.

This kind of analysis is also found in Shuham (2012). Towle (2013) relies on the 'fact' there are large numbers of people born within a common time frame who constitute an age cohort or 'generation', which is then used to 'explain' why change takes place in politics, policies or worldviews, like a shift in political paradigms.

It does not, however, explain how membership in an age cohort translates to a story of generational political conflict or change. There are a couple of problems with these popular stories of generational change. One is relatively small and the other more substantive.

The minor observation is that a large body of credible evidence exists that indicates that most young people tend to share or reproduce their parents' social and political outlook and values. In the mid-twentieth century, it was clear to Hyam (1959) and Jennings and Niemi (1968), for example, that the evidence pointed to the intergenerational transmission of political views and allegiances. That conclusion has been supported more recently by people like Seiden (2009) and Mayer (2012). Seiden found that young conservative Americans overwhelmingly shared the values of their conservative parents, and much more so that than did young American 'liberals' Mayer demonstrated how young 'teens' emulate their parents' values before coming, as part of a process he describes as 'political self-efficacy', to form their own views in the last years of their adolescence (2012).

These writers are not alone in their endeavors to understand the complex issue of how young people form their political views, how they variously engage in political practices, and the role (if any) played by their family, their schooling, friendship networks or their use of traditional and digital media. It is work that highlights the need for caution about overly simple accounts that see a complex and highly variegated process of political development by reducing it to a simple single factor, namely the 'generation' one was born into. That observation segues into a larger observation about the nature of social and political change.

Social order and social and political change have long been central themes in many of the social sciences, like sociology, economics and political science since their origins in the eighteenth and the nineteenth centuries. I will be draw on a number of the traditions that seem to shed the most light on how we can think about change, primarily involving what Schatzki et al. called 'practice theory' (2001). Demonstrated in Pierre Bourdieu's work (1979, 1992, 1990a and b), it is a perspective that shows how our social lives can be understood by paying attention to our 'practices' and the ways in which they which do not change easily or quickly due to its habitual character. For Bourdieu, human practice becomes '*habitus*' typically through the incorporation of inert habits of thought, feeling and action expressed in the ways we talk, live together in families and experience and use our bodies. I develop this point and defend my framing of the problem by drawing on practice theory in the next chapter.

The point of this is relatively straightforward: the idea of practice as *habitus* implies that change is not as easy or as common as many people might like to imagine. In this way, practice theory does not make the mistake that some Marxist social theory, neoclassical economists, technological determinists or commentators and researchers do when they rely on the category of 'generation' in ways that beg the question of change. This they do by seeing generational change as the effect of their favored explanatory categories, be they 'class conflict', the power of technology to shape human behavior, or utility-maximizing rational economic people. I argue that it is not wise to see change or the emergence of new kinds of politics as an effect of generational conflict, or simply as a consequence of the emergence of a new generation of young people.

Having said that, however, it is also unwise to simply dismiss the idea of generations altogether. I agree with Pilcher (1994) and Woodman (2013, pp. 3, 10) that the sociology of generations has been an undervalued lineage. Given that the concept of generations has not received the same attention as other sociological categories like 'class' and 'gender', I argue here that questions about how to think about temporal cultural and spatial boundaries, and the importance of collective identity remain critical to this task.

In this chapter, I propose then to address a series of questions. How did the idea of 'generation' emerge as an explanation for various social and political phenomena? What are some of the distinctive analytic aspects of its use as a theoretical category? In posing these questions, I acknowledge that the category 'generation' shares with other widely used categories in the social and physical sciences a combination of essentialism and 'fuzziness' (Lakoff 1973, Manning 1994, Dietz and Moruzzi 2009). Given this, I ask what are some of the problems entailed in using the category? Can it be used at all? And if it is to be a source of insight, how will that be possible?

My aim is to determine whether we can legitimately say people who share a particular relationship with history by virtue of their chronological age and shared location in historical time allows us to use the language of 'generation'. As I suggest, the meaning of 'generation', like all social classifications, changes across history. Even within the one period, a 'generation' can be characterized in many ways. Given the intrinsically 'fuzzy' nature of such categories, can they be useful? Can we express something general about a group because its members were born to a particular milieu and time, and experienced similar events, even though they experienced them differently?

I now attempt to show, courtesy of a brief excursion into the etymology of talk about 'generations', that we face a long history of conceptual and lexical ambiguity, an opaqueness also evident in discussions about the merit of talking about 'generations' versus 'cohorts'.[4] I then address the evolution of a sociology of generations, beginning with Karl Mannheim (1928/1952), who explored the idea in the 1920s in his attempt to understand social change. For Mannheim, a 'generation'

represents a unique type of social location based on the dynamic interplay between being born in a particular year and the socio-political events that occur throughout the life course of the birth cohort, particularly while the cohort comes of age. (McMullin et al. 2007, pp. 299–300)

As I show later in this chapter, starting in the 1950s a different approach offered by structural functionalist sociologists like Eisenstadt (1956) and Talcott Parsons (1942/1962) to thinking about generations saw a preoccupation with 'youth cultures'. This account relied on an assumption about the inherently agnostic nature of 'adolescence'. It was an approach that owed much to the earlier work of psychologists like G. Stanley Hall (1904), who 'discovered' and propagated the powerful

influential discourse of 'adolescence' as a transitionary period characterized by antisocial conduct and painful angst, storm and stress said to
plague every generation (1904). As I suggest here, structural functionalist sociologists like Parsons and Eisenstadt were excessively concerned
about the maintenance of social order.

I argue that the concept of generation still has some heuristic value
for investigating changes taking place courtesy of new media – a recent
phenomenon involving disproportionate numbers of younger people.
One of the virtues of Mannheim's approach is that he sees the sociology
of generations as an issue in the sociology of time and that we need to
understand how time itself has a multiple nature and that biographical
and historical connections are complex. We also need to pay attention
to the nature of the problem that a sociology of generation is addressing.
As Woodman noted, while a simplified approach to generations risks
seeing everyone who was born at the same time as sharing the same
attributes, this is not the case with the sociology of generations: identifying divisions within a generation has a history back to Mannheim's
discussion of generational units and has the added benefit of being
able to trace both change and continuity but not as binary opposites
(Woodman 2013, p. 8.2).

I begin with the idea of generation itself.

Etymology of generation

The ambiguities that continue about how to best to think about change
and development can be seen in the evolution of the categories and
meanings associated with generation. As Nash noted, while the first
definition of generation in Webster's unabridged dictionary was still
'procreation' into the 1960s, 'our most secure standard for defining
a generation rests on the Greek root of the word, *genos*, whose basic
meaning is reflected in the verb *genesthai*, 'to come into existence', and
as she notes,

> That moment when a child is born simultaneously produces a new
> generation separating parent and offspring – *gonos* ergo *genos* – and
> the very concept educes the paradox of an ever shifting threshold in
> time. (1978, p. 1)

Does 'generation' mean the reproduction of what already exists, or
does it signify the possibility of something new? In either case, how do

we understand the mechanisms operating in the processes that talk of generation denotes?

In most Anglo-European languages the idea of generation was used to denote processes of creation or the bringing of life forms or being into existence, as well as the existence of what we would now call age cohorts. It referred variously to the act of procreation, to parenting and to producing offspring. Other related words like 'stem', 'beget' or phrases like 'to give rise to' (something that did not previously exist) were other ways of saying what 'generate' means.

The idea of generation (in Greek as *gennítoras* or γεννήτορας) is found in Greek classical texts produced by medical and scientific writers like Hippocrates, Aristotle and Galen (Cobb 2006, pp. 17–23) and also by writers and poets like Homer. For Aristotle, whose portrayal was especially influential, generation was central to his ideas about change, 'potentiality and actuality'. It was also central for understanding processes of coming into being (production), or passing away, corruption and decay. In his *On the Generation of Animals*, Aristotle spoke about sexual reproduction and the process of biological development. He asked whether things come into being through causes, through some prime material, or whether everything is generated purely through 'alteration'. For Aristotle, the principle common to art and nature was

> As many things as come to be by nature or by art come to be by means of a being in actuality from that which is potentially such as that being. (734b pp. 22–23)

According to Aristotle, it is the male who generates in another, the female (716a pp.14–15).[5]

Likewise in Homer's *Iliad* (Book Six), Glaucas replies to Diomedes's questions about the source of his courage and skill thus:

> Greathearted son of Tydeus, why do you question my lineage
>
> As is the generation of leaves, so too of men:
>
> At one time the wind shakes the leaves to the ground,
>
> but then the flourishing woods Gives birth,
>
> and the season of spring comes into existence.
>
> So it is of the generations of men, which alternately come forth and pass away.

Like the English usage, ancient Greek and Latin terms for generation (*genos, genea, genesis, gone, genus, generatio,* etc.) carry various meanings, from birth and reproduction to age, time of life, cycle of life, race, family or even species. All these words stem from a common Indo-European root, *gen,* the fundamental signification of which is 'to come into existence'. As Nash notes,

> Like the verb to be, generation requires an adjective of context, a predicate of relativity, before it takes on meaning. Used sometimes with complacency ('my generation'), sometimes with belligerence (*your* generation), and even with affection, as when Telemachus vows his friendship to Peisistratus by reason of their similar ages, generation marks allegiance, time. (1978, p. 3)

The Greek *gennitoras* became the Latin *generationem,* or the noun *generatio,* or *generator,* which refers to that which causes, generates or produces. 'Genital' or genitalia, from the Latin *genitalis,* denotes generation or birth, and into the mid-fifteenth century, generation was used as a noun to name the reproductive or sex organs. Equally, the verb *regenerate* referred to the idea of making over again, or to 'be born anew'.

In the same period, medieval English speakers began using the word *generacion* in ways similar to modern English, namely, to refer to a cohort or mass of people born around the same time, or people who are the same step removed from a common ancestor. In this more modern and sociological sense, we see incarnations of the idea of 'generation' used in French (*generation*), in Italian (*generazione*), Turkish (*jenerasyon*) and Russian (*rehepalina*).

In its modern usage, generation is applied to many areas of life and in a variety of disciplines and fields of practice. In music, for example, the 'generating tone' is recognized as the common chord or fundamental note from which all other sounds are produced. In mathematics, 'a generator' is one element from which other components can be inferred. Similarly, as a design principle in areas like programming, a generator code prescribes or sets initial boundaries that produce specified outputs in the form of values or action. Likewise, in engineering and manufacturing, a generator is a piece of equipment used to change or convert one form of energy (e.g., coal or sunshine) into another (electrical energy).

By the early twentieth century, a discernible discourse about young people couched in terms of 'generation' was evolving. In sociology and the social sciences generally, the concept of generation – or social generation – began to refer to more than family, kinship groups or clans, by denoting all people born around the same time who are said to share similar characteristics, dispositions and values while growing up. Usually the age span specified is determined by the number of years between a parent's birth and that of their children (usually 25 to 30 years). In this way, the older denotations of generation as procreation were absorbed into a more sociological approach to what had once been rendered in terms of discourses about 'biology' and 'time'.

Mannheim's work came to be an important attempt to construct a sociological theory of generation.

Enter Mannheim

The German sociologist Mannheim is best known as the author of classic and highly influential works on the sociology of knowledge, for example, *Ideology and Utopia: An Introduction to the Sociology of Knowledge* and *Man and Society in an Age of Reconstruction* (1940–1952). He is also acknowledged to have produced the 'most systematic and fully developed treatment of generation from a sociological perspective' (Pilcher 1994, p. 482). He was one of the first modern theorists to develop a sociological account of generation as part of his endeavor to develop an alternative to the Marxist and traditional Idealist ideas on social change.

Mannheim was a Hungarian-born philosopher turned sociologist, who studied and worked Germany, Paris and London, and was one of the many intellectuals exiled from his homeland to Germany in 1925 after the Bella Kun-led insurrection staged in Budapest in 1919. Soon after that, in 1933, with the rise of Nazism in Germany, Mannheim once again was forced to flee, this time settling in England. Mannheim's intellectual resources included a sympathy for Marxism reflected, for example, in his sociology of knowledge. Mannheim approached the sociology of knowledge as an inquiry into the social and existential conditioning of knowledge by locating it in a specific sociohistorical space. Mannheim also saw generational location as a key aspect of the existential determination of 'certain definite modes of behaviour, feeling and thought' (1928/1952, p. 291). This combination of different, even contradictory, ideas is evident in arguments that the worldview of a group, whether they be a 'class' or a 'generation', is shaped by their socioeconomic position or in the case of a generation, their historic location.

He also drew on distinctive German traditions like phenomenology to shape his appreciation of hermeneutic questions, interpretation and interest in tracing the relationships between macro- and micro-analysis.

Mannheim was also strongly influenced by the German hermeneutic tradition and by writers like Wilhelm Dilthey (1833–1911). Dilthey decisively rejected mid-nineteenth-century positivism and what he saw as the misplaced enthusiasm by writers like Auguste Comte, John Stuart Mill and Buckle for using the 'natural sciences' as the model for the 'human studies'. Instead Dilthey emphasized the role of human emotion and imagination in human life and in intellectual attempts to make sense of social phenomena. In developing his own account of the 'proper' methods to be used by researchers in the 'human sciences', Dilthey drew on a combination of Kantian philosophy and romanticism. He focused on describing the 'worldview', which he argued shaped the 'lived experience' and the 'historical consciousness' of historical subjects. According to Dilthey, our experience of the world and of our self are bound together and historically conditioned by collective or cultural symbolic and emotional practices.[6]

That focus on understanding and interpretation in turn led to the idea that scholars ought to rely on individual-psychological and collective social-historical description and analysis to obtain deeper insight into human expression (e.g., text, music, art and creators in their contexts).

I now turn to Mannheim's (1952) account of the social and his notion of 'generational units'. Mannheim offers a sociological approach. As he argues,

> Were it not for the existence of social interaction between human beings – were there no definable social structure, no history based on a particular sort of continuity, the generation would not exist as a social phenomenon: there would be merely birth, ageing and death. (1952, p. 291)

With this in mind, Mannheim developed an account of generation that was understood as a cohort of people of the same/similar age, who grew up in the same time and whose characteristic aspirations, ideas and experience were shaped by the zeitgeist of that time. In his book *The Problem of Generations* (1952), first published in German, he drew on a synthesis of Marxist and phenomenological intellectual traditions to argue that our location in a sociohistorical time helps establish the parameters of our formative experiences and has an impact on our physical and psychosocial development in ways that affect who we are, who we become and what we do. He argued that each generation has a distinctive historical consciousness that is shaped by specific historical events. Generation in a sense is a consciousness (zeitgeist – or spirit of the time) that guides their approach to the world. Those historic events or trends are said to help explain why one generation differs from others and how change takes place. This concept seemed to offer a useful beginning for thinking about change.

Yet Mannheim argued for understanding time as a social phenomenon. In this way he anticipated later studies of time (e.g., Adams 1990), which saw it as a multilayered and complex part of social existence, enabling him to see generation as a marker of time past, time future and of historical change. Far from describing time as positivists tended to do, as an external, measured 'objective' phenomenon, Mannheim, like his hermeneutic predecessors, understood time to be an internal and 'subjective' experience. This in turn enabled him to acknowledge the need to recognize the diversity and disagreement that are conditioned by the different social, cultural and geographic locations within a generation. As he explained,

> within any generation there can exist a number of differentiated, antagonistic generation units. (Mannheim 1952, p. 306)

In this way a generation includes groups in which there is disagreement, but who nonetheless belong to each other because they are oriented toward each other. For Mannheim, 'generation units' imply a binding connection between members.

In developing his concept of generation, Mannheim used a class analogy, offering a dialectic approach to change, but without a reliance on causal explanations. Like class, the concept of generation was used to identify a particular group. Rather than an individual's location in the economic system of production, it was a demographic reference and location in specific structural and temporal positions in the age structure.

Those born into a particular time (or milieu or 'field of action') were said to share similar life experiences as they grow up. Furthermore, one's earlier years were seen as formative and 'transitionary' as the young person leaves the natal family and enters the 'adult world'. This formed part of the developmental story reinforced by 'scientific narratives' about stages of development and 'adjustments'. Formative development is particularly relevant because it is when we develop and consolidate values and worldviews that are sustained into adulthood. It is said to be those initial values or framings that provide the prism through which subsequent events are seen and interpreted.

Participation in *historic events* (particularly if they occur in times of rapid change) were said to produce a generation as *actuality*. Like class, one's age position is a distinct and objective fact that the individual may or may not recognize even though he/she may have a sense of sharing a space in the sociohistorical process. This is not to suggest that all 'members' of a generation share the same characteristic attitudes and consciousness, because their exposure to events and how they interpret and experience them are not of the same quality or intensity. Mannheim recognized that each of us interprets events or acts in different ways from our peers. Historic events affect people differently according to their particular geography, gender, religion, class and so forth positioning. This is what Mannheim meant when he referred to the idea of generational units.

For Mannheim, involvement in significant events during our formative years predisposes us toward certain ways of thinking and being, and in doing so creates generation potentiality. In this way a sense of generation can be created by generation members' consciousness of their shared history and subjective feelings (Hammarstrom 2004, pp. 46–47).

Mannheim opted for explaining political stability and change by reference to the political actor's place in the life cycle:

> individuals who hold membership in the same space and age group would share common space and time location in the socio-historical process, these commonalities would delimit their experiental situations and hence produce a common attitude, activities and behavior. (Mannheim, cited in Zody 1970, pp. 18–29)

Since Mannheim, it has been was widely argued that it is through consideration of one's age and the context in which one grows up that we can better understand political opinion, stability and change. Furthermore, assuming the existence of different generations, it seems to follow that there must be generational conflict. According to some, the population was stratified into generations. Empirically, however, the idea that there exists a life-cycle-driven basis for change and the political antagonism between the generations has been effectively contested (see, e.g., Connell 1974, pp. 177–185, Bourdieu and Passeron 1977). 'Reproduction' theorists, for example, observed how cultural heritability offered a much more powerful factor to explain why particular people believe and act as they do (Bourdieu and Passeron 1977, Bourdieu, P., 1990a and b, Connell and Ashenden 1982).

As with social class, change is seen to take place through a dialectical process between younger and older generations as they contest power and resources. And while this approach may have heuristic value in identifying intergenerational tensions and alliances, it is limited as an explanation for change. Whether framings of a dialectic antagonistic relationship between generations, or, in the hands of functionalists, framed 'anomie' or failed socialization, neither fully explains innovation, transgression or social change.

Mannheim was also critical of the overreliance on biological explanations of social phenomena like change, arguing that proponents of such a view fail to pay sufficient attention to the 'fabric of social processes' in favor of those biological accounts (1952, p. 278). One explanation for that tendency is that embedded in biological accounts is the popular, but mistaken, assumption that laws of nature exist that work to govern the structure of the universe and that those laws can be used to explain both natural and social phenomena. It is an interpretation that relies on the seductive capacity of the episteme of the physical sciences and methodologies, and more specifically on materialism, reductionism and determinism, which as I explain in more detail in the next chapter, are inappropriate for explaining social phenomena (Makkreel 1975, Flyvberg 2001).

After Mannheim

As I already indicated a number of writers since Manheim have adopted the vocabulary of generation, and tried to apply it to understanding a range of social issues. One important strand of discussion and theoretical development addressed the problem of how to secure social order and the reproduction of the social order by subsuming the idea of generation into a discussion about 'antisocial' 'youth cultures' – or 'youth subcultures'. This youth culture literature presumed a relationship existed between one's age and political attitudes and behavior.

The American sociologist Parsons (1944/1966) was very effective in promoting a sociological account of 'youth' and 'adolescence' in terms of a natural development model. According to this approach, 'youth' is a universal phase or experience that can best explained in terms of functionalist sociology and biology. For Parsons, and colleagues like Eisenstadt, certain differences between 'young people' and the adult population could be identified and used to explain change and deviance (1956). Although he did not attempt to develop an explicit theory of generations, his account of a youth culture worked in some of the ways that the idea of generation has worked. Parsons those differences developed culturally or generationally and were informed by commonly shared values, aspirations and practices.

However, Parsons argued that youth cultures were largely irresponsible and deeply antagonistic to adults as teachers and parents (1942/1963, p. 32). The concept of youth cultures or youth subcultures built on the idea of 'the adolescent' and classic sociological accounts of 'society', which until the 1960s were predominantly functionalist. Youth culture was typically used to describe young people as rebellious, difficult and a problem to themselves and to others (see Parsons 1942/1963).

Throughout the 1950s and 1960s, many social scientists agreed that young people as 'adolescents' came together in opposition to adult authority. Other American sociologists, like James Coleman (1961) who wrote *The Adolescent Society*, argued that young people were part of a

a relatively autonomous culture, controlled internally by a system of norms and sanctions and largely antithetical or indifferent to that offered by parents, teachers and clergymen. (1961, p. 4)

For Parsons and Coleman, the young generation, or youth culture, were essentially deviant, formed through extended age segregation in which 'the adolescent is dumped into a society of his peers' (Coleman 1961, p. 4). Berger concurred, warning how they were also dangerous, especially to those who were interested in maintaining the prevailing social order:

youthfulness is excess; it is implicit or incipient disorder; for society it is a 'problem' that requires handling, control, co-option or channelling in socially approved directions. (1963, p. 331)

Other sociologists, like the Polish-born Shmiel Eisenstadt, studied age groups and social change. Eisenstadt worked in Israel and the United States across the middle part of the twentieth century. Often described as the sociologist of youth, he wrote the influential book *From Generation to Generation: Age Cohorts and Social Structure*, which first appeared in 1956, in which he examined the 'alienation' of youth, 'youthful rebellion', generational conflict and the role of institutional change and new 'behavioural patterns'. As a functionalist he examined 'the problem of youth' in modern societies, drawing on the work of Parsons and arguing that experiences of particular generations (such as migration, persecution etc.) were significant in shaping their worldviews, intellectual interests and politics.

In the 1960 and 1970s in Europe and the United States and also for those who looked toward those countries saw examples being set by student action in places like France, a new generation of leaders and movements including antiwar protests various civil rights movements and sexual liberation movements by women and gays. Indeed 'the age of dissenting youth' has been fixed in the popular memory and academic treatment of the 1960s and the early 1970s. This era apparently was dominated by radical new musical styles and offensive rock bands, by countercultural clothing and long hair, by the search for sexual freedom and liberation (Altman 1987), and by the rise of a narcotic drug culture. Radical antiwar and anticonscription protests by outraged, outrageous revolting students, and endless demonstrations 'about anything and everything', have become the dominant and lasting icons of the period (Bear 1970, pp. 155–159). In those heady days, many young people who questioned the dominant values of their society were also attracted to 'counter-hippie cultures', which were in turn perceived by many onlookers as a direct threat to social order. And then as now when young people were perceived as a threat or as victims, the tendency was to speak in generalizations.

For some, it was a framing informed by the dominance of neo-Marxist thinking at the time, which saw change in terms of conflict or dialectical interaction. For others, it was a fear of subversion. Indeed, analysts produced many explanations to account for the rise of 'the radical youth movement' internationally. Many advocated the view that student dissent and pacifism from the mid-1960s on were fronts for subversion or fifth-column activity directed from the Kremlin in Moscow. Others saw it as juvenile vandalism said to be inherent in adolescence.

One favored explanation for this rapid growth of youth activism and rise of a 'new left' movement in the 1960s was the idea of the 'generational gap' and generational conflict. Contemporary discussions of the youth (student) movement of the 1960s as well as later, focused directly on this notion of a generational conflict in which a certain commonality of age became the dominant explanation for the distinctive forms of action (Charlesworth 1969). Considerable use was also made of terms like 'generational politics' or youth culture, which by the mid-1960s and early 1970s were achieving widespread currency in the social sciences. A generation gap or generational conflict between those under and those over the age of 25 as the fundamental and underlying basis for the rise of those youth oppositional movements. For *some*, such explanations suggested that those conflicts were nothing to be alarmed about since they had been going on since time immemorial, and that they expressed inevitable, even biological or psychological Oedipal factors working between the generations. It was a framework shared both by those who were sympathetic toward youth movements generally, and those who saw them as threat, as 'delinquent' or 'deviant'.

For conservative theorists like Feuer (1968), the youth-student movement was generational and rooted in a psychoanalytical account of the Oedipal struggle of 'sons' against their 'fathers'. For neo-Marxists like Marcuse the capacity for Oedipal struggle was only possible for social elements not yet incorporated into the 'repressive tolerance' of consumer capitalism and 'technological rationality'. Youth assumed a privileged role in his revolutionary scenario as 'outsiders' who were able and willing to do what the working class had failed to do because as workers they had been co-opted by capitalism (1967). However, for others, the generational struggle and revolting young were understood as rooted in a natural and long-standing antipathy or antagonism between the generations (Charlesworth 1969). According to such accounts, revolt was so natural that there was almost something wrong if the young were not rebelling against the older generation and the society into which they were born.

While the structural functionalist tradition came under heavy and sustained attack, it nonetheless continues to inform a great deal of contemporary commonsense as well as expert understandings of youth, society and social change. Indeed it can be said that this discussion of generations and youth culture evolved into the discourse of 'youth at risk', which revived, albeit in slightly different language, the very old stereotype of youth as inherently troubled and troublesome. Some contemporary writers now offer nonlinear models of human development that challenge older conventional ideas about human development and their claims of predictable and stable 'transition' and more or less common linear patterns and stages of human development experienced by all regardless of their backgrounds. These accounts refer to more fluid individualistic and multiple pathways that are complex, progressive, regressive, backward, forward, up-and-down change – all depending on the 'individual'.

Added to this is the idea that 'social risks' are reflective of broader changes to major social institutions like the labor market that began in the early to mid-1970s. Social risks associated with 'transition flows' between various kinds of employment statuses (part-time, full-time, fixed term and continuing paid work) and nonmarket activities (child care, community participation, education) acknowledges that not only patterns of development but also general patterns of living and working no longer follow a traditional linear model understood in terms of successive phases of education, marriage, work and retirement, but rather involve more complex transitions and 'social risks' that occur across the life course. Thus, risks are no longer seen as located primarily in the 'precarious transitionary' period of adolescence to adulthood (e.g., Winterton 2004). Conservative writers like Hakim speak of individual choice and lifestyle preferences as determinants of this change (2002). Others explain this 'fluidity' by referring to a generation that has been rejected, deceived and shortchanged by decades of neoliberal policymaking and politics and who have given up on the idea of a 'good life', which has been understood conventionally as home ownership, employment and associated benefits and their own family (Mizen 2005, Howker and Malik 2013).

Interpretivist and neo-Marxist and feminist critics

This kind of functionalist approach to understanding 'society' and young people with its emphasis on stability dominated until the early 1960s, when it was challenged by a an array of critics drawing on symbolic interactionist, feminist and neo-Marxist theoretical frames. Running in parallel with these critiques was a challenge mounted by those working from the interpretivist tradition: the social constructionists, poststructuralists and postmodernists.

In Britain, the Birmingham Center for Cultural Studies (CCCS) (Clarke et al. 1976, Brake 1985) provided a stable of neo-Marxist writers interested in questions of change and the role of young people. For the CCCS generation was synonymous with youth culture, it was not seen so much a reaction by youth to adult authority, but part of a larger phenomenon, namely class conflict. For these writers, youth culture was part of a class conflict and more specifically a 'working-class' phenomenon.

Rather than promoting revolutionary struggle against capitalism and an exploitative labor market, 'rebellious working-class youth' expressed their frustration and revolutionary impulse through football riots, street fights or loud music. These local 'youth cultures' engaged young people in struggles for space in cities and streets that were increasingly controlled by corporate private class interests (White 1990).

Some feminists influenced by this tradition pushed the critique a little further, critiquing the CCCS account (and youth culture literature generally) by observing a myopic interest in the experience of boys and young men. Feminists like 1980 (pp. 37–49) and Carrington (1993) argued the youth culture literature in the hands of both functionalists and neo-Marxists simply ignored young women.

One of the other major challenges directed at the long-standing structural functionalists came from a coalition of symbolic interactionists and social constructivists. Drawing on European philosophical traditions like phenomenology, in the 1960s writers like Blumer, Berger and Luckmann (1964) and Ciccourel (1969) rejected the structuralist functionalist approach promoted by the functionalists, by some feminism and neo-Marxist, their emphasis on structural explanations of change and uncritical use of social categories like 'class' and 'patriarchy'.

For symbolic interactionists, social reality, social categories (delinquents, the mad etc.) and social institutions were seen as socially constructed (made up by people). They referred to the ways in which social institutions like education, family, the church, as well as techniques like social statistics were used to create and secure social order. They also challenged claims about scientific methods and the idea that they were objective and could offer an objectivist approach, using counting and numerical analysis that provided an accurate account of the social world.

This was not possible because categories (youth and subcategories like youth cultures) do not refer to things that are material or natural. Moreover, the role of power cannot be ignored in understanding how knowledge about these groups is developed and maintained. In short, how we see, understand and know the world is not by reporting what exists, by extracting from nature what is there, it is made and negotiated by people. In challenging scientific claims, they argued for the use of interpretive techniques. A further different, but parallel, critique came from writers like Michel Foucault (1964), Jean-François Lyotard (1984), Rose (1991) and Hacking (1998), who also questioned claims to scientific status by the social sciences.

Additionally, a broader challenge came from writers informed by postmodernism and cultural studies. Their interest was in the way media images, or discourses produced by experts and scientists, assume control of how social problems and groups are represented. It is an approach that challenged the popular tendency of constructing stereotypes and generalizations. They too challenged the use of structuralist arguments and their reliance on abstractions like society, class and patriarchy to explain change and social processes.

Thus, a variety of social constructivist, postmodernist and poststructuralist writers promoted a critical attitude toward the use of categories
like youth or youth culture and generation. (This is not to suggest there
was agreement between those traditions, but that together they offered
a critical approach to the dominant functionalist worldview.)

In part due to this body of critique, I suggest there is now at some level
a greater awareness of how knowledge is created and historically specific
and thus a little more sensitivity about how we talk about different kinds
of people like Generation Y or the child.

Later writers who worked from these traditions drew attention to the
role of cyberspace and electronic communications and how new identities and new forms of collective action evolved (Melucci 1996, Hopkins
2002, Aapola, Gonick and Harris, 2005). In this work, attention is given
to the deeply political nature of categories like youth culture and generation, and also how ideas like cultural citizenship can provide useful
insight into ways of understanding politics more generally: in terms
of style, music and subcultures (Harris 2001, Giroux 1997). New music
forms, styles and identities have been recognized as political activities
because they can challenge entrenched social practices and institutions
like the family (conventional relationships), institutions and power
relations. These political practices are evident in more recent forms of
feminism like 'girrlzines', in the 'gurl scene movement' and with 'Riot
Grrrls', which entail the claiming of space and creation of new social
and political identities. This can be seen in new spaces made available
through the Net, in which young people have opportunities to narrate
themselves, to speak from the actual places where their experiences and
daily lives are mediated in ways that are largely denied to them in the
traditional public sphere (Bessant 2003, pp. 39–48, Meekosha 2002,
pp. 67–88).

In what follows, I extend this line of inquiry, asking whether the
language of generation and generational politics can be used for research
into new civic spaces to discover whether we are witnessing the development of new forms of politics and change, and to consider the role of
young people. Here I make a case for a theory of generation, suggesting
that it can provide a useful concept for understanding processes of political renewal.

Generation: between essentialism and fuzziness

There are a few considerations for thinking about and using a category
like generation. The first is that there are problems when trying to

operate with an essentialist understanding of age cohorts. The second consideration is that we need to accept the fuzziness of all categories. In both cases there is value in being thoughtful about the relationship between words used to name the things we encounter in the material world and the social phenomena we encounter in the human world.[7] Essentialism involves certain ways of thinking about both the things of the world and the ways we name and know them.

Essentialism

Much discussion of gender, sexuality, race, age, or ethnicity involves claims that certain characteristics are fixed traits that define that group and all its members, and tends to discount variation among group members. We rely on essentialism in popular discussions whenever it is proposed, for example, that certain characteristics can be attributed to everyone subsumed under a category (e.g., 'all women are caring', 'teenagers are irresponsible' or 'all Afro-Americans have rhythm'). Psychology writers like Gelman, outlined how children and adults construe classes of entities, particularly biological entities, in essentialist terms – that is, as if they had an immutable underlying essence that can be used to predict unobserved similarities between members of that class (2005).

To be clear, essentialist thinking holds that, for any specific entity and the class or category there exists a set of attributes that are necessary to its identity and function. As Spinosa and Dreyfus argued, essentialism makes two general interlocking claims. One is about the nature of the world, and the other is about the nature of knowledge (1996, p. 736). Speaking ontologically, the world refers to things that fall into particular kinds or types. A claim about knowledge is made when we say we can recognize types (of a thing) as an example of (the thing). In short, we are making a claim to knowledge when we refer to categories or classes like (cats, mammals, minerals, fauna) and to the nature of the world when we talk about real things (actual cats, rocks, plants). Thus, essentialism is the practice of being able to identify a set of 'fundamental attributes which are necessary and sufficient conditions for a thing to be [considered] a thing of that type' (Ntumy 1990, p. 64). Or as Fuss argued, 'Essentialism is most commonly understood as a belief in the real, true essence of things, the invariable and fixed properties which define the "whatness" of a given entity' (2013, p. xi).

While essentialism has its origins in Western philosophy, over the centuries it has clearly become a very popular practice. Plato and Aristotle are usually credited with early versions of essentialism. Plato offers an early theory of how all known things and concepts have an 'essential' reality that makes those things and concepts what they are. This he referred to as an 'idea' or a 'form', and understood as their essence that makes those things and concepts what they are. Similarly, Aristotle proposed that all objects are what they are by virtue of their substance and that the substance is what makes the object what it is. Since the ancient Greeks, many later philosophers in the Western tradition have been essentialists (e.g., René Descartes, Baruch de Spinoza, Gottfried Wilhelm Leibniz, Immanuel Kant and Edmund Husserl).

Ntumy's observation of the process of establishing an essentialist category may also assist in understanding what is involved. Establishing an essentialist category entails first being able to distinguish the object in question from other objects. This is done by identifying the specific distinctive parts of it that allow one to recognize its intuitive innate essence and then characterize the object within a concept that permits the definition to move to a discursive understanding (1960, p. 65).

The distinctive qualities or attributes used to identify a thing are seen as permanent and inhere in its essence, and are thus unchangeable.

The critiques of essentialism are substantial. Given the focus and scope of this chapter (and book), a detailed account of that literature would divert attention from the primary aim, which is to establish whether the idea of generation and generational politics is useful for understanding what is currently taking place with new media and young people. With that in mind, I refer to the work of philosophers like Searle (1979), who pointed to the problems with essentialist thinking, arguing that it is possible to have a case when it is claimed that something is an instance of the type (e.g., a baby boomer born between 1945 and 1964), but they do not satisfy what we would take to be the normal specifications of the type (e.g., they do not adhere to the values and other attributes said to characterize this generation).

Furthermore, something can meet all the specifications and still not be an instance of the type.

What category or type something falls into is not settled by a defini-tion implicit in the thing. Too often when we are talking about human action and social contexts, such definitions do not work because what something is or becomes is determined by the social context and the meanings given to it by the various participants. What is can for example is often determination by those who have authoritative positioned at that particular time and it is their account that comes to define the type (e.g., Spinosa and Dreyfus 1996, pp. 128–129).

Thus, the problem of talking in a general way about generations or a specific generation like Gen Y and baby boomers as if they possess some kind of essentialist qualities becomes clear. The absence of clear, well-defined and agreed-on chronological boundaries is just one of the deficiencies attending generational discourse and analysis (e.g., Smola and Sutton 2002). The critique of essentialism suggests that this deficiency and many others will be a permanent problem. In its place there is a convincing case for a need to see all of categories less as essentialist types and more as inherently fuzzy categories. Perhaps this is how the category of generation can be best understood and applied. Before arguing that case, I need to pay attention to the idea of fuzzy categories.

Fuzzy categories

Many writers, including linguists, philosophers and psychologists, drew on the work of Ludwig Wittgenstein to conclude there is value in acknowledging the fuzzy nature of categories (Neidenthal and Cantor 1984, Smithson and Verkuellen 2006). As mentioned, Wittgenstein recognized that vagueness is entrenched and pervasive in language, is unproblematic and even useful (1953, pp. 104–108). In discussing the category 'game', he highlighted the problems associated with using any category, claiming it is often not possible to draw a clear line between categories that allows us to distinguish between, say, animal and human, or man and woman. For example, what do all activities that are named a game have in common that allows us to distinguish it from all other activities? The category or definition should allow us to know whether or not an activity is a game, but does it? The problem arises when we discover there is no Platonic Socratic inherent essence in the activities deemed to be games. What we tend to see instead is that there are not thing/s common to all the activities in the category of games, but a series of similarities, resemblances or relationships.

Wittgenstein used this discussion to consider the problem of language use, which he argued could be resolved by seeing language use as a 'language game'. This led him to argue that language is a rule-guided activity: linguistic rules form the logic of sentence structure and composition that lie beneath the surface of language. In this way, language requires a mastery of techniques about the application of rules that determine what can be said meaningfully. They determine what can be said without drawing sharp boundaries. This does not lead to problems until language is subjected to tests using logical principles. Since Wittgenstein, many cognitive theorists and researchers have highlighted the vagueness of our categories (Hofstadter and Sander 2013). In short, an essential vagueness or fuzziness characterizes all our categories. This is a view that presents a major departure from the traditional, classical view of categorization.

Proponents of that classical approach maintained that all members of a category share a single, complete set of defining features (Neidenthal and Cantor 1984, pp. 6–7). This idea is central to the essentialist tradition, and is required to create a clearly defined category. Proponents of this tradition say that is possible to identify a set of attributes or qualities or functions in things that allow us to talk of an entity (group of people, animals, inanimate objects).[8]

Zadeh's approach to fuzzy set theory highlighted the role of vagueness in our perceptions and conceptions of reality phenomena (1965). This early work informed cognitive scientists, who starting in the 1970s argued that the capacity of humans to meet the criteria established by the classical view of categorization was difficult, if not impossible. Rosch et al., for example, showed how our capacity to develop and apply taxonomic categories or classes suffers from 'imperfect feature nesting' (1978). This means that an attribute that considered to be associated with membership in a given category, like the trait 'fly' with the concept 'bird', is not applicable to a member of a more specific subcategory, such as the category 'emu' or 'chicken'.

As Neidenthal and Cantor (1984, p. 7) note, 'The properties assumed to be true of categories and taxonomies, according to the classical view, are in fact characteristic of very few ... in the environment'. Similarly, writers like Lakoff[9] demonstrated that natural categories do not define animate or inanimate 'objects' into clearly bounded categories (1978). The fuzzy structure of natural categories, and the flexibility with which they are used by nonexperts, becomes apparent in classification systems based on attributes of people (e.g., taxonomies of personality traits, mental illness, intelligence). In these areas, even the experts have had considerable difficulty establishing traits to create 'well-defined' psychiatric diagnostic taxonomies' or to classify personalities (see Frances 2009, Kirsch 2010).

In summary, then, all categories (species, fruit, youth or generation) are inherently fuzzy and indeterminate. As Arendt argued, social categories do not have a 'thing-like character' (1958, p. 9). When we talk about a generation, we are using socially constituted categories (e.g., Gen Y, baby boomer, unemployed, student etc.) and do so by relying on explicit or implicit criteria.[10] Yet we need these categories and use them because they provide indispensible pragmatic sense-making functions. There is a pragmatic and arbitrary character to all categories, whether they refer to physical or natural inanimate entities like rocks and minerals or to sentient creatures like cats and dogs or to social categories like the unemployed or Generation X. This discursive-constitutive character of categories always exists when we use language (or discourses) to represent the world.

In short, while generation is a word we now take for granted and too readily assume it has generally agreed-on meanings, like most social categories, it is a fuzzy concept. Yet generation, like all classificatory categories, is not amenable either to an essentialist logical deductive process or to empirical adjudication to determine definitively whether membership in it depends on certain traits or whether the traits said to characterize a specific generation like Gen X or millennials actually and conclusively determine who belongs in or to the category. Given all this, it is advisable that care is taken to recognize essentialist thinking when using categories like generation. Social categories like generation or working class have a 'made-up' character. They are instituted by people, typically experts and governments, who say there are certain properties or features common to all those deemed to fit the classification (Hacking 2000). As such, these classifications do not refer in the same way that our categories refer to physical objects that exist in time or space (like the category tree or rock does).

Is it possible to develop and use the concept of generation in ways that assist in understanding social change and that avoid the pitfalls of essentialist thinking and reductionism, to say nothing of prejudicial stereotypes? If it is, how might this be done and can it be done in ways that are useful for research into whether or not we are seeing new sites of political renewal courtesy of new media?

If nothing else, we need a category like generation for understanding change processes. This is relevant to any kind of empirical or qualitative research because before anything can be investigated, it needs to be identified and conceptualized. There are plenty of categories that do not refer to anything that can be described or seen in a direct way (e.g., crime, madness or unemployment). To accommodate the fact that social categories emerge discursively and are *discursive in nature* (that is, they are made up), researchers have to operationalize categories. This refers to a process of starting with something that has no empirical qualities and then constructing proxies that can be substituted for the idea that can be described and in many cases measured. In short, researchers have to establish a criterion that allows the category for which there is no actual empirical referent to be named. Once that is done, research can proceed.

Conceptualizing generation is difficult because when we use such nouns to denote abstract ideas, we attempt to name things that do not exist in an objective sense. We also rely on definitions over which there is often little consensus. The abstract nature of the concept also makes describing generation a complex task (i.e., What *kinds* of people fit the category? What is it that makes the 'a kind'?). As mentioned in the last chapter, this challenge is often overlooked due to naturalistic thinking, or commonsense assumptions that such entities are relatively easy to identify because it is assumed they exist in an objective sense.

Conclusion: generational analysis?

Can a credible account of generation be developed? The difficulties associated with this task are compounded by the relative absence of consistency and agreement about what is meant by a generation. Using the popular conventional criteria, like birthdates, we could say generation refers to a specific age cohort. This approach, however, has raised questions about what birthdates and time frames should be used, and the rationale for those dates. Similarly, what other criteria might be used (e.g., what are said to be defining bundles of attitudes and values, identity or work practices)?

The fuzziness that we need to acknowledge about our use of generational categories includes a number of dimensions. Firstly, we do not have one clear and stable definition of a particular generation or what we mean essentially by generations. Rather, we have a loose consensus that generation refers to a demographic cohort defined according to a chronological time – specifically, birthdates. (That said, while birthdates are used, there is no consensus about the rationale used for deciding on particular dates). Secondly, we find that a number of other attributes are used. Howe and Strauss (2000), for example, point to three attributes when they identify a generation in terms other than years of birth. The first includes perceived membership based on the self-perception of membership within a generation that begins during adolescence and coalesces during young adulthood. The second element is those common beliefs and behaviors that include the attitudes (toward family, career, personal life, politics, religion etc.) and behaviors or choices (made in regard to jobs, marriage, children, health, crime, sex, drugs etc.) that characterize a generation. Finally, they point to a common location in history and the role played by the turning points in historical trends involving a major shift in politics of a community from social liberal to neoliberal politics and significant events (e.g., the Vietnam War or the war on terror after September 11) that occur during a generation's formative years in adolescence and young adulthood.[11]

Drawing on Mannheim, I now argue that if certain events or social conditions are significant enough, they shape what Bourdieu calls 'fields of action', which in turn mark and inform those who were exposed to those who were 'events' in their formative years in ways that forge particular *habitus*, particular sensibilities, indelible dispositions, ways of seeing and being (1990b). It is to the spelling out of this framework that I turn in the following chapter.

4
Coming of Age in a Digital Neoliberal World: Generation and Politics

The idea of generation is open to many interpretations and uses. Some writers use it to explain why societies remain resistant to change, such as when anthropologists argue that generations are the glue that bind aboriginal societies in time, 'connecting speaker and listener in communal experience and uniting past and present in memory' (Hulan and Eigenbrod 2008, p. 7). Others use the idea of generation to explain why dramatic change occurs. Jones, for example, argued that the baby-boom generation was 'history's decisive generation' responsible for most of the important changes in America since the 1960s (1980).

Does the protean quality of a category like generation, which is seemingly able to explain everything and anything, actually mean that it explains nothing? Many theorists have worried about the value of the generational idea. Some point to the fuzzy and porous nature of all categories that seek to generalize about people. Some say generalizing about age cohorts or generation is even more vacuous than using identity markers like religion, ethnicity, class, sexuality, race or gender to explain large and complex processes of political or social change. Those influenced by the 'linguistic turn' (Rorty 1991) or by poststructuralism and postmodernism (e.g., Jamieson 2002, Clark 2004) argue against the use of essentialist categories and explanations, maintaining that people are best understood by virtue of their membership in many different collective groups, enabling many different identity markers.

Making sense of what is happening in our own time remains a central task that requires sharp thinking, and today our reliance on catch-phrases and clichés seem more prolific than ever. Journalist, authors of best selling books, academics, entertainers, song writers and 'ordinary' people depend on cliches about 'generations' to talk about change and the lives of different people. This is something Hannah Arendt warned us about as she spoke of the damage done to our thinking by a reliance on stock-phrases and adherence to conventional standardized codes of expression. She spoke of how such language confuses, obfuscates, and makes the task of figuring out what is going on difficult. While observing Eichmann's trial in 1961 for his crimes against humanity she observed his reliance on cliché-ridden language in the witness box as he had done in his official life. She connected that language use to his incapacity for independent and critical thought, to his 'authentic inability' to think beyond or manage situations in which routine procedures did not exist. George Orwell similarly warned how 'double speak', how words with official definitions that are used 'badly' and words that are vague that slide in their meaning cloud our thinking and encourage us to see in particular ways.

Can we say something meaningful about a group just because its members were born into a particular time? Given what Arendt and Orwell said, we may want to avoid talking about generations on the grounds this corrupts language and degrades our thinking. Yet further thought suggests that talking about generations may have some value.

So the questions linger: Does the concept of generational change have any value? Can we talk meaningfully about generations as collective actors? If we can, how can this be done in ways that acknowledge the objections and problems in doing so that were highlighted in the previous chapter?

Here I make the case for talking about generations in ways adopted by Karl Mannheim. It will be recalled that Mannheim (1923) argued that some events are of such a scale and significance that they constitute benchmark historic events, which in turn shape or impinge on the lives of whole generations of people, but not with the same effect. He identified the Napoleonic Wars, major famines and economic depressions as examples of such events. Events like this, he said, provide a common framework of experience that can shape the distinctive attitudes, values, social projects or dispositions of different generations. We can appreciate what is now taking place by acknowledging the impact of patterned large-scale arrangements, how they constrain and open-up choices, how they enable and disable our capacities. We can also acknowledge what phenomenological intellectual traditions offer for understanding meanings and perceptions.

With this in mind, it is possible to argue that our location in a sociohistoric time establishes the parameters of our formative experiences. This informs our development in ways that affect who we are, who we become and how we act. Thus each generation has a distinctive historical consciousness, or spirit of the time. It is shaped by specific historical events that guide our approach to the world. Provided we are mindful of certain qualifications and the inherently fuzzy quality of social classifications, it is possible to talk meaningfully about generation.

I begin this chapter by arguing that the late 1970s and early 1980s proved a watershed for many Western and developing nations because three distinct historic events or processes took place that made possible new kinds of social relations and practices. These events created conditions significantly different to earlier decades. They touched and shaped the lives of those born since then. First was the emergence of an authoritative policy paradigm referred to here as neoliberalism. The second was the advent of new digital media, which rapidly took on a global reach. Finally, we see the impact of globalization, a process involving complex economic and cultural effects, the impact of which was both immediate in historical terms and global in its reach. Each of these events, considered either separately or together, was comparable in scale and significance to the benchmark historic events Mannheim wrote about.

In what follows, I outline the distinctive aspects of these three processes. These three historic events were experienced by many of those born after the late 1970s. However, several important points need to be emphasized from the outset.

Firstly, the idea that a given generation has been touched by particular events or some large-scale process like a war or revolution does mean we can assume that the effect is homogenous or univocal. Mannheim did not claim or assume that a historic event or experience like a war, depression or revolution had an homogenous effect on the generation experiencing it, or that that everyone in that generation interpreted it in the same way. Indeed, Mannheim pointed to the diversity of a generational effect, as sometimes 'antagonistic' generational units respond to different social, cultural and geographic events in different ways. A generation includes groups who are different and who disagree, but who are nonetheless oriented toward each other because they have experienced some process or event. As I show, the evidence that a category like generation helps highlight does not suggest that those people born after the late 1970s share in any way the same political dispositions, opinions or values. What they do share is the experience of unavoidable and major processes that had an impact on their lives. My task is to attempt to make sense of the complex patterns of response and sensemaking on the part of that generation born after the late 1970s.

Secondly, a category like generation can only be useful for understanding and explaining certain kinds of human action if a distinction is made between using the category of generation *as if* the use of that category itself provides an explanation, and using the category *as a heuristic* because it sensitizes the researcher to look for certain things. Seeing the generational category as an explanation is illegitimate because it ignores the complexity. Here I use the idea of generation as part of a heuristic to look for evidence and to help make sense of complex processes; its value will need to be demonstrated.

In the second part of the chapter, I indicate how those born after the late 1970s and who came of age in a globalizing world dominated by neoliberal policies and increasingly touched by the availability of digital technology experienced these novelties. I identify five key effects. One is the extension of the dependency traditionally associated with being a child or an adolescent. A second effect is the growing gulf between the promises of education and the benefits said to flow from the neoliberal model of human capital theory, producing many graduates who find it exceedingly difficult to get work in their fields, or what some are calling 'graduates without a future' (Mason 2011). There is also evidence that increasing numbers of young people are socially and economically disadvantaged. Thirdly, the availability of digital technology is reshaping the sensibilities, modes of relating, the identities of young people as well as the experience of being young. Finally, in political terms a complex shift is taking place. There is credible evidence that many who came of age in this period embrace an individualist neoliberal political sensibility. At the same time, there is also evidence that other young people have developed an oppositional stance to various aspects of the political and economic status quo.

I turn to the first historic event: the transformation of sociopolitical and economic cultures that took place the late 1970s and the early 1980s that was promoted by neoliberalism.

The rise of neoliberalism since the 1970s

By neoliberalism, I refer to a series of ideas and beliefs that see everyone as an economic actor and everything as an economic activity. Neoliberals characteristically view government as destructive of the free market and promote the idea of individuals who should be left free to do as they see fit. Neoliberals see social relations as if they are market relations, encourage generalized competition, and even transform the person into an enterprise or a brand. In this paradigm, government is the enemy of the market and the free individual.

While many Western nation-states have been subjected to a 'neo-liberal cascade' (Connell 2013) over the last decades, understanding this cascade is not straightforward. One favored approach is that associated with the Marxist tradition, which sees clusters of ideas like liberalism or Christianity as an ideology. Ideology is said to be a form of 'false consciousness' designed to confuse those groups who are disadvantaged by the way the distribution of resources work. This approach draws on Karl Marx's observation that 'The class which has the means of material production at its disposal has control at the same time over the means of mental production' (Marx and Engels 1965, p. 50 (Marx, K., and Engels, F., 1965, *The German Ideology*, London p. 50)). From this perspective, the 'ruling class' effect their social reproduction by generating 'dominant ideologies'. Those ideologies function by claiming, for example, that the economic interests of the ruling class serve the interests of the entire society.

Notwithstanding the modern cliché that Marxism is now obsolete or passé, Terry Eagleton is right in his claims that ideology-critique is indispensable for understanding and resisting the way certain ideas like neoliberalism now operate, especially when those ideas inform the policy practices of our governments (2011). There is value in this, provided it is accepted that an ideology is not simply a false representation of reality or a lie. This is one of the confusing aspects about what the idea of ideology means (Elster 1985). As Shelby observed,

> ideologies do not characteristically work by providing us with outright false representations, for if they did, we would not be able to coordinate our actions through them as effectively as we do. (2003, p. 165)

Geuss identified three different dimensions required for carrying out a critique of ideology (1981). The first is *epistemic*. Any social consciousness can become an ideology because of certain epistemic problems. This requires establishing whether there is evidence for any of the claims made by proponents of the ideology. Neoliberals may claim, for example, that all citizens will be better off under a fully functioning free market. Is that the case? An epistemic critique of an ideology is able to illuminate problems like a lack of evidence, inconsistency, logical invalidity or a lack of conceptual clarity in the articulation of the ideas in question. Secondly, a *functional* critique of an ideological consciousness is able to highlight the negative social consequences that its acceptance has for a given society or a social group – like the justification of harmful social relations or social practices. This dimension of an ideology critique requires that a proponent of an ideology (e.g., neoliberalism) needs to be able to demonstrate what effects the ideology has. Finally a *genealogical* critique of ideology focuses on the negative features of the history, or the etiology of the belief system. This kind of critique involves carrying out a genealogical or historical inquiry into the ideology. For example, the belief system may have been adopted because of the influence of dominant class interests or some other social group. Was that the case? Alternately the historical analysis may show the belief system has some unfavorable origin that tarnishes it in some way (Shelby 2003, p. 164).

This three-dimensional critical analytic informs some of the investigations of neoliberalism as ideology and its impact on modern policymaking (Steger 2002, Vietta 2013, Dardot and Laval 2013).

Many have claimed that neoliberalism is just an ideology and an economic policy in that it represents and promotes the interests of certain elites, including corporations and wealthy individuals and families. Dumenil and Levy argue that

> Neo-liberalism ... expresses the strategy of the capitalist classes in alliance with upper management, specifically financial managers, intending to strengthen their hegemony and to expand it globally. (2013, p. 1)

One insight from such a three-dimensional critical analytic is that neoliberalism is more than an ideology designed to deceive. As Dardot and Laval argued, neoliberalism does shape people's lives, beliefs and actions (2013). If neoliberalism is *destructive* of rights, institutions and human goods, as Dumenil and Levi claim, it is also *productive* of social relations, ways of living and even people's values and sense of self. Neoliberalism clearly shapes our existence and the ways we lead our lives and relate to ourselves and to others. In this way neoliberalism is best understood as a 'myth' (Midgley 2003) or a rationality (Foucault 2008). Neoliberalism is an influential source of rules and reasons for organizing a way of life, using in this case the norm of generalized competition to prescribe human conduct, and the model of enterprise as a model of subjectification. Hence, the importance of the neoliberal preoccupation with freedom: neoliberalism persistently uses the motif of freedom to persuade individuals to conform to neoliberal norms *of their own accord.*

We also need to explore the ways in which neoliberalism-as-ideology operates in real ways, but does so in ways that reveal epistemic problems. They include the absence of evidence to support some of its contemporary claims, which helps obscure some of the most damaging consequences of its implementation.

Thinking about in these ways neoliberalism matters is because it has shaped a new policy paradigm that has been progressively implemented since the 1970s initially by a variety governments in the developed world. Whatever the political party in government over the past few decades in Australia, the United States, the United Kingdom or parts of Europe, the neoliberal advocates for reform were committed to experimenting with the new policy paradigm. In this regard the enthusiasm was bipartisan. Leading advocates for neoliberal reform included the Hawke-Keating 'laborist' governments in Australia (1983–1996), various 'libertarian' and 'Third Way' governments in the United States, like Ronald Reagan (1981–1988) and Bill Clinton (1992–2001), and new right and Labour governments in the United Kingdom (e.g., Margaret Thatcher 1979–1991 and Tony Blair 1997–2007).

In developing countries in Asia and South America, neoliberalism was forcefully applied by Western proponents through a mixture of policy transfers and direct negotiations between indebted nations and major banking institutions. The beginning of this can be traced to the United States' threat of military action against Arab nations in 1973 following the decision by these nations to implement an oil embargo, and what is generally described as the oil crisis, which had the effect of cutting off oil (petrol) supplies to the West. It had an immediate effect of increasing the price of oil dramatically, which had a global impact. The subsequent decision to filter Arab petrodollars through financial institutions and invest as high interest loans to developing nations. Soon after, many governments defaulted on the loans because the interest rate increased, and we saw the Third World debt crisis, which threatened the global financial system. The United States intervened to reengineer the International Monetary Fund (IMF) to ensure that developing nations would repay their debt. Various deals were struck in which indebted poor countries agreed to follow the neoliberal path, to deregulate their economies. The idea was that such reforms, called 'structural adjustment', would stimulate their economies, thereby allowing them to repay the money borrowed from Western banks.

Structural adjustment programs meant adopting the same neoliberal policies Western nations had implemented. This included reducing government spending on public services or selling off and privatizing public assets and natural resources. All this, it was argued, would 'free the market' and stimulate the economy. These plans failed in many cases to stimulate the economy: in most cases these policies increased inequality and poverty. One thing this approach was effective at was enabling Western financial institutions to take advantage of low wages, deregulated labor markets and cheap public assets to invest in these developing countries.

In the new order in the first world and the developing world, governments progressively introduced local variants on a core array of policies. These include attempts to reduce government expenditures and taxes, deregulate various markets, including the finance and labor markets, slash public sector employment, deliver balanced budgets or even create surpluses, sell off (or privatize) public assets, reduce 'welfare dependency', contract out government services and activities or make public services more efficient by importing the practices and language categories of private business.

In the developed world, governments introduced policies like the user-pays principle (which, e.g., means university students pay for their education), weakened any systems that protected workers from economic exploitation, as well as undermined the role of trade unions, cut tariff protection for manufacturing industries, made getting unemployment benefits harder to access and generally downgraded the quality of health, welfare and public education systems.

These policies have been justified by the persistent and persuasive use of a vocabulary of 'markets' and 'economic rationality', using code words like 'individual' and 'freedom', which invariably take precedence over whatever governments do or whatever people mean when they talk about 'public goods'. Neoliberals have so far been successful in seeing ideas like justice, human rights or equality as words used to camouflage or promote the evils of the 'nanny state', 'the politics of envy', or 'government interference'.

By definition, those people born after the late 1970s had nothing against which to compare the way their lives were shaped in the 1980s through to the 2000s by this powerful set of ideas. But as I show, the effects have been significant for all that, and also somewhat paradoxical.

The second historic event of the past three decades was the explosion in the presence of digital technology and the rise of the Net.

New media and digital connectivity

The widespread spread of digital technology is the second historic event of the last three decades. The application of early forms of digital computing and communications to businesses and governments in the 1960s and 1970s soon after saw the spread of digital technologies into homes and communities across the globe, a move extended in the 1990s with the development of the Internet. By 2013, 41% of households across the globe were connected to the Internet, with half of them in the developing world (78% of households in the developing world were connected to the Internet by 2013 (International Telecommunication Union 2013, p. 90).

As I already indicated, it is easy to overstate the extent to which young people can be seen as 'digital natives' or as the leading or most enthusiastic users of the new technologies. Even so, research on the demographics of new media use shows how young people are more likely than older cohorts to use new media. In the United States report that the different trajectories of new media take up and its use in politics across the youth population shows that large portions of young people across ethics groups have access to the Net and use it to communicate with family friends, and pursue their various interests. Contrary to conventional views about the influence of socio-economic inequality and its impact on access and use of information and communication technology, the Youth Participatory Politics survey of 15- to 25-year-olds, which involved 2,920 participants and was conducted by Mills College, found that 'young people across racial and ethnic groups are connected online (Cohen and Kahne 2012). They also found that 78% of those surveyed sent messages and chatted on line, and that overall 64% engaged in 'interest driven activity' in a given week. Forty-four percent engaged in at least one act of participatory politics, and participatory politics was equitably distributed across different ethnic groups with 'overwhelmingly, white (96%), black (94%), Latino (96%) and Asian American youth (98%) (vii–viii). In this way it can be argued that digital social capital is more democratic.

What is clear is that from the early to the mid-1980s, increasing numbers of people have spent increasing amounts of time using the Internet, playing electronic games, chatting and engaging in online friendship groups, mobilizing political action, and creating, modifying and consuming content.

Globalization

The third historic event of our time is globalization. Saying what globalization is is no easy task. In spite of its buzzword status, globalization remains an ambiguous, even nebulous, concept and one about which there is little agreement either about how to best characterize it, or to explain it. It is a classic example of a 'fuzzy category' in the sense that establishing any consensus about its boundaries and defining characteristics is problematic.

In what follows, I cherry-pick from some of the standard accounts of globalization to establish what some or most commentators agree constitutes or defines globalization (Steger 2002, Giddens 2002, Sen 2002, Stiglitz, 2002, Kohler and Chaves 2003, James 2006, McGrew and Held 2007, Hay 2007, Jones 2010).

Steger distinguishes between globalism as an 'ideology' and globalization as a 'process'. Globalism as ideology is the now-dominant ideology, which promoted 'globalization as process' as the inevitable and natural destiny of 'successful' economies (2002). This distinction helps clarify the links between globalization and neoliberalism, which are not always immediately self-evident or clear. As many observers point out, those who advocate economic globalism tend to be neoliberals, who see market liberalization as a natural or inevitable dynamic (e.g., Glyn 2006, Chomsky and McChesney 2011).

With that distinction in mind, it seems best to see globalization as a process that combines the adoption of a neoliberal policy frame and that relies on highly efficient networking digital technology through the Internet, generating new patterns of economic and cultural activity and connectedness. As economic activity, globalization involves globally connected agriculture and resource extraction, manufacturing, the growth of an information economy and flows of capital in increasingly intensive ways.

This conceptualization of globalization does not therefore sanction seeing it as something akin to a natural event like a forest fire or tsunami: it is a complex process driven as much by government policy as by the decisions taken by corporate elites, technologists and designers, and by the willingness of consumers to buy new kinds of services and products. It is also important to point out that globalization relies on state-sponsored policy processes. This is because the globalization of markets is a product of government policies designed to free trade by introducing policies that erode tariff and other regulatory barriers and lead to the large-scale deregulation of commodities, capital and labor markets. The neoliberal policy framework actively enables businesses to assume a global character. While it is true that many corporations have a transnational character, a move to minimize the impact of national taxation and other regulatory regimes, like industrial relations law, minimum wage conditions or health and safety regulations, many governments have obliged by not intervening. Globalization also relies on transnational agencies like the IMF, the World Bank and the World Trade Organization, which advocate for free trade and deregulatory policies and the evolution of multilateral agreements and treaties (like North American Free Trade Agreement, Association of Southeast Nations, Free Trade Agreement), which ostensibly abolish restrictions on the free trade and movement of goods and services.

The second enabling dynamic operating in globalization as a process is the way in which increasingly networked digital technology has facilitated mobile financial, currency and investment markets, as well as the production and sale of products that move around the globe in highly fluid and speedy ways. We now have new worldwide integrated and interdependent arrangements for production, consumption and finance that have seen markets assume an increasingly global quality, and that have promoted dramatic shifts in the supply of labor on a global scale (Panitch and Gindin, 2012). One example of this is the 'world car', in which the design of a car occurs in one country, sometimes by more than one automotive company; the parts are manufactured in several countries; and the car is assembled in other countries and then sold all over the world. Another is the ways markets emerge for the supply of foods like oranges, which once had limited availability based on climate. These products can now sourced all year around. The emergence of the Internet as a site of online retail activity promises to exaggerate this trend.

In sociocultural terms, globalization denotes the intensification of social relations, the shrinking of time and space facilitated by increasingly rapid global interchange. Globalization in this sense refers to the interchange or flow of worldwide social and cultural practices, pushed by the global reach of old media and technologies (like film, television news and music) overlaid by the newer digital affordances of the Internet and, more specifically, by social media like mobile phones and platforms like Twitter, Facebook, chat rooms, blogs and the like. These networked technologies enable changes in a number of domains (social, political, cultural and economic) and have done so globally in ways that have affected most aspects of our lives including.

I now identify some of the major effects these three historic events had on those born since the late 1970s.

The effects?

From the late 1970s to the early 1980s, the sensibilities and the experience of being young and the status of being young have changed significantly, and in ways that point, as Mannheim (1923) suggested, to the influence of some of the historic events of our time. One key effect has been an extension of the dependency associated with being a child or adolescent in the modern period. Secondly, we see a growing gulf between the promises of education and the benefits said to flow from the neoliberal model of human capital theory and investment, leading to a phenomenon in which many highly qualified graduates struggle to secure work in their field, and there is serious social disadvantage resulting from increasing youth joblessness and underemployment. Thirdly, the availability of digital technology is reshaping the sensibility, social relations and identities of young people. Finally, in political terms we see a shift taking place. On the one hand, there is evidence revealing how many young people embrace an individualist neoliberal political sensibility. On the other hand, there is evidence that many oppose the prevailing political arrangements.

In making this argument, it needs to be acknowledged that those born after 1980 have not experienced the process of change uniformly. Charting the experience of change is difficult.

This is because there is the slow and often invisible or opaque nature of the change process itself, which can make it difficult, to say, 'I experienced this event in this way'. Those who have only known the world since these processes began cannot be said to have experienced change. All that can be said is that compared with previous generations, the experience of those who have come into the world after 1980 is different. The quality of the experience of change is affected by the absence of any other experiences enabling comparisons to be made by those experiencing, in this case, processes of major political, technological, sociocultural and economic change. Saying how a generation experienced a given – or a set of – historic event/s is difficult, given the vast range of the cultural or interpretative resources available to interpret their experience. These resources include the various prevailing political beliefs, a variety of religious and ethnic affiliations, the gendered *habitus* and resources available courtesy of their class and educational experience. Each of these enables us to interpret our lives and experience in a diversity of ways.

In the early twenty-first century and for increasing numbers of people in Western countries, the desire of Barrie's character Peter Pan not to grow up, to 'remain a child forever' is no fantasy, but an involuntary option. Late adolescence and early adulthood, as those who came of age in the West in the 1950s to the early 1970s experienced it, no longer exists in the way it once did.

Peter Pan and the never-never land of adulthood

One key effect of the above-mentioned events has been the extension of the dependency that once characterized childhood and adolescence in the modern period. Increasing numbers of people in their mid to late-20s now find themselves unable to achieve the life deemed to define 'adulthood'. This deferment of adulthood is based on interdependent changes occurring in different vectors of contemporary social life. Increasing numbers of 20- to 30-year-olds now spend more time in education or training. Increasing numbers of people under 30 are also excluded from the full-time labor market, which affects their capacity to be economically secure, access the housing market or develop a career with confidence. It is a shift based on changes to social sensibility and anxieties, explicable in terms of the wholesale adoption of neoliberalism, and associated events like the near complete collapse of the full-time youth labor market in the mid-1970s in many Western societies. That collapse, in conjunction with a series of new policies and laws like those aimed at increasing the time spent in education, has contributed to the prolongation of adolescence.

In the mid-1970s in most Organization for Economic Cooperation and Development (OECD) countries as youth unemployment soared, the relevant policy 'problem' was defined as a crisis involving 'falling education standards' or 'failing schools'. The explanations for youth unemployment and the failing economy were located firmly in the education system. Equally, problems' like poor education and training standards, youth homelessness, youth at risk, high youth unemployment and even a sluggish economy, could all be remedied by investing in human capital and by restructuring national training and education systems to remedy those deficits. As a result, in most Western nations we witnessed a succession of major changes to curricula, the rationalization of education institutions, the development of new training programs and the retention of more and more young people for longer periods of time in education institutions. These policy initiatives were directed toward ensuring participants remained actively ready for work. It has been a project at odds with the realities of the actual number of jobs available.

For people who do attempt to live independently, they need to survive on a junior or trainee wage rate, which in some countries is as low as $3.00 an hour. For those without work, the option in countries like Australia is to try to access social security income or what is now part of a system of 'youth allowances' paid on the condition 'the client' demonstrates an interest in becoming 'job ready' or 'actively' engaged and meets other eligibility requirements. In countries like the United States, such social insurance is not an option, while in the United Kingdom, the government is threatening to withdraw housing benefits and job seekers allowances for those between the age of 18 and 24. Typically youth allowances are means-tested against parental income and assets and are conditional on compliance with participation requirements like agreeing to 'employment pathway plans', attending workshops and so forth. In this way income support became dependent on government employment services closely monitoring the work ethic of young clients through various administrative strategies like 'activity testing'. Thus, in an era of a resurgent economic liberalism and small government, the instruments of governmentality were extended and refined, with severe penalties for noncompliance.

All this had the immediate effect of increasing the dependence of young people either on their families or the state (Settersten et al. 2005, Howker and Mailk 2013). In consequence, we see a new phase in the life cycle emerging between adolescence and adulthood, for which some such appellation as 'dependultcy' may be appropriate (Bessant 1994, pp. 28–39, Bessant 1995, pp. 27–29, Arnett 2000).

A number of activities, statuses and legal entitlements functioned in the past, and continue in part now, as transition markers on the pathway to relative adult independence as it was understood. Those markers included social norms and legal definitions of the age at which criminal liability can be assigned, unrestricted access to alcohol, cigarettes or to cinemas, and the age at which a person can earn adult award wages or own and drive a car. This also includes the age at which a person can have sexual and marital relations, the right to vote or hold public office and assume full citizenship status. Typically in the West, these events took place between 16 and 21 years of age. Twenty-first birthdays were once significant public celebrations of entry to adult status.

Prior to the mid-1970s in most Western countries, getting a full-time job served as a central marker of adult status, especially for young men. For much of the twentieth century, when the distinction between the 'citizen (male) worker' and the 'citizen mother' dominated, paid employment played an important role in finding young men a place in their communities as financially independent adults. The first full-time job customarily provided an income and important means of social participation. It also played a role in establishing a relatively stable adult identity underpinned by occupational status and economic security. Paid labor offered a steady and generally secure source of income, and other economic activities became possible, leading to a relatively independent lifestyle. For most young women in context paid labor usually meant access to a more ambiguous status as 'citizen mother-to-be'. Paid work for young women was a transition separating one period of childish dependency and another acquired with a husband and children.

If adolescence once marked a transition between childhood and adulthood, we now observe an extended and significant different transition as young adults remain dependent on the families and become 'dependults' (Furlong and Cartmel 1997, Settersten et al. 2005, Howker and Mailk 2013). Basic to this process is the way young people now spend more time in schools and universities and face increasing difficulties in getting jobs, which would enable them to lead satisfying and economically secure lives.

In short, there is evidence of an amplification of dependence, childlike irresponsibility and a relative absence of freedom (real choice) for increasing numbers of young people in developed nations. This has occurred in parallel with the emergence of new social problems and social identities. In many Western nations, increasing numbers of young people now rely more and more on their family of origin (that is, if they have a family and one that is willing and able to support them) than was the case in the decades just prior to the 1980s. The PEW Research Center reports that in America, a record number of people aged 18 to 31 are living with their parents due to declining employment, increasing education enrollment and declining marriage rates (Fry 2012).

Unemployment and social disadvantage

Secondly, while young people have not been the only age cohort to bear the brunt of neoliberalism, those born since the late 1970s have been hit hard by the rising tide of economic and social inequality mapped by Wilkinson and Pickett (2009), the OECD (2011) and Oxfam (2013). The fact that they spent their formative years in this milieu is also significant in terms of its impact.

People born in the late 1970s and since have been especially affected by neoliberal policies. One consequence is that new age structures and statuses have emerged as a result of neoliberal policies and practices in the decades since the late 1970s (Harvey 2005, Ball and Olmedo 2012, pp. 85–89, Connell 2013, pp. 99–112). In particular, we see a double-whammy effect of the neoliberal policy framework and the new economy, which that includes the creation of a generation of graduates without a future in employment and evidence that some young people are facing the effects of systemic social inequality (Mason 2011).

Following decades of high rates of employment in the post-1945 years, most Western economies from the late 1970s began experiencing high levels of unemployment with a disproportionate effect on young people. Policymakers accepted the premise that more education was vital for addressing the unemployment problem including high rates of youth unemployment (e.g., Council of EU 2006). Human capital theory informed claims that education and training are were the determinants of factors in each country's economic performance and collective social well-being.

Human capital theory underpinned the commitment to develop competitive knowledge-based economies (e.g., Becker 1964/1993). Acceptance of an 'active society' policy by European policymakers was based on the premise that more education was vital for addressing the socioeconomic and demographic challenges of an ageing population, high numbers of low-skilled adults, and high rates of unemployment, and youth unemployment in particular (Council of EU 2006). Yet the neoliberal advocacy for human capital theory failed to demonstrate how economic growth is promoted by increased education. Human capital theorists cannot show how increasing access to education – to the point of guaranteeing universal access to higher education – can achieve the socioeconomic objectives assigned to it. In particular they have failed to say how increasing education and training increases the supply of jobs and generates increased wealth or national income.

In spite of dramatic increases in education participation in places the EU the United Kingdom or Australia since the 1990s there has been increased income inequality, matched by increases in the unemployment and underemployment of people under thirty. The evidence shows that this cohort have borne the brunt of this increase in inequality fuelled by high levels of unemployment, underemployment and precarious part-time work, leading to an erosion of incomes.

Young workers confront increased unemployment and underemployment. As ILO data suggests: in 2013, 74.5 million people in the 15-to-24 age group were unemployed worldwide, this is a 13.1% youth unemployment rate – twice the global overall unemployment rate. In Australia, by 2014 the youth unemployment rate among 15- to 24-year-olds was

12.5% or twice the 'adult rate' representing a near threefold increase since 2008 (ABS 2014). ABS data also indicates that at least a quarter of part-time workers are underemployed. According to the European Foundation (2009, p. 11) the decade 2000–2009 saw an increase in part-time employment in Europe increased. By 2009, 18.8% of workers in the EU worked part-time, representing an increase of nearly 3% in ten years. By 2012 this increased to 19.3% (European Commission 2012, p. 32). By 2012 the trend was clear: full-time employment was contracting, driving down employment while part-time employment was continuing to grow. In 2012 19.3% of the workforce was part-time (ibid.). In addition to very high total and youth unemployment rates in many countries, young adults, aged 25–34 are facing more pronounced unemployment and under employment than do 15–24 year olds.

One result of all this has been a vicious cycle. As the labor market deteriorates, the precarious nature of the labor market in combination with creeping credentialism and the continuing enthusiasm for human capital theory combines to corral large numbers of jobless or underemployed young people in postsecondary educational institutions. We now have educational systems in many developed countries where just trying to get an education itself generates more inequality. This is not just because the state has steadily withdrawn financial support for higher education, it is also because in the context of mass higher education most students have to bear the burden of heavy tuition debts and too often either fail to complete and else graduate with credentials offering neither a satisfactory educational experience or the kind of job for which they were trained (Stiglitz 2013). Stiglitz points to the net effect in terms of a loss of educational opportunity for too many people from lower socioeconomic backgrounds who are severely disadvantaged in terms of the quality and value of the education they receive and their diminished capacity to enter the labor market (Stiglitz 2013, pp. 244–245).

It is a shift that had the greatest impact on those from lower socioeconomic backgrounds. Old ideas about individual responsibility resurfaced under economic liberalism with significant implications for disadvantaged groups and those with limited resources to practice self-responsibility. Reduced funding for housing, homeless services and allied support services had a significant impact on many disadvantaged people who relied on them. As Settersten et al. (2005) have observed, those from more affluent families have been able to manage the shift more readily than more economically vulnerable families (see also Howker and Mailk 2013).

Among the other effects of the consequences of the toxic combination of neoliberal policies and a globalizing economies include 'youth homelessness', evidence of a range of problems including teen suicide, increased drug and alcohol use, violence and mental illness especially although not exclusively among young people from disadvantaged communities. Millions of people, a disproportionate number of them young people, in the 'global marketplace' are now unemployed or can access only precarious employment. It is a situation that is disruptive to becoming independent and is socially destructive (OECD 2013).

This situation also makes young people more susceptible to the impact of socioeconomic forces (debt, disinvestment in public infrastructure, demographic shifts etc.) over which they have no control and the economic dependency it promotes which directly undermines their capacity to assume 'adult' independence and have some real sense of control over their lives (Settersten et al. 2005). According to Howker and Malik, this is taking place as policy and people's attitudes toughen. If British experience is anything to go by, rather than being sympathetic toward the plight of those 'doing it tough' respondents to a national attitude survey were more skeptical of about whether welfare recipients deserved income support during periods of economic crisis (Howker and Malik 2013, pp. 10–11).

Finally we have witnessed the promotion of new kinds of surveillance and regulation with particular attention given to young people. Historically 'youth' have been represented as the source of 'respectable fears and anxiety' as hooligan, delinquent and now as 'youth at risk' (Pearson 1983, Kelly 2000, pp. 463–476, Bessant, Hil and Watts 2005). With the erosion or fragmentation of modern institutions (education, work, family) that traditionally played a crucial supervisory-cum-socialization role in what was characterized as the notoriously risky 'transition' from childhood to adolescence to adulthood', concern has mounted about new risks associated with 'youth' (Kelly 2001, pp. 23–33). As sociologists like Beck (1991) argued, late modern societies that have embraced the individualist values characteristic of neoliberalism have seen the rise of a discourse and practice of risk. This has seen experts and the state increase their interest in surveillance and management (e.g., curfews, use of ultra sonic 'youth deterrent' technologies like 'Mosquito').

At the same time, new networked communication technologies open new ways of being and communicating in the world.

Online ritual and digital sensibilities

There has been a considerable discussion and speculation about the effects of the new technology on the identity, behavior and sensibility. Does engagement with online technologies lead to a hollowing out of our capacity of to interact with each other socially or to a loss of intimacy as some have argued?

As classic sociologists like Durkheim and Mauss argued, social rituals create and solidify social ties, consolidate a sense of collective identity and render ways of living meaningful and valuable. Rituals involve taking simple, everyday activities like eating, planting crops, welcoming new members into a community or saying farewell to the dead and the transforming them into symbolic, transformative or 'magical' practices. Technologies and various media including drugs (psycho active substances like mescaline, mushrooms), dance, music and images have long played a central part in these rituals.

In the twentieth century people used newspapers, radio and later television to access the world as news and as play: advertising language and imagery also enable us to engage the world magically, for example, through the process of commodity fetishism. Durkheim argued that people who want access to the sacred realm and the gods rely on collective practices or rites, which are socially constructed projections of the community. More recently Goffman demonstrated how rituals are used to position the 'self' in the social world by both conveying messages about our self and managing the impressions we make on others and shaping the interactions we have with others (1967). Steeg Larson and Tufte drew on ethnographic research to show how old media like newspapers, radio, and television provided vehicles in which social life was shared, experienced and expressed (2003, pp. 90–106). Lounge room rituals like family members gathering at specific times of the day to sit on the sofa and watch TV can work to create a particular sensibility and identity.

Contemporary anthropological and ethnographic research has started to reveal the ways the new media creates and reproduces patterns of sociocultural order across time and space especially by engaging the expressive potential of ritual. Today many 'old media' rituals like listening to the radio, reading the newspaper or watching television have been supplanted to a significant degree by new practices enabled by interactive digital media. The constitution of new kinds of (virtual) space opens many new ways of being. For example while contemporary rituals mediated by electronic communications are characterized by their ordinariness, they also provide new freedoms by establishing new, and relatively safe 'virtual spaces'.

Since the mid-1990s and especially since 2000 millions of young people engage in new everyday rituals centered on 'sacred objects' like the laptop, the iPad, or mobile phone establishing contact with sacred sites (Facebook, Instagram, micro-blogs, instant messaging, and other social media sites). Simple activities like sitting down to check emails, playing games online or sharing Facebook, downloading film and music have become ritualized practices that have transformative effects linking participants attention to specific sociocultural orders that transcend the actual time and space occupied physically (Steeg Larson and Tufte 2003, p. 90).

The evolution of new rituals arising from the use the new media offers insight into how globally large numbers of people have come to share particular ways of being and how we can talk about community and more specifically generation in meaningful ways (Carey 2009). These rituals have less to do with the formation of cohesive groups and more to do with networks of individuals and groups each with their own local expressive orders, divergent views and interests, but who nonetheless share certain dispositions and interests. In particular the affordances of the new media enable the transcendence of traditional constraints of real physical space and time. When this is ritualized it induces new ways of being in the world and of relating to others.

On the one hand these new media intensify the experience of listening to music, catching up with friends and relatives, or catching the latest 'news'. Researchers point to the ways rituals like game playing, sharing intimacies, mobilizing political action through the Internet, or just 'hanging out' in social media sites often take place in emotionally and politically charged spaces and point to the ways these practices become more than a momentary escape from or suspension of everyday life separated off into special space (Boyd 2008, 2014). These 'virtual' activities build new social bonds.

New media opens new ways to be creative. Boyd points to the ways many young Americans use new media to explicitly create online profiles or self-portraits, photographs, video, 'likes' and 'dislike', demographic information and blog posts which can be changed in response to feedback and according to the context (2014). Others make and post short films. YouTube makes possible the huge volume of online activity detected in 2013: two billion videos are watched every day, hundreds of thousands of videos are uploaded daily, and 24 hours of video are uploaded every minute. We have seen examples of young people like Justin Bieber, Jackie Evancho, Venetian Princess or Travis Porter composing and releasing songs for free as the start of highly lucrative careers.

The way such processes evolve in a person's life is suggested in the case of 'Noah', now in his thirties. Noah fell in love with what quickly became a sacred object to him. He first encountered a computer at the age of six in the early 1980s when an Apple appeared in his classroom. It was a piece of technology imbued with all kinds of magical powers that gave him access to a world he had not known existed. In Noah's case it began with the 'boy's own adventure', the adventures of *Carmen San Diego*, an educational games about heroic detectives and villains. It was a decisive, and perhaps given the emerging digital context, an inevitable moment replicated across the globe by many others just like Noah. Through his teens Noah sat at his computer in his bedroom most nights as his family slept. He 'played' and chatted initially using local dial-up local Internet access, Bulletin Board System (BBS) and personal home pages. To overcome the problem of slow and limited access he and his 'mates' hacked ISP addresses with unlimited open access like the local university to call international numbers and the world free of charge. They also sometimes engaged in 'phreaking', a practice that entailed posing as a female to men online to gain access to their computers and accounts. Alternatively they would build zombie networks or botnet (a collection of programs) to gain and secure access and control of IRC channels by the backdoor.

In this way he accessed an unlimited and accelerated both the speed and scope of his access offering undreamt of variety of music, film and a world of ideas. With the launch (in 1999) of Napster (one of the first online peer-to-peer audio file sharing services) Noah shifted to multi-user chat systems like IRC (Internet relay Chat), and connected with 80 million people to talk swap music and ideas.

With the roll out of cable he was downloading at speeds of 10mb per second and accessing material like artists anthology of work, sometimes 30 years of work, in 30 minutes. Noah spent his night and much of his days listening to hundreds of songs, many of which were unreleased or obscure. What he experienced was an entry to a vast, new 'no worries', world where money was not needed. For Noah and boys like him it was an experience that opened a new world affording a hitherto unimaginable cultural awakening. This effect was augmented when he began to download books. Noah was able to create his own digital library amassing some 500,000 books ranging from planting a herb garden to quantum physics. It allowed him unmediated, and unimpeded access to an amazing world of ideas and information he otherwise would have been excluded from or at best had limited entree. It was opened a magical rich world in which he read, learned, played and thrived, it was also a world Noah did not have access to in the 'real' world because he, like most of his friends, were not from families with the financial or cultural capital that could provide access to such an enchanted treasure trove of cultural riches.

By the late 1990s these more playful activities saw Noah's activities and interests segue into politics. He recalls how he and one of his friends came across an Internet provider address which they figured was located in Belgrade. That night NATO started bombing the Serbian capital. While he was watching it live on CNN, Noah started chatting to some of his new friends in Belgrade, asking them what was happening and what it felt like to be in that situation. He described it as surreal. He recalls how one girl was scared and seeking information from him via the new as to what was going on. I relayed to her what I was watching on CNN. We're so far apart, but suddenly the world felt a lot smaller.

In these ways new media offered opportunities to hang out, share and communicate, to explore the world to play, gossip and grumble to each other, to enter the world of war and politics albeit electronically in ways that are otherwise constrained. Ritualised use of new media can produce lasting moral emotional dispositions, schemes of perception, thought and action that sustain certain ways of being and capacities (Boyd 2014).

Digital media compensates for the difficulties certain groups (and especially young people) traditionally faced when accessing or using actual public space, given the extended governance aroused by 'respectable anxieties' about young people trying to use actual public space (Griffiths 2013). In this way new media provides young people with escape routes into safe and fun spaces where they are able to roam relatively free from the constraints attendant on being the less powerful party in asymmetric relationships with older people – like parents, teachers or security personnel who typically get to say what you can and cannot do, when you do it and how you can do it. In these ways new media can work to integrate, to *orient participants toward each other* in ways that allow us to talk in terms of a generation (Boyd 2014).

The new media affects our capacity to make and communicate with each other, to understand or make sense of ourselves and the world while transforming sensibilities like the etiquette of social interactions or traditional ideas about privacy. It also seems to affect the evolution of political sensibilities.

Political opinion: a neoliberal subjectivity

The political subjectivities of those born since the late 1970s has been affected by the experience of growing up in societies dominated by a neoliberal policies and economies which have flourished since the 1980s. Yet what researchers have started to reveal points to a paradox. If researchers like Alloway and Dalley-Trim are right, young people who belong to 'Gen Y' (i.e., born between 1982 and 2003) have 'overwhelmingly adopted a neoliberal discourse' with effects on their dispositions, aspirations and expectations (2009, pp. 51–55).The paradox is: how is it that this generation at once the generation most disadvantaged by neo liberal policies are the generation most likely to support those policies and values?

Alloway and Dalley-Trim argue that this generation talks about 'choosing' to become the author of one's own life, of being self-directed, self-actualizing and on taking on one's own life as a 'do-it-yourself' project (2009). These new 'individuals' identify themselves as 'active', as leading their lives through acts of (regulated) choice. Howker and Malik's account of the 'Jilted Generation' also offers an age-based analysis which shows that many young people are 'tougher', more individualistic and antistatist than older age groups (Duffy in Howker and Malik 2013, pp. 12–13). According to Howker and Malik this generation gives priority to neoliberal rules about competitive advantage and imperatives like promoting the free market (2013). This is said to find expression in an uncritical acceptance, if not promotion of the 'user-pays' ethos, and restricted access to civic goods such as public health care and education.

Opinion surveys in the United Kingdom have found that young people are at the extreme in terms of 'individualistic attitudes' (ibid.). Young people are less supportive than other age groups of spending on social expenditure on national health, welfare and public services on which they may be especially reliant. This appears to be because they worry about having to raise higher taxes to pay for these social expenditures (Duffy, in Howker and Malik 2013, pp. 12–13). According to this analysis young people are more likely than other age groups to be suspicious of 'the poor' believing they are jobless and disadvantaged because they are both 'lazy and unlucky'. As Howker and Malik put it,

These results are remarkable because ... the jilted generation are much more likely to consider themselves poor and to be reliant on benefits aimed at the poor. (Howker and Malik 2013, p. 14)

The neoliberal ethos also appears to have been successfully embedded in their thinking about social assistance and welfare policy. Neoliberal principles that have reshaped industrial relations like the systematic dismantling of formalized practices for collective bargaining, institutional provisions for arbitrated minimum employment conditions, wage controls and industry protection in favor of deregulation and workplace 'flexibility' seem to be accepted by many young people (Muller 2006). Reportedly many young people see waged work as precarious and as requiring constant flexibility as the acceptable norm. However the idea of having a secure job with related benefits is believed to be an unlikely prospect while secure employment is rejected as being too confining. While those surveyed were described as confident and robust, they were said to be relatively unaware of the social impact of new media and globalization and remained committed to the belief that their fate is self-determined (Alloway and Dalley-Trim 2009, p. 53, see also Dusseldorp 2006, Muller 2006).

Why is a political belief system like neoliberalism that serves to justify an increasingly unequal social order and which has damaged the well being of many young people still respected by those who are disadvantaged by it? How do we understand the apparent paradox highlighted by Howker and Malik (2013) that the generation born after the late 1970s:

hold a peculiar set of beliefs: more likely to seek to cut to all welfare programs including those on which they ... most rely; more likely to consider themselves poor but less likely to want state help; more likely to be unemployed but less likely to than any other cohort, but perhaps more likely to feel that it's the fault of idle behavior rather than of bad luck. (Howker and Malik, 2013, p. 14)

One way of interpreting this complexity we now see is to draw on Raymond Williams who pioneered the study of popular culture. Williams distinguished between what he described as 'residual', 'dominant' and 'emergent' structures of feeling. These refer to the ways that different ways of thinking, feeling and being coexist and coincide sometimes complementing sometimes grating with each other. This seems useful given the evidence that suggests that while some young people support a neoliberal worldview even as they are disadvantaged by it, others are opposing neoliberal policies.

Political opposition

Finally alongside evidence of a neoliberal political subjectivity among some young people, is evidence about the role of young people in developing an oppositional politics. While the neoliberal imaginary has told a seductive story about its capacity to produce economic growth and prosperity for all, the reality for many has been quite different. Experiencing of mounting unemployment and unemployment, inequality and poverty, student debt loads, unaffordable housing and the global financial crisis after 2008 have encouraged antagonism toward the state and to 'normal', that is, neoliberal politics. These differences may also reflect that fact that evidence gleaned for example, from the United Kingdom does not readily translate to other countries like the United States.

According to one PEW survey, young Americans aged 18 to 24 years are more 'liberal' or 'progressive' than the country as a whole. They have a favorable view about the role of the state (including the value of government regulation), although they also entertain positive views of business. They also report a dramatic generational divide along party lines with young people being more likely to identify as Democrats rather than as Republicans especially when compared those who are now in their 30s and 40s (Keeter 2006).

American research by Zukin et al. (2007) inquired into the degree to which different age groups had developed their own political and civic outlooks and styles of engagement. They identified four discrete generations in the early twenty-first century:

- Dutifuls: those born before 1946
- Baby Boomers: those born between 1946 and 1964
- Generation X: those born between 1965 and 1979
- DotNets: (aka Generation Y, GenNext, millennials) those born between 1980 and 2000

They began by distinguishing between 'political' and 'civic' engagement. Civic engagement they defined as engagement in community problem solving, volunteering, involvement in charitable causes, member of a civic group (ibid. 2007, p. 73). Participants were labeled politically engaged if they took part in two or more political activities defined as voting, volunteering for a political group, trying to encourage someone how to vote or vote in a particular way, wearing a political message (button, car bumper sticker, carrying a political campaign sign for a candidate), or making a financial contribution to a political party (Zukin et al. 2007, p. 69).

These researchers found there were important generational effects that influenced the kinds and degrees of political and civic engagement. While there is diversity amongst the two generations born after the advent of neoliberalism those born since 1979 and 2000 (Gen X and Dot Gen) exhibited lower rates of political participation. However when it came to civic participation researcher reported different generational responses and higher civic engagement for those born after 1979 and 2000 especially when compared with their political engagement. Those born between 1980 and 2000 (DotNet) in particular, for example, displayed higher levels of civic engagement compared to those born before 1946 and were more active than other generations when it came to charitable causes (Zukin et al. 2007).

The young people surveyed recognized how corporations and the private sector enjoyed considerable influence over own their lives and the sovereignty of the state (Zukin 2006, p. 170). A critical finding was that young people form the Dot Net generation they interviewed believed that 'the market' was incompatible with and counter to democratic practices (e.g., participation). Reportedly young people saw the power of corporate interests as beyond the reach of the state, beyond any form of democratic accountability (Zukin et al. 2006, Dahlgren 2009b). This disillusionment or what by some has been called 'value dissonance' between young people and political elites has been used by some writers to talk of problems such as the erosion of public trust in democratic institutions, low youth voter turn out, the 'crisis in democracy' and the alleged apolitical disposition of younger people (Bastedo 2012).

These findings have been replicated in Australia. Lyons and Tilling (2004) interviewed young Australians and found they were aware of and concerned about political issues. They found they had an awareness of global issues and saw how they might be affected by them. They did not like evidence of increased poverty, inequality, or global conflict and felt empathetic toward those most negatively effected. Reportedly they experienced a sense of empowerment mediated through the new media, 'forming a stronger network of youth' while at the same time some they expressed a sense of powerlessness they felt in being able to change the things they do not agree with (Lyons and Tilling 2004, pp. 42–51).

Conclusion

Mannheim's notion of generational units helps provide some understanding of what is going on now. As Mannheim argued disruptive or large scale historic events touch the lives of generations but not necessarily with the same effect. Mannheim observed how those who spent their formative years in the same context did not interpret and experience events the same ways. Germans who grew up during the Napoleonic wars of the 1800s responded differently: some became liberals and others romantic conservatives.

I made the case that provided we are mindful of some important qualifications, we can talk about young people as a generation. The three historic events namely the rise of neoliberalism, the digital revolution and globalization, that characterized the global milieu from the late 1970s until now created conditions that are significantly different to earlier decades. These events have touched the lives of young people born since the late 1970s, and those events have helped generate new experiences, sensibilities and customs.

Yet there are limits as to how far we can generalize about these generational effects. This is why I turn to case studies (in Chapter 6) which sacrifice the ability to generalize to a smaller tighter focus that allows for more detailed analysis, one that pays attention to the complexity and diversity at play.

5
A Heuristic, or a Guiding Framework

Future historians may regard our time as one characterized by a coming together of significant events: the Internet and associated digital media, and concern about 'what's wrong with democracy' (Zakaria 2013, Baumann 1999, Furedi 2005, Hay 2006, Hay and Stoker 2009, Ginsborg 2009). This takes place in a context of repeated instances of large numbers of people engaging in new and high-profile forms of political activism that rely on new digital communications media. How can we best interpret these developments that mark our time?

The past few decades have also seen a rich and vast array of descriptions and explanations about the relationship between young people, new media and prospects for social, economic and political change. One feature of this has been the confidence with which this description and prognosis has been offered. American experts surveyed by the Pew Research Center in 2011, agreed that the generation of young people referred to as the 'Millennials' were

> growing up hyperconnected to each other and the mobile Web and counting on the internet as their external brain will be nimble, quick-acting multi-taskers who will do well in key respects. At the same time, these experts predicted that the impact of networked living on today's young will drive them to thirst for instant gratification, settle for quick choices, and lack patience. (Pew 2012)[1]

Is such certainty warranted? Indeed one reason for writing this book is to highlight the complexity of what we see before us. It is why I now draw on the writings discussed in the earlier chapters, gleaning insights about change, politics, generation from writers like Pierre Bourdieu, Jürgen Habermas, of his critics like Dahlgren, Keane and Frazer and, of course,

Mannheim. This exercise entails extracting key ideas from their writings on generation, politics and change and using that to formulate questions that provide a heuristic or guide. I then use that heuristic to discover and figure out what is happening in the case studies that follow, to determine the political nature of the actions taking place in those sites.

However, before I sketch out a heuristic scheme, something needs to be said about this approach as a method.

Method: 'The world outside and pictures in our head'

I begin by recognizing how it is when we interpret the world in all its complexity that we create mental or cognitive maps that are representations of our social and physical environment. These are maps that are reliant on categories or concepts. A heuristic helps us see those categories more clearly and overcome the tendency to see them as stereotypes, a tendency that can perpetuate illusions and inform poor political judgment and practice (Lippman 1922).

The heuristic framed in this chapter offers a set of rules or guidelines that in the form of questions that have been formulated from the rich intellectual and practical treasure trove of thinking set out in the earlier chapters.

They are questions that encourage a focus on specific aspects of a situation, in this case, politics, change and the role of new technology. It is a heuristic that will help me intuit, form judgments and figure out what is going on. I note too that while heuristics can help us discover and interpret events, they can also create biases because they encourage a focus and thereby affect the choices we make. In response to this, I note that the problem of bias is not unique to this approach. Indeed, no research is or can be impartial, dispassionate and objective, and any such claims are both misleading and dangerous. To paraphrase Stephan Jay Gould, impartiality even if it were attainable is undesirable is unattainable because we all have backgrounds, interests and beliefs. He argues it is dangerous for a researchers to imagine they can be neutral because it encourages us not to be vigilant about our personal inclinations and their influence, something that risks our falling victim to prejudice. Thus to take a leaf from Gould's book, objectivity, operationally defined, is fair treatment of material and not the absence of preference. Indeed recognizing and acknowledging our preferences as we work is critical if their influence is to be recognized, constrained or countermanded and if that fair treatment of material and arguments is to be achieved (Gould 1981, pp. 36–37).

Moreover, we do not deviate from good research practice when we identify and use our preferences, experiences and interests to decide what subjects, writers and ideas to pursue. As Gould notes, life is too short and potential studies infinite. And 'we have a much better chance of accomplishing something significant when we follow our passionate interest and work in areas of deepest personal meaning' (ibid. p. 37). This approach does, of course, pose the risk of prejudice, but the gain in dedication can balance or counter such a concern, particularly if one remains committed to the principle of treating the material fairly and acknowledges one's own interests and preferences.

I did not take up this study void of personal curiosity or politics. Like all researchers, there is a relationship between the private and the public (Habermas 2009, p. 23). And while that connection is clear to me, the space constraints of this book and the need for discipline or focus means that I do not have the luxury of offering a full account here. What I can say is that what I am politically is reflected in the things I stand for and that I am interested in. They include

- how people treat each other. (e.g., that civic decency and public respect for imagination and knowledge are valued);
- what is justice and what kinds of laws we should have;
- that people who are not well off ought to have deliberate state intervention or collective support;
- that minority groups (e.g., young people) should not be subject to prejudice and bullying;
- that freedom and political autonomy are critical for a good society and a good life, including the protection of our rights to speak truth to authority.

This said, I acknowledge how the ideas and material in this book mesh well with my politics. Indeed, this recognition caused me to be extra attentive when I selected the case studies, the key writers used in this book and the analysis of that material. I believe I can and have been fair with the material used and particularly how it has been used to develop an argument, and that the evidence supports the arguments and insights that are made (Gould 1981). I believe our democratic cultures are in strife and that we are now seeing important political shifts sponsored by new media. This can be seen on many new sites where the playing out of prejudices and the exercise of power between traditional power-holders and newcomers hold a key to understanding what is going on. I recognize the inherent resistance to change, but that it does nonetheless occur. I believe that the philosophers G. W. F. Hegel and Hannah Arendt were able to identify important aspects of change by recognizing the role of natality and how the old is incorporated into the new. I believe that our milieu plays a powerful role in forging our *habitus* and that it can promote and resist change and, importantly, the capacity of our imagination to create new ways of seeing and being.

Returning to heuristics as a method, and how they provide guide or mental shortcuts, I refer to the work of the American writer and policy adviser Walter Lippmann (1889–1974) and specifically his psychological theory of stereotypes that helped illuminate how we work as emotional problem solvers and decision-makers by relying on quite limited cognitive resources, or what subsequently came to be known as 'bounded rationality' (Lippmann 1922, Simon 1979, Kahneman 2003). Lippmann elaborated and defined several categories (e.g., Cold War) and coined the terms 'stereotype' and 'blind spot', arguing that we are more likely to believe the fixed ideas and pictures in our heads about what we see than to make a judgment based on critical thinking. Stereotypes, he argued, reflect social values, and are what come to mind when we think of a particular social group. In short, they are simplified mental images of a class of people or objects in the world that subject us to partial truths (1922). Stereotypes are important because they provide material for the construction of our mental models and tend to be quite rigid and resistant to change. Stereotypes about people constitute one class of these cognitive structures.

Lippmann wrote about the 'pseudo environment' or what today is referred to as 'a mental model' (Johnson-Laird 1983). These pseudoenvironments act as a bridge between inner ourselves and the real world. We develop them because the real world is too complex, too big and fleeting for direct experience and knowledge. Thus they are fictional cognitive representations of the world, and as such as are subjective and biased. Having said that, they are amenable variously to forms of human manipulation, reasoning, and problem solving.

Lippmann's other cognitive category, the blind spot, which is relevant here, is an analogy to the perceptual illusions generated by the visual system. These are gaps between the external facts and internal mental representations, resulting in cognitive illusions that lead people to make misguided choices.

For Lippmann, it was important to develop critical reflexivity about our stereotypes and blind spots, and he invested a lot of faith in the work of intellectuals' engaging in economic research, political analysis and psychological study of pseudo environments, blind spots and human error. Recognizing that it would take several generations to accomplish this, he pinned his hopes on the enrichment of the educational system. 'As a working model of the social system becomes available to the teacher, he can use it to make the pupil acutely aware of how his mind works on unfamiliar facts' (Lippmann 1922, p. 408). Higher education could assist students by preparing them 'to deal with the world with a great deal more sophistication about their own minds' (pp. 408–409). Above all, a systematic study of human error was imperative because it 'is not only in the highest degree prophylactic, but it serves as a stimulating introduction to the study of the truth (p. 409).

The subsequent interest in and development of Lippmann's account of social stereotypes has been erratic. Some later psychologists like Gordon Allport claimed Lippmann was wrong because he

> tends to confuse stereotype with category. A stereotype is not identical with a category; rather it is a fixed idea that accompanies the category. For example, the category 'Negro' can be held in mind simply as a neutral, factual, non-evaluative concept, pertaining merely to a racial stock. (1954, p. 43)

This depends on the conventional or classical view of category, which sees a category as a discrete set of attributes that define membership independent of the pictures in our head (Johnson-Laird 1983).

Lippmann's work anticipated more contemporary work that claims all social categories are fuzzy and that we develop new understandings or insights by establishing a similarity between new experiences, facts or cases and existing pictures and categories in the head (Rosch & Mervis 1975; Medin 1989). Based on experiments on categories, researchers argued that categories have the best examples or prototypes that provide ease of classification and other aspects of reasoning (Rosch and Mervis 1975). As Lippmann's psychological theory implied, the pictures in our head are actually part of the structure of our cognitive categories.

Thus, to move beyond a possibly simplistic or even a dangerous reliance on stereotypes, we need to understand categories as fuzzy and in more reflexive ways using what the Greeks called heuristics. This is one way to respond to the complexity of the world and refine our categories in more reflexive ways.

For the Greeks, heuristics referred to the ways in which we find things out or discover a solution to a problem or a mystery. The use of heuristics might sound sophisticated, but it is not. Heuristics simply entails the use of accessible, applicable information, rules or rule of thumb, or sensitizing questions to help solve a particular problem or make discoveries

Although much of the work of discovering heuristics in decision-makers was done by the Israeli psychologists Tversky and Kahneman, the modern idea of heuristics was introduced by Nobel laureate and economist and psychologist Herbert Simon. Simon was fascinated by the way humans solved problems, and he showed how we use what he called 'bounded rationality' (which is a less rational than the formal forms of rationality found in mathematics or logic). He coined the term 'satisficing' to refer to the ways we tend to seek solutions or accept choices or judgments that are 'good enough', even though they could be developed into much more highly refined forms of rational analysis. Doing the latter is my purpose here. I will develop a heuristic framed primarily as a series of questions.

In what follows I identify some questions that I use as a heuristic to identify, interpret and understand the evidence I have gathered so as to address my key questions. As mentioned, the aim is to draw from the previous chapters certain key insights and use these to develop a kind of checklist or a rule of thumb. These insights constitute questions that will help highlight *who* is doing *what* and *how* we might understand what some people are doing now as they engage with various kinds of new media. I am particularly interested in understanding whether these activities constitute 'democratic' practice and whether we are seeing the opening up of possibilities for new forms of politics.

The heuristic is offered to explore three connected points of inquiry. They are the value and relevance of generation as a valid interpretative category, what the practices of people born since the late 1970s reveal about the prospects for different kinds of new politics, and the extent to which the new forms of communications do (or do not) make these political practices and change processes possible.

In short, do we see evidence of a generation shaped by 'exceptional historic' circumstances? Is there evidence in the various cases studies of change and, if so, what kind of change is taking place? Do we see new media being put to particular use involving forms of deliberative democratic practice (Habermas)? Is there evidence of a new political/social imaginary interested in autonomy (Castoriadis)? I now work through these questions.

Generation

Courtesy of pop sociology, pop psychology and the marketing industry, the idea of generation now enjoys a commonsense status. It is generally been assumed that when we speak of generation, we share agreed-on meanings, and that generation can be used to explain social phenomena like why everyone born after 1979 is 'constantly connected young adults who thirst for instant gratification and often make quick, shallow choices' (PEW 2012).

As I argued, like all social categories, generation is a fuzzy concept. Generation has a classificatory purpose, and is not amenable to an essentialist logical and inductive analysis. It is also not amenable to empirical adjudication for determining membership, or whether the traits said to characterize a specific generation like (Gen X or millennials) actually determine who belongs to that category.

Given this, it is advisable that care is taken to recognize essentialist thinking because generation, like all social categories, has a 'made-up' character. Categories are instituted by people, typically experts and governments, who say there are certain properties or core features common to all those deemed to fit the classification (Hacking 2000). As such, these classifications do not refer to 'things' in the same ways that categories refer to physical objects that exist in time or space (like the category tree or rock).

With this in mind, I reiterate my earlier argument that it is possible to develop and use the concept of generation in ways that assist in understanding sociopolitical change and that avoid the pitfalls of essentialist thinking, reductionism and prejudicial stereotypes. The question is how such a category can be used for empirical investigation, how it can be recognized and analyzed.

I note also that we need categories (like generation) for understanding change processes. This is relevant to any empirical or qualitative research because before anything can be investigated, the 'it' we want to study needs to be identified and conceptualized. As mentioned, conceptualizing generation is difficult because when we use such nouns to denote abstract ideas, we attempt to name things that do not exist in an objective sense. This is also why there is so often little consensus about what defines a category. There are plenty of categories that do not refer to anything that can be described or seen in a direct way, but that certainly have very real and often physical effects (e.g., crime, unemployment, violence). To accommodate the fact that social categories emerge discursively and are *discursive in nature* (they are made up), researchers have to operationalize categories. This refers to a process of starting with something that lacks empirical qualities (like visibility, sound, tangibility, smell or taste) and then constructing proxies that can be substituted for the idea, which can be described and in many cases measured. In short, researchers have to establish a criterion that allows the category for which there is no actual empirical referent to be named. Once that is done, research can proceed.

The fuzziness we need to accept when using generational categories has a number of dimensions. To begin, we do not have one clear-cut and stable definition of a particular generation or what we mean by generations. Rather we have a general, loose consensus that generation refers to a demographic cohort defined according to a chronological time – specifically birthdates. (That said, while birthdates are used, there is no consensus about the rationale used for deciding on particular dates.)

Secondly, a number of other attributes (beside birthdates) are used. Howe and Strauss, for example, point to the following three attributes they use to identify a generation in terms other than years of birth (2000):

- membership based on the self-perception of membership within a generation that begins during adolescence and coalesces during young adulthood
- common beliefs and behaviors that include the attitudes (toward family, career, personal life, politics, religion, etc.) and behaviors or choices made in regard to jobs, marriage, children, health, crime, sex, drugs, etc.) that characterize a generation
- a common location in history and the role of turning points or historical trends that involve major shifts in politics within a community from (e.g., social liberal to neoliberal politics) and significant events (e.g., the Vietnam War or the war on terror after September 11) that occur during a generation's formative years in adolescence and young adulthood)

Drawing on Mannheim, I argue that if certain events or social conditions are significant enough, they help shape what Bourdieu calls fields of action, which in turn mark and inform those who were exposed to those events in their formative years in ways that forge particular kinds of *habitus*, particular sensibilities, indelible dispositions, ways of seeing and being. That said, this is not to be read as implying that a given event like the Great War or the global financial crisis of 2008 produces the same responses among a given generation. For any event we will see divergent understandings and responses. The only thing a generation shares is the exposure to a common large event: how they experience and make sense of it will depend on all kinds of structural and serendipitous factors. Accordingly, and this is a critical point, we cannot assume that

- we can use the generational idea as an explanation in its own right, or
- that all those said to belong to a generation share the same dispositions or attitudes or do the same kinds of things in the same kinds of ways.

With the heuristic and Mannheim in mind, I ask:

1. Generation	Is there evidence of a distinctive generation, defined less as a group of people who share a singular set of defining attributes, traits or dispositions and more in terms of a range of reactions or dispositions shaped by exposure to a number of exceptional historic events?

The second central theme in my inquiry is the relationship between the generation of people born since the late 1970s and whether we are seeing new kinds of politics. Investigating this involves several separate questions: one critical question relates to political legitimacy. Another is about the usefulness of a revised conception of deliberative democracy in a revitalized public sphere (or civic space)? The third is how we can identify and understand the idea of political change.

The political: deliberative democracy

Contemporary interest in new politics, and particularly the role of young people, begins with the idea that political relations and activities conventionally understood to characterize Western democracies are in a state of crisis. I argue that many of the assumptions and questions in the literature and commentary that make this claim are problematic and require conceptual clarity.

As some research indicates, attempts to 'measure' the degree of young people's political disengagement or alienation assumes, usually implicitly, that the researchers and the young people 'share a common understanding about the definition and meaning of politics' (Henn et al. 2002, pp. 168–169). As critics have pointed out, these studies overlook important questions, like what young people see as political (Henn et al. 2012, McCaffrie and Marsh 2013, p. 113). Indeed as McCaffrie and Marsh argue, 'a pervasive problem with the mainstream participation literature [is that] a restrictive conception of politics forces a restrictive understanding of participation' (2013, p. 116). If we want to discover what political activities young people are engaged in, it may be useful to take a step back to think about the idea of politics, the political and new politics. Yet as Leftwich observes, asking an apparently simple question like, what is politics? 'is not as straightforward as it may at first seem, and raises many further and difficult questions' (2004, p. 1).

One difficult question relates to the issue of legitimacy, which is understood as referring to what a political and social order needs to promote if its citizens are to believe or feel that that order is fair and just. In short, political legitimacy is the general acceptance of a government's authority, and without that, rulers lose their mandate or capacity to govern.

The idea that Western societies face a crisis of legitimacy and have come close to a collapse of the entire system has become so commonplace that it is almost a cliché. One aspect of this concern relates to the viability of a public sphere, the space in which the formation of public opinion takes place, and a process deemed vital to a functioning democracy (Habermas 1989, Cohen 1989, Elster 1998, Dryzek 2010). Another concern of this kind relates to evidence, especially since 2001, of the inclination of avowedly liberal states to declare 'states of exception' or 'states of emergency' in the face of security threats posed by terrorism or war and to derogate fundamental rights and rule of law principles (Agamben 2005, Dyzenhuus 2006, Ackerman 2006).

A third dimension of concern about political legitimacy is evident in the fact that in many contemporary societies there exist processes of 'will formation' that enable elite political and economic players and specialist technicians of communications (public relations experts and journalists) to exercise their power to deliberate, while also using gate-keeping practices to reduce the capacity of ordinary citizens to deliberate. In so doing, they reproduce major inequalities in the circulation of ideas and opinion (Wolin 2008).

The legitimacy crisis was a central preoccupation for Habermas, expressed in what he called the 'post-metaphysical crisis' and evident in his writings about the breakdown in the ways people historically dealt with questions of fact and value. As Regh explained, this refers to 'the problem of dealing with a social reality on the one side and a claim of reason (which is sometimes belied by the reality) on the other' (in Habermas 1998, p. 8). As Habermas observed, Bockenforde one of Germany's foremost legal philosophers, posed a disturbing question when he asked 'whether the pacified, secular state is reliant on normative presuppositions that it cannot itself guarantee' (2009, p. 101). Bockenforde was implying that modern states, especially those committed to a liberal utilitarian ethos (which is relativistic and individualistic) are not able to regenerate their ethical foundations through their own resources. For this reason they may come to rely tacitly on traditional religious traditions, to which they are formally committed to ignore due to injunctions to separate church and state.

Habermas' response to the problem constituted by the decline of traditional authority and concern about the ethical void that characterizes liberal orders and their economic, legal and political systems was to develop an account of rational and deliberative practice. According to Habermas, it is through processes of deliberative rationality that modern states can produce a 'fragile form of collective identity among citizens' that can provide a normative legitimacy courtesy of civic solidarity. Yet as mentioned in Chapter 1, many critics have engaged with Habermas' insistence of consensus, highlighting its faults and offering other 'defending politics' in terms of 'politics of action' (Keane 2009, 2012, Crick 2005).

Indeed as Keane points out, we need a political communication processes suited to the fact we are 'living in an age marked by large-scale adventures of power that touch and transform the lives of millions of people and their bio-habitats in unprecedented ways citizens and that are "powered by silent complacency", institutional dysphasia, group-think, willful blindness, unchecked praise and anti-learning mechanisms'

(2012, p. 660). In his argument for 'the early warning principle of communication', he states that

> It is not just that it no longer indulges bland rationalist (Habermasian) fantasies of conjoining citizens into harmonious agreement, or that it is no longer wedded (as earlier justifications of freedom of communication were) to a First Principle, be it Truth or Happiness or Human Rights or God, Public Service or the Common Good. Suspicious of organized silences and arbitrary power, a champion of the weak against the strong, especially when the weak find themselves silenced by the strong, the early warning principle of communication is politically meaningful in a wide range of contexts. It is on the lookout against all forms of arbitrary power, wherever they take root. (p. 666)

Other ideas central to Habermas' work include the public sphere, discursive rationality, and deliberative democracy' (i.e., the idea that if a norm or decision is to be considered legitimate, it should rest on the proviso that everyone affected by the decision could accept the consequences of their observance of it – and that those with an interest would prefer that decision to any alternative). For any norm or action (decision) to be valid and legitimate, it needs to be justifiable within a moral-practical discourse. Only then would it conform to Habermas' 'ideal speech situation' (1998).

In these ways Habermas argues that the solution to the crisis of legitimacy is to engage in deliberative activity because rational consensus making provides a basis for authority. For this reason, communicative action is critical for democracy and political legitimacy.

> The disenchantment and disempowering of the domain of the sacred [accompanies] a release of the rationality potential in communicative action. The aura of rapture and terror that emanates from the sacred, the spellbinding power of the holy, is sublimated into the binding/bonding force of criticizable validity claim. (Habermas 1987, p. 77)

Habermas' account of the public sphere was part of an intellectual project designed to clarify and explain how we can provide good reasons for practical beliefs and judgments as well as political decisions. His notion of a 'Kantian pragmatism' inspired considerable interest in establishing the epistemic, normative and social conditions that enable rational deliberative practices and in turn a democratic polity (1974, 1984, 1996). For this reason, the question of whether or not Habermas offers an adequate account of the political is especially important.

In Habermas' attempt to detail rational practice, he addressed the metaphysical crisis of meaning (i.e., the loss of traditional theological authority narratives). This was done while remaining faithful to the idea of democratic politics and also avoiding a slide in the direction of authoritarian populism, as was the case with earlier German critics of liberalism like Weber and Schmitt. Habermas wanted to merge the requirements of rationality with legitimacy by producing a set of rational techniques and protocols that he said can be used to produce value rationality (Mouffe 1998, Benhabib 1994).

Habermas was committed to specifying the nature of rational communication and its relevance to democracy, thus his interest in rule formation, and in identifying and clarifying the rules or norms he said underpinned rational discourse or ideal speech (e.g., listening, turn-taking, relative equity between participants etc.). Habermas offered a discursively grounded communication theory that he said was able to enable value rationality. As mentioned, his perspective of course has attracted considerable debate.

Given the scale and significance of his contributions, it is not surprising that Habermas attracted much critique, most of which provides ideas that can be used to augment and modify his accounts of deliberation, rationality and the public sphere. For this reason, that body of work is critical for the heuristic I have in mind (e.g., Dahlgren 2009, Geuss 2008, Keane 1995, pp. 1–22, 2009, 2012, Fraser 1995). For as Keane points out, the conventional idea of a single public sphere in the context of the digital age is likely to disappear in favor of a concept of plurality of spheres somewhat like a 'complex mosaic of differently sized overlapping and interconnected public spheres' (1995, p. 8).

These conditions of deliberative democracy and a public sphere that is inclusive of critiques informs the following questions that I have used to formulate a heuristic for the case studies.

Is there evidence of more participation on relatively equitable grounds, and is that a necessary condition for democracy?

2. The Political: Deliberative democracy

Is there evidence of deliberative democracy or collective deliberation and action?

Is there evidence of expanded forms of deliberation where participants value listening to each other and encourage new styles of action and creativity (e.g., new forms of literature equivalent to epic poems that see the expansion of language to include comedy, political commentary, theological speculation etc.)?

Is there evidence of a variety of technical and other means available and being used to enlarge participation, which insures that values like equity, fairness, openness and a pluralism of views are promoted? Do new media expand our opportunity for deliberation?

Is there evidence of expanded Forms of Deliberation?

Are deliberative democratic processes enlarged and open to a diversity of groups in which a range of communicative spaces are valued?

Is there relative Equal Participation?

Do significant power differences exist? Are they acknowledged or ignored and bracketed-off, 'as if' all participants are social equals when they are not?

What effects do inequities have? Do they help reproduce inequalities or traditional social imaginaries?

Are power disparities (e.g., disparities in resources, experience, status) mitigated?

Do the public spheres or civic spaces favor elite discourses and rationality? (e.g., Are they characterized by specified rational principles and rules and what are the implications of that?)

Is there a plurality of publics? If there is, do they have a better chance of promoting the ideal of extending participation and parity than does a single public sphere?

Does it allow for an inclusive network of multiple competing publics as opposed to a single restricted public?

Are marginalized and excluded groups included (e.g., minority groups like young people, children, women) sphere?

Are participants comfortable articulating matters using their own words, when they are comfortable expressing countering interpretations of their own identities as well as those of others?

Are they guarded by gate-keeping practices like those who are employed by editors who censor and limit access?

Is there freedom from coercion and is there enhanced autonomy?

Is there evidence of collective will formation?

Yet all this does not deal with the question already referred to of how we will know that we are seeing a process of political change. For that I turn to the work of Cornelius Castoriadis (1997), who offers a different account of the prospect for political renewal, grounded in our capacity for imagination and creativity.

The political: change and autonomy

Castoriadis introduces the prospect of change with his idea of a new imaginary, and in doing so offers a challenging account of how the new becomes possible. Central to his work is the inexplicable process of creativity, which human imagination makes possible and which results in the constitution or creation of our own world (Castoriadis 1984b, p. 5). It is his emphasis on creativity and the work of the imagination that adds an important counterfoil Bourdieu's emphasis on the conjunction of change and continuity in his theory of practice (see Chapter 2) and to Habermas' steadfast views about the importance of observing a universalistic conception of rational deliberation.

I am not suggesting that Habermas is compatible with Castoriadis, but rather that the idea of putting them together is akin to trying to square a circle – something that is not possible due to a basic incommensurability. I simply suggest that Castoriadis' emphasis on how change, and especially political change, as an expression of creativity and imagination offers another line thought. As I argued earlier, Castoriadis focuses throughout his work on the question of *autonomy*, which goes well beyond the conventional liberal preoccupation with individual freedom, pointing to a collective understanding of freedom involving the processes and conditions in which a society comes to recognize that its values are its own creation, not inevitable or 'given' (by 'God' or nature etc.).

Castoriadis argues that 'the imaginary of the society... creates for each historical period its singular way of living, seeing and making its own existence' (1974, p. 2). Overstepping any explanation of how this happens, he says that these imaginaries arise out of the imagination of people and assume a persistent and institutional character represented in the system of meanings that shape and govern the social or political order. One consequence of this is that people unconsciously absorb and make these imaginaries their own: the result is well-ordered conventional beliefs and conduct that make possible what he calls *heteronomous* societies. We may well believe that we exercise our own judgment, but in reality how we see and act are shaped by these overwhelming social processes. In this way, most people are heteronomous because we judge on the basis of convention and public opinion (2007, p. 75).

For this reason, thinking about and questioning the social imaginary operating in a heteronomous society tends to be 'an exceptional occurrence' and has only been encountered twice, and only within the European and Greco-Western traditions. The first centers on the evolution of the classical era in Athens when the Athenian polis saw the birth of democracy, philosophy and tragedy as well as the arts and sciences. The second 'project of autonomy' that Castoriadis identified can be found in the onset of the 'modern period', in that time conventionally referred to as the European Renaissance, which spanned from the fourteenth to the seventeenth centuries (2007, pp. 77–79). Achieving this represents a 'tremendous historic break'. When this does happen, we see rich and rare instances of creativity.

If we do not wish to resort to transcendental factors to explain their radical transformations, we must postulate or assume a power of creation, *vis a formandi*, inherent in both human collectives as well as in individual human beings (Castoriadis 2007, p. 72). The radical transformation of society can only come from individuals who want their *autonomy* on both a social and an individual level. They achieve this by continuously preserving and augmenting their autonomy, which involves working to cultivate individuals who aspire to having their independence, by taking responsibility for themselves and encouraging as many people as possible toward that end. Without this creative political work, social change cannot come about.

With this in mind, I formulate the following questions for the heuristic frame:

3. The Political: Change and autonomy	***Do we see evidence of political autonomy?*** This may take the form of heightened political autonomy in either the individual and/or the collective? It can be evident in the capacity of people to make self-governing judgments rather than decisions based on convention and public opinion. It can be seen in the degree to which people are willing to question truth claims, and in their preparedness to speak out and exercise positive freedom, to 'stand up' and say 'the tribe's' representations and commonsense worldviews need rethinking, the laws and powers are unjust, and we have to create new arrangements.

continued

In short, political autonomy and movement toward change
can be seen in the extent to which the citizenry is populated
with self-reflective individuals who demonstrate an interest
in uninhibited critical thought, frank debate and work on
autonomous political projects. (This might take the form
of activities directed toward promoting a self-legislating
society.)

Are processes of will formation understood as norm creation
both subversive and transgressive, and do processes of will
formation highlight the generative capacities of the social
imaginary?

This can be evident in the extent to which claims
that sources of legitimate authority are derived from
nonhistorical or divine sources are queried and contested.
Evidence of a radical imaginary can also be seen in the
creative forces and new forms of being that people bring
into existence.

The reference here is to ontological creations in the form of
new worldviews, linguistic and innovation in language, art,
and music and new ways of being.

Is there a generational dimension involving younger people's
exploring the possibilities of autonomy?

I now turn to the case studies.

6
Democratic Renewal, Pussy Riot and Flash Gigs in the Kremlin

Pussy Riot is an anonymous Russian female punk collective made up of young women who have achieved global fame for their high-profile protests directed at the Putin regime. Founded in August 2011, they hit the world stage in February 2012 when five of their members used the Christ the Saviour Cathedral in Moscow as the site for one of their anti-Putin 'flash gig' performances.

Pussy Riot was galvanized into action by the presidential election due to be held in early March 2012. This election had already provoked a lot of public discussion about Vladimir Putin's record in office (1999–2012) and the legitimacy of the election itself.[1] There was heightened concern about the use of secret police tactics by the presidential office, a fear fueled by Putin's former life as a high-ranking KGB operative. There was concern about both specific events like the contract killing of oppositional figures (including the journalist Anna Politkovskaya, who was murdered in 2006) and a fear that the KGB was no longer subordinate to the government and enjoyed too much power. All this fueled disquiet about the prospect of a neo-KGB Soviet dictatorship (Kryshtanovskaya 2004).

On 21 February 2012, and 11 days before election day, five members of Pussy Riot, including 22-year-old Nadezhda Tolokonnikova, 24-year-old Maria Alyokhina and 30-year-old Yekaterina Samutsevich, their faces covered by colorful balaclavas as was by now their usual practice, entered the 'sacred' space of the altar. This is an area of the church reserved for priests only (and forbidden to women). They began singing a 'punk' prayer 'Holy Mother of God, chase Putin away'. Described variously as a 'flash' or 'guerrilla' gig and even a 'concert', their form of political activism draws on the practice of punk rock as it was performed in the United Kingdom and the United States during the early 2000s. The five women sang for one minute and thirty-three seconds and were prevented from continuing by church security officers. Later that day, and following their release from the Cathedral, they mixed a video of their performance with a more elaborately scored soundtrack and scenes recorded elsewhere days earlier, and released their musical video on YouTube.

In spite of the fact that there was no service being held in the Cathedral at the time, nor was there any threat or actual damage done to person or property, conservative Russians and the Russian state reacted savagely. Andrei Kuraev, a senior deacon in the Russian Orthodox Church, wrote on his blog on the day of the Pussy Riot performance:

> I would offer them some *bliny* (traditional Russian thin pancakes), pour them a cup of honey wine, and invite them to come back for the forgiveness ceremony. And if I were a layman elder, I would also give them a fatherly pinch ... To bring them back to their senses ... And it's *Maslenitsa* time (the week before Lent in the Orthodox calendar, similar to Mardi Gras): the time for the social cosmos to turn upside down. (cited in Bernstein 2013)

On the same day, Maksim Shevchenko, a well-known journalist and television presenter, was much tougher: 'I think Orthodox women should catch and flog these little bitches with birch rods. Let them also have a "performance"' (cited in Bernstein 2013). An influential conservative intellectual, Egor Kholmogorov, likewise proposed that

> If I was working for this church, I would first call the TV crews and then undress them, cover them with feathers and honey, shave their heads, and kick them out to the freezing cold in front of the cameras. (cited in Bernstein 2013)

Twelve days later, the young women were arrested on charges of 'crude violation' of social order, extremism, religious hatred and 'hooliganism'.[2] The formal indictment ran to 2,800 pages. On 21 March 2012, the Patriarch of Moscow and All Russia, Kirill I, condemned Pussy Riot's actions as 'blasphemous', saying:

> The Devil has laughed at all of us ... We have no future if we allow mockery in front of great shrines, and if some see such mockery as a sort of bravery, an expression of political protest, an acceptable action or a harmless joke.

Their trial in July 2012 ended with the three Pussy Riot members' being sentenced to two years in prison. In the indictment, presiding Judge

Syrova argued that Pussy Riot's performance could be interpreted in only one way, that is, as a crime, an act of hooliganism and an expression of religious hatred:

> On the whole by realizing this act [Pussy Riot] clearly and unambiguously expressed their religious hatred and hostility towards one of the currently extant religions – Christianity – in an obviously disrespectful manner, devoid of any moral foundation (Syrova 2012, cited in Voronina 2013, pp. 73–74).

And yet as von Gall observed, it is a problem that in Russian legal literature there are 'generally no clear-cut definitions of the two formal elements of the crime, i.e. hooliganism and religious hatred' (2013, p. 3). The legal niceties aside, the point was a political one: the sentence, which criminalized dissent, was clearly designed to send a clear message that dissent was not a viable option. It also provoked worldwide criticism, and as Western critics pointed out, the tactic of repression was not going to work. As Zizek put it,

> their message is, ideas matter. They are conceptual artists in the noblest sense of the word: artists who embody an Idea. This is why they wear balaclavas: masks of de-individualization, of liberating anonymity. The message of their balaclavas is that it doesn't matter which of them are arrested – they're not individuals, they're an Idea. And this is why they are such a threat: it is easy to imprison individuals, but try to imprison an Idea. (2012)

The other members of the group reportedly fled Russia, fearing persecution. Subsequently appeals were made, but only one member (Samutsevich) had her sentence suspended. Tolokonnikova, and Alyokhina were released from prison in December 2013, just three months short of their two-year sentences.

Their will to dissent does not seem to have been dampened. Both Tolokonnikova and Alyokhina were among the group that performed as Pussy Riot on 19 February 2014 during the Winter Olympics in Sochi: they were attacked with whips and pepper spray by Cossacks employed as security guards (Miller 2014). They remain unrepentant. As Tolokonnikova says,

> As for Vladimir Putin, we still feel the same about him. We still want to do what we said in our last performance for which we spent two years in prison: drive him away. (cited in Circa 2014)

This case study provides a bounded case involving a collective of young people engaged in a political struggle against powerful, established and well-resourced power elites: the Russian government, state security forces and the Russian Orthodox Church. The questions addressed in this chapter draw on the heuristic frame to provide an investigative framework and thematic narrative. The Pussy Riot case invites a range of questions about politics and young people, power and politicians, and traditional key stakeholders in major social institutions as they each create and respond to the challenges of new media, new forms of deliberative practice and political action, and as they also encounter the experiences referred to as globalization, neoliberalism (in its Eastern and Western forms) and the rollout of new media. Whether Pussy Riot expresses what might be described as an 'ethics of a generation' requires that we consider whether the politics of dissent they have articulated around ethical demands that arise from a particular situation is something that helps orient others experiencing similar injustices.

I begin by asking who and what is Pussy Riot?

The evolution of Pussy Riot

Pussy Riot is a Russian feminist cooperative. While it began with approximately a dozen activists and musicians, it has always had a somewhat fluid membership. As one of its members explained,

> We often change names, balaclavas, dresses, and roles inside the groups. People drop out, new members join the group, and the lineup in each *Pussy Riot's* guerilla performance can be entirely different. (interview with Langston 2012)[3]

The group's dissent is expressed, as so often has been the case in Russia, in forms and ways that are distinctly 'intellectual' and performative in nature.

It is significant that some of its founding members, like Tolokonnikova and Samutsevich, had been members of Voina (Russian for 'war'). *Voina* was a street-based performance art group founded in 2007 and dedicated to staging subversive art performances or 'happenings'. Voina is known best for two of its 'events'. One was called 'Fuck for the Heir Puppy Bear'. This happening was staged in February 2008 in the run-up to the election of Russian president Dmitri Medvedev to protest against what Voina described as a corrupt presidential election. The performance 'starred' five couples, including an eight-months pregnant woman, 'having sex' next to a taxidermy display of a bear in the Moscow's Timiryazev State

Museum. Given that the Russian word for 'bear' is *medved*, the target of the happening was obvious: the sexual activity around the stuffed bear in one interpretation became a mock 'fertility ritual' symbolizing hope, new life and pointing to the rebirth of the political system. In another reading it could be taken to imply that 'we are all fucked by the Putinist system'. As one Voina member, Alexey Plucer-Sarno, put it, the event was: 'a portrait of pre-election Russia: everybody fucks each other, and the puppy bear (Medvedev) looks at that with an unconcealed scorn' (2 March 2008).

The event created a scandal that provoked predictable outrage and disgust from various 'moral brigades'. The event was photographed, videoed and published online. It also became a controversial topic for discussion in blogs and mainstream media. The slogan 'Fuck for the Heir Puppy Bear' went on to have an afterlife, reappearing on banners in later protests.

The other famous happening, which was videotaped and posted on YouTube, involved Nadezhda Tolokonnikova, who participated in a happening called 'Kiss the Cop', in which members of Voina forcefully kissed policewomen on the street.

Voina has been charged with more than a dozen criminal cases. Ironically the Russian Ministry of Culture awarded the group its 'Innovation' prize in the category 'Works of Visual Art' in April 2011.

In August 2011, after mounting conflict inside Voina, Nadezhda Tolokonnikova and Yekaterina Samutsevich left and founded Pussy Riot. Like Voina, Pussy Riot was formed in opposition to the increasingly anti-democratic, authoritarian and corrupt Russian government led by Putin since 1999.[4] Pussy Riot was founded with an explicit commitment to both promote human rights, gender equity and freedom of expression in Russia and to protest the authoritarian and antidemocratic tendencies that have characterized the Russian state since Putin's rise to power (Pussy Riot n.d.). According to Pussy Riot member Serafima, its founders had come to feel by 2011 that Russia

> needs a militant, punk-feminist, street band that will rip through Moscow's streets and squares, mobilize public energy against the evil crooks of the Putinist junta and enrich the Russian cultural and political opposition with themes that are important to us: gender and LGBT rights, problems of masculine conformity, absence of a daring political message on the musical and art scenes, and the domination of males in all areas of public discourse. (cited in Langston 2012)

The group has protested against decrees making public meetings and protests illegal.[5] They have campaigned against the arrest and imprisonment of protesters and political opponents, as well as state censorship and surveillance of the Internet and the censoring of art, literature and free speech. They have also protested the 'overly cozy' relationship between the Russian Orthodox Church and Putin.[6] As I will argue shortly, Pussy Riot does this by using provocations subversive of rationality and by creating a political theater with a cast of judicial, church and political officials playing out high drama on the global stage for all to see.

While being the child of Voina, Pussy Riot has drawn on a range of intellectual, cultural and musical influences. They point to the legacy of earlier American punk rock groups like Sonic Hero, the 1990s Bikini Kill and Riot Grrrl movement. Garadsha, a member of Pussy Riot, claims, for example, that 'in terms of feminist musical acts, activism, and community building we do give credit to the Riot Grrrl movement' (interview with Langston 2012). While strongly influenced by punk, Pussy Riot also draws inspiration from feminist theory and political action:

> In feminist theory that would be de Beauvoir with the *Second Sex*, Dworkin, Pankhurst with her brave suffragist actions, Firestone and her crazy reproduction theories, Millett, Braidotti's nomadic thought, Judith Butler's Artful Parody. (Pussy Riot member Serafina, cited in Langston 2012)

They have also identified with anarchism, dedicating one of their songs ('Kropotkin Vodka') to the nineteenth-century Russian prince Pyotr Kropotkin (1842–1921), who founded an important Russian tradition of anarchism.

Like their musical predecessors and consistent with their own political commitments, Pussy Riot's members write songs using provocative political lyrics and with titles like 'Egyptian Air is Good for the Lungs', 'Do Tahrir on Red Square, 'Putin Pissed Himself', 'Death to Prison', 'Freedom to Protest', and 'Fuck the Sexist, Fuck Putin's Henchman'. The titles alone point to the political nature of their project and suggest why their music has provoked the ire of the Putinist regime and the Russian Orthodox Church. Equally, as Russian have intellectuals noted, the Pussy Riot style of performance art clearly fits into a Russian tradition. The art critic Irina Kulik actually nominated the punk prayer for the Kandinsky Prize in 2012, an action that led some of her colleagues to call its artistic merits into question. Kulik herself saw Pussy Riot's performance in the Cathedral of Christ the Saviour as a continuation of the tradition of political, absurdist and anticlerical actionism (Kulik 2012). Curators of the 2013 exhibition 'Pussy Riot and the Russian Tradition of Art Rebellion' in the Prague MeetFactory art center, agreed when they situated the collective's work in the tradition of Russian politically engaged art.

Pussy Riot has created a distinctive style of dress and performance that provokes indignation and anger among traditional Russians, and delight and admiration on the part of their supporters. Dressed in distinctive neon balaclavas, bright monochrome snug-fitting dresses and brightly colored tights, their performances divided Russian society as they became internationally recognizable courtesy of their 'events' that filled the airways in the mainstream and new media. They have specialized in ignoring police warnings and heaping scorn on 'sacred' religious traditions.

As for their public performances or flash gigs, these are mostly done quickly and take place with little if any prior notice in spaces like city squares, on trams, and even on prison rooftops. Typically the sites they select are politically significant. In late 2011, for example, Pussy Riot performed on the prison roof of Moscow Detention Centre No. 1, singing 'Death to Prison – Freedom'. They did this to protest against the imprisonment of reformer Alexey Navalny, the 'face of the [Russian] opposition movement', profile blogger and dissident, as well as to draw attention to the Russian state's 'zero tolerance' policy on political opposition.

Band members remain cautious about detailing their performance schedules out of concern that security personnel will disrupt them. As performers they work anonymously both to protect themselves from unwanted attention and because anonymity enhances the collective nature of their project. As one Pussy Riot member, Garadzha, explained, anonymity allows any one member to be replaced with another:

> *Pussy Riot* has to keep on expanding. That's one of the reasons we choose to always wear balaclavas – new members can join the bunch and it does not really matter who takes part in the next act – there can be three of us or eight, like in our last gig on the Red Square, or even 15. (Interview with Langton 2012)

Her Pussy Riot colleague Kot added 'if the repressive Putinist police crooks throw one of us in prison, five, ten, fifteen more girls will put on colorful balaclavas and continue the fight against their symbols of power' (interview with Langton 2012). Once their performances are over, no time is lost in editing and posting videos of the recitals on the

Internet. YouTube videos documenting their live performances high-light their sexualized, jerky dance moves that typically climax with a solidarity salute. These images have spread like wildfire in Russia and globally.

Digital politics in a globalized world

The politics of Pussy Riot has clearly taken advantage of the new media. Apart from offering them a global reach, the medium offers the imme-diacy and connectivity that both fuels and defines the information age. It provides users with the capacity to translate text into any language in an instant. Equally, while the digital divide remains and excludes some, it is becoming increasingly available to more people. In this way the new media that Pussy Riot relies on has worked to facilitate the exchange of ideas and images and enlarge participation in political practice on an unprecedented scale.

Their access to a medium like YouTube enables them to render in vivid and immediate ways their outrage at the specific injustices expe-rienced by ordinary Russians. Both of Pussy Riot's original punk prayers had a fixed place (Elokhovo Cathedral and the Cathedral of Christ the Saviour) and time (February 2012). They lasted under a minute and, as is clear from Pussy Riot's recording that was uploaded to YouTube, were viewed by small audiences present in the two cathedrals. However, the act of recording these events and then uploading them onto YouTube transformed what were originally brief site-specific performances into a political/artistic performance that can be reproduced and viewed on the Internet an unlimited number of times. By creating a permanent and an accessible record of the punk prayer, Pussy Riot made it avail-able to mass audiences, thus increasing its impact and outreach and turning their local protest into a global event. As Mayer (2013, p. 147) has insisted,

> Pussy Riot's musical performance is only one aspect of the activist performance strategy of *Voina*... with its visual clarity, punk attitude, and lyrical power – it is the action that drew both the coercive atten-tion of the government and subsequently the supportive attention of the international community.

The fact that Pussy Riot received worldwide attention, while so many other Russian dissidents continue being persecuted and receive rela-tively little critical attention may be explained, in part, by Pussy Riot's

capacity to control the way they both communicate and mobilize political support by sharing their cultural-artistic and political interests far
and wide in the evolving participatory cultures sustained by the Net.
Equally, the Net does not by itself explain too much.[7] Their political
visibility owes as much to their ability to create powerful images, and
make their activism and performing art highly visible as it does to the
affordances of the Net.

In this way Pussy Riot is using the virtuality of the internet to reim-
agine the nature of political space. What has proved decisive in the
Pussy Riot case has been their access to and use of a cyber platform,
which opened space previously not so extensively explored in post-
Soviet Russia while posing a challenge to the complacency found in the
West. In this respect any exercise in positioning Pussy Riot politically
needs to begin by understanding that while critical of the contemporary
Russian state, they are equally critical of Western liberal capitalism, especially in its latest neoliberal versions. Their politics are as disapproving
of Western capitalism as they are of the contemporary authoritarian
Russian corporate state. As Nikitin (2012) noted, 'Pussy Riot's dissent
does not stop at Putin. It will not stop if and when Russia ever becomes
a "normal" liberal democracy'. What Pussy Riot wants

> is something that is equally terrifying, provocative and threatening
> to the established order in both Russia and the West (and has been
> from time immemorial): freedom from patriarchy, capitalism, reli-
> gion, conventional morality, inequality and the entire corporate state
> system. We should only support these brave women if we, too, are
> brave enough to go all the way. (Nikitin 2012)

The social imaginary informing their action is evident in their acknowl-
edgment of the need for individual accountability for the harm perpe-
trated not only by Putinism but by neoliberal states in the West. It is
evident in the acceptance of their own moral responsibility for the ways
criminality and unlawful ventures have been normalized in Russia's
political culture and to what they, and others in the opposition movement, came to see as Russia's 'uncivil order'. It is evident in their rejection of love and deference to authority. They enact a new imaginary by
drawing attention to the state of a social order in which responsibility
for others is largely absent and often consciously rejected. It is evident
in the ways they have highlighted the law breaking by the political-
executive elite (referred to in both Soviet and post-Soviet Russia as the
nomenklatura), the granting of privileges, the blatant disregard for the

rule of law and the increasing practice of creating fantasies to please the populace and to deny the truth.

All this is a new imaginary in the sense that it does not buy into the idea of there being a political binary between Russia, conceived of as a post-Soviet authoritarian, even criminal, society on the one hand, and the West, characterized as a set of morally and politically exemplary liberal democratic and capitalist regimes on the other. Much to the disappointment of some Westerners (and I expect some Russians), Pussy Riot does not accept or promote such a benign dichotomy. In spite of all the talk by neoliberals, about the virtues of accountability and auditing, neoliberalism actively discourages moral accountability and political autonomy as much as Putinism even as it reveals a similar willingness to descend into the lawless use of war, terror and abuse of human rights whenever it needs to or an equivalent capacity to privilege the needs of its elites (Rawlinson 2010).

None of this, of course is to deny the saliency of the challenge posed by Pussy Riot to their immediate Russian context.

Creating political space

The political space in which Pussy Riot operates in Russia is a long way from being the kind of deliberative or inclusive space people who live in Western liberal democratic societies like to imagine they enjoy access to. In Russia, a plurality of open publics does not exist. There is one formal single sphere, membership of which is tightly controlled and restricted to the officially sanctioned. This is evident in the ways elite discourses are favored within the mainstream media and key social institutions like schools and universities (e.g., the use of revisionist history). It is evident in the actions of 'gatekeepers' like administrative and legal workers as they censor dissent and limit access to information, making the prospect of inclusive participation unlikely. It is evident in the introduction of laws and polices designed to depoliticize Russian society by restricting the capacity of people to either deliberate or to criticize. Russia has seen the use of policy mechanisms like

new treason laws criminalizing the distribution or receipt of material the government considers 'sensitive',
new antiblasphemy laws and other legislative reforms that outlawed protest and that made civil disobedience illegal,
crackdowns on dissident groups and individuals, and various intellectual and artistic activities,

moves to deny access to certain information available through new media. (this included the censorship of Pussy Riot videos),
use of intellectual property rights laws to justify raids on advocacy groups (members of advocacy groups were charged with software piracy and had their computers seized). (Levy 2010)

Pussy Riot's interventions are clearly designed to challenge the Russian state's interest in suppressing dissent, and to close down deliberative space and new civic spaces involving street art, theater, music and the free use of new media. The recent history of attempts to criticize the resurgent Russian Orthodox Church is also a history of state-sponsored repression. *Ostorozhno, religiia!* (Beware, religion!) was a provocative exhibition staged at the Sakharov Centre in Moscow in 2003 that challenged the role of the Orthodox Church by parodying icons and other Orthodox symbols. The exhibition can be viewed in light of the Russian and Soviet history of iconoclasm in the context of art, as elaborated by Bodin (2011). The organizers were subsequently fined for violating article 282 of the Russian Criminal Code: 'Incitement of National, Racial, or Religious Enmity'. A similar sentence was also handed down against the organizers of the exhibition *Zapretnoe Iskusstvo-2006* (Forbidden Art-2006), which displayed artworks at the Sakharov Centre that had been banned from state museums, including caricatures of Jesus Christ (Bodin 2009, p. 256). It is not surprising that as Serfima, one of its members says, it is perfectly reasonable to describe Russia as

a 'third world dictatorship' akin to 'Libya under Gaddafi', and 'North Korea under Kim Jong-un'. To us, Russia under Putin, aka 'the National Leader' is no difference. (Serfima, cited in Langston 2012)

Pussy Riot has proved to be successful in using new media to build social bonds and spontaneous solidarity that bought support from a range of political leaders and other powerful friends. Spontaneous expressions of solidarity in Russia and across the globe saw their symbolic emblem, the colorful balaclava, placed by supporters on the heads of statues around in public squares. In cities like Kiev, topless female activists took a chainsaw to a large cross bearing the figure of Christ in the center of the city (Radia, August 2012). In Zurich, protesters climbed the Grossmuenster Cathedral to attach the Pussy Riot banner. Meanwhile, balaclava copycats targeted cathedrals and churches and other religious symbols in protest. New digital sites were established to support Pussy Riot (e.g., 'Free Pussy Riot' http://freepussyriot.org), all of which augmented participation and civic space, keeping open the flow of information. Opportunities for the exchange of ideas and debate about issues of public concern, namely questions of justice and democratic practice, were debated and in these ways augmented participation.

This response also included public engagements from a number of high-profile figures who had their attention and who were listening. Politicians like Germany's chancellor Angela Merkel was certainly listening, something that became apparent after she publicly questioned Putin at a Moscow business forum about the decision to imprison Pussy Riot members. It was an inquiry that provoked the ire of President Putin, who defended their imprisonment by accusing Pussy Riot of 'anti-Semitism' (Euronews 17 November 2012). He also referred to a mock execution performed by Voina in 2008, in which Nadezhda Tolokonnikova, later to become a Pussy Riot member, participated. According to Voina, the aim of the performance art was to highlight and protest against the plight of non-Slavic migrant workers and to draw attention to what they saw as the systemic bias experienced by minority groups in Russia. Putin's misrepresentation of the political message behind the event in his response to Merkel provoked a backlash in the mainstream and news media, with bloggers and others accusing him of deliberately misinforming the German chancellor (e.g., Gutterman 16 November 2012).

Fellow Pussy Riot member Nadezhda Tolokonnikova explained their aim was to augment debate, to dissent and renew politics. Their action was

> a form of civil action in circumstances where basic human rights, civil and political freedoms are suppressed by the corporate state system...We've put on our political punk concerts because the Russian state system is dominated by rigidity, closedness and caste. And the policies pursued serve only narrow corporate interests to the extent that even the air of Russia makes us ill. (Tolokonnikova, cited in Taylor 10 August 2012)

Yet this reference to the way 'that even the air of Russia makes us ill' should not be taken too seriously. As will become clear, Pussy Riot's politics draws on some deep streams of Russian culture and tradition. The oppositional politics of Pussy Riot is clearly evident in their feminism, in their DIY (do-it-yourself) punk rock music and in the ways they highlight female sexual agency and power. Yet the potent appeal of Pussy Riot's political performance art derives a lot from its dance with Russian tradition and its attempt to synthesize the old and the new by reclaiming valued traditions and practices.

Generational politics: dancing between the old and new

In their closing statements in their trial at the Moscow Khamoviniki District Court in July 2012, the three members of Pussy Riot on trial described their actions as rooted in the tradition of Russian avant-garde dissent. They named the great Russian novelist Fyodor Dostoevsky and the famous Russian writer and poet Aleksandr Vedensky as influences on their own creative political action. While considering the prospect of her own exile and imprisonment in a Russian labor camp, Tolokonnikova said in court that

> Katya, Masha and I may be in prison, but I do not consider us defeated. Just as the dissidents were not defeated; although they disappeared into mental institutions and prisons, they pronounced their verdict upon the regime. The art of creating the image of an epoch does not know winners or losers. It was the same with the OBERIU poets, who remained artists until the end, inexplicable and incomprehensible. (2012)

She went on to talk about how Pussy Riot claims to be 'students and heirs' of Vedensky, founder of Russia's last avant-garde OBERIU group, who were purged in 1937 (2012). She also went on to describe how Dostoevsky had faced a firing squad – an act that was far more than an artistic achievement.

This self-aware reference to Russian tradition points to Pussy Riot's highly sophisticated dance between old and new.

We see something of the way that Pussy Riot imagines the relationship between past and present in their choice of venue and the form that their flash gig performance in the Cathedral of Christ the Saviour took in February 2012. This performance points to the peculiar combination of a secular and a religious dynamic at work in their protest. Firstly, the punk prayer both hijacked and resignified the Cathedral as a site of political protest rather than simply treating it as a site of religious worship. However, in politicizing the space of the Cathedral, Pussy Riot was also recalling the marriage of state and church, a relationship that engendered the original building. The Cathedral was co-opted in political discourses from its inception (Suchland 2012). Originally built in the nineteenth century to commemorate Russia's victory over Napoleon, the original Cathedral had always served a dual function as both a site of worship and as a memorial to a national military victory.[8] Likewise the consecration of the Cathedral in 1883 just happened to take place on the day of Alexander III's coronation (Winterbottom 2009, p. 18). After the Cathedral was blown up by the Bolsheviks, Joseph Stalin built the Palace of the Soviets, an equally monumental building to glorify new Soviet and secular values. In Putin's Russia, and after a new cathedral was built, state and church are most noticeably brought together at Easter services led by Putin and attended by prominent Russian officials.

By broadcasting their performance of the punk prayer on the Internet, Pussy Riot was both echoing and subverting the practice of televising this televised ritual on national television. In effect Pussy Riot was 'damaging the brand', a point actually conceded by the prosecutor Samutsevich, who argued in her closing statement that Pussy Riot had violated 'the integrity of the media image that the authorities had spent such a long time generating and maintaining' (Hecksinductionhour 8 August 2012).

Yet that does not do justice to the significance of the performance. Pussy Riot's parody of a church service, compared by one witness to antireligious campaigns of the 1920s and 1930s, indeed, parodies Orthodox rituals practiced in religious buildings. Yet their hijacking of forms of religious ritual for political protest is itself a critical commentary on the Russian Orthodox Church's failure to stop symbolic usage (and thus resignification) of its churches for political agitation and as a stage for political candidates like Putin to use to enhance their electoral appeal. Pussy Riot has cast their desacralization of the Cathedral as a stage both at the moment of their performance and in front of a global mass audience on the Internet as an attempt to reclaim it from the state as a protest arena and thus to restore to the Church the aura and moral authority it once had when it was being persecuted by the Soviet regime (Richters 2012). They did this through 'obscene' provocation of the Russian state, the Church and the police, by pointing to the hypocrisy of the state and clergy, to the ways in which traditional power holders themselves acted offensively, and to the ways they ignored and ridiculed the rule of law and the constitution. Zizek makes this point:

> What is a modest Pussy Riot obscene provocation in a church compared to the accusation against Pussy Riot, this gigantic obscene provocation of the state apparatus which mocks any notion of decent law and order? (2012)

In effect Pussy Riot's choice of the Cathedral as their venue also paradox-ically comes from a position of faith that invests this site with meaning. Steinholt writes that 'the self-professed atheists of Pussy Riot failed to convince their audiences of the main prerequisite' for a critique of the Russian Church namely, 'its foundation in sincere faith' (2013, p. 124). The group's appeal to the Mother of God serves, for example, as both a reminder of the highest authority to the onlookers and a genuine act of supplication. Indeed, parts of the punk prayer that address Virgin Mary 'sound earnest and respectful' (p. 123). This is also one way to make sense of what is both significant and highly unusual for a punk group, namely the fact that the opening melody for this song was based on Sergei Rachmaninov's *Ave Maria* from his Opus 37 *All Night Vigil*. The decision to title another song 'Virgin Mary Mother of God' and to describe it as a 'religious hymn' can be read as a move to reappropriate the old, to reclaim the Church, and Russian religion and culture gener-ally, which had been corrupted. It was also a highly effective rhetorical device that involved the use of traditional Russian Orthodox hymns to create something new and different. In doing so they directly challenge those claiming to be the authoritative voice of the Russian Orthodox Church and culture.

In a religious context, hymns play an important ritualistic role in their decision to call their song 'Virgin Mary Mother of God', and a hymn takes on special significance. It created a parody that worked to communicate their message that the Church and its teachings ought to be dynamic, not static, and that it should not be the exclusive purview of the clergy. While they were iconoclastic, Pussy Riot members explained that their actions were intended to defend cherished Russian beliefs and religion by drawing attention to the corruption in the Church, by denouncing its 'patriarchal superstructure' and by pointing to the hypocrisy in the form of the close relationship between Putin and the Orthodox Church. As Pussy Riot member Yekaterina Samutsevich explained in her closing statement at the Moscow Khamovniki District Court, they were not motivated by religious hatred – as accused. They were trying to

> unite the visual imagery of Orthodox culture with that of protest culture, thus suggesting that Orthodox culture belongs not only to the Russian Orthodox Church, the Patriarch, and Putin, but that it could also ally itself with civic rebellion and the spirit of protest in Russia. (2012)

Likewise for Nadezhda Tolokonnikova,

> It was our search for truth that led us to the Cathedral of Christ the Savior. I think that Christianity, as I understood it while studying the Old and especially the New Testament, supports the search for truth and a constant overcoming of oneself, the overcoming of what you were earlier. (Tolokonnikova)

Maria Alyokhina also complained that for too many Orthodox leaders, 'the Gospels are no longer understood as revelation but have become a source of quotes that can be deployed to serve their own interests' (Alyokhina 2012). Samutsevich summed up their position simply:

> We dared to present as image Orthodox culture and the culture of protest without the blessing of the Patriarch, and in doing so, encouraged intelligent people to consider whether Orthodox culture didn't just belong to the church, the Patriarch and Putin, but might also be on the side of the civil revolt and protest movement in Russia. (Samutsevich, cited in Dugdale, n.d. 2012)

In this way Pussy Riot symbolically reclaimed the site not only for protest but also for religious worship! In this way Pussy Riot has made a particular kind of claim on Russia's past. If their choice of venue points to the old, their embrace of the new includes the ways they have used bricolage to create new 'compositions' and make their political case.

For what *is* new about Pussy Riot's politics is evident in their distinctive style. This style is best described as a kind of intellectual, political and visual bricolage created as they 'pirated' from various sites past and present. In this way their performance art can be seen as artistic political 'heterogeneity', the product of what is now sometimes referred to as remixing, the product of scavenging and borrowing dissimilar material, ideas, and objects from disparate sites and disciplines that is typically seen as opposite to create new compositions, cultural forms and identities. Taking a synoptic view of the performances, Pussy Riot has borrowed from commercial advertisements, propaganda, pop culture, serious social theory and philosophy, public relations, human rights, religion, the radical Left and elements of conservative politics, and bohemianism using sophisticated new technology to create a coherent political message about the value of genuine democracy and the value of a strong civic culture.

This bricolage is closely attuned to some of the more distinctively Russian aspects of their identity. On the one hand there is the concept of 'fool for Christ', or 'holy foolishness' (Russian: *Iurodstvo*), which is deeply rooted in Russian culture. Beat argues that

> In claiming inspiration from such holy folly, *Pussy Riot* allies itself with a long theological and artistic tradition in which the fool's 'passion, openness, and naïveté' expose official hypocrisy. (2012, p. 21)

Equally many have seen in their distinctive style similarities with Mikhail Bakhtin's famous account of carnival. Their famous 21 February 2012 cathedral performance of 'Holy Mary, Drive Putin Away', calling for the removal of Putin, took place in Shrovetide week and more precisely on 21 February, which is Mardi Gras day.[9] This is a day customarily reserved for confession and a sanctioned day of riotous celebration, when traditionally the church has encouraged revelry, gaiety, carnival escapades and clowning around (Mirovalev 2012). This politics of dissent and renewal, of calling on the past to create and renew imaginaries is evident in Pussy Riot's carnivalesque style, in their choice of locations and the timing of their actions. Their carnivalesque live actions are designed, as Bakhtin (1941) argued regarding manifestations of the carnivalesque in earlier periods in European history, to simultaneously expose and subvert the core assumptions and practices of the dominant culture by combining absurdity, jesting and chaos. This is exemplified in their punk hymn 'The Virgin Mary Mother of God' draw on a traditional feminist call to arms and solidarity among sisters as well as playing on the Russian Orthodox cult of Mary:

> Virgin Mary Mother of God |Chase out Putin.
> Chase out Putin. |Chase out Putin...
> Holy Mary Mother of God |Be a feminist to us.
> Be a feminist to us. |Be a feminist...
> The most holy Mother of God is at the rallies with us,
> Virgin Mary Mother of God.
> Chase out Putin |Chase out Putin. |Chase out Putin.

This was a plea to 'Mary' for help, as a woman and as a mother. As Bernstein (2013) has argued apropos of the pungent language used in their lyrics,

This catalogue of linguistic brutality suggests the radical power of *Pussy Riot's* use of words. Where *Voina's* physical and visual performances, including a staged orgy at a state museum and a phallus graffiti on a Moscow landmark, had drawn critical attention, it was the 'Punk Prayer' that galvanised the government to action. The effect of the combination of the (female) body and the powerful intervention into religious language is evident in the doublespeak counter-measures then employed by the prosecution, and in Putin's suggestive use of the term *shabash*, which confers an eldritch power on the performance.

The synthesis of the old and new, the playful use of traditions like carnival and constant references to Russian political history is always on show in their sexualized party style and in their mocking provocative dance. It is apparent in their costumes, the brilliantly colored dresses, bright tights and 'super-hero' balaclavas. Their use of masks also worked to communicate political-historical connections reminiscent of the disguises worn in masquerades and in theater. It is a style that connects with Guy Fawkes, the sixteenth-century Catholic terrorist who attempted to blow up the House of Lords with gunpowder and which led to the custom of 'firecracker nights' (Guy Fawkes night celebrations), a night of revelry and explosive craziness. The oppositional and transgressive nature of Pussy Riot's politics was evident in their exuberant 'fun' style, and in the public nature of their actions. At the same time, the masks and anonymity also worked to symbolize a connection with more recent protest movements – especially the global Net activist movement known only as Anonymous, and to Occupy Movement and WikiLeaks in which such masks are commonly used. This is to say nothing of its resonance with vigilante figures of the superheroes and heroines genre like Wonder Woman, Superman, Batwoman and Batman. In this way the balaclava connotes a direct association with a crusader – superhero action dedicated to fighting for the good, and associated propaganda that includes stories of courageous public-spirited deeds, fighting villains, and the restoration of truth and justice. In these ways the mask not only provided protection through anonymity, it also tapped into a popular imaginary with universal appeal, especially for many young people. The fact that balaclava masks have now been co-opted by the fashion industry, for some, highlights their effectiveness and appeal.

Their embrace of the carnivalesque was evident also in their deliberate breaching of rules, like swearing and breaking the dress code in church. It was evident in their outspoken claims that Putin's constitutional changes were corrupt, along with similar claims that the church-state relations breached the constitution because it declared Russia to be a secular state.

They aired serious issues, but did so in a satirical, carnivalesque style. It was a light-hearted approach to communicating heavy messages about state crime, the corruption of the political elite and a Church that had lost its way. They had a playful yet intense style made more powerful by the way it was juxtaposed to the serious, grey, male-dominated political style of traditional power holders.

Yet while their performing art and the different forms their politics took were imaginative and ethically charged, they did not offer an entirely new form of literature or art such as that equivalent to epic poems like Dante's *Inferno*, a work that expanded language to include comedy, political commentary, theological speculation and so forth.

Similarly, their first song, 'Release the Cobblestones', called the past to the present with its launch on 7 November 2011, the anniversary of the 1917 Russian Revolution. Likewise, their song 'Kropotkin Vodka', dedicated to Pyotr Kropotkin, a nineteenth-century prince and cofounder of anarchism, was also a statement about their politics and connection with Russian political history.

While what they propose is not totally new, they do promote change by preserving and raising elements of the past to transcend into a more open form of politics, something new to their context. In this way new worldviews and change were taking place through processes that both preserve and change through bringing together various elements of the old and the modern.

Art as politics

Pussy Riot uses performance art as a vehicle for expressing the ethics of a generation by both channeling and shaping the ethical-political perceptions of their audience. Their politics as direct action are designed to promote a new sociopolitical subjectivity interested in self-determination. Their interventions highlighted a subjectivity informed by their ethical relations with other persecuted minorities, like gays, lesbians and dissidents.

Pussy Riot draws on a medley of dissident political genres and actions to create public platforms that put them in the international spotlight and opened up forums for dialogue, which at least to some degree made official power holders accountable if only in the sense that they saw the occasional need to justify their actions.

Working within the avant-garde tradition, their work is both impassioned and high risk. They draw on a range of styles of resistance movements, including feminism (e.g., the suffragettes) and neoanarchist movements. They also draw on links with punk rock and identify with other eminent dissident individuals and social and revolutionary movements like the American civil rights movement. While they were clearly anarchic in their political style and made explicit references to the Russian anarchist Prince Kropotkin, they are not conventional anarchists preoccupied with freedom exclusively, as traditional anarchists tend to be. Rather, they are preoccupied with the idea and praxis of that kind of responsibility that 'arises from situational injustice'. Critchley distinguishes this 'infinite responsibility' from 'unlimited freedom' (even though the responsible action might lead to other freedoms). While he does not specifically refer to Pussy Riot (but does talk about similar groups), this formulation nicely characterizes the ethico-political stance of Pussy Riot.

The use of public spaces for unsanctioned public performances is conceptually central to Pussy Riot's protest art. Before the controversial punk prayer, Pussy Riot was already notorious for the formal dimension of their performances, in particular, for their choice of venues rather than the lyrics of their protest songs. For instance, the collective staged hit-and-run-style gigs in the Moscow underground, on the roof of a trolley bus, in Red Square and in the Moscow Elokhovo Cathedral, where they recorded a fragment of the punk prayer days before their later performance in the Cathedral of Christ the Saviour. None of these earlier performances, however, resulted in lengthy prison sentences. Indeed, Elder points out that the eight members of Pussy Riot, detained by the police after the performance in Red Square, were given administrative fines rather than '15-day jail sentences often doled out to those who stage illegal protests' (2012) and were subsequently released. More importantly, none of the witnesses of the first punk prayer in the Elokhovo Cathedral thought to report Pussy Riot to the police. Instead they called a priest, who consecrated the part of the Cathedral used by unwanted visitors (Syrova et al. 2012, p. 17). The first significant criminal charge was brought against the collective after its performance specifically in the Cathedral of Christ the Saviour.

Pussy Riot's political interventions offer something new in their immediate context: they disturb the sense of stability that exists for some by questioning key institutions in ways that produce volatility and uncertainty. They achieve this by highlighting how key institutions like the Church, the state and the law are socially created, as opposed to being natural entities derived from extra-social forces they cannot influence. In this way Pussy Riot encourages moral responsibility and political autonomy in a society that is largely closed off. Their actions remind citizens of their capacity to free themselves from 'external compulsions', and in so doing take on responsibility for being responsible in their particular situation (Rawlinson 2010, pp. 144–145). They encourage a capacity to 'speak to power', and a recognition that people influence their social institutions and challenge official practices and accounts of modern Russia.

They have expanded the forms of deliberative practice to include dissent and conflict, and in this way, there is an interest in listening to and understanding alternative positions. Obviously there is not much interest on the part of the state and church in dialoguing with reaching consensus with Pussy Riot.

Conclusion

Russia is not an open society. Moreover, any prospect of augmenting deliberative practice and political autonomy is unlikely in the short term, in large part, because traditional power holders are committed to thwarting the creation of a genuine civil society. Pussy Riot is part of a larger opposition movement made up of alliances of prominent political activists from various walks of life, including lawyers, business people, authors and politicians. That opposition includes 'national democrats' like Alexei Navalny; liberal politicians like Ilya Yashin, Boris Nemtsov, Dmitry Gudkov and Ilya Ponomarev; and ordinary citizens like Maria Baronova, as well as youth movements like Oborona and street art collectives like Voina. This opposition is engaged in everything from traditional oppositional practices like standing for office in elections and the documentation and publication of reports detailing official corruption, to the exchange ideas and mobilization through social networks (e.g., LiveJournal, websites and Facebook) and other media, to organizing large protests, all coalescing around the common objective of promoting an open society, which necessarily entails countering what they see as Putin's determination to destroy democratic institutions and establish an authoritarian police state.

Russia is yet to manifest any sustainable culture of autonomy approximating the kinds of epochal transformation that Castoriadis had in mind in his account of the social imaginary. This is true in spite of moments like the decade after the Bolshevik Revolution of November 1917 when Russian artists, writers, composers and filmmakers felt free to achieve a culture marked by unprecedented vitality and exuberance (Cook 1995), or the painful renaissance of nonconformist art in the decades after Stalin's death in 1953, which saw work produced by the Lianozovo Group or the artists associated with the 1974 Bulldozer Exhibition (Dodge and Rosenfeld 1995).

In some ways Pussy Riot can be seen as part of an older 'youth cultural' or 'subcultural' tradition that included a rich history of youthful creative-cum-political action starting with the Beats of the 1950s, the rockers, mods and hippies of the 1960s and 1970s, and punks that took off in the 1970s. Unlike Pussy Riot, they performed in real time and space with 'happenings', concerts, displays of fashion or street fighting, relying on more traditional technological media like the press, audio recording, television and videos to spread their message. Pussy Riot, like most forms of contemporary music and politics, relied heavily on digital communication like Facebook, YouTube and other social media to broadcast their music and their message and to mobilize global and local support. As one Russian journalist observed, they have developed a new kind of politics based on everything

> From their name, pitched to shock and attract the western media, to their instantly recognisable look...their message (concise bursts of feminist agitprop with just enough of a tune to pass as a song), to their method of distributing this message via social networks...to their pointedly academic statements to the court, which David Remnick called 'a kind of instant classic in the anthology of dissidence'. (Idov 2012)

Pussy Riot has also recognized how the same technology they relied on for political communication was also used to facilitate surveillance of themselves by Russia's police and security agencies and to support repressive activities that dampened dissent. Such actions take on significant meaning in the context of a politically repressive society where protests and advocacy for civil rights (e.g., gay and lesbian relations) are illegal, and in a society with a long history of severe punishment for political dissent, including Siberian exile, the use of gulag camps, torture and execution. When you cut to the chase, two young women were imprisoned for near on two years for singing and dancing in church in a way deliberately designed to provoke the ire of the power elite. Equally as I have argued here, Pussy Riot has worked hard to refresh and remotivate a long tradition of carniva-lesque humor and nonviolent warfare by generating new forms of civil disobedience, and to revitalize the idea and practice of direct democracy (Critchley 2012). This has involved Pussy Riot in making a particular kind of claim on Russia's past, something signified by their most famous performance in the Christ the Saviour Cathedral. If their choice of venue points to the old, their embrace of the new has seen them use bricolage to create new 'compositions' and inhabit cyber-space as a platform from which to motivate a new kind of ethical and political energy.

In this way they are responding to what Critchley calls 'situational injustice' in ways that both elicit and invigorate a new kind of 'ethical energy' relevant to their politics. This ethical energy flows through similar but dispersed groups in Russia in ways that contribute to a home-grown politics of resistance, while also motivating and connecting globally with a plurality of similarly situated antiauthoritarian groups (Critchley 2012). In this way Pussy Riot, like many contemporary activists, is having a positive political effect by countering the motivational ethical deficit, institutional anomie and overall anaesthetized experience of modern life that has become so prevalent in Western liberal democracies and 'transitional' political systems like Russia (Deleuze 1990, 1991).

Pussy Riot also offers a new imaginary that rejects determinist thinking, or the idea that we are humanoid automatons stripped of moral autonomy and agency. A new imaginary is on display in the way they give expression to the ethical dimension of their lives – and by implication of ours, and in their recognition of their moral agency and outspoken rejection of the commonsense idea that the constitution of our individual and social identity lies outside ourselves. A new imaginary is evident in the intense focus on maximizing freedoms and displays of a collective interest in the questioning of traditional institutions and their significations.

Indeed, the point of their message has not been lost on people in liberal democratic communities. As Mayer notes, people in the West may well be broadly accustomed to thinking of liberal democracy 'and the new globalized digital democracy – as being largely benign and as a level playing field for open discourse, enhanced by the diversification of media and platforms' (2013, p. 148). Yet Pussy Riot has drawn our attention to the 'chilling effect' of so-called liberal democracy, and crystallized a pervasive sense of concern about the authenticity of our democratic order.

And they reinstate a regard for humor. Pussy Riot is animated by an imaginary committed to the right to dissent and expressed in critique, direct action and performing art. In keeping with their satirical style, Tolokonnikova says, 'We have different ideas about a bright future, and we don't want a shirtless man on a horse leading us into that bright future' (2014).

7
The Graduate's Future and Neoliberal Education: New Generation Politics on the Campus

On 17 December 2008, students enrolled in the New School of Social Research in New York occupied the university's cafeteria. The New York protests took place just after Greek police killed Alexandros Grigoropolous a 15-year-old protester in Athen's anarchist Exarcheia neighborhood, igniting a wave of occupations and rioting across Greece. The New York protest was precipitated on 10 December 2008, when 74 of the New School's senior professors passed a vote of no confidence in New School president Bob Kerrey, a vote confirmed when on 15 December, 98% of the university's full-time faculty again voted they had no confidence in Kerrey.[1] Two days later, over 100 students barricaded themselves in the cafeteria on the campus, while hundreds more waited on the streets outside demanding Kerrey's resignation. The students soon enlarged their occupied area, blocking security and police from entering the building. At 3:00 a.m. the next morning, the students left the building after Kerrey agreed to some of their demands, including increased study space and amnesty from any actions performed during the protest. He did not agree to resign or accept the most elements on their list of demands.

The 30-hour occupation saw the resurrection of the kinds of direct democracy politics of student protests in the late 1960s. More significantly, this was a new kind of politics that would recur again and again in the later Occupy Wall Street Movement and anti-austerity protests. One eyewitness understood this new aspect when he said that if the students 'turned the space into a cross between a town hall and Trafalgar Square', it was also a space where the new technology abounded:

Students shared laptops, batteries and phones. They were in constant contact with the world beyond the cafeteria, posting communiqués on the Web and e-mailing manifestos and updates to allies. (Moynihan 2008)

The deliberative style that defines some of the later protests was also evident:

On the final afternoon of the occupation, the students held one of their biggest meetings and also began using a form of shorthand sign language to communicate: waving both hands in the air indicated agreement; pointed index fingers meant somebody had a fact to convey; and fingers forming a triangle were meant to remind others to stick to the point. (Moynihan 2008)

In January 2009, a student organization called The New School In Exile issued a threatened to shut down the university on 1 April unless the president and chief operating officer were removed. On 10 April 2009, students, mostly from the New School but also from other New York colleges, reoccupied the building at 65 Fifth Avenue, this time holding the entire building for about six hours. Once again, the students demanded the resignation of Kerrey. The New York police arrested the occupiers the New School students involved were then suspended. The police 'over responded', as students who were not directly involved in the occupation were pepper-sprayed or beaten and arrested. On 26 August 2010, the board of trustees appointed David van Zandt to replace Kerrey and become the eighth president of the New School.

As Yannis Theocaris (2011, p. 162) noted, young people's political engagement has prompted intense and polarized debate among academics, policy analysts and journalists. Academics and journalists alike have had no trouble talking about young people variously as the 'lost generation', the 'jilted generation', 'the apathetic generation', the 'indulgent generation', 'Generation me' and even the 'Dumbest generation'. And yet as others have pointed out, we have also seen young people play a leading role over the past decade in democratic and protest movements using new media as a technique to mobilize and organize political campaigns (e.g., Zuquete 2011; Solomon and Palmieri 2011). What has been dubbed the 'Arab Spring' saw popular protests involving large numbers of mainly young people using new media (Solomon and Palmieri 2011). A local protest movement that began in Tunisia when Mohamed Bouazizi, a 27-year-old Tunisian man burned himself to death on 16 December to protest the corruption of Tunisia's government, spread to Egypt in 2010, triggering similar movements across northern Africa in Yemen, Syria and Libya in 2011. In South America, student protest activity in Chile increased to the point that The *New York Times* dubbed 2011 the year of the 'Chilean Winter' as student groups began demanding major changes in educational, environmental and energy policy (Barrionuevo, 2011).[2] In the United Kingdom, as young people began disengaging from conventional electoral politics, some began to mobilize popular protests: a million people marched against the Blair government's decision to wage an illegal war in Iraq in 2003 (Rees 2011). We have also seen the digitally facilitated Occupy Wall Street protests in the United States, and the emergence of movements like the *indignados* across southern European countries to protest the imposition of neoliberal austerity policies (Schwartz-Weinstein 2013).

These large-scale and often spectacular protest movements have attracted considerable discussion and debate about the political role of young people, their use of digital media, and potential of these experiences to recast the very meaning and experience of democratic politics (Dahlgren 2007; Aitchinson 2011; Rheingans and Hollands 2013). Yet surprisingly little attention has been given to the less dramatic but no less significant campaigns of resistance mounted by students like the two rounds of occupation at the New School in 2008–2009; the occupations of the University of Leeds, the University of Sheffield, London Metropolitan University and many other schools in 2010; or the student strikes in Quebec during 2011 and the spring semester of 2012 protesting fee increases. As Schwartz-Weinstein (2013) notes, the importance of the student movements was that while the Occupy movement did draw direct inspiration from Medan al-Tahri (Cairo's Liberation Square) and the *indignados* of Madrid's Plaza del Sol, the political language of Occupy Wall Street:

> was cribbed directly unevenly from slogans scrawled on banners, pamphlets, and walls in a series of student occupations of universities in New York City and across California.

Little sustained attention has been given to the use of digital technology in new kinds of politics emerging in schools and universities, where a large proportion of young people now spend much of their lives. In these institutions, young people confront significant asymmetries of power and the seemingly never-ending exercise of neoliberalism's extending its reach as a mode of government (Dardot and Laval 2013).

In this chapter, I remedy this relative omission. My focus here is on students engaging publicly and deliberatively with teachers, managers and others about matters in which they have a direct interest, namely their education. This is why I focus firstly on *Rate-my-Teacher/Professors* websites. The second is a case study of 'University X', which details events that actually took place in two different universities in response to changes to the academic programs in which students had enrolled. [3] I amalgamated these events to protect the identity of those involved as well as the institutions. In both cases, some harm was caused to a number of participants, legal cases were pursued, people lost their jobs, some students were excluded from their programs and disciplinary action taken.[4] I chose these cases because they are well bounded and provide context-dependent examples of students using digital technology to develop political responses to situational injustice (Critchley 2011).

To make sense of these cases, I draw on the heuristic frame (set out in Chapter 5) to help determine what is happening, to establish whether digital technology promotes participation and debate in ways that facilitate democratic practice. What kinds of political processes are in place? Does the use of digital media promote a new public spheres, or what Dahlgren calls 'civic cultures' that enable young people in secondary and higher educational institutions to engage in deliberative practice? Are expanded forms of deliberation evident, one that is also open to a diversity of groups? Are new styles of action and creativity encouraged? Are power disparities mitigated? If so, how and to what effect? Is there freedom from coercion? Is there evidence of some shift in the way politics is being understood and practiced?

While this chapter contributes to the existing body of empirical and theoretical work on the relationship of the Internet to 'public spheres' and deliberative democracy, it also contributes to larger debates about the prospect of new political practice and the role of new media in facilitating democratic processes, political resistance or even the evolution of a new radical imaginary involving new forms of being.

I argue that we see here a direct expression of a generation shaped by the alarming effects of neoliberalism. As Connell (2013, p. 99) argues, education systems all over the world have been affected by the rise of neoliberal ideology and practices of government, which she calls 'the neoliberal cascade' (also Harvey 2005). In the case of highly visible protest movements and the less visible student activism addressed here, we see political processes directed at publicizing and protesting ongoing attempts to impose or expand neoliberal and authoritarian government in schools and universities. As Mason argued, a central figure in the occupations and uprisings between 2008 and 2012 is a 'new sociological type: the graduate with no future' (2011). One of the unintended consequences of neoliberalism and the systematic devaluation of higher education and the degradation of the 'human capital' that it is erroneously claimed it produces[5]:

> is to make debt-saddled university graduates and those who see such a subject position as their own future, the focal point of a global set of communicable and communicative struggles. (Mason 2011; see also Dardot and Laval 2013)

While digital media is clearly 'at the forefront' of new kinds of evolving public spheres (Dahlgren 2009), what is not so immediately apparent is the politics that are at work. As I suggest, while it appears that the activities in these domains do align somewhat with Jürgen Habermas' model of deliberative democracy, they also point to a new kind of politics shaped by nonliberal democratic assumptions involving a commitment less to consensus and more to a politics of dissensus. Although it oversimplifies things somewhat, we see in the two case studies in this chapter, as well as in the Pussy Riot project in Vladimir Putin's Russia, in the various recent student occupations, and the evolution of movements like Anonymous as a global network of net activism, less of Habermas' model of deliberative democracy and more of politics as networks of antiauthoritarian groups making ethical demands in response to particular situated wrongs. What can be seen is an imbrication of political practice and tradition of political theory and resistance signified by Debord (1967), Michel Foucault (1979), Bataille (1985), and the Situationist International, Agamben (1993), the journal *Tiqqun*, Deleuze and Guattari (1983), Negri (2003) and Critchley (2012).

I turn now to the case studies.

Case studies

RateMyTeacher, RateMyProfessors websites

RateMyTeacher and RateMyProfessors are user-generated virtual spaces built for students by students. They are sites in which students evaluate and talk about their teachers, managers and other professionals (e.g., counselors) in schools and universities (http://au.ratemyteachers.com). There are also options for rating their 'easiness, helpfulness and clarity' and 'overall quality' on a scale from 1 to 5. Additional space is added for commenting and deliberating about the institution itself (http://

www.ratemyprofessors.com/SearchSchool.jsp) (It is also available on Instagram option).

Rate My Professors was established in 1999 as TeacherRating.com by John Swapceinski, a software engineer in California, and modified in 2001 to Rate My Professors. It is said to offer:

> The Internet's largest listing of collegiate professor ratings, the site reaches approximately 10 million total college students each year, who use the free service to plan their class schedule, and rate professors on attributes such as helpfulness and clarity. (http://www.prnewswire. com/news-releases/mtv-networks-mtvu-agrees-to-acquire-ratemy professorscom-53560002.html)

Rate My Teacher was first established in 2001 by Michael Hussey (who soon after sold it as a business). He says he started it so students could appraise their teachers, and in particular the 'stellar ones' (Hussey CNN interview, YouTube http://michaelhussey.com). He continued, saying the site is:

> changing the way the world looks at education by providing students with the unique opportunity to critique their teachers. For students, RateMyTeachers.com is first forum to publicly expose ineffective teaching or broadcast praise for stellar teachers. For truly committed teachers this site serves as a gauge for evaluating their own teaching methods. Dedicated teachers will benefit from the honest, anonymous feedback generated by our users. ... RateMyTeachers.com is the first website of its kind and is maintained by thousands of student volunteers. A new world is upon us – embrace it and thrive. (Hussey 2001)

Like Rate My Professors, Rate My Teacher was sold by Hussey and has since passed through the hands of a number of owners (http://www. linkedin.com/in/michaelhussey).

Since then, replica spaces have been developed and the practice of rating 'my' teacher-professor has expanded globally (RateMyProfessors. Com; see also, http://my, .net.au, Blue Book + and UniYu, www.sylla-busrate.com). The reach of the sites is extensive. By 2010, Rate My Teacher, for example, claimed 'over 11 million teachers had been graded (http:///www.ratemyteachers.com). It also claimed to profile 7,500 institutions and 13,000,000 student-generated commentaries on teachers and institutions in the United States, Canada, Australia and the United Kingdom. By 2014, it was estimated that Rate My Professors was getting more than 5 million visitors per month (Walker 2014; http://www.usato-dayeducate.com/staging/index.php/pulse/sites-like-rate-my-professors-earn-mixed-grades-on-campus).

Most sites provide codes of conduct advising participants to restrict discussion to their experiences. There are rules for participation, and those interested are warned that improper postings will be removed, and that any threats will be handed to the 'authorities' along with the participant's IP address. They are also advised to remove identity markers. 'Thousands' of volunteer students work as moderator entries ensuring they comply with the 'rules of conduct' (http://au.ratemyteachers.com/info/Terms). Teachers have the option of clicking the red box if they believe comments made about them or others are inappropriate. This triggers a second review of the entry, and if it is found to be a breach the rule or if it is libelous or defamatory, it is removed (Hussey interview 2003, CT New Untube video). Some sites have space for teachers to reply on the site or by registering separate accounts. Alternatively, teachers can also respond in text or video via sites like Professor Strikes Back.

The declared purpose of Rate My Teacher:

> is to be a resource for students. Where else can you find out what others think of an instructor? Is he/she a good teacher, do they challenge you, are they fair? When you have the option of choosing a teacher, wouldn't you really like some information? It also gives you, the user, a place to voice your opinion. It gives you a place to make a difference in your education. (http://www.ratemyteachers.com/faq#17)

Some Rate My Teacher-style sites have been co-opted and used for parents to find out about schools. Some also involve parents and school staff – with some parents assuming the administrator role on behalf of the school (http://www.ratemyteachers.com). In this way the sites can be used to promote the school. In 2014, apps for phones and tablets were introduced by university administration to review and rank professors and university services generally in 'real time'. At Tel Aviv University, Professor Yoav Ariel, the dean of students, explained how the app is turned on by the teacher when he/she enters the classroom. Students are asked questions about how interesting they found the class, and how they rated the lecturer's performance. Lecturers then receive the rankings straight away, which are made anonymously. Students also have the option of talking with each other online about the class without the teacher's being able to see the conversation. From the perspective of one student, the real time or immediacy of the feedback is much more valuable that the more traditional end-of-semester student evaluation:

> During the semester, problems come up and when the time comes to fill out the assessment form for the lecturer, they are no longer relevant or have been forgotten. (cited in Skop 2014)

Rate My Teacher/Professor was set up for students to have a voice, hear each other's views, get advice, exchange information and deliberate (Hussey CNN YouTube http://michaelhussey.com). The sites provide space in which students can and do speak freely, and *to some extent* without fear or favor, about matters in which they have an interest. Indeed, anyone with an interest in education can participate. Commenting on 'Jackamo' had this to say:

> She is nice and a pretty good teacher, but it's the end of term 3 and she hasn't marked any of our assessment or she hasn't bothered to hand back any forums. (http://forums.whirlpool.net.au/archive/638392)

This site and others like it provide forums for staff and parents to hear about the various teaching practices that are used and other aspects of the institution. They allow participants to contribute to debates and to form opinions. From a student perspective,

> giving kids a voice is a good idea i had some teachers who would not listen to kids. ie they believed they explained things right and i disagreed, and maybe if a forum like this had been available students could have gotten concerns across with out the fear of reprisal. ('Felicity', http://www.ebroadcast.com.au/eblah/m-1178196840)

Not surprisingly, sites like Rate My Teacher/Professors have not been welcomed by all. This has led to moves to block and close some sites down. At Yale University, two students, Peter Xu and Harry Yu, established Yale Blue Book + as a website that compared courses by reportedly allowing 'students enrolling for the semester at Yale to see how courses had been rated numerically in student course evaluations'. In 2014, Yale University closed down 'Yale Blue Book +'. According to Xu, Yale administrators felt they knew best about how students should use data, about how students should choose their courses, and basically wanted to enforce that on students, and we felt that students should have control over their own education. (cited in HuffPost Live 2014)

The issue seems to have been that their 'online course catalogue' efficient, user-friendly usurped the university's own directory with reportedly 'more than a third of the undergraduate student body – used it to choose their courses'. This was an action that led to a full-blown public campaign involving the use of blogs, Twitter and advocacy groups like the Electronic Frontier foundation centering on the issue of free speech (Kaminer 2014; see also Walker 2014). The dean of Yale College finally issued an open letter in which she stated, 'In retrospect, I agree that we could have been more patient in asking the developers before taking the actions that we did'. She continued,

> Although the University acted in keeping with its policies and principles, I see now that it erred in trying to compel students to have as a reference the superior set of data that the complete course evaluations provide. That effort served only to raise concerns about the proper use of network controls. (Miller 2014)

Attempts have been made to ban students from using these kinds of sites at educational institutions, and instructions have been issued prohibiting their use of the sites outside school. There are also reports that students have been punished by their schools for using Rate My Teacher (Hussey interview CT News 2003). In Australia, for example, the Australian Queensland College of Teachers and the Western Australia teachers union have called for the sites to be either controlled or closed. In the United States, teacher unions have been lobbying government for the closure of the sites. In New York State, United Teachers went so far as to apply for a court injunction to shut down the sites. Requests were denied on free speech grounds. In the United Kingdom, teachers unions 'demanded' the removal of a YouTube video, arguing that 'teachers have had enough of the various online pranks and tricks that kids pull on teachers' (http://www.techdirt.com/articles/20070801/092449.shtml).

Student activism at University X

As Bernstein observed some time ago, the principles of the market and its managers are more and more shaping the policy and practices of schools and universities (1996). Aronowitz and Giroux also point to the ways in which the neoliberal university 'appears to be indifferent to ideas, forms of learning, and modes of research that lack commercial value' (2000). Tatto describes some of the consequences of moves to remove control of education from teachers and academics by using arguments about efficiency and accountability. What we have seen is the subversion of the very *telos* or intellectual raison d'être of the university. Courtesy of this worldview, the requirements for knowledge and critical thinking have been subverted in favor of the production of knowledge, online delivery, large classes and the employment of untrained, cheap, casual part-time staff (2007). The modern neoliberal university relies on 'market' criteria like 'student demand' (the popularity of a subject) and 'the vocational relevance' of a program to effect major changes to the curriculum and learning and teaching practices. This results in the closure of 'areas of study that do not translate into substantial profits get[ting] marginalized, underfunded, or eliminated [which leads to] downsizing in the humanities' and the closing of small 'boutique' programs that fail to meet the market criteria (Aronowitz and Giroux 2000, p. 332). Generally those developments have not been contested – especially by students.

These observations are relevant to what happened at University X when senior administrators decided to make major changes to a professional degree program in ways that avoided the more traditional processes of consultation and consensus making with both the teaching staff and the students enrolled in the professional degree program. Dissenting staff members were disciplined, leading to industrial action. Student concerns were initially expressed using conventional means like informal and formal internal complaint and dispute resolution processes (e.g., complaints to teaching staff, deputations to managers and meetings with them). The students complained they had not been informed about the major changes to the program, adding that they were being shortchanged and were not receiving the education they had been promised when they enrolled. Moreover, they complained that the institution had failed to consult with them and that it was deceptive in its reporting about the program to relevant statutory agencies charged with regulating the professional sector and to the public more generally. Students argued the university was being 'evasive with information and withhold[ing] it from people in order to lure potential applicants ... '.

It did not take too long for students to complain that their expressions of concern were not being taken seriously. Students claimed they had made many unsuccessful attempts to bring the issues to the attention of the administration, but to no avail:

> We have brought these issues to the school's attention since 2006 in e-mails, class meetings, letters, etc., and the school appears not to do anything (ibid.) ... [The] administration refuse to answer any questions students ask about these or other matters despite repeated attempts to seek an explanation prior to the census date [which is when students can withdraw from the program without financial and academic penalty].

Some students and staff directly affected by the changes were disillusioned at what they saw as a lack of basic fairness or justice, leading some staff to resign their positions as teachers or, in the case of some students, to canceling their enrollment. For others, however, this disappointment fueled an 'ethical energy' and galvanized a commitment to a politics of resistance. The result was action that remotivated some staff and students by challenging what the students saw as antipolitical attempts to manage them. As Critchley argued, initial disappointment, in this case about the poor behavior of neoliberal managers, segued into something else, filling up the hollowed-out spaces experienced as 'motivational-moral deficits' with the university-as-institution, which now led to positive and politically enriching activism (2012). The result in this case was an activism that invigorated politics by going beyond the traditional forms of political engagement, which both encouraged more deliberative engagement and challenged the deeply authoritarian impulse at work in this university.

Some of the students turned to digital media to voice their concerns, establishing blogs and websites that hosted commentary about 'the problems', updates, relevant newspaper and journal articles, videos, cartoons and photographic images. The sites were used to exchange information, to deliberate, to organize meetings and to mobilize action. Electronic petitions were also posted, along with a log of claims. The sites were regularly updated and links provided to other relevant sites. Students posted critiques about the quality of relevant academic programs in addition to allegations of nepotism, incompetence or maladministration and other forms of 'academic dishonesty'.

Students also used a preexisting Facebook account as part of their political action. These digital sites provided multiple spaces for active engagement by participants, who listened to each other, vented steam, joked and engaged in purposeful discussion. The sites became so popular that within a relatively short period of time, the debate about the issues began spilling over into 'real space', drawing in relevant government departments and oversight bodies, professional associations, politicians, and the media and, of course, the media department within University X and senior administrators at the institution.

Not surprisingly, some university administrators were not happy about the public criticism and responded to the complaints defensively, declaring them to be inaccurate and slanderous. Lawsuits of various kinds were threatened, and some were filed against students, leading to retaliatory legal action by students against administrators. (In these cases, the courts refused to support the applications by the university administrators.) Legal action was also taken by the university representatives against Google to have the it remove the student blogs and Facebook accounts from the Internet. University administrators also responded by taking disciplinary action against some students and threatening them with expulsion.

I now consider some of the implications of the cases involving the Rate My Teacher/Professors websites and University X.

Generational politics

Most participants establishing and using the new digital sites were young people under the age of 30, and many much younger, while those toward whom the critiques were directed tended to be older. In this sense there is clearly a generational dimension in both case studies. This was evident in the ways in which younger participants felt at home in the new sites, how they were able to fill up that space, use language they were comfortable with, express their views and listen to others. The generational dimension was evident also in the reluctance of older players to cooperate or reciprocate in that same space – almost as if doing so was to cede power. While some retreated to the sites where their power was relatively secure, others set up their own web pages to contest.

In one instance, university administrators did respond by posting counterclaims on their own website that countered student claims, describing them as slanderous and incorrect. This was followed up with legal interventions designed to remove the student postings. On 17 April 2011, University X filed a lawsuit in the X Court against the owner of the blog – Google. They also filed for a temporary restraining order, requiring Google to remove the items that were critical of the faculty members. In a hearing on 28 April 2011, Judge X of the X District Court rejected that claim.

Debate and expanded participation?

One of the main reasons students gave for participating in the Rate My Teacher/Professors websites was to exchange ideas, hear about the experiences of peers, and get information about how to handle difficult situations, what subjects to take and which instructors to avoid or search out.

To achieve this, a variety of new modes of deliberation were used, which included posting commentaries, blog dialogues, Facebook, wikis, message boards, podcasts, Twitter, YouTube and videos. Students could deliberate amongst themselves, and others with an interest in the issues could also participate. Instructors, parents and administrators, indeed anyone curious about learning and teaching, could respond.

The same can be said of the University X case study. The students most directly affected by administration decisions voiced their views, heard responses and debated in ways they were not previously able to and in ways that were less subject to limitations imposed by more powerful parties (adults as teachers, parents, managers).

In both the University X case and the Rate My Teacher/Professors websites, the affordances of the Net created forums for discussion between students and between students and teachers and others about various aspects of learning and education. In effect, space for deliberation was augmented and the new media were used to open up sites for deliberation and engagement. The networked nature of the Net meant that anyone with an interest in education, good management of public and private institutions and access to the Internet could participate. Recalling the deliberative space that students had access to prior to the development of these sites and using that as a baseline gives a clear indication of how new media augmented opportunities for deliberative practice.

One minor caveat to be noted is that there was an age restriction on one site. Rate My Professors, intended for postsecondary students, required participants to be over 18, and for Rate My Teacher, participants needed to certify they were over 13. This was not, however, a requirement for participation in other rate-my-teacher sites, or in the University X case. In the Rate My Teacher/Professors websites, deliberation was constrained somewhat by formats that restricted some of the spaces for feedback or to provide other information. Having said that, if participants wanted to have ongoing conversations, they had the option of connecting to linked spaces, associated chat rooms or blogs. Indeed the availability of a 'constellation of communicative spaces' encouraged exchanges of information and ideas. In these ways, these new digitally mediated sites actively worked to expand participation.

In student-sponsored sites, the expert and more socially powerful voice was not privileged. I note too that references to popular culture were frequently used along with colloquial 'nontechnical' language, which made the sites youth-friendly. In the Rate My Teacher sites, that exchange sometimes broke into commentary about the charm and personal appeal (or otherwise) of a teacher.

In these ways the forums invited groups traditionally excluded from discussions about matters like teaching practices and the administration of schools and universities. And while this may not have always entailed cool, sober, rational debate, it nonetheless expanded participation in ways inclusive of groups (students) that were traditionally excluded from deliberative practice.

In both case studies, the Internet was instrumental in promoting interaction and encouraging participants to identify themselves as social agents capable of thinking and acting relatively independently and in ways that overcame some of the constraints imposed by their educational institutions (e.g., the authoritarian culture, the absence of a forum for voicing their views in ways that informed decisions). While theorists like Habermas remain skeptical about the capacity of the Internet to enhance deliberative practice, these case studies how digital technology can move us beyond a narrow definition of the 'public sphere' by helping build and sustain civic cultures (Dahlgren 2009).

In the University X case, participants identified as members of groups interested in a range of political issues related to higher education, which included equity, corruption, academic fraud, the value of debate and what they saw as wrongdoing in their educational institutions. In one university site, students openly declared their commitment to 'positive change' in the community, and went on to explain what that looked like. This interest in broader social issues was also apparent in some deliberations that incorporated major political-ethical issues like the marketization of higher education and its impact on learning and the status of students as consumers.

Similarly, student concerns were aired about transparency or a lack of transparency, along with complaints about the absence of consultation or deliberative practice in the university and what students saw as failures to consult with or inform them about matters in which they had a direct interest. In these ways, deliberations that were available through new media were imbued with powerful moral emotions that connected to questions of justice and that saw students position themselves in opposition to neoliberal politics that characterized their universities, or what Dahlgren described as the consumerist or commercial interested devoted to 'uncivic economism' (2009).

While inclusivity and an enlarged participation are vitally important for building a democratic culture, these along are not enough. The context, or more specifically, the political-ethical culture of the space in which deliberation took place and the quality of that participation itself also needs to be factored in. Even if there is 'acceptance' of a decision by all those affected by it, and even if we attain agreement, whether that then enhances or diminishes democratic practice depends on how the accord was attained. Deliberation per se and more inclusive deliberation may not reflect a more democratic process nor better decisions or the truth.

This brings us to the question of freedom, equity and power. On this point I note the general recognition of the significance of equity and freedom by a range of political theorists (see Chapter 1). Here I am interested in the degree to which participants were free to dissent and also in their capabilities in respect to dissent (e.g., capacity to mount argument, assemble relevant evidence, offer ripostes etc.). Are participants free in both the negative and the positive sense of the term? If they are free from the exercise of overt constraints on their freedom (e.g., coercion), were they also free from more subtle forms of constraints, including the limitations we place on ourselves, like self-censorship?

Pervasive and subtle pressure imposed by peers and others can lead to extremism and consensus about falsehoods. Indeed, history is littered with examples of communities deliberating seemingly openly to produce social harmful decision. As Sunstein observed, it is quite common for deliberating groups to fail to obtain the knowledge, information and ideas the members of a group have. One reason for this is that groupthink can reflect a predisposition toward a certain outcomes that causes the group to fail to explore alternative possibilities, to promote unthinking conformity and dangerous self-censorship. In the case of the Central Intelligence Agency (CIA) and its 'predisposition' to find a serious threat from Iraq, Sunstein reported on the Senate committee's finding that the CIA:

> demonstrated several aspects of group think: examining few alternatives, selective gathering of information, pressure to conform within

the group or withhold criticism, and collective rationalisation. (cited in Sunstein 2006: 12)

He continued, the Senate committee found that the agency demonstrated 'a tendency to reject information that contradicted the presumption' that Iraq had weapons of mass destruction. Because of that presumption, the agency failed to use its own formalized methods 'to challenge assumptions' and 'group think', such as 'devils advocates' and other types of alternative or competitive analysis (Sunstein 2006, p. 13).

Thus, while we may be inclusive and have many participants, the question remains: were participants able to present a strong case for competing views? In the university case study, alternative views were not elicited or encouraged by administrators of the institutions; rather, they were actively discouraged, courtesy of a clear disposition to find a serious threat to the program area and the university, and thereby represented dissent as illegitimate and warranting disciplinary and legal action.

This points to questions about the degree to which consensus is valued, expected or indeed required as an outcome of debate. Was there pressure to follow the party line? Was consensus making privileged over and above dissent, or was dissent genuinely valued? Was it actively or subtly discouraged? Was it considered important for reasons that go beyond the fact that counterpositionings (dissent) are necessary for reaching consensus?

Democratic politics

Discussion about the value of an enlarged and inclusive deliberative space has, since Habermas, relied heavily on Immanuel Kant's principle of universalizability. It is an idea that holds that in order for a norm or decision to be ethical and valid, we need to ensure that everyone affected by it can accept the consequences of its observance and that those with an interest prefer that decision to any alternative. It is assumed that the more encompassing that space, the more people engaged in the debate, the more likely it is that the process itself and any outcome (e.g., decision) will be ethical and legitimate. Yet while 'the more the merrier', enables those affected to have a say, I argue that the culture or the nature of relations within that space is also critical for determining the legitimacy and ethical status of the debate and ensuing decisions. In saying this, however, I do not suggest the debate ought to conform to Habermas' requirement for rational deliberation.

The insistence on the requirement of rationality is constraining and ignores the role that a variety of 'nonrational' attributes and activities can play in the enhancement of democratic politics (e.g., art, satire, displays of emotion such as anger and laughter). In the effort to understand human action, we have seen an overreliance on a rational and cognitivist bias that has had the effect of overlooking the influence of emotions (Barbalet 1998). The idea of human action as rational, whether it be understood as instrumental or goal-oriented action (e.g., economic transaction) or as value rational action, also overlooks the creative or constitutive role players (e.g., of experts) in 'discovering' or constituting the problem, while at the same time overlooking the contingency of politics and its disorderly, variable and unexpected qualities. It ignores the value of phenomenological inquiry, which can produce insights into the role of confusion, misguided conduct, accidents, deliberate deception, ignorance and malevolence in politics. Finally, this preoccupation with rationality ignores the role of power and 'governmental rationalities' that operate and their impact on politics. For these reasons, I am critical of the liberal humanist notion of social action, whether it comes in the form of a positivist or as an interest in the subjective experience because it is assumed human action is rational. It is assumed the capacity to reason is critical for politics and our political institutions. It was certainly considered critical for Habermas' 'communicative rationality', which he pictured as a 'unifying consensus building force' or discourse in which participants might begin from their own subjective views, but soon overcome those in 'favor of a rationally motivated agreement'.

How then can we interpret claims to be rational? How can we interpret a contribution to a debate, like the following extract from the university case study? On the face of it, it seems to offer a sober, self-reflexive contribution to dialogue in which the participants learn from each other and from themselves. It appears to be thoughtful and reflective of the participant's own *habitus* and cultural knowledge, and appears to question assumptions we take for granted.

> In January, the...program did a 'self assessment' that they reported to the...professional board. Amongst other lies, ...it states: ...Students are required to attend 80% of classes in the first two years and full attendance is mandatory for students in the third and fourth...years. Attendance is monitored by students signing into classes...and is part of the evaluation of students....This meets the...[professional bodies] requirement" for 80% actual attendance in all courses".

Full attendance is NOT enforced. ... The attendance monitoring is also a lie, as students in the first two years are actually encouraged not to go to certain courses by lazy professors. ... [The] curriculum makes extensive use of active learning methods such as problem-based-learning and small group teaching in ... years given the small class size, and promotes self-directed learning in its students consistent with its stated mission.

> Self-directed learning is DISCOURAGED. Class time can be approximately 50 hours per week and people commonly stated that going to classes left them with inadequate time to study on their own.

Is this an example of communicative rationality?

The limitations of the idea of the individual as rational and autonomous have been explored by many, from Friedrich Nietzsche and Sigmund Freud to more recent accounts by postfoundationalist theorists like Jacques Derrida (1978). Although there are differences in their respective analyses, these writers challenge the liberal humanist view by emphasizing the multiple, even contradictory, forms that identity can take. And while these critiques have their own weaknesses, one strength is their attention to the multiple dimensional and dynamic aspects of our being. The idea of positionality or subject positions, for example, acknowledges how different aspects of who we are (i.e., masculine, Muslim) provide the content of subjectivity in ways that go beyond traditional notions of the self or the individual as rational stable and coherent.

Postfoundationalists also point to the ways in which language is used to construct or describe certain types (rational, well balanced, shy, foolish), as if those descriptors refer to actual things said to be inherent in us, which determine and explain our actions. The value of this insight becomes apparent when we realize that these descriptors of our actions have no meaning if they are removed from their social context. In saying this, I do not deny we have particular dispositions, but rather the liberal idea of the individual as rational independent and stable, and the idea that actions originate from internal psychological structures ignores the generative role of the social and particularly the role of language. Moreover, they cannot account for the contradictory nature of our self.

Sociologists like Max Weber, who promoted a sociology of action, and phenomenologists like Schutz provide a basis for developing a better understanding of politics as action that is negotiated and mediated through collective symbols (language) and informed by systems of meaning and belief (religious beliefs and ethical aspirations). And while Weber tried to defend the idea of action as rational action, Schutz acknowledged the presence of multiple actors, and in doing so made it obvious why the idea of simple linear causality had to be dismissed in preference for more complex accounts of social action as negotiated, contingent and processual (Schutz 1973, pp. 214–226). While these writers provide a beginning, the work of later theorists like Norbert Elias, and particularly his writing on a figurational model and process sociology, holds promise for those interested in analyzing the politics of a particular site (1978).

With all this in mind, I return to the question of whether deliberative space has been expanded. We can point to an extensive repertoire of communicative styles used in both cases. While some of these did fit Habermas' category of communicative rationality, many did not, and instead appealed to participants' aesthetic and affective dispositions. Humor, poetics, irony and satire were deployed to inspire and provoke powerful political emotions, to provide sardonic amusement and to affirm biases and predispositions. As Dahlgren notes, emotions and aesthetics do matter because they can play an effective persuasive role in political communication; they can influence how we see, feel and think. Participants described the sites as fun, enjoyable and 'cool', and as a way of 'checking out' each other's views (http://www.ratemyprofessors.com/About.jsp). The site is also reportedly used for fun and play between teachers and students. Reportedly, teacher Matthew Julius, an associate professor of biological sciences at St. Cloud State University, United States, writes a number of comments about himself on Rate My Professors. He says his 'page is peppered with gags',

> which he composed purely to amuse his graduate students. Mr. Julius says he and his colleagues take great sport in posting remarks about themselves and each other on the site – so much so that it has become a medium for their inside jokes. (cited in Montell 2006)

In both the university and the Rate My Teacher/Professors cases, we saw expanded forms of deliberation that were open to a diversity of groups. Yet augmented deliberation on its own may not be enough if there is little or no interest on the part of participants in listening to each other.

Listening to each other

In the university case, students actively participated in the digitally mediated sites, listening, exchanging information and debating. The content included descriptions of 'the issues' in contention along with rationales for the students' stance. There were regularly updated, and more serious deliberations were often interjected with comedy, using film, music and cartoons. The regular use of funny caricatures and parodies added comic relief while communicating serious political messages. Other time-honored styles of political communication, like mockery depicting mangers as villains or fools, were incorporated into this new domain, working to engage people, provide a laugh, poke fun and provoke those targeted.

Within this expanded range of communication, most participants were interested in listening to each other. While some students listened with an interest in understanding each other's positions at a linguistic, intellectual and emotional level, this was not the case with all participants.

Institutional managers, however, were reluctant to respond to any of this content. Rather, what we saw was an example of traditional power holders using 'administrative or organizational rationality' to exercise power in ways designed to hijack and frustrate any burgeoning deliberative practice. This included, for example, decisions to carry out reviews of the program in the midst of student complaints about administrative decisions. The reason or rationale for such actions was, however, so unclear that it even caused the chair of the review panel, an external individual recruited for the task, to officially query the university's rationale:

> I'm still unclear as to the terms of the review. It would very helpful if you could you send through any documentation that explains the basis for the review and its charter or governance and any guidelines on what it is hoping to achieve etc. As I raised at the … meeting, I'm still unclear as to why the course is being reviewed at this time and what its purpose is? I do hope the review is about promoting and maintaining the future of the course as a … qualification as this is very important to the sector. As the longest running … course in the country I'm sure I don't need to remind you of the iconic status of the degree to the youth work sector and to the many graduates now in very senior positions in NGOs and government around

[the country]. To see the course downgraded ... would be extremely disappointing.

Also as I raised at the ... meeting it is still unclear to me why the review panel does not have any of the long-term teaching staff sitting on the review panel? This seems an anomaly given that the teaching staff have, I assume, been the ones who have developed the current subjects and know the content and presumably will be the ones that will have to develop and teach any new subjects that may be recommended by the review? It does seem to be a bit odd to be reviewing the course without the long-term coordinator and teachers involved? Having sessional or temporary staff on the review does not seem to be adequate. As such, can more be done to include these staff, or is it at all possible to put the review on hold until such time as the staff could participate? Or is there an urgency to the review's timing?

Thus in the university case, it seemed that administrators may have been listening to student deliberations, but were genuinely interested in reflecting on their own position or in trying to appreciate the issues from the perspective of the students.

Yet while some of the engagement was not collaborative and did not meet the criteria for 'communicative rationality', the use of new media by the students was effective in ensuring they could voice their views and that they were heard. The new sites provided a forum in which the students and others could debate and which forced university administrator to respond, albeit in ways that did not invite further debate.

Indeed in most responses, university administrators were defensive and antagonistic and refused to respond within the new domain, preferring instead 'actual space' inside the university or in legal administrative domains where they seemed more at home, and where they enjoyed greater power. The responses came in various forms, as 'advice' (warnings) about the legal action and pending disciplinary action if students continued with their action. Responses also came in the form of action designed to counter student claims, but without direct interaction with students. One such response was the employment of public relations consultants for the purpose of 'crisis management' and to prevent damage to the university 'brand'. This particular strategy entailed giving the program area in question a public profile. It was a rather circuitous but nonetheless often effective attempt to usurp or contest the students' agenda. The university-sponsored public relations campaign entailed the recruitment of a small number of leaders in the relevant field of professional practice to present keynote speeches in a bid to usurp student initiative and persuade public opinion. In note that such attempts to appropriate or contest oppositional views may be explicit, but more often than not they are made invisible or presented as something other than direct engagement in the debate or than agenda setting. In this way the belief is maintained that administrators or indeed any participant remains rational, distanced and apolitical in the process (Yeatman 1990).

The Internet and equal deliberative participation

Relative discursive equality characterized all sites. Participants demonstrated the linguistic and technical competence needed to engage in debate, and there appeared to be no subordinate or marginalized groups. New media provided civic space so that anyone who wanted to participate had ample opportunity to speak, ask questions, provide information and express opinions. Indeed, a pluralism of views was on full display, something that previously did not exist. Equity and fairness could also be seen in the observance of courtesies like listening and turn-taking when speaking. All of these behaviors conform to the Habermas-Dahlgren taxonomy in which participants ought to have relatively equal capacity to deliberate and that civic space is recognizable by values like equity and openness that encourages a pluralism of views.

The disembodied nature of cyberspace has a particular advantage for those historically excluded by providing particular conditions that help overcome long-standing exclusionary practices. That is, virtual space offers choices about whether participants reveal aspects of their identity in ways that cannot be avoided in embodied public spheres. Discrimination on the basis of age is less likely if participants choose not to disclose their age, and in this way the option of anonymity the Net offers can counter certain discriminatory practices and inequalities that characterize actual public spheres.

In addition, the university case participants filled up space using the language and modes of communication with which they were comfortable, something that had not been their experience in formal institutional forums where agendas and regulations were set by traditional power elites. I note that when traditional power holders participated in the Rate My Teacher/Professors sites, their institutional power did not automatically transfer into that space.

These examples of what was happening in the case studies demonstrate the role of digital media in opening up civic spaces and promoting change in the political culture of the institutions.

Digital media, autonomy and coercion

Compared with the constrained and tightly managed formal venues in which students traditionally participated in educational institutions, digital sites provided far more opportunity for them to speak freely and purposefully, but did not provide complete autonomy from undue pressure or intimidation, and in this way created civic space. While greater opportunity to speak freely did exist, coercion, threat of discipline and other sanctions were very present and caused some participants in the university case to be intimidated and some to withdraw partially, and in some instances completely, from their involvement. This coercive capacity was possible in the university case because the student body was relatively encapsulated, and participants more readily identifiable.

In the Rate My Teacher/Professors sites, the situation was different. Complete anonymity was recommended and became the norm, allowing participants to deliberate without the inhibitory fear of retribution. To help counter the prospect of retribution, participants in the American-based Rate My Professors site were assured their name and email address would not be revealed (http://www.ratemyprofessors.com/faq.jsp#). Nonetheless, offline actions designed to curtail participation in Rate My Teacher sites were taken. They included embargoes on the sites, with some school principals instructing students not to participate at school or at home. Such directives, in conjunction with the use of software filters, were some of the strategies used to prevent participation. Students knew too well that school authorities monitored the sites and that if they disobeyed, repercussions would follow. Yet, such attempts to curtail deliberation overlooked the subversive capacity of both students and the Net. More technically savvy and motivated participants were well able to use Web proxies and other techniques to get around bids to close off deliberation.

In this way the technical capacities of knowledgeable users to avoid detection and thereby subvert attempts to intimidate and restrict their participation demonstrates the capacity of the students to use technology in ways that enhance their autonomy and freedom from coercion, conditions that both Habermas and Dahlgren consider important for deliberative practice.

Having said this, I note that some traditional power holders made incursions into Rate My Teacher sites, resulting in its 'colonization'. In some instances, authorities took over the sites completely, assuming a management role (e.g., giving parents administrator roles), and in doing so transformed the sites. Part of the rationale for this action was so that parents, teachers and administrators could get 'real, honest opinion about how good (or bad) a particular instructor really is'. In this way the deliberative nature of sites was lost as they became management and public relations exercises (Boswell n.d.). While threats to Net neutrality and deliberative capacity posed are present, it is too early to tell whether those influences are likely to undermine the democratic potential of new media. Like any political space, virtual space is political. Moreover, it is a new terrain in which the norms and rules of the game are not yet set (Papacharissi 2010).

In the university case, participants assumed they had a right to speak openly about matters of public interest. After all, they argued, universities have a declared commitment to critical and free inquiry and debate. Yet in spite of the official commitments to critical inquiry, some authorities proved to be sensitive to open deliberation and public scrutiny. As events unfolded, student participation intensified, attracting a wide audience. It was a successful new platform that provided a new stage for students to air their grievances in full public view, something that provoked the ire of those being criticized, spilling offline and making relationships between participants and some administrators intense and even hostile. Clearly some traditional power elites struggled in coming to terms with student access to these new public forums, rejecting their legitimacy and right to raise matters as they did. It is worth mentioning at this point that little or no effort was made by those critiqued to engage students on their own turf. Nevertheless, it was the case that students and staff from other universities, as well as professionals from relevant fields of practice did participate in the site.

A full defense strategy was deployed, including formal disciplinary actions like official warnings, suspensions, expulsions and threats of various kinds, in addition to various legal interdicts – all directed toward constraining further deliberation. This action was effective in rendering some students silent, while for others it provoked righteous anger. In the university case, a small group of participants were identified as ringleaders and held responsible for mobilizing action and for generally causing bother. They were subsequently called to disciplinary meetings, given warnings and informed that further investigations into their conduct would continue.

Surveillance was a further example of undue influence that had an inhibitory impact. In the university case, technical specialists were contracted to carry out reconnaissance into the online activities. Surveillance included monitoring emails, identifying Internet Provider addresses and trawling the Internet for evidence of 'radical activities'. Such surveillance worked to create a sense that one was being watched, or that one might be watched, and in this way it had a powerful self-regulatory and inhibitory effect. Having said that, surveillance did not cause participants to abstain, but made them cautious about how they participated.

In addition, traditional power holders successfully applied to Google to have the students' Facebook site removed on the grounds it infringed copyright. Students had remixed graphics, incorporating copyrighted icons and the official logo. Use of copyright law was an effective exercise of power that inhibited debate by closing the site.

Administrators also responded to student claims by postings statements on their own websites, describing student complaints as slanderous and incorrect. This was accompanied by a series of legal interventions designed to remove postings. The institution also filed a suit against the owner of a blog that students were using, calling for a temporary restraining order that required the owner to remove items critical of the faculty. Students appealed, and in a hearing the judge rejected the institution's claim. Meanwhile, students transferred their blog to a new provider, continuing the critique:

> Rather than investing in fixing the corruption at the X, ... [the] School has decided to pay lawyers to make a feeble attempt to once again cover up the continued abuses of the American medical students.

Other legal action followed, aimed at having material removed which students contested the orders and at the 11th hour the university withdrew.

Some time later, a senior administrator at the center the disputes ventured into digital space. Yet rather than deliberating with the students, she established a separate blog, and while there was no discussion about the issues the students had raised, some whom the manager believed were participants were named and described as troublemakers. Not surprisingly, this action did not contribute to reaching consensus, but aggravated the situation, with the matter spilling once more offline and into the legal system.

Internet security programs such as Microsoft AntiSpyware and Norton Internet Security may have blocked RateMyTeachers because it feels it is unsafe to visit. If you have Internet security software installed on your computer, make sure it is not blocking access to this site http://www. ratemyteachers.com/faq#17.

In summary, while it seems that digital space in some instances enhances autonomy and freedom from coercion, it also needs to be acknowledged how coercive actions can and do spill out into actual space, which has an inhibiting effect on participants' capacity to be involved online. What the case studies also reveal is that while digital technology facilitates political communication and promises enhanced civic engagement, it can also be the same technology that allows traditional power elites to engage in information technology surveillance, to be coercive and to pursue disciplinary and legal activities that have the effect of dampening participation and dissent.

Political autonomy

Evidence of heightened political autonomy is evident in the ways students engaged in both the University X case and the Rate My Teacher/ Professors websites. Political autonomy was exercised by the students, who challenged the long-standing asymmetric power relations between themselves and administrators. The significance of this development can be appreciated by referring to the conventional reporting practice, which was one-way. Teachers exclusively wrote the school reports on students, typically with little if any opportunity for the students to have a right of reply, and in many cases they did not know what was said of them until their parents read the report. This is not to suggest there complete political autonomy, but simply a movement toward a change in power disparities in some contexts, which has a spillover effect in real space even if that is only evident in the fact that 'the privacy' of the classroom has been breached and teaching staff are aware that their teaching practices could very well be scrutinized publicly by their students.

Indeed, the prospect of being 'cyber-baited', which is filmed at any time without one's knowledge, and for that to footage end up in the public domain for all and sundry to see has a virtual panopticon effect, which certainly has the potential to change the ways people conduct themselves. In this way it can influence the teachers' conduct and the power relations between students and teachers. As Foucault pointed out, being exposed to constant surveillance through subtle, and not so subtle, mechanisms has a powerful and effective inhibitory or self-regulating effect. Indeed, knowing we are, or may be, observed is a disciplinary technique in itself. It is a coercive power that results in teachers' self-monitoring and possible changes in behavior toward students. As Foucault explained,

> He who is subjected to a field of visibility, and who knows it, assumes responsibility for the constraints of power; he makes them play

spontaneously upon himself; he inscribes in himself the power relation in which he simultaneously plays both roles; he becomes the principle of his own subjection. (1977, p. 104)

In the university case, political autonomy was also on display even in the capacity of students to make self-governing judgments about aspects of their education and governance of the university. This was evident in their willingness and capacity to question truth claims, and in their preparedness to speak out and exercise positive freedom. They were prepared to stand up and say 'the tribe's' representations and common-sense worldviews need rethinking, the laws and powers are unjust, and we have to create new institutional arrangements.

University X's disaffected students used new media to initiate public debates about the quality of their that offered specialist education to 'overseas' students. They claimed the program did not 'appear to meet the requirements of the national Federal Financial Aid', and argued that a lot of the reporting data was false. It was claimed for that

> x program continues to have an abysmal rate of postgraduate placement with an annual revenue stream exceeding $3,000,000/year. Most often, the...students are...[enrolled] as a hope of last resort to become a physician after being rejected from all...schools [in their homeland and elsewhere]. After investing in excess of $100,000/each into their...education, most of the recent graduates [have trouble securing an internship and work].

Conclusion

The cases used in this chapter indicate how the use of digital space by students can go some ways toward altering their status and challenging the asymmetric power relations that characterize contemporary educational institutions in ways that promote democratic practice.

While new media has not made an immediate difference to the political landscape and administrative practices of schools and universities, there is evidence it is encouraging student participation and opening new civic spaces and that is holds the promise of altering how politics gets done in those institutions. All that said, change toward a more genuinely democratic culture in schools and modern universities is likely to be a slow process and one beset by many obstacles. Thus, what the case studies hint at is the ways in which new media is a catalyst for political renewal that is creative and encourages democratic practice.

8
The *Stop Online Piracy Act* Case

One case that demonstrates the complexity of how politics and new media work is the attempt by the US Congress to pass legislation in late 2011 called the *Stop Online Piracy Act* (SOPA). Its supporters claimed the legislation would protect the profitable film and music industries from online piracy by bolstering enforcement of copyright laws, especially against foreign-owned and operated websites.[1] While the proposed legislation initially received broad support in Congress and the relevant policy-making communities, that backing was short lived. Introduced on 26 October 2011, the SOPA became the object of unprecedented opposition that was mounted using various forms of new media.

Initially it was framed as a defense of commercial and national interests, and specifically of a traditional business model based on the sale of film and music products like cinema tickets, DVDs and music CDs. The public response to the SOPA quickly turned the proposed legislation into an assault on the competence of certain lawmakers and the right to freedom of speech, one of the most powerful rights enshrined in the US Constitution and in American popular culture.

During November 2011, a storm of online discussion and online protest, and various forms of electronic direct action erupted, initiated by websites like Reddit and Wikipedia (United Kingdom), underwriting the establishment of new websites and followed up by interventions by big Net players like Google, Mozilla, and Flickr. This loosely structured electronic opposition ultimately involved approximately 115,000 websites. Supporters of the SOPA were targeted with denial-of-service attacks, Internet 'blackouts' and 'brownouts', and campaigns designed to shift customers away. Google punished Go Daddy, a prominent e-business and SOPA supporter by degrading their online visibility by lowering its ranking in their search engine.

A virtual strike was staged on 18 January 2012 in protest against the SOPA as websites partially or fully blacked out their sites and disabled services for 24 hours (Garner 2012). Wikipedia claimed 182 million people saw its anti-SOPA banner. Sites like Google and Mozilla, darkened their logo and released further calls for action campaigns to encourage users to protest. Similarly, when users accessed Craigslist, they encountered a 'Stop SOPA' flash page. This wave of online protests was accompanied by street-based demonstrations in late 2011 and early 2012 in cities across America, including New York, Seattle and San Francisco.

The SOPA was effectively killed off just two and a half months after its introduction when on 18 January 2012, President Barack Obama vetoed the legislation. Obama's office declared,

> We will not support legislation that reduces freedom of expression, increases cybersecurity risk or undermines the dynamic, innovative global Internet... [Moreover any proposed] laws must not tamper with the technical architecture of the Internet through manipulation of the Domain Name System (DNS), a foundation of Internet security. (Espinel et al. 14 January 2012)

Two days later, House Judiciary Committee chairman Smith formally announced that his committee was indefinitely postponing plans to pass the bill.

In considering this case, I address the following questions: Is what happened in this case evidence of a renewed public sphere, courtesy of new media? Is this a case of generational politics? Is there evidence of a renewal of politics or of a new kind of politics that might begin to look like a radical imaginary? What does it suggest about the emergence of a new imaginary or political sensibilities embodied in novel practices courtesy of digital media?

I begin with a brief overview of the legislation and outline what the designers of the law intended. I then ask whether an analysis framed in terms of a 'networked public sphere' provides insight into the SOPA case (Blenker 2006). I offer a description of some of the deliberative processes that took place in virtual space in the process as a prelude to the development of strategies that established a loose but effective coalition that shaped public opinion and mobilized action to powerful effect. I argue that we also see evidence in this case of a generational politics as I map the players in the ensuing debates and protests. Finally, I ask whether the fate of the SOPA indicates the emergence of a new political autonomy of the kind foreshadowed by Cornelius Castoriadis? As I argue here, the complexity of the interests represented and the kinds of representations by both supporters and antagonists of SOPA suggest, there are a number of contradictions operating in a contest between different conceptions of freedom.

The case: the Stop Online Piracy Act movement

The SOPA was introduced on 26 October 2011 in the US House of Representatives. The SOPA (or Bill 3261) was draft legislation introduced by the House Judiciary Committee chairman, Congressman and Republican Lamar Smith from Texas, and a bipartisan group of 12 cosponsors.

The SOPA designed to authorize the US Attorney General, the US Department of Justice and copyright holders to seek a court order against any Internet site or domain to cease and desist activities considered to be infringing copyright. The Act would authorize a plaintiff to seek remedy for the 'theft' of US property by giving an IPS notice to cease providing a service to the accused site within five days. 'Stolen property' included unauthorized possession and trafficking of sound recordings or video online, counterfeit labels, goods or services.

The proposed legislation made it a felony to access or upload any material like videos, photos, music, films, correspondence etc.) that contained any copyrighted material. The proposed remedies seemed simple yet far reaching. Central to the legislation was the proposal that when a court authorized and issued a cease and desist order, on receipt of that notice the provider was required to prevent their US customers, who were subscribers to the website in question, from accessing the 'offending' foreign or American sites. Search engines like Google or Yahoo were also required to prevent offending sites from being served as a hyperlink. Additionally, payment processes involving banks and credit card suppliers could be intercepted to block financial transactions between US customers and the offending site. Action could also be taken to prevent online advertisers from providing ads to foreign websites. All these legal remedies could be undertaken within five days of the issuing of the order.

The case for the bill, according to its supporters, was that the legislation would protect America's national interest. It would do this by targeting 'foreign rogue' companies and sites, which it was argued, were the primary perpetrators of 'egregious' piracy. This was a major problem because the use of copyrighted material and products without permission was undermining the national economy and costing US companies millions of dollars in lost revenue. There were also serious associated problems like job loss. This issue was framed in moral terms as a problem of theft and unfairness. Supporters of the SOPA claimed to be looking after the 'national interest' by defending it against foreign and domestic 'pirates' who kept stealing the creative and intellectual property and hard-earned gains that rightfully belonged to American creators and investors.

For major pharmaceutical companies like Pfizer, it was argued that this was in the 'public interest by protecting citizens from being hoodwinked by forged websites selling counterfeit or deliberately misbranded medicinal and therapeutic products.

Supporters of the SOPA included large corporations like Rupert Murdoch's News Corporation and its subsidiary, 20th Century Fox; pharmaceutical companies like Pfizer; key industry and lobby groups like the Motion Picture Association of America, the National Association of Broadcasters, the American Federation of Television & Radio Artists and the US Chamber of Manufacturers; and some entertainment industry unions representing actors, musicians, stagehands and other workers.[2]

On the face of it, these groups constituted a well-equipped even formidable power bloc uniting around clearly articulated common interests and acting as they had on many occasions before, as a single political force enabled by extensive resources and experience.[3]

However, the opposition they faced demonstrated itself to be even more effective. The legislation faced intense opposition from a loose coalition of well-informed, large, diverse, highly active and motivated groups and large numbers of individuals who built on and extended a sophisticated and effective communication network and a highly effective campaign of opposition. It was a coalition that included small and large relatively new technology and Internet companies;[4] First Amendment and prodemocracy advocates;[5] many savvy computer enthusiasts; some business people, including venture capitalists, academics,[6] creative artists;[7] and many well-organized interest groups like the Internet civil liberties group Electronic Frontier Foundation, hacker groups and Anonymous. As it eventuated, this coalition was able, after a series of high-profile actions and protests, to defeat the legislation barely two and a half months after its introduction.

In what follows, I begin to address the questions above and which arise from a heuristic designed to draw out some of the conceptual and theoretical conundrums we encounter in an age dominated by the new media. I begin by asking whether in this case opposition to the SOPA provides evidence of a public sphere or a networked public sphere?

The networked public sphere

Benkler did much to develop and refine the idea that new media promoted and renewed the public sphere and effectively challenged the monopoly of capital-intensive media industries involved in producing newspapers and electronic radio and television news (2006). He uses the term 'networked public sphere' in acknowledging new media as an agent of transformation (2006). He argues there are two fundamental differences between the new networked information economy and traditional mass media, which are the 'network architecture and the cost of becoming a speaker'.

> The first element is the shift from a hub-and-spoke architecture with unidirectional links to the end points in the mass media, to distributed architecture with multi-directional connections among all nodes in the networked information environment. The second is the practical elimination of communications costs as a barrier to speaking across associational boundaries. Together, these characteristics have fundamentally altered the capacity of individuals, acting alone or with others, to be active participants in the public sphere as opposed to its passive readers, listeners, or viewers. (Benkler 2006, p. 212)

Pointing to the affordances of the World Wide Web, like the creation of a networked public sphere, is not intended to emphasize the role of technical assets or tools, but to highlight the social production practices that these tools enable. The networked public sphere refers to an alternative arena for public discourse and political debate, an arena less dominated by large media entities, less subject to government control and more open to wider participation.[8] Again, as Benkler argues,

> The networked public sphere is manifest as a complex ecosystem of communication channels that collectively offer an environment that is conducive for communication and the creation of diverse organizational forms. This digital space provides an alternative structure for citizen voices and minority viewpoints as well as highlights stories and sources based on relevance and credibility. (2006, p. 9)

We can observe quantitative and qualitative changes. To begin, anyone can be a publisher, including individuals, educational institutions, and nongovernmental organizations (NGOs). Far more people can now do what traditional speakers in the mass-media environment (i.e., government and commercial entities) had long been able to do courtesy of their access to economic resources. As Benkler points out, the cost of sending an email to others or to an entire mailing list of people interested in a subject, the cost of establishing a website or a blog, the 'cost of being a speaker in a regional, national, or even international political conversation' courtesy of new media is 'several orders of magnitude lower than the cost of speaking in the mass-mediated environment' (2006, p. 214).

Culturally and psychologically the experience of being a speaker, as opposed to being a listener and voter, affects the identity of individuals and the culture of participation they can adopt.

> The easy possibility of communicating effectively into the public sphere allows individuals to reorient themselves from passive readers and listeners to potential speakers and participants in a conversation. (Benkler 2006, p. 213)

The political effects of all this can also be significant. The networked public sphere serves to moderate one major problem when the commercial mass media claim to operate a platform for the public sphere: namely the excessive power it gives its owners and their capacity to mobilize popular sentiment to serve a narrow band of interests or values.[9]

Two things can be said. In the case of the online opposition to the SOPA, we see striking evidence of the ways the new media supports rational and deliberative processes associated with Jürgen Habermas' theoretical specification of the 'public sphere' as well as Benkler's networked public sphere. The quality of the deliberative process mounted by those concerned about the SOPA played a crucial role in this political outcome. They presented superior arguments to those used by supporters of the SOPA as evidenced by, among other things, the political outcome. Equally, and this points to a limitation in Habermas' original formulation of the public sphere, those opposed to the SOPA used new media not only to talk about the SOPA but also to mount a highly successful activist political process. As will become clear, the networked public sphere when it was mobilized to discuss and then thwart the introduction of the SOPA, functioned to severely abridge the power of both major media companies and the US Congress. In effect, we see a complex process that involved both deliberation and action. The first involved the long-term development of networked communication enabling highly engaged actors to inform themselves and create a conversation about the problem. The second stage, which erupted in

November 2011, involved widespread mobilization as a rapidly growing network of individual activists and organizations confronted both the US Congress and the corporate sponsors of the SOPA.

In what follows I offer an outline of the deliberative process involved in the SOPA case, providing some insight into the scale and character of what took place, then summarize the arguments presented by opponents and supporters before turning to an account of the activist use of new media as a political space considered as generational politics.

The *Stop Online Piracy Act* and the public sphere

Benkler provides a unique insight into the 'how' of both the deliberative and the political processes (2013). Benkler et al. compiled, mapped and analyzed the *Combating Online Infringements and Counterfeits Act* (COICA)-*Stop Online Piracy Act*[10] and the *Protect IP Act* (PIPA) debates starting in September (2013). This work makes it possible to get some understanding of the ways the deliberative process developed in the networked public sphere. Benkler et al. researched 9,757 stories relevant to the COICA-SOPA-PIPA debate from September 2010 through the end of January 2012 and then mapped this against the unfolding story of the SOPA (2013).[11]

This mapping exercise revealed two distinct but connected processes: the first involved the long-term development of networked communication that enabled highly engaged actors to inform themselves and create a deliberative process about the problem. The process began with a small number of very engaged individuals and organizations discussing the moves to regulate online activity for more than a year, before a period of rapid expansion starting in November 2011 and building to the subsequent eruption in January 2012. The second stage, covering the last two months, saw widespread mobilization as a gradually growing network of engaged actors and organizations informed, directed and engaged with a surge of interest and mobilized activation on a much larger and broader scale.

The initial stages of the debate were hardly noticeable compared with the peak of political activity. The deliberative activity began at a low level and included many 'quiet' weeks before becoming a national political movement in early 2012. The process of deliberation began with the introduction of the precursor to the SOPA called the COICA, introduced in September 2010 in the US Senate. This was a bipartisan project led by Senators Patrick Leahy and Orrin Hatch and backed by all major content and copyright industries involved and by the US

Chamber of Commerce. The basic framing for this proposed law was that it would save millions of jobs and billions of dollars, bolstered by claims that these objectives and the legal approach had broad bipartisan support.

The counternarrative that informed the protests of January 2012, and decisive abandonment of the legislation, began immediately. West Coast tech media websites raised the alarm, especially *CNET* and *Wired*, which were the first sites to report on the COICA critically on 20 September 2010, joined by *Techdirt*. In the following week, action shifted from tech media to NGOs, including the Electronic Frontier Foundation, GovTrack, and to a lesser extent at this stage, the left-leaning Demand Progress. The network of individuals and organizations that discussed the COICA grew in November. By the end of the month, nearly 100 entities had entered the discussion, including 20 tech media sites, an equal number of general media organizations and dozens of bloggers. At this point, the right wing of the blogosphere began its case against the COICA, marking the emergence of a left-right online coalition that was sustained until the legislation was defeated.

Right-wing resistance was facilitated by Patrick Ruffini of Engage LLC, a consultant specializing in building online campaigns for the political Right and which launched Don't Censor the Net, a special purpose online advocacy organization created to oppose the pending legislation. Epitomizing the bipartisan nature of the opposition to the COICA (and later, SOPA and PIPA), Ruffini continued his collaboration with David Moon and David Segal of the left-leaning Demand Progress throughout the campaign. Right-wing libertarian blogs and organizations like the Cato Institute and Atlas Shrugs, and prominent right-wing political blogs such as Hot Air, Instapundit, and Red State.

More intense online discussion was triggered by the introduction of the PIPA in the Senate on 12 May 2011 by Senator Leahy, who introduced the bill on the Senate floor. Senator Ron Wyden declared himself a vocal opponent of this bill and placed a hold on it on 26 May 2011, while raising a general alarm that he might 'not be able to hold back the flood'. Tech media like *Ars Technica, Techdirt* and *CNET*, and independent organizations like Electronic Frontiers in California and Public Knowledge and the Center for Democracy and Technology (CDT) on the East Coast provided highly detailed critical commentary. Don't Censor the Net developed an online petition opposing the PIPA.

In October 2011, the SOPA was introduced by Congressman Lamar Smith of Texas. Washington DC groups like Public Knowledge, and Senator Wyden (who had helped to defer the COICA the previous autumn and the PIPA a few months before) emerged as online groups, including tech media sites (e.g., Ars Technica, eWeek, GigaOM, and TorrentFreak) responded to this legislative development.

The three most important newcomers to the maps during October were Wikipedia, Fight for the Future (FftF) and Open Congress. At this stage, Wikipedia played a more deliberative role. (The protest activity that would emerge three months later was still some months away.) Any links to Wikipedia were, for example, to the articles that provided descriptions of the SOPA and the PIPA, not to mobilization or talk pages. Fight for the Future and OpenCongress, both cofounded by two mille-nials, Tiffiniy Cheng and Holmes Wilson, began to play a central role in the controversy that would continue until the end of the campaign.

In this week, Fight for the Future launched a popular video in the anti-SOPA-PIPA campaign that was in part informational and in part polem-ical, while urging viewers to take action by contacting legislators. Fight for the Future also provided a platform for artists and musicians to sign an open letter to Congress. Open Congress offered a complementary mode of access to the written materials on the Act, again with a point of contact and an option to 'vote' publicly on the proposal. However, by the start of November 2011, the deliberative process was moving into serious activism. I return to that process later in this chapter.

Given that these arguments were so decisive, it is necessary to provide a synopsis of the key arguments mounted against the proposed legislation.

Arguments against the SOPA

The anti-SOPA case offers a classic example of what George Lakoff described as the 'politics of reframing' (2004). Framing simply refers to frames as 'mental structures of thought' that shape how we see the world and how we act (Lakoff 2004, p. xv).[12] We all engage in framing all the time. All words in all languages are defined or given meaning by reference to frames, which deploy and rely heavily on metaphors and analogies. In politics, frames are part of competing moral systems that are used in political discourse and in charting political action. In the political process, because all politics is moral, framing is a moral enter-prise: it says what the character of a movement or party is.

In the campaign against the SOPA, activists immediately framed opposition to the legislation as a defense of the 'information commons', as writers like Lawrence Lessig (2004a, p. 229) had previously done. This framed the debate in terms of an open access movement, using metaphors like 'information commons' as 'a resource to which everyone within a relevant community has equal access'. In this commons, citizens and researchers can 'read, download, copy, distribute, print, search, or link' to the full text of articles, 'without financial, legal, or technical barriers other than those inseparable from gaining access to the Internet itself' (Bailey 2006, p. 14).

The open access movement therefore aligns with an interest in equal opportunity and freedom from ignorance. Like the public domain, open access empowers individuals by giving them the means to be better informed. An informed public is the prerequisite of a functioning democracy (Gurman 2009, p. 3). What they presented was a powerful moral argument against the SOPA.

In this way the attempt to defeat piracy involved the supporters of the SOPA defending copyright law, which provoked those who valued the information commons to defend it against the SOPA. Thus, the campaign against the SOPA was able to frame the debate in terms of public benefit. The first frame of that narrative was public empowerment. By increasing access to information (through shorter copyright terms that allowed more intellectual works to enter the public domain, through more open access, through an expanded notion of educational fair use and by giving libraries the right to curate and preserve digital resources), the information commons increases the spread and growth of knowledge. The ability to research freely and widely benefits not just the individual but society as a whole. The notion that not only the elite but all people ought to have opportunities to benefit from scholarly learning is an argument for democracy, and it is an argument difficult to counter in a country that identifies itself as democratic.

In this frame the promotion and protection of copyright by major publishers assumes a cast that is not only antidemocratic but threatening to liberty, truth, justice and the 'American way'. The fact that journals are distributed and licensed predominantly by just a few commercial publishers means that those publishers are relatively free to raise prices. Supporters of open access point to unfair price increases for electronic serial subscriptions to journals, or to the restrictive access provisions in licensing agreements. Suber, speaking for the Scholarly Publishing & Academic Resources Coalition (SPARC) claimed that 'in more and more countries, an aroused public is ready to fight', and that this is 'something we haven't seen in the entire history of copyright law' (2008).

Thus, what started as another attempt by powerful corporate interests to legislate to protect their intellectual and creative property rights and interests was quickly converted to an attack on freedom of speech. A broad coalition of opponents saw in the SOPA an assault on the American right to freedom of speech. It was this framing that characterized much of the discussion of the SOPA, although other kinds of arguments would be made against the proposed law.

The SOPA: antagonistic toward free speech and destructive of the Net as a public sphere and creative commons

Opponents of the SOPA declared it be a danger to the protected right of free speech as outlined in the First Amendment to the US Constitution.[13] In particular they claimed the seizure powers under copyright law were not exercised with due regard for First Amendment considerations. It would 'chill' protected speech and undermine the openness and the free exchange of information, all of which is constitutive both of democracy in general and the Net in particular. The SOPA would negatively impact the free exchange of information and ideas critical for a democratic culture. As Tribe argued, the SOPA would curtail 'one of the greats tools of freedom' in the world – namely, the Net (2011).

SOPA opponents pointed to the ways the legislation enabled the delegation of power to suppress speech with prior notice or a judicial hearing to a private party. This would discourage fully protected lawful speech because parties would be fearful of SOPA violations and penalties. It would shut down sites that had not violated copyright or trademark laws. It would introduce 'sweeping changes' that went well beyond addressing the issue of piracy to blockade noninfringing content. The blacklisting of sites would deny US audiences the ability to access constitutionally protected information.

The bill also extended the power to copyright holders to stop activities like advertising and credit card transactions. In doing this it delegated to copyright holders the power to suppress free speech, enabling a private party and taking material out of publication on the Net. This infringed not only First Amendment rights but also the 'prior restraint doctrine' embedded in the Constitution that prohibits the silencing of free speech before the court has rules for that to occur. Moreover, it would enable the ad hoc and extra-judicial use of criminal sanctions that basic rule of law principles in American courts had maintained should not be applied without prior and specific, case-by-case judicial determination.

The opposition also argued that the SOPA had the effect of denying people who wished to protest, long upheld in the United States to be a component of the right to free speech, by making use of protest tactics like 'Denial of Service Attacks' (DoS) tools by making them illegal

(Palfrey 2011). It would make innovative projects like the TOR project (which created encryption technology) illegal. The effect of this would be of particular concern for dissident groups, in both democratic societies like the USA and in autocratic regimes like China or Iran who rely on this technology to protect their anonymity and safety. These arguments doubtless played a key role in persuading pubic opinion to reject the SOPA.

Equally damaging were arguments that the architects of the SOPA did not know what they were doing either legally or technically. These kinds of arguments point to the danger of people from one generation, in this case those promoting the SOPA engaging politically and intellectually with a world with which they were not fully conversant. As we will see, the defeat of the SOPA owed much to the level of technical and intellectual mastery of the issues possessed by those opposed to the legislation.

The SOPA breaches existing laws

A second set of arguments addressed a range of legal and technical issues. Opponents argued that the SOPA would be unenforceable. The proposed legislation would not work because it would not stop copyright infringements. Opponents pointed out that people could still access blocked sites by using the IP address rather than the name. Proxy servers could easily and successfully obstruct copyright enforcement (Electronic Frontier 2011). Moreover, given the porous nature of the Net, pirate websites would simply reappear under a different name.

Further, the SOPA had the effect of overriding existing copyright protection law, which had not been found to be either ineffective or illegal. As opponents pointed out, there was already a bevy of laws that had proven successful in protecting copyright, like the *Digital Millennium Copyright Act 1998*, which provided the basic legal framework critical to making the US Internet so successful.

In addition, the SOPA was said to be legally improper. The bill required recipients of an order to comply with it immediately, action that would include blocking businesses or groups access, and stopping the servicing of websites exclusively on the basis of a unilateral allegation of infringements and without any independent review, fair hearing or judicial finding of guilt. There were many practical and definitional legal problems. Opponents pointed to the ways it would be difficult to test government allegations, particularly in respect to foreign sites, the owners of which would not be required nor compelled to present themselves to a US court. The vagueness of many of the definitions in the proposed legislation was problematic (e.g., Would a 'foreign infringing site' described as a domain name but registered through a nondomain registrar outside the United States count as foreign even if it was administered by a US company and hosted in the United States?) The idea of 'theft of US property' was another definition that generated concern. The way the theft issue was framed meant that an entire website, which might consist of millions of pages and links, could be targeted even if only one page was the cause of an allegation. This would cause major problems for global sites that rely on user-generated content like Facebook, Twitter, and YouTube blogs (in which users post photos music, videos, video commentary or blogs). It would have had a major impact on cloud computing services and social networking, which would affect millions of people.

The absence of knowledge of an infringement by a website owner was deemed by the draft legislation to not be a defense. Those responsible for sites would be required to actively police themselves to make sure infringements did not take place. This was action that would impose substantial self-monitoring obligations.

Opponents also pointed to the many practical and technical problems in the SOPA that would 'break' the Internet. They argued that the SOPA would create serious technical problems by undermining the 'technical architecture' and cohesive structure of the Net. Web browser software applications like Firefox, Internet Explorer and Safari, which retrieve, locate information and direct people to locations, would become liable under the legislation and subjected to denial of access. As experts like Stewart Baker, former assistant Department of Homeland Security argued, this would have the effect of damaging the functioning of the domain name service (DNS) system, which provides the basic regulatory foundation for Internet security by enabling the blocking of access to browsers from resolving to a domain name address (Baker 2011). Undermining the would also damage the basic security of the Net.

The SOPA is bad for business

The final set of arguments against the SOPA pointed to its likely negative effect on e-business. It was argued that if passed, the SOPA would mean that the mere act of filing a notice that accused a site of theft, even if the court found subsequently that there was no infringement, would close down many businesses. It would create an incentive to comply with the request rather than fight piracy, cut off and close down businesses because it could be used by an individual competitor or company to cut off business of others. Opponents insisted that the SOPA would discourage innovation and creativity by deterring Internet companies from exploring new kinds of communication and from hosting and linking to a third party. It would slow down technological innovation.

Furthermore, there was no mechanism for the restitution of websites, lost business, damage to reputation or lost earnings if they were harmed by allegations and associated actions. This meant that ISPs would have a strong incentive to shut down websites and/or terminate business with sites simply because they had been accused of the theft of US property (Tribe 2011). A business could be cut off before it had the opportunity to respond. In addition, the SOPA did not require the ISP to restore the services (even if the company served a counter notice).

It would also make companies liable for the actions of their users. The self-policing obligations that would follow should the SOPA be passed meant that user-generated content would impose a large liability and repress business and user-generated sites in particular (e.g., YouTube, Flickr, Vimeo). As Booz and Company (2011) pointed out, the effect of giving responsibility to host websites for detecting and policing infringements would weaken the existing 'safe harbor' provision for host websites under existing DMCA legislation. It would deter entre-preneurs and stifle venture capital and angel investors (Lukas Biewald, CrowFlower). According to one business consultancy company – Booz and Company – which interviewed 200 venture capitalists, they would not invest if the government passed 'tough new rules allowing websites to be sued or fined for pirated digital content posted by users' (http://www.booz.com/global/home/press/article/49953717).

Some also predicted that SOPA would encourage many cloud and web computing companies that host services to move outside the United States so as to avoid lawsuits (Christian Dawson, CEO ServInt).

Many of these arguments were hard for SOPA supporters to counter or address effectively. Equally, the wide sweep of arguments, some encom-passing Net freedom and the right to free speech, the various legal-tech-nical arguments and the business effects of SOPA indicate that a broad coalition of interests could gather around a common purpose, namely the defeat of SOPA. This is precisely what happened when deliberation moved into action.

Political activism

The deliberative phase rapidly moved into a process of heightened activism within weeks of the introduction of the SOPA. This is not to ignore the continuing process of critical commentary. In early December 2011, for example, Eric Goldman's blog received attention for his assessment of the newly proposed the *Online Protection and Enforcement of Digital Trade (OPEN) Act*, providing a compilation of his past anti-SOPA posts, and explaining why he opposed the SOPA (2011). A *Stanford Law Review* article authored by Lemley, Levine, and Post (entitled 'Don't Break the Internet') likewise attracted a lot of attention. But increasingly we see deliberative talk converting into political activism (2011).

As mentioned, Wikipedia, Fight for the Future, and Open Congress joined the fray in late October 2011. The nature of the process began to change, especially when Fight for the Future (cofounded by two millenials, Tiffiniy Cheng and Holmes Wilson) launched video urging viewers to take action by contacting legislators. Fight for the Future also provided a platform for artists and musicians to sign an open letter to Congress. OpenCongress offered a complementary model of access to the written materials on the act, again with a point of contact and an option to 'vote' publicly on the bill A White House blog petition, Stop the E-Parasite Act, appeared as a result of links from Mashable to the petition page.

The level of online activity increased dramatically as groups like Fight for the Future, Participatory Politics Foundation, Demand Progress with Public Knowledge, the EFF, and the Mozilla Foundation established a site called American Censorship became their push for intense online activity.

The marked increase in online activism against the SOPA culminated in American Censorship Day on 16 November 2011. It was organized to coincide with the first hearing of the SOPA by the US House Judiciary Committee. By this time some Internet companies had begun blocking certain sites and displaying 'Censored' stamps in their place. As part of the American Censorship Day protest, the blogging site Tumblr, offered a mass mobilization platform that automatically connected individuals to their congressional representatives. Growing activism was also evident in sites like the blog politechbot.com, which on 15 November 2011 published an anti-SOPA letter written by professors, a letter from Internet and technology companies and a letter signed by members of the international civil and human rights community.

On 15 December 2011, the House Judiciary Committee held its first mark-up session on the SOPA, and Representative Darrell Issa and Senator Wyden introduced the OPEN Act in both the House and the Senate as an alternative to the SOPA – as well as to the PIPA. On 21 December 2011, the House Judiciary Committee released a long list of corporate supporters of the SOPA, perhaps hoping to bolster the claim that the legislation was good for business and innovation. In response, we now see the use of a tactic that proved to be very successful: Internet users self-organized to pressure Internet companies to publicly reverse support for the legislation or to take a public stance opposing the bills. On 22 December 2011, a single Reddit user initiated a major online mobilization to boycott the Net registrar GoDaddy for its support of the SOPA and PIPA. (Go Daddy quickly retreated and abandoned its support for the legislation as consumers began to change the domain name registrar they used).

Goggle, Mozilla, and Flickr soon followed suit. Within a short time over 115,000 websites joined to support mass boycotts of SOPA supporters like GoDaddy, and Internet Corporation for Assigned Names and Numbers (ICANN) were orchestrated with a number of specific days set aside beginning on 22 December 2011 ('Move Your Domain Day') dedicated to having people transfer from pro-SOPA companies and associations. The effect was such that a number of against pro-SOPA businesses changing their minds and withdrawing support for the bill. In conjunction with this, in late December 2011 Google also reacted against a prominent e-business and SOPA supporter (GoDaddy) by degrading its online visibility by lowering its ranking in their search engine. Some sites recommended that users contact and write directly to politicians, organizations and individuals supportive of SOPA. To speed up action, contact details were provided (e.g., Gizmodo, http://projects.propublica.org/sopa/) and in some cases pro-forma letters were also drafted to encourage participation. Feedback was also encouraged to promote deliberation and the further exchange of ideas and information.

Gaming sites like Joystiq, mommysbest.blogspot.com, majorleaguegaming.com, and Rock, Paper, Shotgun, among others now joined the anti-SOPA campaign. In particular, Joystiq's actions epitomize this dynamic: the site pointed to a post by game developer Nathan Fouts at Mommy's Best Games, in which he encouraged game developers to determine their bosses' stance on the SOPA and urged the gaming community to lobby the Entertainment Software Association (ESA) to cease its support of the SOPA.

Online protest was accompanied by actual street-based demonstrations in late 2011 and early 2012 in cities across America, including New York, Seattle and San Francisco. In early 2012, the online protest intensified with Internet 'blackouts and 'brownouts'. Reddit supported links to a call to action on 10 January by its administrators ('Stopped they must be; on this all depends') as well as announced its decision to black out Reddit on 18 January 2012, and included links to the various campaign sites. Wikipedia was now serving as both a source of information and a platform for action. Wikipedia founder Jim Wales discussed the initiatives and debated the role that the online encyclopedia should play; these talk pages included deliberation as to whether the SOPA was so dangerous to the open Internet that Wikipedia might shut down in protest for a day. The White House garnered attention that week with a blog entry entitled 'Combating Online Piracy while Protecting an Open and Innovative Internet' as senior White House officials responded to the online 'We the People' petitions against the SOPA and related bills and announced that the White House, while sensitive to the problems posed by online piracy, did not support the proposed legislation.

Websites were used to collect petition signatures, with the Google petition alone recording over 4.5 million signatures (Netburn 2012). The public sphere was further expanded, courtesy of blogs like the 'Stop the new American Censorship' (http://stopthenewamericancensorship.org). Individuals motivated to act wrote as individuals, like 'MaaseyRacer', who wrote to withdraw his membership from one of the unions supporting the SOPA.

> After seeing this list. I have just written and given notice that I will not be renewing my Graphic Artist Guild membership because of their support of SOPA. I am also writing my local chapter president and I hope that more graphic artists and designers jump on board and do the same. The Internet has created a huge amount of opportunity for graphic designers and artists, I would hate to see that be threatened in any way. PS Does anyone have a suggestion of a domain registrar that opposes SOPA? After seeing this my company will be leaving GoDaddy, We have 100s of our and client domain names hosted there as well as SSL certificates. (MaaseyRacer 2011, Replied to Same Biddle, 21 December http://maaseyracer-old.kinja.com/)

Coordinated action was planned to coincide with the first hearing on the SOPA in the House of Representatives, scheduled for 18 January 2012. On 17 January 2012, and just before the scheduled reading of the bill, the White House made a public statement that it would not be supporting the legislation because it 'reduces freedom of expression, increases cybersecurity risk, or undermines the dynamic, innovative global internet'.

Notwithstanding this presidential veto, the planned day of action went ahead on 18 January 2012, when a virtual strike was staged nationally to protest against the SOPA. Major digital companies like Wikipedia, Reddit, and BoingBoing partially or fully blacked out their sites and disabled services for 24 hours (Garner 2012), and posted notices in opposition to the proposed legislation. While Google's landing page remained operable, it offered a link to its 'End piracy, not liberty' petition page. Petition drives were also carried out, with Google collecting over 7 million signatures. Sites like Google and Mozilla then darkened their logo and released further calls for an action campaign to encourage users to protest. Wikipedia reported more than 162 million people read its banner notification. Companies that supported the SOPA, like the Recording Industry Association of America (RIAA), were boycotted or subjected to denial of service attacks Similarly, when users accessed Craigslist, they were presented with a stop SOPA 'flash page'. Soon after, an estimated 4 million people emailed Congress to voice their objections about the bill (Wortham 2012: McSherry and Samuels 2012). This was accompanied by an estimated 14 million emails from concerned voters to politicians opposing the SOPA (Weisman 2012).

Generational politics

American academic and activist Lawrence observed the generational character of the contest that determined the fate of the SOPA (2012). As he explained, it was a classic a case of 'new generation' politics. The origins of the opposition to the SOPA can traced back to the 1990s. It was then that Congress began the practice of 'restoring' copyright to works that had entered the public domain. The US Supreme Court also heard cases and made judgments in cases like *Eldred v. Ashcroft*, which upheld this practice.

As these legal cases were litigated, they helped fuel a growing and broad-based movement that was increasingly skeptical of what is viewed as 'copyright extremism'. Students who camped outside the Supreme Court for seats to hear the argument in *Eldred* were outraged by that decision, which fueled the recognition that copyright law had gone too far. It helped build the activist organizations that would fight copyright extremism – from the Electronic Frontier Foundation to Public Knowledge. As Lessig explained,

> Outrage about that decision only fueled the recognition that copyright law had gone too far. It helped build the activist organizations that would fight copyright extremism – from the Electronic Frontier

Foundation to Public Knowledge – and it will be a constant source of education for a new generation just coming into the field. (2012)

According to Lessig, this new generation was largely responsible for the 'extraordinary' victory achieved on 18 January 2012:

> After months of rallying activists of all stripes, including liberals and conservatives, technology companies and free software activists, protest against SOPA and PIPA achieved critical mass. With the support of the traditionally non-activist Wikipedia, the Internet community staged a powerful and effective shut down of critical parts of the web, awakening millions to the fight that had been brewing for almost a year. (2012)

A credible case can be made that there were indeed generational factors operating that shaped the political contest over the SOPA.

Drawing on Mannheim's discussion about the role of 'historic events' in creating generations and change, I argue that the advent of digital media constitutes such an historic event, that from the early 1980s digital media began incrementally to change the milieu with global effect. It did so extensively and quickly so that those raised in the following decades grew up in settings that were different in significant ways from those of their forebears. It was an historic event with global reach. Thus, the question of age and generation is significant for understanding how and why the SOPA case developed as it did.

This becomes apparent when we examine obvious demographic facts like the make up of the 112th US Congress, which sat between January 2011 and December 2013. In the House of Representatives, there were 241 Republicans, 198 Democrats (including five Delegates and the Resident Commissioner) and two vacant seats. The Senate had 47 Republicans, 51 Democrats and two Independents, who caucused with the Democrats. As Manning notes, the average age of Members of the 112th Congress, although lower than that of the previous Congress, was among the highest of any Congress in recent US history (2011). This trend was so noticeable that the *Wall Street Journal* wrote about the 'greying of Congress' as it provided data showing that the 111th and 112th Congresses were among the oldest in US history.[14] The average age of Senators at the beginning of the 112th Congress was 62.2 years. The average age of members of the House at the beginning of the 112th Congress was 56.7 years (Manning 2011). Even the average age of new Members of the House, including a Delegate and the

Resident Commissioner, was 48.2 years. The youngest Representative, as well as the youngest Member of Congress, was 29-year-old Aaron Schock (R-IL), born in 1981. The oldest Representative, as well as the oldest current member of Congress, was Ralph Hall (R-TX), born in 1923.

If most elected representatives in the United States were born in the 1940s and 1950s, long before the advent of digital media, the opposition was on average significantly younger. Unlike the Congresspersons, the opponents of the SOPA by and large came of age in 'fields of practice' shaped by 'the digital age'. Google, for example, was founded in 1998 by two 21-year-olds, Larry Page (born 1973) and Sergey Brin (born 1973). Similarly Wikipedia was launched in 2001 by two young men in their mid-30s (Jim Wales (born 1966) and Larry Sanger (born 1968). Likewise. Facebook was founded in 2004 as a social network site by a group of undergraduates all in their early 20s, that is, Mark Zuckerberg (born 1984), Eduardo Saverin (born 1982), Andrew Collum, Dustin Moskovitz (born 1984) and Chris Hughes (born 1983).

Again, and to be clear, I am not suggesting that age by itself somehow determined the actions of the contestants. I am suggesting that the *habitus* and the 'mental structures' of key opponents of the SOPA were informed by the milieux (field) in which they spent their formative years, and those milieux were different in significant ways from those of the corporate and political community promoting the SOPA.

This mattered because many people in their sixties do not have the repertoire of knowledge and competencies needed to critically assess or to create content using the available technology compared to those born after the popularization of the Net, who tend to have this capacity and who have a better understanding of the language and the technologies used, the potential of this new 'networked public sphere'. This is of course only true as a general trend, and there were exceptions. One stand-out example of intergenerational collaboration and an exception to the age-related literacy norm for those who are 60 plus can be seen in the partnership between two founding editors of the Canadian *Adbuster* magazine. It is 69-year-old Kalle Lasn and 29-year-old Micah White who have been held responsible for launching and orchestrating the New York Occupy Wall Street protests (Gerbaudo 2012). What I am arguing is that the literacy levels for older people with regard to their ability to use the Net is the exception rather than the norm, and in the SOPA case this helps explain, in part, what happened. That difference between the two camps and its significance became increasingly apparent as the debate evolved.

At this point I note also that the SOPA debate was not drawn along simple party lines. Opposition to SOPA proved to be bipartisan, with support coming from both Democrats and Republicans or Left and Right.

New politics?

How can we understand this turn of events? Was this an example of democratic renewal or a new kind of politics?

One feature of the campaign against the SOPA was the absence of formal organizational structures on the part of the opposition. This is often the case with digital political processes. There was never any central coordinating body, leadership structure or organizational hierarchy. Like the Occupy Wall Street movement, the self-directed and spontaneous character of the action made it different to embrace or use more traditional models of political organization and action (Gerbaudo 2012).

What happened was the result of an unplanned, yet very real, intersection of various autonomous political projects drawn together by a network of deliberation and critique and the sharing of a common interest, namely preserving the free character of the Internet, which is usually referred to as the principle of 'Net neutrality'. That said, Cramer provides a powerful critique of some of the peculiar ways the libertarian and right-wing opponents of the SOPA understood the principle of Net neutrality (2013).[15] The networked public sphere provided new and effective methods of engaging in flexible, fast communication that fostered an assembly of groups and individuals, interacting and constantly swapping information and ideas. It also provided a formidable way of organizing political action. What resulted was an arrangement that enabled participants to be less constrained by standard bureaucratic requirements of traditional politics such as administrative control or the pursuit of approval for action from boards of management and consensus (Gerbaudo 2012). And perhaps this in part explains why the anti-SOPA alliance was able to move so swiftly and nimbly in taking action and in opening up new space for deliberation. In this way we observed a relatively new style of organizing politics in play, one that was also reliant on new media and that incorporated elements of old and new politics.

Another significant feature of the anti-SOPA campaign was the way it drew on new sensibilities related to freedom and creativity offered by the Net and the responsibility to foster this freedom and creativity using the affordances of the Net (Kelty 2008). Groups like the Free Culture

Movement, Creative Commons, Fight for the Future, the Internet Defense League, Question Copyright, the free software movement and the 'free music movement' were just some of the groups making up a 'collective' of interest groups. All were and are dedicated to the promotion of digital rights and an 'ethos of freedom' to share and create works using digital media, and to support protest actions aimed at securing those ends. As such they oppose the social harm caused by distribution monopolies. They treat traditional copyright law as an obstacle to knowledge production and artistic, scientific and business creativity and innovation.

Yet as I argue here, the case of Lessig is illustrative of a larger complex point. What we saw in the opposition to the SOPA was a mixture of new and old politics.

Founder of *Creative Commons*, and an influential law academic whose analysis of the legal underpinnings of the Net architecture (which he calls Code 1.0 and Code 2.0) has been influential, Lessig ostensibly epitomizes aspects of a new approach to creativity. *Creative Commons* is an NGO established by Lessig, (born 1961), Abelson (born 1947) and Eldred (born 1943) in 2001. *Creative Commons* has its headquarters in California, and is devoted to expanding the range of creative works available for others to own legally and to share. The organization has released several copyright licenses known as 'Creative Commons licenses' free of charge to the public. By 2008, there were an estimated 130 million works licensed under the various Creative Commons licenses, which allow creators to communicate which rights they reserve and which rights they waive for the benefit of recipients or other creators. Creative Commons licenses do not replace copyright, but are based upon it. They replace individual negotiations for specific rights between the copyright owner (licensor) and licensee, which are necessary under an 'all rights reserved' copyright management, with a 'some rights reserved' management employing standardized licenses for reuse cases in which no commercial compensation is sought by the copyright owner. The result is an agile, low-overhead and low-cost copyright-management regime, profiting both copyright owners and licensees. Wikipedia uses one of these licenses.

While Lessig was not himself a prominent player directly involved in the anti-SOPA campaign, he has played a decisive role in shaping the politics of opposition over the preceding decades as an advocate for Net freedom. This might suggest that Lessig's approach to online creativity is the harbinger of a new political or social imaginary. Is there here an underpinning for a new kind of politics? It is difficult to answer this in a simple yes or no way.

On first appearances Lessig, who established *Creative Commons* and is skeptical of government intervention, appears to be an unconventional libertarian. (He clerked for both Richard Posner and Antonin Scalia).[16] He also calls himself a 'constitutionalist' who believes that the modern American republic has been corrupted.

With one foot in the tradition of republican political theory represented by Aristotelian and Roman political theory, and the other in the twenty-first-century Internet, Lessig is not so much heralding a new politics as advocating for a hybrid politics.

I note here how republican theory is characterized by a preoccupation with liberty or freedom and the fear of political corruption based on dependence. This is a dominant concern of the modern republican tradition, from Machiavelli through to Americans like Thomas Jefferson and Gore Vidal.

Contemporary republican political theory has been given fresh life by a group of writers – Skinner, Viroli and Pettit – who define liberty as the absence of dependence. According to Pettit,

> Being unfree consists rather in being subject to arbitrary sway: being subject to the potentially capricious will or the potentially idiosyncratic judgment of another. Freedom involves emancipation from any such subordination, liberation from any such dependency. (1997, p. 5)

Lessig's concerns about 'dependence corruption' are linked to concerns about the gross inequality that has emerged in the United States over the last 30 years. His view is that this inequality is not just the result of market forces (he is not opposed to inequalities developing in the free market) but also of government interventions into the economy purchased by lobbyists. Enormous wealth transfers have occurred because of state capture in the form of institutional 'dependence corruption' largely created by the demands of campaign fundraising.

Fighting against overreaching legislation like the SOPA is all well and good, Lessig says, but it is just another twisted branch from the tree of corruption that is the American political system. To do any good, it is best to focus on its rotten core: the moneyed interests that have hijacked the inner workings through corporate lobbying, favors-for-favors campaign financing and other under-the-table deals. Whether one is looking at wealth disparity, the environment or even the recent rash of violent police action against peaceful protesters, it can all be traced back to the folks for whom the government truly works:

the problem with our government is that we have a Congress that's dependent upon funders. And that dependency leads Congress to do things they otherwise wouldn't be doing – spending time worried about bank swipe fees rather than unemployment or budget deficits. It also leads Americans to believe that Congress is just bought, as the vast majority of Americans believe, which makes them cynical and less engaged, and therefore leaves the fox guarding the hen house. That's not a corruption violating any federal law, that's a corruption that I call 'dependency corruption'. (Lessig 2011)

Unlike those who see corruption merely as instances of individual abuse of public office, Lessig sees a more pernicious form of corruption caused by a systemic misalignment of dependence. To use one of his favorite metaphors, the framers of the US Constitution meant for representatives to be dependent on the people alone, just as a compass is dependent on the earth's magnetic field. But the current system is akin to a compass in which the casing has been magnetized, causing the needle to deviate from north – there is a miscalibrated dependence. Lessig thus expresses the view that the republic has been 'lost'. The remedy is a (limited) return to origins, with a new constitutional convention:

When government disappears, it's not as if paradise will take its place. When governments are gone, other interests will take their place. ... My claim is that we should focus on the values of liberty. If there is not government to insist on those values, then who? The single unifying force should be that we govern ourselves. (Lessig 1998)

Lessig's solution is to realign this dependence through a scheme to democratize campaign finance without either limiting speech or suffering from the problem of other public financing laws in which people's taxes pay for speech with which they disagree.

Finally, it seems in this way the anti-SOPA campaign was different from many other contemporary actions that were as reliant on new media as it was to inform and mobilize dissent. The anti-SOPA campaign was not like the Occupy Wall Street Movement, the 2011 Spanish *indignados* protests (15 M Movement) or the London student protest movement. Unlike these campaigns, the SOPA campaign was not mobilized in opposition to neoliberalism or in protest to the effects of the global financial crisis and to austerity measures. In the SOPA case, it was not about taking on the power of the corporate sector. On the contrary, some of the key players in the SOPA opposition were 'new capitalists' themselves who joined forces with a diverse range of individuals and groups to advance their own interests. They joined forces to create a plurality of unusual, if not an incongruous assembly of, players. This produced a coalition grounded in multiple interests that would in many settings clash. I refer for example to the unusual mixture of multinational companies – new businesses – dedicated to securing their own and American global economic dominance, aligned with new media activists of various kinds.

These included anarchists, hackers typically opposed to capitalism, a medley of (e.g., promoters of open-source software), members of 'a techno-utopia political culture' (e.g., hacker groups like Anonymous) and more 'respectable' university-based research centers. It was what might be best described as a rich political bricolage brought together by a shared commitment that overcome their substantial differences, which led to cooperation based on a common and explicit interest in securing Net freedom.

Conclusion

The SOPA case involved on the one hand an alliance of traditional power holders comprised of experienced Washington policy makers who joined forces with the equally long-standing and powerful Hollywood entertainment industry and a number of fellow travelers, all of whom were united by their interest in regulating the Internet and securing the status quo. On the other there was a loose coalition of relatively new e-businesses (Google, Wikipedia, Facebook) specializing in Internet services and products. These entities along with thousands of other smaller businesses, associations, interests groups and individuals formed a cohesive and powerful opposition alliance against the bill.

Most of those incorporated into this opposition were well equipped in terms of their intellectual capital as it related to digital technology and new modes of political communication. This stood in stark contrast to the relative absence of these qualities in proponents of the legislation. It was something that played a key role in the defeat of the SOPA as its supporters incriminated themselves and caused major embarrassment to themselves by having to admit to ignorance about the practical and political implications of their proposal.

9
The Digital, Indigenous Art and Politics

Roebourne, or what the Ngarluma people call Ieramugadu, is the oldest township established in 1866 as a 'non-Aboriginal town' in the remote Pilbara region of Western Australia (Edmunds 2012). It is some 1,500 kilometers north on the North West Coastal Highway from Perth, one of the most isolated large cities in the world.[1] The Pilbara is home to about 50,000 people, most of whom live in and around small urban centers like Roeburne, Port Hedland, Karratha and Newman.

The Pilbara is an elongated rectangular region that runs from the coast along the Indian Ocean deep into the interior of northwest Australia. It is a vast region stretching over 502,000 square kilometers, covering ancient mountain ranges, craggy precipices and deep gorges estimated to be at least three to four billion years old.[2] The dominant color of the land is a deep red-ochre sharply contrasting with the deep cobalt blue cloudless sky. Dry and hot for most of the year, the countryside can change abruptly win winter and spring with flushes of color and life that blossoms into impressive displays of wild flowers that spring from nowhere, then disappear as fast as they arrived. The coast is also littered with estuaries, mangrove systems and billabongs, creating wetlands that in the cyclone season can become floods, and which sustain a rich ecosystem that sustains a diversity of fish and other life (Barber 2005).

The Pilbara is also the site of several important contemporary cultural projects involving young indigenous (Ngarluma) people's using the new digital media. One of these is the Big hART 'Yijala and Yala' project and involves the production of an interactive digital comic series called the *Neomad*, a title that, among other things, playfully reworks the older idea that Australian Aboriginals once were 'nomads'. Another contemporary cultural project is the body of video work being produced by

Tyson Mowarin, a Ngarluma man from the Pilbara. According to one Australian government website Mowarin is a

> a digital storyteller from the Murujuga coastal region of north west Australia, [[whose use of] technology] has become the medium that could help ensure his ancient cultural traditions and language flourish well into the future. (Australia Unlimited 2013)

Both projects are supported by funding from Woodside Energy Ltd., one of the world's largest producers of liquid natural gas, which is engaged in extracting oil and natural gas from the Northwest Shelf. As part of a mining agreement with the Australian government, Woodside pays $434 million to support cultural heritage in the Dampier Archipelago and Burrup Peninsula region of western Australia. Some of that money is being used to fund these indigenous cultural projects.

These projects produced by young people speak to cross-cultural engagements and social interactions mediated by new media technologies. But what do they say? Do they tell us anything about Ngarluma culture or being Ngarluma? Given a long history of difficult political relations between indigenous people and a larger, dominant 'white' culture characterized since the 1850s by white 'settlement' and black dispossession 'justified' by a complex mélange of 'white' racial assumptions and policies, what are the political issues at stake in these projects?

Given the long-standing practice of seeing modern media as a vehicle for Western cultural imperialism and sociopolitical domination, what, if anything, do these projects imply for the politics of Aboriginal-nonindigenous relations (Tomlinson 1991, Said 1993, Hamm 2005)? There are also questions about the relationship between 'traditional' and 'modern' culture given the tradition of social inquiry into the role of communication media as a mode of 'imagining and imaging communities'.[3]

Can we see these projects as new practices and new forms of cultural production that inquire into what it means or be indigenous (Deger 2006, p. xix)? Do the Ngarluma people display what Deger says is evident with another Northern Territory indigenous community, the Yolngu, who work with new media: it is not 'a loss of culture nor of the Yolngu becoming Western [so much as evidence of] the enduring genius of the Yolngu imagination' (2006, p. xx)?

Do these projects say anything about the interplay between media, technology, perceptions and our imagination – particularly when we consider the work of Castoriadis and Appadurai (1996)? What role, if any, can these projects play in ameliorating the common Aboriginal experience of a loss of agency, purpose and dignity, respect, direction and hope?

In short, what value do practices using new technologies taken from the dominant culture have in promoting – or diverting – a politics aimed at enhancing Aboriginal moral autonomy?

Before I address these questions by engaging my heuristic, I provide some local context.

The context

The history of the Pilbara, like much of Western Australia, and Australia generally, is one of dramatic change in the way of life of people who lived in the region for around 45,000 years before confronting a process of dispossession that began in the 1860s.[4] Indigenous Australian people are heirs to a rich tradition of cultural activity going back perhaps 45,000 years and are the custodians of a land hosting the world's highest concentration of ancient Aboriginal petroglyphs, or images, etched into hard rock and paintings of people and now-extinct animals, as well as ceremonial sites (Department of Environment n.d.).

The first dispossession of the people living in the Pilbara began with the British pastoralists who started trekking overland from Queensland in the 1860s, a process that peaked in the 1880s. It was a time when pastoralists expected the large populations of local people to provide a plentiful supply of cheap labor (Bolton 1958, p. 28). At the same time, governments and experts confidently expected Aboriginal people to die out. This view drew on a social evolutionary perspective that condemned the 'Aboriginal race' to *'predestined* extinction' due to either an assumed racial extinction, or *a new* admixture which gradually filtered out the 'black blood' (Francis 2009, p. 94).[5]

As it eventuated, the indigenous people in the Pilbara were not exterminated, but did experience dramatic change. Pastoralists like John Forrest, who established a 230,000-hectare station called Minderoo in 1878, used the legal power granted to them by colonial governments, which led to the indigenous people's giving up their traditional hunter-gatherer lifestyle.[6] This was done by coercing them into station camps on the pastoral stations and pressing them into service by requiring them to labor for basic food and clothing rations. In effect the government licensed a system of indentured labor in the pastoral (and pearling) industries for Aboriginals in the Pilbara around 1900, which Olive (2007), for example, describes as slavery.

Complaints about European violence and mistreatment saw Australian governments pass legislation in 1905 abolishing the unlimited power given to pastoralists over Aboriginals and shifting responsibility for their protection to government agents. Like many remote Australian country towns, a de-facto apartheid system was also established in key townships like Roebourne and Karratha that included curfews and the confinement of Aboriginal people to out-of-town native reserves.

Yet the Pilbara, even in the first half of the twentieth century, was unusual. In spite of, or perhaps because of the reliance by pastoralists on a regime of severe punishment to maintain discipline, the first strike by indigenous people in Australia took place in 1946 in the Pilbara (Olive 2007). It was a strike that lasted over three years and saw Aboriginal pastoral workers walk off the stations in protest of low pay and bad working conditions. This was action that points to a region with an unusual history of politicized activity.

The second major process of transformation began in the 1970s, when vast reserves of iron ore, oil and natural gas were discovered in the region. Today the region is primarily known for its rich supply of natural resources (iron ore, natural gas and oil), the mining of which has generated hundreds of billions of dollars for the Australian economy and lined the pockets of some of the biggest companies and wealthiest people in Australia, like Gina Reinhart and Andrew 'Twiggy' Forrest.

The Pilbara became the site of a complex interaction between mining companies that took advantage of these discoveries and more politicized communities of indigenous people motivated by national black civil and land rights movements of the late 1960s.

In 1967, the Australian government bowed to popular support and agreed to count Aboriginals in the census and give them voting rights as citizens, but not land rights. In 1972, four young Aboriginal activists planted a beach umbrella on the lawns in front of the Australian Parliament in Canberra, sat under what they called the Aboriginal Tent Embassy and began a protest against the Australian government's refusal to recognize Aboriginal land rights (Feltham 2004). In 1992, after ten years of court cases, the High Court, in the *Mabo vs. Queensland* case, formally determined that Aboriginal people had native land title rights.[7] Given that local people in the Pilbara had stayed to live and work on the pastoral stations until 1966, a strong case could be made for native title. When native title became a possibility, the boundaries of each language group became a recognized geographical reality, and claims were registered with the National Native Title Tribunal. At the start of the twenty-first century, indigenous people numbering around 6,000 (out of a total population of 50,000 in the Pilbara) were still pressing their claims for land rights. People identifying variously as the Innawonga, the Banyjima and the Nyiyaparli peoples made a native title claim under the name chosen for their representative body, 'Gumala', meaning 'All Together'. The Ngarluma and Yindjibarndi people, the original landowners of Roebourne and the surrounding area, were granted native title in 2005.

Yet while some progress on land rights was made, most of the indigenous people were excluded from the economic benefits of mining in the Pilbara. The Pilbara is crucial to Australia's long-running resources boom. Twenty-four of the 34 mines currently operating in Western Australia are in the Pilbara, with production capacity in the Pilbara totaling 478 million metric tons per month.[8] In 2013, the value of Western Australia's mineral and petroleum sector reached a new record of $113.8 billion, which was 15% above 2012 (Western Australian Government 2013). The succession of mining booms meant new mining towns and large numbers of people flocking into the Pilbara as short-term, fly-in-fly-out mining company employees working block rosters, as employees of allied infrastructure businesses like ports and rail systems earning very large wages, and as government Aboriginal 'support workers'.

As mining companies like BHP Billiton, Fortescue Mining Group and RioTinto have acknowledged, the continued development of the Pilbara as a site of tremendous mining wealth has largely bypassed the indigenous people.[9] While the mining boom encouraged some changes to social sensibilities, which saw indigenous people relocated from the fringe camps into the towns, the local people did not get significant economic benefits from the mining industry. In 2005, for example, Rio Tinto commissioned a study that highlighted the persistent levels of economic exclusion of indigenous people from employment in the Pilbara region. In response, that company thought the solution was to initiate an Indigenous Employment Strategy encompassing education and support programs, mentoring and cross-cultural awareness training. This strategy included the development of land use agreements with Pilbara Traditional Owners, which was focused on strengthening a mutual commitment to increasing the employment and work-readiness levels of Pilbara Aboriginal people. By 2010, of the 12,000 people employed by BHP Billiton in its Pilbara operations, 700 were indigenous. Rio Tinto, in 2010, was employing 700 indigenous workers in its Pilbara operations, comprising 6% of its overall workforce. Government social security benefits have long provided a stable, albeit meager, income for most local indigenous people.

Whatever efforts, genuine or token, mining companies made to address the exclusion of indigenous people from the new economy, the people were concerned about the noneconomic impacts of mining, some of which went directly to their cultural identity, others to the impact on the land.

There have been significant debates about the virtues of having the area heritage listed, and disputes about threats to the natural environment and to heritage sites posed by further industrialization, tourism and old-fashioned vandalism like graffiti.[10] For local volunteer groups like Friends of Australian Rock Art (FARA), the presence of the mining industry presented a major threat to their cultural heritage:

> nearly 20 per cent of the rock art precinct has been destroyed or disturbed in recent decades to make way for the Northwest Shelf gas processing plant, a fertiliser plant and other industry activity on the Burrup. (Hugo – Chair, cited in Laurie 2012)

Hugo continues to warns that more will disappear as petroleum companies like Woodside bring more gas offshore on at Burrup peninsula and if explosive plants are built on the Burrup by other oil and gas corporations.

Indigenous communities are divided on the value of mining. Local communities have been engaged in debating how to relate to multinational mining companies like RioTinto and Australian companies like Fortescue Metal Groups. Some local communities, as local native title-holders, remain divided over the wisdom of accepting millions of dollars and other royalty payments and 'incentives' from mining companies in exchange for access to their land and the extraction of resources. Other communities have welcomed mining and seen benefits like financial payment and training by profiting from their hard-won land rights and the land's valuable resources, replete with moral justifications about individualism and how their 'participation' in the mining booms provides a way of reducing the kinds of social problems found in many indigenous communities.

Finally, indigenous communities still struggle with the consequences of a long history of racialized interactions in the Pilbara. In the 1980s, Roebourne was infamous for the incidence of Aboriginal deaths in police custody. Many of the communities with significant Aboriginal populations continue reporting abuse of alcohol and other substances (petrol sniffing), as well as major social problems like high rates of family violence.

Some of these debates center on the impact of Western economic and cultural practices on local culture and kinship ties and whether the new economy will solve what some neoliberal commentators call 'welfare dependency' by restoring respect and autonomy or whether it will exacerbate these problems. If we accept the assumptions embedded in problem-setting activities that locate the various 'problems' described as 'welfare dependency' arising in 'failed' societies this 'neoliberal' normalization option is presented as a solution.

Others, however, think the market solution to welfare dependency is not so rosy an option and that the adoption of a neocolonial-cum-neoliberal worldview by some Aboriginal people is likely to cut the taproot of kinship and cultural duties and obligations. Framing the problems facing indigenous communities as internal to Aboriginal culture or seeing Aborigines as incapable of self-government is unhelpful.

Here we see traces of a familiar binary of alternatives said to define the future of indigenous peoples of Australia: hang on to tradition and the Dreamtime or give it all up and accept a Western lifestyle, economic integration and sensibility. This binary choice has its neoliberal advocates, like Noel Pearson, who argue for the embrace of modernity, as well as its Aboriginalist advocates, who urge the retention of tradition.

Pearson is a key indigenous leader from the Cape York Peninsula and has long promoted a key plank of neoliberalism: governments need to get out of the way so individuals can take responsibility:

> If individuals, families and communities are going to take charge or their own future, then there has to be a displacement of responsibility by those who've filled the gap. Bureaucracy has got to retreat. ... Because of our passivity, other people have intervened [and] government service delivery and government intervention ... disempowered our people. (Pearson 2005, p. 5)

For Pearson, this involves accepting another key element in neoliberalism, namely ending the 'culture of welfare dependency', which he says means 'we've got to refute the idea that we have an inalienable right to dependency. We don't have an inalienable right to dependency' (2005, p. 6).[11] For Pearson, this means acknowledging that if there is a tension between economic integration and retaining a culture that is based on 'a strong inherited and ongoing connection to ancestral lands', then the lesson across the world that all attempts to create societies that are not integrated with metropolitan centres of economic growth and culture have failed. (p. 3)

For Altman, who is an advocate for 'sustainable Aboriginal enterprise',

white Australia has bought the now-dominant narrative that self determination has been a failure and that it is high time that Aboriginal individuals take responsibility. This is a message promulgated by Noel Pearson and echoed in the nationally-dominant Murdoch media (where Pearson has a regular column). (2011, p. 1)[12]

On the other side of the binary, writers like Davidson (2011) and Langton (2012) argue that the market model will exacerbates the problems facing indigenous people. The lure of mining money will increase dependency – and become 'a sexier version of welfare':

if wealth earned from mining can bring about solutions to community problems, then perhaps it is worth chopping up a Dreaming story, trashing a piece of wild and stunning coastline, fencing off some rock art. The tragedy would be if, in fifty years time, the problems had not been much solved and people had lost those deep connections to country, to that other way of interpreting the world. (Davidson 2011)

Langton, another key indigenous leader, argues that

Mining is the only significant industry in remote [indigenous] communities and dependence on it may leave these communities in a precarious position when operations stop. High levels of dependence on mining can be detrimental for indigenous and rural and regional communities, so development aimed at increasing economic diversity is needed. (2012, p. 1)

These alternatives help define the context of the projects in this chapter. What exists is a lack of consensus about these issues on the part of local indigenous communities.

Both the Yijala Yala Project and Tyson Mowarin's work highlight important and complex issues about the online media, the nature of politics and the role of generational factors. These projects are thrown into sharp relief within a setting characterized by the long-term, often traumatizing, effects of a racialized *habitus* central to a field of asymmetrical power relations and interactions between black and white people in the Pilbara.

There is no doubt that long-standing black-white relationships and administrative and policing practices like curfews underscore how the persistence of racist assumptions can discourage indigenous people from imagining new or choosing between alternatives that are not framed by the apparently contrasting choices of embracing either tradition or modernity.

Or can we, as Edmunds suggests, see these projects as elements in a historical moment as a local indigenous community 'encounters modernity' and decides to accept an alternative hybrid option that entails reimagining a culture (2011)? As Edmunds explains, this is an imagining that has been tried by other indigenous communities and requires a capacity to picture ethical values that 'would be needed to overcome despair and lead a meaningful life in a new world'. It is an option to which a philosopher like Nussbaum also appeals in her arguments about human development (Nussbaum 2010). It may be that the case studies offered here provide some insight into what such a reimagined indigenous culture entails.

I now turn to the task of providing a short descriptive account of the work of Tyson Mowarin and then of the Yijala Yala Project.

Tyson Mowarin

Tyson Mowarin is a young Ngarluma man, now in his early thirties, who makes video film, interactive storybook cartoons, blogs and websites.[13] He says he uses the new media to reclaim and promote indigenous knowledge and culture. He is the creative director of The Digital Dreamtime Project, which incorporates a number of ventures like the iCampfire.tv, which is designed to promote storytelling. This is a web-based project

> designed to be what we call a 'Living Breathing archive of Aboriginal Culture and History' as opposed to a sleeping archive like a traditional library so that we can document, create and use our knowledge today and not just in the distant future ensuring that our knowledge is still used daily. (Mowarin, 2012)

Mowarin also founded Weerianna Street Media, which is an indigenous company whose main activities are to promote learning about local culture, to enhance the 'indigenous experience', to collect and record traditional landowners' language and other aspects of culture, and to fuse all that with new media. It does this by engaging local communities and corporate businesses to create art in forms such as film and photography.

Mowarin worked at the Ngarluma Aboriginal Corporation in Roeburne and produced material for indigenous television (the Yaarnz program) and wrote and directed a series of short films, including *Mabuji* and *Ngurra Wanggau*, for national television. Other films he wrote and directed include love stories, like *Ngurra Wanggagu*, which is set in the Pilbara and which offers an intimate portrait of a Pilbara family as they spend their day fishing and traveling across country to visit friends.

In 2012, he screened a documentary that records other aspects of indigenous life. This time it was the practice of spearmaking in the film *Jurdi Jurdila*, for which he won an award in cinematography. To do this, he filmed his cousins walking 'the country', locating the right kinds of woods to make spears (Leahy 2012).

Ngurrara iPad comic

Another part of Mowarin's project has been his interactive storybook called *Ngurrara*. This has been produced in collaboration with his nonindigenous Big hART Yijala Yala Project illustrator, Stuart Campbell.[14] The project was financially supported by the mining company Woodside Pluto, courtesy of a Conservation Agreement brokered by the Australian government.

Mowarin also created a series of iPad apps that include the small children's graphic novel mentioned above, *Ngurrara: A Ngarluma Story*, and a 'welcome to country' app. This app takes the form of a short video showing some of the protocols used in some communities as a custodian of the land makes a statement showing respect to the traditional landowners, to welcome visitors or greet people at the openings of special events (Mowarin 2012. Finally, as a composer of music he wrote 'Murru's Our Ways, Our Stories', which is performed by indigenous singer John Bennett and which was nominated for the West Australian Music Industry Association's WAM Song of the Year in the Indigenous category (see also his CD of songs, *BLACKLOCK*, on local Gumala Radio). Aside from digital media, Mowarin is also involved in setting up a new family business, Buriyamangga Enterprise Pty Ltd, to supply a database of indigenous workers for fields like mining and civil earth works, public transport and project management.

The Big hART Yijala Yala Project and Neomad

Big hART is a not-for-profit Australian art company founded in Burnie (Tasmania) in 1992, which has initiated a large number of community arts development projects. Since 2000, it has supported more than 15 projects, many in Tasmania and in remote outback settings in the Northern Territory and Western Australia. In 2010, it established the Yijala Yala Project in Roebourne.[15] The Big hART Yijala Yala Project began promoting indigenous art as an evolving, living culture (Big hART 2013). As Edmunds explains,

> They did this using film, text, translation, recordings, songs, music, iPad apps, NBN focused material, photography, and performance. Over 300 workshops were held in the first year, with over 25 adults and 250 young people, including workshops at the prison and school. A women's choir produced a Christmas DVD for 2010. In 2011, four Roebourne people went as part of the Big hArt contingent to the International Community Arts Festival in Rotterdam. And in July 2011, Yijala Yala, involving performance, film by and with young people, and music was presented at the Woodside Plaza auditorium in Perth. It was just one part of an ongoing process in what the participants refer to as the Cultural Resources Boom. (2012, p. 167)

While it received initial funding from the federal government's Department of Families, Housing, Community Services, and Indigenous Affairs (FaHCSIA), it now receives much of its funding from Woodside Energy Ltd.[16]

The *Neomad* series, which is one component of the larger Yijala Yala Project, brings together Australian Aboriginal children aged between 10 and 15 years, indigenous elders and non-Aboriginal creative workers to produce stories about the past, present and future that are told through new media, using interactive comics and games and videos. It is an intergenerational and cross-cultural project that has local children and their communities working with Big hArt Youth Workers and professional artists like cartoonist Sutu (Stuart Campbell), producers (Deb Myer) and other artists and technicians.

The Yijala Yala Project adapts stories from the local indigenous communities by scripting and creating animated interactive comics and storybooks like *Neomad*.[17] This is 'interactive fiction' that links elements of a video, a game and a book to a website and is available as an iPad app. It also involves a mix of graphics animation and live-action film. Young indigenous children have worked with Big hART youth workers and creative workers to create interactive digital comics and online games featuring two sets of characters, the boy *Love Punk* gang and the girl *Satellite Sisters* gang. They are described as a 'motley crew' of 'tech-savvy' heroes who take off on epic adventures and find themselves confronted by terrifying creatures. The two small gangs of brave and 'intrepid travellers' bent on doing good in the world and fighting 'the good fight' carry messages from wise characters like 'little Bird man' about important issues, such as the need to keep a balance between industry and nature. They are identifiable by their punk gear and distinctive face paint – rather like the teenage Mutant Ninja Turtles (Whispering Gums 2014).

Set over three episodes, Neomad follows the story of the Love Punks and the Satellite Sisters, techno savvy young heroes from a futuristic Roebourne in the Pilbara region of Western Australia, who speed through the desert full of spy bots, magic crystals and fallen rocket boosters branded with a mysterious petroglyph.

When you click 'Play' on the home page, it starts with a live-action sequence set somewhere in the Pilbara, involving a group of indigenous boys. They are the Love Punks and they feature in Episode 1. They tell us, 'When you see a star fall at night, be sure to welcome it to the land for the star brings new life'. The story is set in 2076 and concerns the Love Punks who chase a space robot (oops, space bot) across the sky, only to find, when it crashes to earth, that it bears the image of an ancient petroglyph. What does this mean? Episode 2 begins with quite a different live-action sequence involving the *Satellite Sisters*, who are indigenous girls, learning about the importance of their ancestors. Like Episode 1, this sequence progresses into an animated comic, which you can read as text or click on the speech bubbles to hear the characters speak the words.

The aim of the Yijala Yala Project is to connect 'people to place through animation and storytelling...'. It is the 'telling, retelling, and transformation of stories through new mediums [that] connects younger generations with their cultures, and honours the knowledge passed down from Elders' (Yijala Yala Project 2014). They also want to enable local children to flourish by providing opportunities for creativity, by encouraging learning that includes teaching various literacies (linguistic, mathematical, media). The birth of the boy *Love Punk* gang and the girl *Satellite Sisters* gang involves animated characters and live-action sequences based on the children's own lives. The children helped produce and they act in the Neomad productions, are trained in the use of Photoshop and become well practiced in patiently cutting images frame by frame to help create the stories.

Those running the project also say they want to animate and support the interest of Aboriginal children in being part of their culture. The narratives have their roots in 'dreamtime' stories, tales imbued with Aboriginal iconography, descriptions of the land and waterways, sacred sites and spirits, all of which are fused with nonindigenous modern imagery. It is a project that relies on interactions between different generations and that taps into ancient mythology along with the life-worlds, imagination and voice of local children.

Project leaders also talk about building a rich milieu in which indigenous children have access to basic social goods and opportunities to choose what they value, including prospects for future employment. Finally, as a community development project, they want to enable young participants to have a say about who they are, about their identity as young people capable of engaging with the world and enacting change through animation and new media in ways that are not exclusively defined by their Aboriginality and that open opportunities for them to connect with Asian and Western imaginaries.

How can these two projects be best understood? To address this question, I turn to my heuristic.

Generational politics?

There is no doubt that Tyson Mowarin's projects are animated by someone who is characteristically described as a 'member of the millennial generation' as he deploys a range of digital forms of interactive technologies. On the face of it, so too are the *Neomad* projects that involve young people, some of whom are quite young, who use digital interactive technologies. On closer examination, however, the *Neomad* project suggests that it can less readily be described as the work of the young people as their role is largely defined for them by adults and by the ethos of a larger long-term project called Big hArt.

The argument presented here is not straightforward.

Certain elements that shape the neoliberal imaginary in promoting conceptions and practices of community development seem to inform the *Neomad* project. They work to sustain an age-based hierarchy of power that defines the working relationships between community development workers and the young people whom they mentor, and that is typical of most relations between adults and young people and children.

At the same time, we also see a transforming interest operating in the creative work that makes the *Neomad* project a promising example of contemporary indigenous media work in spite of the structuring intentionalities of the community development project.

Big hArt as a community development enterprise?

The Yijala Yala Project is part of the Big hArt model, which belongs to an older traditional youth development model in which promoting genuine autonomy as a political quality defining young people is not a defining feature. As Rankin and Bakes acknowledge, while the role of young people is central to all Big hArt projects, it is a role determined and predefined by a community development discourse that assumes that disadvantaged or at-risk young people are social problems and that the explanation for this state of affairs is certain deficits of skills, knowledge or appropriate behavior on the part of the young people (1996). This model includes understanding disadvantaged young people within a 'welfarist' discourse of 'social problems' currently shaped by a neoliberal imaginary.

As Smyth et al. note, governments in Australia have invested heavily rhetorically and financially in community engagement activities since the 1980s (2009). For Smyth, 'community engagement' in Australia, and its variants like 'community capacity', 'social capital' and 'social inclusion' are among the ways a neoliberal state attempts to clean up or mitigate the adverse social effects of its own policies at a neighborhood level without having to give up on the neoliberal agenda.[18]

Big hArt belongs to a contemporary tradition of Australian 'community capacity building'. For advocates like Verity, this approach to community development is characterized by the 'empowerment of individuals and groups' within defined 'communities' that a 'progressive' person would find appealing (2007). This includes the development of 'skills, knowledge, and confidence', 'increased social connections and relationships', 'more responsive service delivery' and policies based on identified community needs and solutions (2007). Big hArt offers an example of community development in an era of neoliberal policymaking.

While community development has a long history of attempting to ameliorate the damage caused to those who are disposed or disadvantaged by the economic order, with the advent of neoliberalism in the late 1970s and early 1980s we saw an increase in demand for those interventions. The discursive deployment of 'community' as a seductive metaphor has also been augmented into talk of 'social capital' and become integrally related concept of 'social inclusion' as part of a government strategy to provide support. These are terms that have come to replace words like 'poverty' that governments and some others have become uncomfortable about using.

Since 2008, Australian social policy has been framed by a commitment to social inclusion that saw Australia aligned, somewhat belatedly, with policy imaginaries already widely, if variably, adopted in Europe and the United Kingdom. One reason for concern about this approach is the way its proponents tend to overlook the idea that local communities can act autonomously to express their needs, free from 'shaping' by the interests of government or from big corporations (Craig 2007).

This critique highlights the role of framing in how we understand and respond to experiences of poverty and social distress. In indigenous and nonindigenous communities alike, they variously frame a policy problem by reference to 'community breakdown' and 'loss of virtues' like civic mindedness and faith. This is a framing that makes the 'solutions' obvious: rebuild and reinstate the 'lost' shared ideals that hold society together through education and community development. While this framing has quite different implications for indigenous communities than it does for late modern heterogeneous multicultural communities, it is nonetheless highly effective in directing our attention away from the idea that social and political relations and patterns of exploitation embedded in the order might be central to the distress experienced by those who are not doing too well.

In this way, what are deemed to be authentically community-based or 'bottom-up' programs are state funded (in-house and outsourced), state-regulated programs veiled by discourses about promoting 'local autonomy and other communitarian values' that give the impression that the state is responsive and acting responsibly, but that actually work to obfuscate the political interests that inform relations between the recipients of services, the state and private corporate interests (Mowbray 2005, p. 257; see also McDonald and Marston 2002).

The popularization of the communitarian ethos that emerged in the 1980s and that inspired 'Third Way' thinking saw a revision of traditional social democratic concern about equality by emphasizing 'social capabilities' and by offering a mixture of economic liberal monetary policies with some regard for social equity. It relied on the language of morals to talk up social responsibility and reciprocal obligation, emphasizing community building, neighborhood renewal, reciprocal obligation and participation to counter the emphasis on rights. It has been a popular ethos that has been highly effective in delegitimating concern about moves to minimize the political agency of minorities and address ethnic-based inequalities.

Among the new meanings attributed to community is a neoliberal politics that serves 'to minimize state responsibility for the support', and that obfuscates 'the central individualist and contractual core of [the neo-liberal] regime of welfare' (McDonald and Marston 2002, p. 7). For Cass and Brennan, the idea of 'building community' provides a 'misreading of disadvantage' (2002). As they explain, such talk of 'community' implies the problems people experience are caused by deficits in 'their commu-nity' or themselves, which disguises the ways in which

> disadvantage is economically, politically and socially constructed by the operations of financial markets, labour markets and housing markets and by government economic and public policies. (p. 257)

What needs to be addressed, if we are serious about a decent society and good life for citizens, are 'the underlying market and policy causes of these unequal spatially concentrated distributions of income, capital and employment opportunities' (p. 257).

Finally, the contemporary preoccupation with evidence-based policy encourages community development enterprises to produce evidence that projects work, something that assumes such an exercise can provide an objective – scientific – assessment and that thereby adds legitimacy to claims that the interventions are effective in mitigating social distress and their causes.

Does Big hArt provide an example of contemporary neoliberal commu-nity development? Or are we seeing action that promotes the capacities of young indigenous people to articulate a felt sense of historic injustice that has a living legacy, or a demand that flows from various experi-ences of contemporary wrongs, to claim autonomy and political self-determination?

Big hArt reports regularly refer to 'young offenders and teenage victims of domestic violence' and other 'marginalised' and 'dysfunc-tional' young people who become the 'target' of their community devel-opment projects. The dysfunctions of the young people whom these programs target include educational deficits like a lack of basic skills, social deficits like school truancy, low self-esteem and self-harming behaviors like drug and alcohol abuse. Big hArt's development model also envisages that its adult workers and experts will address these defi-cits and become the source of 'advocacy and mentorship to achieve behavioral change' and enable 'increased options for people who are multiply disadvantaged'. This community development model positions the project as a professional and adult-led intervention. The Big hArt model itself requires two key people – an arts mentor and an organizer or producer. Participants work with the skilled mentor for 23 weeks in core groups of 20 (with up to 100 second-tier participants who are involved intermittently throughout the program). 'The mentor guides the participants through pathways of personal learning and skills development'.

The kinds of social relations and the power asymmetries in those relations are reflected in interviews with the creative workers who lead the Neomad project. These interviews represent the capacity for autonomous cultural production that is open to the young people. In an interview on his own blog, Stuart Campbell, or Sutu the Yijala Yala Project graphic artist-cum-teacher, describes his day behind the scenes in the making of *Neomad*:

> I wake up and go to the office, in 40 degrees weather outside. I have until 2 pm to smash out as much of my own work as possible and then after that we have the little kids running around who we try to teach Photoshop to. They color in the comics that we are working on together.

When asked about his current project, he described how he had been working on the Yijala Yala Project for the last two years, defining it as an intergenerational arts project based in Roebourne.

> I'm the Digital Media Producer, and I manage all of the digital media content. When I first arrived I didn't have a plan. So I met with the community and talked with them about what they wanted to do, and it became apparent straightaway that the kids were all passionate about video games, so the first project became about producing a video game titled 'Love Punks'. 14 main kids initially helped out. Over four months 50 kids created over 2000 frames of animation, which meant that they learn the skills, and become little Photoshop masters.

> It got picked up by a bunch of media and magazines around the world, we got so many unexpected positive results with it, and the community are really happy with it.

He continued:

> I have been working on the project Neomad... this is a 3 part series, sci-fi film, that has a similar theme to the Love Punks video game, to get the kids to be organically involved. The story goes from the dessert to the new cosmos. Every episode comes with a behind the scenes documentary, where the kids talk about the making of the comic which you can find it here which is now available on iTunes.

The 'main intention'

> was to go into the communities and get to know them and meet their families, as well as get them involved and interacting in our projects to establish a positive connection. The big motivator is if they want to be in the comic they have to colour themselves in. We draw the scenes and the kids colour them.

Referring to the national and global distribution of these stories, he explains,

> I was contacted by Bucheon International Comic Festival in South Korea and invited to exhibit my work for The Nawlze, I told them to check out the current project that I was working on Neomad. When I told them all about the project, they were excited and they mentioned that they had a kids comic festival in Bucheon, and that they would love for the Neomad kids to come over, so they paid for me and two of the kids from Roebourne to go over to South Korea, gave us a fancy hotel for a week, and gave us a spending allowance. The coolest thing was that I was one of three international guests, the other guests, included the Vice President of Marvel Comics, so we got to hang out with him for the week. Everyday I was going out with some amazing veteran like the Miyazaki's of comic writers in Korea it was like a weird dream. ... We aligned the first episode launch of the Neomad with the Bucheon International Comic Festival in South Korea, at the kids festival, that coincided with a two-day workshop where me and the Love Punks Nathaniel (Future Smash) and Maverick (Garruwara – Shooting Star) were teaching local kids how to draw their own characters, amongst a bunch of other international kids.

Big hArt is committed to providing evidence that its model works. It makes many quality assurance declarations about its efficacy as a welfare intervention that produces outcomes (Big hArt 1996, p. 4). It says it sees itself as providing

> 'life training' and self-affirming experiences for the projects' participants, whose experience of family, school, the labour market and the justice system has mostly been dysfunctional. (p. 8)

Big hArt measures its success by pointing to specific and quantifiable outcomes:

> Previous Big hART projects have resulted in a decreased incidence of vandalism and violent behavior. In one group of twenty participants, criminal activity decreased from one offence per week at the start of the project to one offence in ten months by its completion.

It also claims that

> Valuable outcomes for the participants include: improved mental/ emotional health; suicide prevention; family reintegration; crime prevention, vocational training and youth employment.

While these observations imply a critical view of the Yijala Yala Project, it is not a good idea to write it off because of what might be seen as a 'structure determines agency' explanatory or an analytic account that tends to conceive of human beings as automata following the dictates of 'social structures', leaving little room for political agency and the individual's critical capacity and moral choice. This requires theoretical explication that involves attention to indigenous media practice.

Indigenous cultural production and the politics of culture

In terms that resonate with Cornelius Castoriadis' account of change and the imaginary, Jay pointed to 'a paradigm shift in the cultural imaginary of our age' (1994, p. 3). This relates to the ways we understand what it means to live in a world known and experienced through images, especially since the late 1990s, when digital images became available on a scale and intensity without precedent.

On the one hand, Hamilton (1992)[19] argues that new digital and visual technologies involve turning from 'the rationalising modes of modernity...toward a different grasp of knowing itself' (1993, p. 5). Similarly Walter Benjamin and recent theorists like Michael Taussig (1993) provide an account of how *mimetic* reproductive media and technologies initiate a new 'kind of modernity'. Martin Heidegger's (1977) essays on 'The Question of Technology' and 'The Age of the World Picture' develop the idea that technologies 'enframe' the world, producing new relations between people and between people and things, which can objectify or master the world in ways that produce a new sensibility *and* an ontology. These writers emphasizes the idea that culture (and the recognition of cultural difference) is a product of history and technology. They understand phenomenologically that technologies like digital media mediate the relations we have with things and other humans *and* that the refractions of perception that these media create simultaneously produce a particular kind of world *and* sensibility for dealing with that world. Hamilton explains,

> what's on the emergent visual-aural culture of the twenty-first century creates the context for what is known and hence finally for what is. (1992, p. 5)

In short, they are sating that these technologies produce new experiences and knowledge that provide new foundations for culture and subjectivity.

On the other hand, 'nonrepresentational' thinking (Thrift 2009), or what Deger (2006, p. 35) refers to as the 'post-linguistic turn', has encouraged an investigation into relationships between ways of seeing, experiencing and engaging in the world *and* the production of subjectivity and power. In short, it moves us away from representational theory and the academic convention of trying to reveal and understand meanings and values that we then analyze, interpret to discover the ultimate representation – truth– and toward a disposition or focus on what happens, toward an interest in how life occurs through practice, through embodied movement and expressions of shared everyday experiences.

This interest in the gaze and surveillance was evident in Michel Foucault (1979) and Jacques Lacan (1978), and much of that work was inclined toward a semiotic strategy. Implicit in the new nonrepresentational framing is a move to bypass the linguistic and semiotic assumptions found in a lot of representational theory and the tropes of reading and decoding. That semiotic focus segued to an interest in the phenomenology of embodied experience and the visualizing of experience. In a context where the focus is on relations of power that operates between, for example, a dominant non-indigenous culture and indigenous communities and their cultures like Ngarluma, this shift includes an interest in 'the relations of looking' (Gaines 2000).

This paradigm shift has implications for thinking about indigenous art and politics. Predominantly the anthropological and political frame has seen 'indigenous culture' as passive and something 'acted on' by dominant Western or European technologies and media forms. Thus the relations of indigenous culture to Western culture mimicked the larger asymmetrical power relations operating between the West and relevant indigenous communities. Yet even as this complacent account was produced, minority and disenfranchised peoples in many parts of the world, often encouraged by anthropologists (e.g., Worth and Adair 1972), began experimenting with media production that was available as a result of the affordability and increased accessibility of portable media and recording equipment (Deger 2006, p. 37).

In Australia in 1982, the Australian Institute for Aboriginal and Torres Strait Islander Studies supported Michaels in studying the effect of television on remote Aboriginal communities. By 1986, however, Michaels had worked to help enable the Warlpiri community establish their own pirate radio and television facilities, and he was arguing against the cultural imperialist framework that was then dominant. The Warlpiri were reading Hollywood films and making television in ways that were informed by their own cultural dispositions and perspectives (1986). Michaels argued that the Warlpiri used the new technology to 'encode relationships and meanings' derived from the ancestral and make videos that were full of meaning and open to interpretation (Deger 2006, p. 39). Thus, rather than undermining traditional cultural practices and concerns, video and television production as it was used by the Warlpiri was enhancing the prospect of a 'cultural future' based on 'traditional values'.

Yet, as Deger's critique implies, Michael's account of a Warlpiri 'cultural future' grounded in their use of new media technology is countered by his framing assumptions (2006). According to Deger, Michaels continues to understand the Warlpiri people's lives and futures in terms defined by their links to and defense of tradition and the Dreamtime. She explains,

> In this way [Michaels] ended up reproducing the very things he was apparently trying to deconstruct, namely the dualistic categories of tradition and modernity, and the reification of the local and the traditional as the source of a cultural 'authenticity' that for so long

have underpinned the analytic logics of anthropology. (Deger 2006, p. 41)

Deger's solution to this difficulty was to try to understand indigenous ways of seeing and thinking that might help refigure or even transcend such conceptual binds (p. 41). Yet while this seems like a productive approach, Deger does not quite deliver on it. To begin, she uses and accepts the mimetic theory of Benjamin (1968) and Taussig (1992), two Western theorists, whose arguments are represented as universally valid. Secondly, and leaving aside Benjamin and Taussig, any attempt to shift to the use of Yolgnu categories seems to shift the difficulty associated with using a Western set of binary categories to a set of indigenous (in her case Yolgnu) categories, a problem made insoluble by her acceptance of the mimetic faculty thesis. Given that this is significant for my argument, it is important to clarify the mimetic faculty thesis.

The mimetic thesis

In a series of essays written in the 1930s, Benjamin argued that humans possess a universal and innate capacity to produce and recognize similarities – and by implication, differences (1978). This is the mimetic faculty. According to Benjamin, it affords a foundational mode of knowing and experiencing the world. As he explained, 'the gift of seeing resemblances is nothing other than a rudiment of the powerful compulsion in former times to become and behave like something else' (1978, p. 333). This faculty is central to human experience, especially in language and writing, and in other forms of creativity like dance, art and music. In his reflections on the technological mass production of images characteristic a time when analogue cameras (and printing) and now digital cameras (and the internet) allow the mass reproduction of static and moving images, Benjamin saw in the use of filmic technologies capacities to produce a 'new schooling for our mimetic powers'. Thus, for Benjamin the mimetic faculty is a combination of the sensuous and the cognitive, thereby rendering our experience of knowledge and the world, including our relations with other people and things, 'intelligible' and coherent.

Until the 1990s, the tendency in anthropology was to see mimesis among non-Western peoples as evidence of a premodern sensibility – or what earlier would have been seen as evidence of the 'savage mind'. A disposition to see the world in terms of 'non-sensuous similarity' (Benjamin 1978, p. 334), which involved finding correspondences and meaning in the shapes of clouds or the configuration of the stars, seemed to be evidence of a premodern or an uncritical cognitive style (Deger 2006, p. 86). Then Taussig's work appeared, which challenged that framing by taking Benjamin seriously, while offering a poststructuralist turn (1993). For Taussig, 'the ability to mime, and to mime well...is the capacity to Other' (1993, p. 19). As Deger (2006, pp. 86–87) and McGilchrist (2012, pp. 247–249) argue, the primacy of dealing with 'the Other' is central to Taussig's reworking of mimesis as opening new ways of understanding similarity and difference.

This approach allows Taussig to understand the intercultural relations and dynamics of power, perception, imitation and imagination that operate in fields of racialized habits. For Taussig, likeness needs difference to push against and recoil from: the self becomes itself through encounters with the other: difference is produced in the encounter with the same. Taussig's insight is that the attempt to copy (mimic) produces difference because all our attempts to mimic must fail to create the original for various reasons. The failures of copying are inherent to the act of mimesis resulting from the technologies available, be they crayon on paper or digital cameras producing images for the Internet. The copy can never *be* the original, no matter what effort is made. Copying does not destroy alterity (otherness); rather, it reveals it. Mimesis thus becomes a dynamic and complex process becoming a dialectical interaction as people are moved by the desire to be close to the other or to be the same by copying. This simultaneously negates and reconfigures distinctions between self and other, colonizer and colonized, or 'modern' and 'primitive' by emphasizing the relationships mediated through a mimetic dynamics of sameness and difference.[20]

To sum up: first, work by McGilchrist (2011) and Hofstadter and Sander (2013) summarizes several multidisciplinary research studies in neuroscience, cognitive theory, and cultural and anthropological studies that provide an evidentiary and theoretical base for seeing Benjamin's work and Taussig's work as prescient.[21] Second, it provides an insightful framing of the artistic work now being produced in the Pilbara, which can avoid the simplistic and unhelpful dualistic categories of 'tradition' and 'modernity'. Seeing Tyson Mowarrin's work or a project like the *Neomad* as examples of mimesis *and* alterity helps us be able to see better what is there.

Ngarluma digital and video projects as mimesis

The Yijala Yala Project and Tyson Mowarin share a few common interests that extend as far as collaboration on some projects. They include keeping local Aboriginal culture alive and dynamic by preserving and contributing their own creative work to their Aboriginal heritage. In this way they are acting politically in subverting conventional and popular ideas about 'real 'or 'authentic' Aboriginal art and the idea that culture is largely dead, and a static single, entity preserved in ancient rock art in a remote country. They do this by highlighting the ways in which Aboriginal art is alive and dynamic and can incorporate aspects of the new as well as aspects of other cultures. They do this by drawing on traditional indigenous stories passed on by elders, and/or by reimagining and recreating through old practices like storytelling and 'walking through country'. Sometimes this is done directly from one generation to the next within the community and in ways that are exclusively or predominantly indigenous in the case of Mowarin (and projects like the Ngurrara, a digital book that, as I explain below, involved the traditional practice and recalling and creating 'memory and stories'). Sometimes nonindigenous intermediaries have played a larger role (in the case of Big hArt), in which creative professionals-cum-youth workers work with children to create new stories and art in the form of comics and videos replete with customary iconography, tales of the land and creative spirits fused with more recent nonindigenous imagery (in the case of Neomad), all using contemporary art forms embedded in digital technology.

These bodies of work are political not only in the ways they subvert conventional notions of Aboriginal art but also in how they debate and challenge dominant social classification or narratives about identity – specifically 'Aboriginal identity'. I note that while there were opportunities also to subvert conventional classifications of the a 'child' or 'youth', the Yijala Yala Project seemed to affirm rather than contest the notion that children could do no or little more than color in and learn lines.

They contest the idea of a 'real' Aboriginal as dark skinned, living off the land in natural surroundings in remote Australia, and skilled in throwing boomerangs and hunting kangaroo or making baskets. They do this by demonstrating the multiple aspects of their own identity as savvy technicians skilled in the art of new media, by highlighting various 'nonindigenous' aspects of their identities, by highly they competent and critical people more than able to exercise political or moral agency.

All this I suggest is deeply political not only because they directly and indirectly participate in debates that contest meanings about Aboriginality, but also because those meanings influence the asymmetric power relations that typically characterize relations between indigenous people, the state and associated experts, and corporate participants. While the political consequences of this may be hard to determine immediately, they do hold some promise for changing the relationship between Aboriginal people, the state, nonindigenous people, and large, well-resourced and powerful mining companies.

Whether any of this results in a politics grounded in a 'felt sense of injustice' that generates resistance and the making of demands on the state or the corporate sector, or a process of political co-option, or some hybrid of both is yet to be determined. At the least, Habermas and his notion of 'human interests' provides a framework that can help us evaluate what is at stake as it distinguishes between three kinds of knowledge and the human interest they embody. There are those technical and calculative forms of knowledge that embody the instrumental interest in control; there are all those kinds of hermeneutic or interpretative knowledge that enact our interest in expressivity and sense making. Finally, there are those ways of knowing that arise out of our pursuit of liberation or emancipation as people seek to free themselves from deception, delusion and socially oppressive constraints that inhibit their freedom or capacity to flourish (1971).

To bring one political option into the frame, we might refer to action taken by the Zapatistas in 1994, a group predominantly comprised of rural Mayan indigenous communities in Mexico after the government appropriated large swaths of land (1.729 million acres) from the local people. In response, the Zapatistas quietly moved down from the mountains to capture a number of towns in southern Mexico that they occupied. They managed to hold Mexican soldiers at bay without weapons – only wooden replicas of guns. They then issued press releases explaining the issue that concerned them and how the unfair land distribution practices motivated their actions. The Zapatistas took a direct stand against neoliberalism and globalization, calling for land, proper housing, schools, jobs, fairs wages, roads and democracy (Jung 2008). The Mexican army retaliated, reoccupying the towns and killing many Zapatistas and a few civilians. The Zapatistas retreated and regrouped. Soon after the Mexican president, Salinas, declared a ceasefire, an agreement followed to engage in formal negotiations between the government and the Zapatistas.

The Zapatistas' action capitalized on networks of destitute people on the land, and in this way they share with many Australian Aboriginal people a concern for fair-minded land distribution and for it not to be sold off to multinational mining and pastoral and other shareholder companies. By 1996, the Mexican government and the Zapatistas concluded peace agreements governing relations between the state and indigenous people. The accord focused on indigenous rights, declaring that 'autonomy is the concrete expression of the exercise of the right to self-determination within the framework of...the national state'. The agreement stipulated that land would be allocated to indigenous people. As Jung explained, by 1996 the Zapatistas had framed their political claims in terms of indigenous rights, thereby binding the concerns of the poorest and most disposed sections of society to the 'cornerstone of Mexican political discourse. Of course, the struggle continued. The government reneged on its agreements and 'reformed' the legislation, repealing its commitment to land redistribution and instead privatizing the land. This, according to the Zapatistas made it easier for multinational corporations to secure the land and exploit resources. So, the struggle went on, and 20 years later Zapatista communities continue working to develop self-government and land rights (Jung 2008, p. 3).

Back to the Pilbrara. The practices identified in this chapter work to generate new Aboriginal identities and to renew local cultures. As they say they want to make a living growing culture. What we have seen is content that incorporates traditional and modern imaginaries replete with Western and Asian myths and popular culture icons. These are practices that encourage thinking, that counter stereotypes of Aboriginal culture and art as ancient, tribal and locked into the past. As Mowarin explains, his *Digital Dreamtime Project*

> has grown and evolved....It's more of what I like to call a living, breathing archive of culture and history, as opposed to a sleeping archive like a library. (Mowarin, cited in Howarth)

Using new media, Yijala Yala Project and Mowarin have established a continuum between the past, present and future, and have connected the local with the global.

He has also used digital technology to engage in politics as they are more narrowly defined, like critiquing the conduct of key political figures. Speaking about the traditional practice 'welcome to country', he observed the following of then-Prime Minister Kevin Rudd:

> Welcome to country is an ancient part of Aboriginal culture and has been used for a very long time when our ancestors used to travel through another tribal groups country or when they would meet up for ceremony. This is why it still happens today and we always acknowledge each other, more and more non-indigenous Australians are doing the same. I was disappointed when it appeared that former Prime Minister in all his good faith could say 'hello' in Mandarin at

the foot of the Great Wall of China but he could not say 'hello' at the foot of Uluru in the Country he is the leader of. (Mowarin 2012)

Similarly, digital media was employed to campaign against policies that erode indigenous culture and livelihood is another way that Mowarin and others have used new media politically, to lobby against policies like the importation of 'Aboriginal products' made overseas in places like China, which are then exported globally, including to Australia (http:// www.gopetition.com/petitions/import-ban-of-aboriginal-products/ signatures-page21.htm).

The Yijala Yala *Neomad* project draws on stories from elders. And Mowarin and those engaged with the Yijala Yala Project share an interest in drawing on Aboriginal oral storytelling practices and histories to create productions for local indigenous, local nonindigenous and global audiences, a practice itself that breaks with the customary law in which certain stories are told only to certain people, typically those who know the storyteller. All this happens in a context of continuous negotiations, agreements, compromises and challenges between local communities, large mining companies, governments and experts. As Mowarin explains, he wants to retell the stories to locals and strangers alike:

> If a city person drives through our country, all they will see is hills, trees and rivers. ... But if you come for a ride with me, I can name those hills, I can tell you where people were born, I can tell you whose families lived on which stations and I can tell you the Indigenous names for the animal that just ran, hopped or flew past. (Mowarin cited in Howarth 2012)

Another interest that Mowarin and the Yijala Yala Project participants share is an appreciation of new media and its capacity to enhance the ways in which local people and their cultures are valued. As mentioned, this work challenges certain ideas about what constitutes authentic Aboriginal art and Aboriginality. This, they argue, will optimize indigenous people's opportunities for a good life, while highlighting the desire of indigenous communities to engage in creative and political expression. It is action that engenders debate about cultural authenticity. It reclaims and recreates Aboriginal knowledge and images. Mowarin explains,

> knowledge is power, and knowledge is identity as well. ... If Aboriginal people don't know who they are or where they are from, then they

are lost. You can call yourself Aboriginal, but you won't feel whole
without your knowledge. (cited in Howarth 2012)

In the case of Yijala Yala *Neomad*, this exploration and image making
fusing ancient Aboriginal and Western futuristic fantasy replete with
indigenous ancestral totem spirits and style zombies roaming the landscape. Both projects highlight the political and elusive nature of identity
and identity formation.

Finally, Mowarin and those involved in the Yijala Yala Project share
a rich cultural milieu. As mentioned, they work in a rich and enriching
setting of 30,000 years of mimetic practice encompassing painting, etch-
ings, storytelling, dance and music. It is a not just a long-ago artistic
setting that they draw on, but rich contemporary artistic milieu of cross-
cultural art projects, including music, film and theater, that provide a
nourishing environment for creative endeavor.

Such identity making is political and creates change. Such image- and
identity making is self-creation that rests on our mimetic capacity to
recognize resemblances and differences that offer ways of knowing and
experiencing the world, which enable us to become and behave like
something else. In short, they are transformative (Benjamin 1978). And
new media provides new pedagogy for our mimetic powers.

In the case studies presented here we saw participants draw on their
affective, aesthetic and cognitive capacities to find correspondence and
to see meaning in the colored palette of the earth, in the curves and peaks
of land formations, and in the patterns of the stars. New media provides
a powerful medium for mime, to make and remake experiences, knowledge and the world. In doing so, their activities brought into being identities that hitherto did not exist. They brought forth different options
for intercultural and power relations, perceptions and imagination that
inform and can interrupt dominant ways of seeing that make up fields
of racialized habits which work to restrict our responses and receptivity
to openness. As such, the projects in this case study are exercises in
change making that evolve and that involve drawing on and preserving
elements of the past to produce new subjectivities and forms of power
in the present.

Mowarin and the Yijala Yala Project work (Neomad) offer examples
of bricolage as they borrowed and remixed from dissimilar material,
ideas, objects from different peoples, sites and normally seen as opposite to create new compositions, cultural forms and identifies. I refer, for
example, to the manga cartoon (Japanese art), science fiction, elements

of traditional Aboriginal narratives, traditional Irish music and even voodoo magic.

Bricolage, however, was not always so prominent a feature. One of Mowarin's early films is *Mabuji*,[22] screened in 2010 as part of an ABC TV.[23] *Mabuji* typifies his tale-based approach to storytelling, an approach that draws on the mimetic gift of his elders. In this case the spirit of 'the old fella'

> Mabuji is the story that my uncles told me about an old fella who died near Nickel River when he was riding a horse. He fell off and he died on the spot. When my uncle was a young guy, mustering out on the station on horseback, they'd come toward Nickel River and they would see, every now and then they'd catch a glimpse at the back of them of this extra rider [the old fella] coming up.

> It's filmed here in Ngarluma Country and I'm a Ngarluma, my mum's a Ngarluma, my family is Ngarluma. This area is pretty unique in the colors and even the heat. They're all characters, I suppose. Yeah, and like I said before, I really wanted the country to be the other character in the film. (Mowarin, cited in ABC 2009)

One of Mowarin's later pieces of work, *Ngurrara*, is a fictionalized historical account delivered in three episodes[24] that reiterates the message that local indigenous people have a 40,000-year-old unbroken connection to their land. To produce *Ngurrara*, Mowarin invited a group of young Ngarluma and the Yijala Yala Project film crew to accompany him on a trip to Deep Gorge at Murujuga. Replicating the traditional Ngarluma practice of storytelling, they 'walked through the story on country', 'travelling the story line while improvising and 'acting out the content'. The young Ngarluma men acted as their adventure was filmed. It was an exercise in their mimetic faculty, designed to see resemblance, to imagine, recall and create 'memories of the stories that may have been otherwise forgotten' (Yijala Yala http://www.yijalayala.bighart.org/neomad/ngurrara/).

Mowarin directed the film and produced photoshots redrawn by Big HArt's illustrator, Stuart Campbell (aka Sutu), who produced a sequence of illustrations of figures, backgrounds and talking balloons for the book. Local young Ngarluma children were recruited to digitally color the drawings using Photoshop. They produced a beautifully illustrated, interactive, computerized children's book incorporating technology that invites the reader to participate in the story. This includes touch options that allow readers to activate the text and hear the audio voices of characters along with translations of the Ngarluma language that are embedded into the text. The story is told from the perspective of three young Aboriginal men as they go about their daily activities of fishing, hunting and carving.[25] It draws on stories from the traditional land-owners of Murujuga (Burrup Peninsula in Western Australia), where the majority of the rock art is located (http://www.icampfire.tv/people-cul-ture/culture/behind-the-scenes-ngurrara-ipad-comic.html). The brico-lage effect of contemporary Ngarluma media is even more striking in the Neomad project.

Neomad narratives

Neomad is a sci-fi fantasy interactive comic. Its use of icons, styles and genres is typically both playful and allusive as it draws on images that suggest superheroes (like Batman), Teenage Mutant Ninja Turtles, science fiction, Green politics, gangsta and rap, even as it also draws on the lives of local people and places in stories about people's relationship to country.

The first Neomad episode, 'Space Junk', opens with shots of a group of young boys who are 'new nomads' and future 'warriors' who fight with slingshots, and who described themselves as Love Punks. The cast includes characters like Ashton Munda as Birdman, Hardcore Hami, Deshawn, General EJ, Jarried, Edwin Dan, Garuwarru, Supamaxie, Future Smash, Baldhead and Born Ready.[26] As they play, they talk of radiation and tell how the world was destroyed and taken over by zombies who eat humans. They engage in an imaginary about the future with 'super smart robots' and the implications of such technology. An alternate optimistic future is also held out with reference to crystal magic. 'Sit back and let me tell you a story', readers are told, and the story begins.

The year is 2076. The story begins with the boys chilling out, relaxing against the backdrop of a junkyard desert landscape replete with rusty pipelines and abandoned cars. They play as they pursue adventure and make discoveries. In the background is a blend of Western and distinc-tive Aboriginal music. It is an adventure story that sees them stuffing themselves into a fast-flying guadcopter spacecraft that takes off into the unknown cosmos. In typical hero-villain narrative style, they are chased by 'baddies', the Segs, with our heroes the Love Punks finally crashing to earth.

When their vehicle crashes, they set off on a further adventure to discover an archaeological landscape replete with petroglyphic images reminiscent of their own homeland in the Pilbara. They go on to make other magical discoveries. Traditional narrative comes into the story as the reader is told that 'old man fire has gone' out. This, we are told, is 'a bad sign', and the chase is on again, with the hero boys off running into large anthills and finding a magic crystal that lifts them up and out as church bell and Doctor Who-style music provides the background music.

In the second Neomad episode, 'The Last Crystal', small groups of seven Satellite Sisters take on a protective Gaia environmental conservation role and rescue their Love Punk brothers, who are in strife with the gods, who are annoyed about their misbehavior. The girl heroes meet up with the Love Punks continue their adventure orbiting the earth and saving from falling space debris. In the third episode, 'Porkchop Plots', in keeping with the hero narrative, the Satellite Sisters and the Love Punks join forces and set off to save some tourists in a spaceship who in Jonah-style have been swallowed up by the Mongkala god of the sky.

This is also a developmental/learning project in the conventional sense that aims at helping participants acquire digital media knowledge and skills, and use software like Photoshop and graphic tablets.[27]

Conclusion

Are the actions identified in this chapter political responses? Are they responses to the dislocating power of capitalism and a history of dispossession? Is there evidence of co-option and depoliticization and processes of normalization typically found in traditional community development enterprises? Or, is what is happening more complex, involving mimesis, the practice of looking, shadowing, imagining in ways that extend art into politics and that result in the kind of self-transformation that leads to new or different subjectivities? I suggest this is evident in part, and as such is a political achievement. It is action that helps create new identities and names and that can be used to exert universal claims organized around those identities. It can work to alter power relations and make demands on the state and corporate entities like global mining companies. It is likely these will not find expression in a Zapatista style of direct action, but nonetheless they can be used to regain disinherited land and go some way toward mitigating the damage caused by generations of dispossession.

The visual and performance art discussed here expresses the imaginative and ethical energies of a generation of young indigenous people in a specific community whose members have long been long caught in the crossfire of competing white colonial and black indigenous interests and experience. It is a politics of negotiation that can contribute to the creation of autonomous political subjectivities, and the discouraging of moral indifferenceAnd while it may not be on the extreme end of the spectrum as Zapatista-style direct action, it does nonetheless encourage a more gentle form of politics of resistance through the exercise of mimetic faculties via art and new media.

Conclusion

The purpose in writing this book was to offer an account of some aspects of contemporary politics and the way some people are now using new media to reanimate politics. The book points to the ways in which increasing numbers of people, many of whom were born in the past few decades, engage politically, but not necessarily in ways recognized as such when judged against conventional ideas about what constitutes politics. What that renewal signifies gives good reason for confidence about politics in the future.

My aim was to promote thinking about the prospect of new political practice and imaginaries while acknowledging the Orwellian risks posed by those interested in 'managing democracy'. What I aimed for was a disposition that resists an overly pessimistic view that new media will be deployed to destroy civic rights like privacy or freedom of speech, but which is not so optimistic as to encourage complacency leading to a failure to countenance darker possibilities.

Yet what is at stake is not just a question of 'dark' or 'light' dispositions. The experiences reported in this book serve as a reminder of why it is so important to be attentive to questions of ethics and power – and to be concerned about how the prevailing neoliberal logic finds its way into all aspects of our with enormous dislocating effects that place our democratic culture and potential to live well at risk.

I argue that the ways many people use digital media create and open up spaces that are filled with new forms of politics, which help in moving beyond the prevailing orthodoxy of neoliberal and its economistic obsessions.

Although it might seem simplistic to reduce such a variable and global phenomenon to a specific nomination, I suggest that what we are seeing may be broadly described as the emergence of 'critical liberalism'. And while I would need to spend much more time than I have saying why I think this is the case, I want to make a small gesture in that direction.

Critical liberals are interested in ethical and political subjectivity in ways that critique and extend conventional understandings of democratic practice. I use the term to apply to a very diverse group of writers like Fraser (1990, pp. 56–80), Pateman (1988), Yeatman (1994) and Young (2000), who inquired into the experience and categories of women and gender. I include writers like Jung (2008), who wrote on indigeneity and culture, and Dahlgren (2009), who wrote on new media and young people. I refer, perhaps more controversially, to theorists like Cornelius Castoriadis (1997) and Critchley (2011), who thought respectively about the role of the imagination and the body as sources of radical change, as well as Keane (2009), who has written extensively on democracy, and Sen (2009) and Nussbaum (2010), who have given thought to the question of justice.[1]

What links these writers is the ways in which each has pointed to how classical and conventional notions of liberalism work to exclude, delegitimate and narrow claims of justice or thwart the legitimate aspirations of people to have a good life. Critical liberalism is an approach that looks for solutions within that broad yet discernibly liberal frame, which continues to sustain a commitment to ideas of freedom, autonomy and justice. Critical liberals promote a radical critique of more traditional expressions of liberalism like rationality and the valuing of consensus over dissent, and reveal and resist the tendency to act 'as if' any democratic society has achieved relative equity either by way of freedom to access the public sphere or to access the resources defining a good life. In effect, critical liberalism deploys a range of critical styles to augment democratic practice.

For critical liberalism, the rules for admission to citizenship, a prerequisite for participation in any society, provide a crucial starting point for assessing the ethical and moral status of contemporary democratic regimes. Davidson argues that

> This is because such rules decide who will be included and who will be excluded from civil, political and social rights, and thus create inequalities between human beings who inhabit the same society…. In turn we are entitled to question critically the grounds they advance for relegating some people and not others to the category of absolute or relative Other. (1994, pp. 111–112)

Questions about who is included and excluded are fundamental to the question of justice because political identity is interwoven with politics that has a determinate telos, like the pursuit of some conception of the good society, especially in a contemporary society with multiple forms and ways of life. Sen is one writer who understands justice as that circumstance in which people are free and have a capacity to choose, live and give expression to their own valued ends: having these rights and capabilities is what justice means (2009). In this respect critical liberalism recognizes (like other streams in liberalism) the value of freedom.

Critical liberalism is thus concerned with bypassing the contemporary ethos of competitive individualism, consumerism and utilitarianism promoted by neoliberals, which relies on abstract defenses of freedom and on the falsehood that free market mechanisms will somehow deliver the basic human goods equitably and effectively. The evidence provided by the OECD (2011) and Oxfam (2013) reveal why this idea is malicious and mendacious. Critical liberalism affirms that justice requires that people have and enjoy rights, like the right to speak freely, to be free from terror and surveillance, and to engage in decision-making that affects them. A good society ensures people have access to basic resources like food, water, clothing and shelter, as well as high-quality education, health, and cultural and leisure amenities. Together these rights and these capabilities provide people with the capacity to become good citizens.

Critical liberals are also less concerned with valuing or promoting consensus. As Jung argues, consensus masks the relations of power and the exclusion on which those relations of power rest, rendering injustice invisible (2008, p. 253). Thus, critical liberalism aims at providing the conditions for contestation and dissent. For Jung, contestation has a signaling and transformative value: 'By exposing injustice it offers a source for comprehending what counts as justice. By challenging the boundaries of inclusion it has the potential to transform them' (p. 253). In each of the four case studies were examples of this commitment to dissent and to challenging boundaries based on markers like age, gender or ethnicity. We saw the use of publicity afforded by the new technology to highlight injustice and to include in terms prescribed by Iris Young the insights and experience of people long assigned to or assumed to have 'structurally inferior positions' (2000).

Finally, critical liberalism proposes there is value in putting questions or proposals on the agenda that have not yet been contemplated or accorded a value within a framework of what is often fake consensus or an abstract defense of freedom, which disguises continuing and fundamental asymmetries of power and the capacity to enjoy a good life.

Critical liberals see political identity formation from a constructivist perspective and praise those forms of political action manifest in critique. They are interested in the emergence of new political subjectivities and how newcomers manage to move from the subterranean level lying beneath the surface of the civic space to articulate their demands, thereby challenging the prevailing arrangements and transforming debate and social and political arrangements, and in so doing highlighting naturalized and invisible power relations and ethics and rules of inclusion.

This is why I focused on the emergence of new political identities that challenge popular prejudices about 'young people' entailed by the popularization of generational labels like Gen X or Gen Y, the millennials, or the Narcissistic generation, or epithets like 'parasitical' 'dumb', and 'selfish' and that represent 'them' as essentially apathetic and 'apolitical'.

While this might suggest that using generational categories is unwise, I made the case that provided we are mindful of certain qualifications, we can draw on Karl Mannheim's central insight that 'generations' are people who share certain common 'historic events', (and as I argued, three such events characterized the late twentieth and the early twenty-first centuries). How a generation responds to given sets of common 'historical' experiences is of course highly variable. This is why generalizing about a generation as if all its members share common attitudes, dispositions, values, aspirations or behaviors that somehow determine their actions cannot be taken seriously. Yet for the reasons outlined in Chapter 4, I argue we can still talk about generations, while acknowledging the diverse ways in which people interpret and respond to certain defining features of a time period.

One historic event referred to in this book was the emergence of neoliberalism, which took place starting in the late 1970s and which saw increasing numbers of young people in Western and developing societies face common experiences that have been formative. Sweeping global effects like neoliberal political and policymaking, along with radical economic and technological change have affected large numbers of people, including those who came of age in the decades after 1980. They have, for example, experienced the effects of government policies and relentlessly restructured market economies. Many have been forced into extended periods of education, and carry increasingly burdensome education fee debts, even as many find themselves excluded from the labor market in growing numbers (Willets 2011). In consequence, many are denied access to affordable housing, and are condemned to dependency and increased life in the natal home. As Howker and Malik argue in respect to young Britons in terms that apply in Europe, the United States and Australia, these are 'the jilted generation' (2013).

We are talking about those who also came of age in a world where the advent of global and networked digital technology transformed long-standing ways of relating socially and engaging in the world. Social etiquette, cultural and educational experience, narratives of self and sexuality are some of the forms of life that are being reshaped, enabling new sensibilities. And for some people, the new digital world opens up the prospect of new kinds of politics.

I noted also the increasing discussion about democratic failure, the sense we are running on empty ethically, the trivialization of real political choice, the arbitrary use of concentrated and increasingly privatized power fueled by anxiety about global issues like poverty and social inequity, war and terrorism, food and water security and climate change. They are issues best understood as the effects of far-reaching changes to the socioeconomic fabric of many communities that have been wrought by neoliberal policies, sweeping technological changes and radical changes in the places and ways in which agriculture, manufacturing and services are provided. They are events that touched the lives of those who grew up in that context (those born after the late 1970s) more significantly than their forebears.

For some people with memories of the way 'things were done' in the 1940s, 1950s, 1960s or 1970s, a sense of 'a world we have lost' can lead to a politics of nostalgia or resentment. For those unencumbered by such memory, the political horizon may look quite different. With this in mind I pointed to evidence of new sensibilities and ethical concerns and political engagement facilitated through novel technology. And while not all that activity involves those born since the late 1970s or early 1980s, much of it does.

I argued there is value in the idea that some young people are now using communication technologies in ways that promise to revive democracy and foster new styles of political deliberation and activism. Clearly global networked digital media are being used extensively to promote the dissemination of information, to encourage deliberation, to promote popular mobilization and to engage in political activism.

While we see a plurality of responses, the four cases presented here all share what John Keane described as a reaction 'against all forms of arbitrary power, where they take root' (2012, p. 666). In each case we saw a politics catalyzed by 'ethical energy' involving political emotions like indignation, righteous anger and even patriotism in response to various wrongs, or simply to express a restless will to escape definition or prescription about the proper ways to be and to behave, and in so doing to forge new identities.

What we saw in each case were collective projects, some on a small scale, some on a large scale, consisting of young people, many of them excluded or marginalized previously, now using the resources of the networked public sphere to participate in a range of creative cultural and/or democratic practices.

As the quite different cultural projects involving Neomad and Pussy Riot suggest, music and video productions were made and posted on the Internet as part of a commitment to the 'art of making public noise'. Pussy Riot's project was animated by a deep sense of 'felt injustice' in the context of state-sponsored criminality and repression that encouraged many Russians to retreat into dissociation or succumb to the growth of an infectious anomie that sucks the life from so many institutions and Russia's political culture – the effects of which surely are not confined just to Russia. The indigenous art projects in the Pilbara make a different affirmation: in this case young indigenous people were no longer content to continue being defined by a reified conception of traditional Aboriginal culture, or by the commodified nihilism promoted by an increasingly corporatized 'Western' art culture that tends to define the value of an image in terms of its resale value. Both the Pilbara cases and Pussy Riot assemble complex new kinds of cultural performance that assert a claim on tradition as they proclaim a new cultural and political possibility. Here bricolage – or remix – both affirms and breaks old models, while laying claim to new forms of performative freedoms, the freedom to be. In each case we also see how some traditional asymmetric power relations are contested, new subjectivities and identities shaped and new ways of thinking encouraged about how politics might be conceived.

Projects of this kind hold as much promise of political renewal as the more traditional kinds of popular mobilization that saw millions of young Americans challenge the US Congress, some of whose members were intent on restricting free access to the Internet, or the less visible exercises in schools and universities initiated by students wanting to hold education managers and teachers to some kind of account courtesy of the Internet.

In each case young people are helping mitigate what Critchley and others identify as a motivational deficit evident in widespread apathy, a crisis of political legitimacy and loss of public trust in power elites that plagues many societies and threatens the health and future of civic cultures. Evident in these responses is the making of new political subjectivities that have clear generational dimensions, coalescing around the still-evolving identities of 'jobless graduates', 'neo-anarchists' and young indigenous people.

These cases also stand in for countless instances found in places scattered as far and wide as New York, Cairo, Paris, Athens, Montreal, Santiago, London, Mexico City, Madrid and Melbourne. There the moral force of claims made by those historically marginalized and by those who bear a disproportionate weight of the 'dislocating effect' of neoliberalism or crony capitalism, reliant or overly cozy relations between political elites and business, are now expressed in emerging global networked public spheres. Against the spirit of organized and managed public silence that is often interpreted as 'consent', but perhaps more often experienced as a 'cold fear' that breeds accessories to bad acts, those who call themselves different names announce a refusal to stay silent and safe in the spaces which Wolin calls 'inverted totalitarianism' (2006).

In this way the responses on display can refresh and offer a remotivating response to the drift and demoralized state of liberal democracy as its stands. This links to art, carnivalesque humor and play of groups engaged in civil disobedience and the renewal of the idea of democracy. Through various forms of direct political action and art – be it visual or performing art – we see new media used to express ethics as a binding force in politics in ways that are quite different from mainstream notions of politics as a practice distinct from ethics.

The book argues that a just and democratic society requires ethical reinvigoration. It is a reinvigoration evident in the various projects described in the case studies. Democratic society requires wholehearted debate, a valuing of politics and dissent. This relies on social practices that are reflective and that break with habitual practice to encourage innovation. It requires recognition of the sociopolitical and psychological obstacles that get in the way of ethical practice. It rests on identifying the connection between ethics and politics and injecting a strong dose of ethics into the ways most people think about politics. In short, this goes considerably further than Jürgen Habermas' classic notion of the public sphere. Critical liberals like Critchley, Dahlgren, Fraser, Keane and Jung (to name a few) highlight these points and the importance of politics as the valuing a diversity of opinion, where 'contrarians are not rebuked' and where people are not sanctioned for raising taboo topics.

If we are to do more than survive, to prevent catastrophes, and are to live well and create politically vibrant cultures, then there is considerable value in examining actions like the ones presented in this book Ethical responses to wrongs, public scrutiny, the questioning of arbitrary power and particularly the privatization of power are what moved those to action. New media was critical and provides the means for those competent and comfortable in its use to counter power elites who cocoon and protect themselves within 'positive' accounts of 'performance outcomes' and improvements typically described in terms of utility value.

Notes

Introduction

1. While I draw primarily on the work of Habermas and Castoriadis here, I also draw on classic and contemporary political philosophers and sociologists like Aristotle, Arendt, Fraser, Dyzenhaus, Keane, Critchley Dahlgren, Papacharissi, Bennett and Dahlberg, the modern work in particular pointing to a common interest in critical liberalism, the democratic value of dissent and sociopolitical change.
2. One meta-analysis by Boulianne demonstrates that once controls are in place for political interest, there is little relationship between Internet use and political behavior (2009). Sherr (2005) and Bauerlein (2008) also argue that engaging with new media has not improved young people's knowledge of current affairs or related information. Equally, as Smith et al. (2012) and Hargittai (2010) argue, the 'digital native' framework (Prensky 2001) ignores important social and educational differences in academic and social Internet use.

1   Politics in the Age of the Digital

1. There was early and substantial interest by many political theorists in the Net: see Grossman (1996), Poster (1997), Kellner (1998), Rheingold (2000), Coleman and Gotze (2001), Sparks (2001), and Dahlberg (2001a and b).
2. Benson, R., 2009, 'Shaping the Pubic Sphere: Habermas and Beyond', *American Sociology*, 40, pp. 175–197.
3. For example, Barber (1984), Dryzek (1990), Fishkind (1991), Cohen and Arato (1992), Walzer (1994, 1995), Bohmann (1996), and Benhabib (1996)
4. Arendt (1958), Habermas (1989). See also Fraser, 1995, 'Politics, Culture and the Public Sphere: Toward a Postmodern Conception', in Nicholson, L., and Seidman, S., (eds.), *Social Postmodernism: Beyond Identity Politics*, New York: Cambridge University Press, pp. 287–314.
5. This has not overlooked Lawrence Lessig's warning that 'cyberspace has the potential to be the most fully, and extensively, regulated space that we have ever known – anywhere, at any time in our history. It has the potential to be the antithesis of a space of freedom' (1998).
6. I am not suggesting a general theory of change of the kind offered by Talcott Parsons, nor a unilinear or a stadial model of progress, but simply acknowledging that through learning we interpret, adapt, improve and build on knowledge in ways that are creative and dynamic. This is different from the Parsonian functionalist's idea that sees practices and knowledge as shared, but as remaining largely unchanged and the culture as static.
7. External constraints include natural or biological influences (e.g., natural habits of a society). For example, the fact that two and two will always make four, and that a chicken and rooster will always produce chickens and not

calves are natural conditions that constrain in the sense that they need to be reflected in social institutions' representations of the world. The same can be said about constraints imposed by language. It is to these external constraints to which institutions need to respond. Other constraints are internal, like the human psyche, which has to be socialized, which entails investing emotional energy into social created and valued objects dispositions, actions etc. The psyche has to enclose itself within a public work and a public time. In talking about the psyche, Castoridias says, 'When we consider the unbelievable variety of types of society known, we are almost led to think that the social institutions can make out of the psyche whatever it pleases' (1997 p. 334). This, he says is true on the proviso that the institution supplies the psyche with meaning. Social imaginary significations tie together the meaning of existence, life, death, the ways of society and the cosmos as a whole. In short, social imaginary significations create the world for the society and shape the psyche of individuals. They create the representations of the world and the place of society in it, as well as the intention or mood (emotions) that pervade social life. Thirdly, historical constraints acknowledge that no society emerges from a vacuum. Pasts and traditions are embedded in social institutions, which can see some (e.g., primitive) societies replicate the past, while for others the 'receiving' of the past is to varying degrees conscious, and what we see is an incessant reinterpretation and recreation of it with differing outcomes. The fourth and final intrinsic constraint is coherence, assessed in terms relative to the whole organization of the social imaginary.

2   How the Light Gets in: Change and Continuity

1. In philosophy alone a vast literature on change exists. In the metaphysics of social, or 'modern', theories of change, we could turn to the detailed analysis of writers like Vico, Charles Montesquieu, French and British Enlightenment theorists (John Locke through Jeremy Bentham), to the counterrevolution (Edmund Burke through Joseph Gobineau), and early sociologists (Henri de Saint-Simon, Auguste Comte, Herbert Spencer, Ferdinand Tonnies, Émile Durkheim and Max Weber). This is to say nothing of G. W. F. Hegel, Karl Marx and socialist theory.

2. Dao talks about the way water in its natural, most gentle and soft form can eventually wear away the hardest stone even though it will take a long time to see the effects of this action:

   > Nothing under heaven is softer or more yielding than water;
   > but when it attacks things hard and resistant
   > there is not one of them that can prevail.

   For they can find no way of altering it. Cited in Xuanming, Y., On the Unity of pluralistic Values, The Bases of Values in a Time of Change: Chinese and Western Studies, in Bunchua, K., Fangtong, xuanmeng, Wujin, Y., (eds), *The bases of Values In A Time of Change: Chinese Philosophical Studies*, the Council for Research and Values, Washington. DC. XVI, p. 345.

3. This is the Hume idea of law as the regular succession of two observable events.

4. Even conservatives like Burke (1729–1797) developed an equivalent conservative account of change when he acknowledged the ubiquity of change, describing it as a law of nature. He argued,

> We must all obey the great law of change. It is the most powerful law of nature, and the means perhaps of its conservation. (cited in Stanlis 1993, p. 86)

Change was seen as an organic project all part of a divine plan ordained by a Creator God. God was said to allow humans to develop their own unique natural qualities shaped by climate, civil customs, religion and other factors, but required harmony between human will and a god-ordained moral law. According to Burke, constitutional law, for example, needed to include a principle of change:

> A state without the means of some change is without the means of its conservation. Permanent political arrangements are meaningful only as they sustain and are sustained by the changing needs of and circumstances of men. (cited in Stanlis, 1993, p. 64)

5. Labor, work, and action are the three central categories in Arendt's (1958) philosophical anthropology. 'Labor' refers to our animal nature *as animal laborans*. It denotes the endless and basic biological processes required to maintain life. 'Work' speaks to our social nature as *homo faber* and points to the fabrication of an *artificial* world of things, and fabricated things that endure temporally beyond the act of creation itself. Work thus creates a world distinct from anything given in nature. Finally, 'activity' defines us as truly free creatures. The political life is the purest expression of our freedom, which begins with our capacity to make new beginnings:

> To act, in its general sense, is to take initiative, to begin 'to lead', and eventually 'to rule' indicates, to set something in motion. Because they are newcomers and beginners by virtue of birth, men take initiative, are prompted into action. Arendt, H., 1958, *The Human Condition*, Chicago University Press, Chicago.

6. Bourdieu's work, developed over five decades has been interpreted in various ways and continues to invite controversy about what he 'really' meant. For some of these differences see Calhoun (1992), Fowler (1997), Wacquant (2005) and Steinmetz (2011).

7. Bourdieu's work on practice is part of a larger project designed to highlight the power dynamics operating in modern capital intensive societies, including the role of symbolic violence in the production and reproduction of cultural social and symbolic capital in institutions like schools and universities, as well as museums and art galleries.

8. At the individual level of action and cognition, it was the psychologist (Jean Piaget) who provided Bourdieu with a way of thinking about the conception of structure at a cognitive-practical level, which provided a matrix to generate action, but which did not involve a theory of an indefinable consciousness from which 'spontaneous' action originates (as in Mead, 1934).

9. 'Capital' of any kind is unequally distributed, a point typically overlooked in contemporary discussions about 'social capital'.

10. While it leaves him open to criticism, Castoriadis does not explain why or how humans possess the powers of imagination. Jürgen Habermas (1987) was one very critical respondent to what he saw as Castoriadis's creation

ex nihilo of figures, forms and worlds, and his refusal to ground his theory in a 'proper' 'sociological' explanation that relies on 'social' processes. This went so far as an alleged misuse of Sigmund Freud, as Habermas argued that Castoriadis located unconscious imagination in a realm prior to language and so fell victim to a psychoanalytic version of subjectivism.

11. Castoriadis argued that Immanuel Kant rediscovered the importance of the imagination and gave philosophy a new awareness of it (1997, pp. 246–272). For Castoriadis, Kant allowed that the imagination is the capacity to present an object even without the presence of that object, thereby freeing the imagination from the need for accompanying sensation (1998, pp. 319–337).

12. External constraints include natural or biological influences (e.g., the natural habits of a society). For example, the fact that two and two will always make four and that a chicken and rooster will always produce chickens and not calves are natural conditions that constrain in the sense that they need to be reflected in social institutions' representations of the world. The same can be said about constraints imposed by language. It is to these external constraints that institutions need to respond. Other constraints are internal, like the human psyche, which has to be socialized, which entails investing emotional energy into socially created and valued objects dispositions and actions etc.

    In talking about the psyche, Castoridias says, 'When we consider the unbelievable variety of types of society known, we are almost led to think that the social institutions can make out of the psyche what ever it pleases' (1997, p. 334). This, he says, is true on the proviso that the institution supplies the psyche with meaning. Social imaginary significations tie together the meaning of existence, life, death, the ways of society and the cosmos as a whole. In short, social imaginary significations create the world for the society and shape the psyche of individuals. They create the representations of the world and the place of society in it, as well as the intention or mood (emotions) that pervade social life. Thirdly, historical constraints acknowledge that no society emerges from a vacuum. Pasts and traditions are embedded in social institutions, which can see some (e.g., primitive) societies replicate the past, while for others the 'receiving' of the past is to varying degrees conscious and what we see is an incessant reinterpretation and recreation of it with differing outcomes. The fourth and final intrinsic constraint is coherence, which is assessed in terms relative to the whole organization of the social imaginary.

13. While Athens is generally and conventionally recognized as the 'cradle of democracy', scholars like John Keane (2009) query this, pointing rather to the Mesopotamian region (now Iran, Iraq, Syria and Persia) as the places were the 'lamp of assembly-based democracy was first lit' (Keane 2009, p. xi).

14. Castoriadis's notion of creation is not equivalent to the epistemic notion of unpredictability, as he clarified (1997, pp. 374–401). An emergence of something out of something else can still be fully unpredictable. Unpredictability might, for example, mean that not all of the relevant producers, factors, or laws of inference are known or knowable. An unpredictable event or phenomenon could still be determined by unknown factors. Unpredictability could be a function of the limitations of *knowledge*. Thus, unpredictability is not equivalent to *creation*. While Castoriadis agreed that knowers are not, as far

as we know, omniscient, he argued that with each creation there emerges something ontologically new, something that is not merely *seemingly* new 'for us' due to some subjective lack of knowledge. Separating radical creation from the merely epistemic notion of unpredictability, Castoriadis defends the notion that creation brings about something *genuinely* new.

3   Change and Generation

1. Those working in the burgeoning areas of life-cycle and life-course studies, e.g., operationalize the idea of generations using birth dates and characteristics to define members of the generation in question. Some of these researchers point to changes in patterns of living and working that see young people no longer following a 'traditional linear model' of 'transition' from childhood, to adolescence to adulthood understood in terms of successive phases of education, marriage, work and retirement. Writers like Coles (1995), Jones and Wallace, (1992), France (2008), Setterston et.al (2005) and Galland (2007) refer to the complexity of social life in late modernity and its impact on the experience of being young and 'patterns of transitions to adulthood'. (Additional ref details: Galland, O., 2007, *Boundless Youth Studies in the Transition to Adulthood Studies in the Transition to Adulthood*, Trans Matthews, T., and Hamilton, P., The Bardwell Press, Oxford.
2. To make things more complex, it seems that Robert Capa first used the term Generation X to describe this age cohort in his title for a photo-essay about young men and women growing up immediately after the Second World War. His images first appeared in *Picture Post* (UK) and *Holiday* (US) in 1953.
3. The Pew Research Center defines the millennial birth range as those born 'after 1980', while a global generational study conducted by PwC (2013) (a network of accounting firms) and the London Business School defined millennials as those born between 1980 and 1995.
4. As Pilcher observed, anthropologists talk about 'cohorts' to refer to people within a specific population who experience the same significant events within a given period of time, while technically speaking, 'generation' is a structural category in kinship terminology denoting the parent-child relationship. Mannheim's approach to 'generation' is really a way of speaking about 'cohorts' (1994, p. 483).
5. In Aristotle's explanation of biological creation, it is the male who contributes the source of movement, or *dunamis* (power). This turns out to be a special capacity to heat that is present in the semen's *pneuma*, or air, which is part of its nature. The semen is merely a vehicle for delivering this warmth. In this way the male makes no material contribution to the offspring. The female contributes the 'prepared matter'. All it needs is the heat from the male, which begins a lengthy and complicated developmental process.
6. in this way Dilthey and Mannheim were influenced by German romantic writers like Johann Wolfgang von Goethe, Friedrich von Schiller, and Johann Gottfried Herder and by theologians like Friedrich Schleiermacher who helped establish the hermeneutic tradition. Kantian philosophy and the romantics (e.g., G. W. F. Hegel) emphasized the zeitgeist, or 'spirit of the time', said to characterize each historical period. There was also an emphasis on the idea

that we are not so much rational, calculating machines located in human bodies, as the Cartesian tradition implied, but culturally embedded actors who engage in 'understanding' and 'interpretation' (*verstehen*). As I explain later, the Hegelian idea of history as a process of dialectical change influenced Karl Marx and in turn informed Mannheim's account of generational change. Older European, and more specifically German, ideas about youth and youth movements like the *Sturm und Drang* period (storm and stress) (1760–1780s) were encouraged by sensibilities displayed in Goethe's novel *The Sorrows of Young Werther* (1774). This extremely popular novel celebrated heightened youthful emotions with European-wide consequences.

7. There is no absolute distinction between the material and social dimensions of our world: we confront each other as material objects as bodies, living in objects like cars and buildings and dependent on material things like food and water or using physical processes like speaking and writing to communicate. Equally we humans attribute symbolic significance to these material entities and processes. .

8. This is possible if certain criteria are met, which include the following
   • Being able to recognize 'the' essences of living or nonliving objects: This, it is said, allows us to see a causal mechanism or to predict and thereby understand behaviour.
   • Because all members share a set of common features, they are all equally suitable representatives or examples of the concept.
   • Since all defining features are necessary, each needs to be equally noticeable in determining the membership in the class or category.

9. See also Rosch and Lloyd (1978), Lakoff and Johnson (1983) and Hofstadter and Sander (2013).

10. This is *not* to say that people seen to be part of a 'generation' or part of any social category (e.g., homelessness) are not real or that their experiences are invented. Rather, it is to say that whatever empirical status these categories possess will be different from those attributed to tangible physical objects (like rocks). There is a difference between inanimate objects – which exist regardless of whether humans exist – and something that is the product of a human activity that would not exist if we did not.

11. The aspects alleged to characterise the collective psychology or behavioral characteristics of this or that generation are always themselves interpreted from particular standpoints, and as such cannot offer decisive and stable identifiers of a generation like Gen Y, baby boomer, or global generation. Additionally it is often the case that the characteristics attributed to those assigned to a social category says more about the observer's own fears, fantasies and prejudices than they do about the lives, experiences and identities of those being described. Indeed, one of the ethical and practical issues this raises is whether the use of age to create generational categories, and the associated search for connections between age and other characteristics, appeals to existing popular prejudices. Finally and in the case of academics the meanings attributed to generation reflect the observer's disciplinary perspectives, his/her habits of mind and theoretical traditions. For anthropologists, generation refers to a family or kinship group who by the same degree are descendants from common forebears. Genealogical histories provide such pedigree accounts, which, at least in the West, record patrilineal rather

than matrilineal descent. Also within these kinship groups are classificatory systems (i.e., great grandmother, uncle etc.), which identify generational relations and help inform social expectations and norms (like deference between kin). As a "fuzzy category", the content and boundaries of generation are not exact, fixed or constant, but change according to the context. This is not to say generation is empty and meaningless, but that it can have various meanings. Sometimes those meanings can be made clearer by elaborating what distinguishes a generation from other concepts, like kinship groups or birth cohorts.

5 A Heuristic, or a Guiding Framework

1. The survey used a nonrandom sample of 1,021 technology stakeholders and critics. The survey was conducted by the Pew Research Center's Internet & American Life Project and Elon University's Imagining the Internet Center between August 28 and October 31, 2011.

6 Democratic Renewal, Pussy Riot and Flash Gigs in the Kremlin

1. That election was significant because Putin had already served as president for eight years (from 2000 to 2008), the full constitutionally mandated term allowed. That length of tenure made him ineligible to serve for a third time as president. Given that constitutional constraint, in 2008 Putin moved to the office of prime minister under the presidency of Dmitry Medvedev where he served until early 2012. It was a position that allowed him to maintain his political dominance, while working to overcome the obstacle to his aspiration for reelection as president. Putin achieved that goal by working to amend the law barring a third consecutive term. Once the hurdle of law reform was complete, he announced his intention to stand in the presidential election for a third time, a move that was greeted with dismay and widespread protest with Russia.
2. Putin went on to win the election the day after the arrest of the members of Pussy Riot. He got 63% of the vote, sparking demonstrations amid concern from local and international observers about the integrity of the election (Vassilieva 5 March 2012).
3. In addition their technical support staff, they are mostly in their mid-twenties to early thirties.
4. In 2012, the Economist Intelligence Unit assigned a democracy index weight of less than 3.9 to Russia, making it an authoritarian regime. Putin's ascent began when he became prime minister (1999–2000), then president (2000–2008) and prime minister (2008–2012), before he was elected again as president to a six-year term in 2012.
5. As is the case in some liberal democratic' societies, protest marches in Russia are illegal unless they have prior official approval.
6. Patriarch Kirill (a former KGB agent) went so far as to describe Putin as a 'miracle of God', as as Kirill used his status and authority as to encourage orthodox Russians to vote for Putin (Hermant 17 August 2012). The announcement

in late 2011 to grant Patriarch Kirril official residence in the Kremlin gener-
ated considerable unease about the relationship between church and state.
Permission for residency in the Kremlin had not been granted since the 1917
Bolshevik Revolution, when the church was disestablished.

7. After all, as Voronina (2013: 80) observes, the Russian Orthodox Church has
been using the Net for a decade or more as it 'actively embraced modern technology and consolidated its foothold in the Runet. ROC 2.0 is run online
with the help of Orthodox television channels, such as the Ekaterinburg
Diocese-owned site called "Soiuz", and the official ROC website Patriarchia.
ru, publishes church news and streams live broadcasts of services during major
Orthodox celebrations'.

8. It was in this context that Mikhail Riazantsev, a sacristan at the Cathedral
and a prosecution witness in the Pussy Riot trial, compared dancing in the
Cathedral to dancing on the grave of an unknown soldier in the indictment
(Syrova et al. 2012, p. 27).

9. Mardi Gras has become synonymous with carnival in places like New Orleans,
Rio de Janeiro and Sydney.

7   The Graduate's Future and Neoliberal Education: New Generation Politics on the Campus

1. The immediate issue was the removal of the New School's provost and Kerrey's
decision to act as provost. Kerrey presided over a major 'development' of the
New School, doubling its endowment to $201 million, while enrollment
increased by 44% to over 10,200, and online course enrollment doubled. The
number of full-time faculty members grew from 156 in 2001 to more than
372 in 2009. His total take-home pay, including bonuses and other benefits,
was $3,047,703, making Kerrey the highest-paid private college president in
the United States (June 2009). Stripling, J., 2012, 'Pay and Perks Creep Up for
Private-College Presidents. Some of the highest paid get cash to cover taxes,
too. 'The Chronicle of Higher Education', 9 December, From chronicle.com/
article/PayPerks-Creep-Up-for/136187.

2. By the end of 2011, polls put public opinion support for the student movement at 79% (Valenzuela 2012, p. 1).

3. I refer to my own earlier work on this topic which referred to some aspects
of the same case study, but which offered an analysis different from that
presented here (Bessant 2013).

4. For this reason, I placed an embargo on the data and relevant scholarly apparatus for referencing the materials used. These details may be obtained from
me on request.

5. For a critique of human capital theory, see Adamson (2009).

8   The *Stop Online Piracy Act* Case

1. My focus in this case study is on the SOPA introduced in the House of
Representatives. I note the US Senate was also addressing cognate legislation,
the *Protect Intellectual Property Act* (PIPA) that was drafted just before the House
of Representatives began considering the SOPA.

2. For a full list of those supporting the bill, see http://www.opencongress.org/bill/hr3261–112/bill_positions.
3. It seems the industry in mid-2011 believed itself immune to public outrage. In mid-2011, an agreement made behind closed doors among several American entertainment firms and ISPs, informally called the 'six strikes' plan was made public. Under it, copyright holders would reserve the right to track the traffic of their files across the World Wide Web, and entertainment firms could order ISPs to punish users merely suspected of copyright infringement, first with stern warnings and ultimately by discontinuing their service. This plan would have no government oversight whatsoever (Anderson 2011).
4. For example, Google, Yahoo, YouTube, Facebook, Mozilla, eBay, LinkedIn, AOL, Twitter, various gaming companies, Reddit, Wikipedia (cofounder Him Wales), PayPal, and Booz and Company.
5. Think tanks like the US Center for Democracy, the Cato Institute, human rights organizations (like Human Rights Watch), Electronic Frontier and the TOR project.
6. Professor Laurence Tribe (Harvard University) and Professor Palfrey (Harvard University).
7. Those involved included Jerry Brito (TIME.co), Marvin Ammori (Affiliate scholar Stanford Law School), Rebecca MacKinnon (New American Foundation), Christian Dawson (CEO of ServInt), Art Brodsky (former Vice President of Public knowledge), No – They can be removed Lukas Biewald (CrowFlower).
8. Sunstein provides an alternative view of the Net, describing it as a place not of refined knowledge, but rather a space that encourages fragmentation, polarization and the destruction of the possibility of common discourse in the public sphere (2002).
9. That said as Benkler et al. (2013) points out the mainstream media did join in the public scrutiny of SOPA.
10. COICA was a forerunner to SOPA.
11. In methodological terms, Benkley et al. (2013) started by mining stories from the Media Cloud collection of blogs and digital media sets, searching for content by matching a set of regular expressions based on the names and acronyms of the bills put forward during this time: COICA, PIPA and SOPA. After doing a manual review of the stories, they followed all the links in these stories to locate other relevant stories. They then discovered connected new stories, accessing their links, downloading the linked URLs, extracting the text from those Web pages, and seeking text that matched the COICA/PIPA/SOPA pattern. They repeated this process until they found no new stories (Benkler etal., 2013).
12. Cramer points out that Goffman (1974) and Tuchman (1978) used the idea of framing to structure, organize and simplify complicated and fragmented news information or public commentary (2013, p. 1078). Entman added that 'framing essentially involves selection and salience' on the part of the framer, unconsciously or consciously (1993, p. 52).
13. The First Amendment says 'Congress shall make no law respecting an establishment of religion, or prohibiting the free exercise thereof; or abridging the freedom of speech, or of the press; or the right of the people peaceably to assemble, and to petition the Government for a redress of grievances'. Free

speech rights have been refined and extended through a series of twentieth- and twenty-first-century Supreme Court decisions that protect various forms of political speech, anonymous speech, campaign financing, pornography and school speech.

14. I note the US Constitution forbids any one under the age of 25 from being a member of the House of Representatives, and anyone under 30 from being a member of the Senate.

15. As Cramer notes, most American citizens equate Internet freedom with network neutrality, as opposed to the largely procorporate view that freedom means service providers' managing their networks in nonneutral ways (Cramer 2013, p. 1087, Scott et al. 2006, p. 22). This highlights what Cramer described as the 'primary disconnect' between domestic policy issues and dramatic political events overseas:

   The ultimate result is rhetorical and practical discord in the U.S. political establishment's framing of who is victimized by governments' actions concerning Internet communications. In unfriendly regimes, the victims are regular people clamoring for a better life; at home, the victims are corporations that want to maintain economic growth and stability. (Cramer 2013, pp. 1086–1087)

16. Posner is a public intellectual and an appellate judge who is famous for his eclectic blend of conservatism, American pragmatism, neoclassical economic model of law – and his fondness for Nietzsche. Scalia has been a Supreme Court justice since 1986, and has a reputation as a formidable conservative, a strong defender of the powers of the executive and an opponent of affirmative action and other policies that see minorities as groups with rights.

9 The Digital, Indigenous Art and Politics

1. Edmunds produced an excellent history of Roebourne (2012, pp. 152–180).

2. In 2013, researchers announced they had discovered the earliest signs of life on earth in the Pilbara. The international team found evidence of a complex microbial ecosystem in well-preserved sedimentary rocks estimated to be almost 3.5 billion years old (Spriggs 2013).

3. For example, Ginsburg (1999, p. 297) associated with Benedict Anderson (1991) and Stuart Hall (1999).

4. Rasmussen et al. (2012) used a whole-of-genome sequence analysis of old Aboriginal hair samples at Cambridge University to conclude that Aboriginals lived in Australia up to 50,000 years before the present (BP), making them one of the earliest known populations of modern humans outside of Africa. Aboriginal Australians seem to have split from the ancestral Eurasian population, migrating out of Africa between 62,000 to 75,000 years BP, most likely crossing into the northwestern part of what is now Australia.

5. As Francis notes, late-nineteenth-century racism in Australia borrowed from diverse scientific and nonscientific sources, many of which continued into the twentieth century. Francis emphasizes a combination of racial prejudice, authoritarian language and the desire to regulate people deemed to be not fully human as the distinguishing features of public discussion and policymaking about Aborigines from the 1880s into the 1930s and later (2009, p. 103).

6. John Forrest's great-great-grandson, Andrew Forrest, is the current owner of Fortescue Metals Group, which has mines in the Pilbara worth tens of billions of dollars. Andrew Forrest purchased Minderoo in 2009 to reclaim it for the Forrest family.

7. The High Court (Bartlett 1993) found native title at common law; the source of native title was determined to be the traditional connection to or the occupation of the land; the nature and content of native title was determined by the character of the connection or the occupation under traditional laws or customs; and native title could be extinguished by the valid exercise of governmental powers provided a clear and plain intention to do so was manifest (Bartlett 1993).

8. The Pilbara makes up about 90% of the state's claim to have the world's largest Economic Demonstrated Resources of iron ore, with 22% of the world's iron ore.

9. There is one small Aboriginal-owned company, Ngarda Civil and Mining, which in 2007 won a $300m contract from BHP Billiton.

10. In 2007, the Australian Heritage Council awarded heritage protection for the petroglyphs and rock engravings to the Burrup Peninsula region and Dampier Archipelago in northern Western Australia.

11. Many indigenous communities continue to question the individualization inherent in Australian welfare policies, which provide individual benefits and payments, or the education and training approaches to land and family management practices offered by companies, which again presume a strong individualized focus rather than a communal focus.

12. Altmann has in mind examples like the Buku-Larrngay Mulka Arts Centre and the delivery of environmental services to white businesses (2014).

13. See, e.g., digitaldreamtime.tumblr.com.

14. Stuart Campbell is the Digital Media Coordinator of Big hART's Yijala Yala Project.

15. Big hArt was established in 1992 by writer and director Scott Rankin and writer and director John Bakes. It works to make sustained changes in disadvantaged communities in rural and regional Australia and to make the problems faced by these communities visible in the public sphere. It also wants to create high-quality cultural activity that promotes personal, community and regional development, and produces high-quality art for local, national and international audiences.

16. For an account of Yjala Yala Projects, see Edmunds 2012, pp. 167–168.

17. The name Neomad implies these are new nomads. The term of 'nomad' has a linguistic history. According to Schmitt, our idea of nomad is derived from the Greek *nemein*, meaning to pasture or graze, while the Greek *nomes* is capturing, wandering, or searching for pasture (1993, pp. 70–71). *nemein* refers to the verb *nemein*, 'to take' or 'appropriate'. (1993, p. 56).

18. For an overview of those policies and their effects, see Dardot and Laval (2013) and Dumenil and Levy (2013).

19. Who adapts Heidegger's (1977) and Benjamin's (1968) theoretical framework.

20. Thus, Taussig helps revise Fanon's (1967) account of the social and psychic dynamics at work in the interactions between white colonizers and 'colored' indigenous people who want to get along with their masters.

21. That work had its origins in philosophical and cognitive theory originating with Ludwig Wittgenstein (1953) and Lakoff and Johnson (1983), and early work on categories (e.g., Rosch and Mervis (1975).

22. This was part of the 'Deadly Yarns' initiative, a partnership between ScreenWest ABC television and the film television institute of Western Australia.

23. Australian Broadcast Commission (ABC).

24. The first episode tells of the first-born son, Mararra, who is shown how to move stealthily across the country to make his first kangaroo kill on his first hunting expedition. The second episode takes the reader across time, located in the last ice age, and tells about another boy hunter's adventure in catching a sea turtle. In the final episode, both boys mark their hunting quests by etching petroglyphs. We are then taken to see an awe-struck modern-day boy discover those images. He asks the elder who is accompanying him how old the petroglyph is, a question that leads to a conversation about the history of their people.

25. Mowarin's *Ngurrara* was awarded a jury selection at the 17th Japan Media Arts Festival.

26. Local child actors in this episode were Ashton Munda, Brody Tahi Tahi, Deshawn Roberts, Eric Wedge, Jarried Ashburton, Edwin Dan, Maverick Eaton, Maxie Coppin, Nathaniel Edwins, Nelson Coppin and Sidney Eaton. Other credits go to Directors: Benjamin Ducroz and Sutu; Writer: Sutu; Creative Producer: Debra Myers; Associate Producer: Elspeth Blunt; Editor: Benjamin Ducroz; Set Design: Benjamin Ducroz; Set Construction: Benjamin Ducroz, Dudley Billing, Sutu; Set Artist: Hiroyasu Tsuri; Costume and Makeup: Chynna Campbell and Sutu; Camera: Benjamin Ducroz, Cavill Schipp; Sound: Stuart Thorne; Script Consultants: Denise Smith and Tyson Mowarin benjamin ducroz, Yijala Yala Project: big-hArt, www.**ducroz.com/yijala-yala-project**-big-hART).

27. It is also worth dwelling for a moment on *Hipbone Sticking Out*, because it is illustrative of the local art, music, dance and creative projects and provides an example of the political nature of local art. It offers a semifictionalized historical account of a tragic aspect of white indigenous relations, namely the issue of Aboriginal deaths in custody, which remains as continuing testimony to a persistent history of racist violence and dispossession. The recent stage show *Hipbone Sticking Out*, produced by Yijala Yala and others from the Ngarluma and Roebourne communities, is illustrative of the ways community members have worked to reclaim and build on the cultural heritage embedded in the landscape and people. This piece of theater transports the audience through time and space by telling the story of John Pat, who is the main character. It is the story of a 16-year-old boy who died in 1983 from massive head injuries while in police custody in Roebourne, and while his death was one in a long line of such fatalities, it was the one that led to a breakthrough. The Royal Commission into Aboriginal Deaths in Custody was established by the Hawke Labour government in 1989 (tabled in Parliament in 1991). In this way it takes on additional political significance.

Use of the narrative device of time travel in this dramatic work also makes a point about history, how it is told and from whose perspective. A spiritual journey through time that is taken by the main character, John Pat, renders this point more accessible and likely to engage a contemporary audience than simply telling the story of John Pat as part of a more straightforward historical narrative.

The style of this theater makes a disquieting political point. The music of *Hipbone Sticking Out* fuses traditional Pilbara songs with other traditional cultural traditions, including Irish sea shanties and the contemporary music of modern pop stars like the American Britney Spears. This kind of bricolage, or overlapping of diverse even discrepant traditions or genres, works to reinforce the time-travel device, offering a musical counterpoint to a storyline that explicitly narrates a journey that the main character John Pat takes, who time travels through European, Asian and Aboriginal history. The music provides an aural counterpart to a history of the world, drawing together the Pilbara, the ancient Greek and Roman gods, the spice routes of China, the coming of the 'ghost people' (Europeans) to Ngarluma country, and the coincidental arrival of slavery and pearling, through the various mining booms up to the present. This musical bricolage reinforces an atypical historical account that is not Eurocentric. It also highlights the continuous history of Aboriginal people's history, while it serves to raise questions about the ethics of cultural borrowing, and asks the audience to think about the distinction between cultural blending and cultural appropriation and what is involved in making a claim to cultural authenticity.

Conclusion

1. To this extent I see dead writers, like Castoriadis (d. 1997) and Young (d. 2006), and living writers, like Sen and Critchley, who are very different in many ways 'as if' they belong to this tradition, a treatment to which they might take exception. Thus I highlight the shared themes and emphases that characterize and animate their work in making that nomination, while acknowledging the importance of their differences.

References

Aapola, Gonick and Harris, 2005, *Young Femininity: Girlhood, Power and Social Change,* Hampshire UK, Palgrave Macmillan.

Abbate, J., 1999, *Inventing the Internet,* Cambridge: MIT Press.

Acton, H. B., 1955, *The Illusion of the Epoch,* London: Cohen and West.

Adam, B., 1990, *Time and Social Theory,* Cambridge: Polity.

Adamson, M., 2009, 'The Human Capital Strategy', *Ephemera: Theory & Politics in Organization* 9:4, pp. 27–39, http://www.ephemeraweb.org/journal /9-4/9-4adamson.pdf.

Aitchinson, G., 2011, 'What Next for the UK's Student Movement', in Hancox, D., (ed.), *Fightback: A Reader on the Winter of Protest,* London: Open Democracy, pp. 314–318.

Alderson, P., 2007, 'Competent Children? Minors' Consent to Health Care Treatment and Research', *Social Science & Medicine,* 65, 2272–2283.

Alloway, N., and Dalley-Trim, L., 2009, It's All about I: Gen Ys and Neoliberal Discourse in New Times', *Youth Studies Australia,* 28:1, pp. 51–56.

Allport, G. W. 1954, *The Nature of Prejudice.* Reading, MA: Addison Wesley.

Altman, D., 1987, 'The Creation of Sexual Politics in Australia', *Journal of Australian Studies,* 20, pp. 76–82.

Altmann, J., 2011, 'Noel Pearson's policies embraced by white Australia, but how effective are they?', *The Conversation* 8 August, http://theconversation.com/ noel-pearsons-policies-embraced-by-white-australia-but-how-effective-are-they-2226.

Altmann, J., 2014, 'Rio Tinto's Gove Plant Never Delivered on Indigenous Hopes', *Crikey,* 13 February, http://www.crikey.com.au/2014/02/13/rio-tintos-gove-plant-never-delivered-on-indigenous-hopes.

Aly, W., 2010, What's Right? The Future of Conservatism in Australia, *Quarterly Essay,* 37, pp. 1–110.

Alyokhina, M., 2012, (Shayevich, B) 'Pussy Riot Closing Statements', http://nplusonemag.com/pussy-riot-closing-statements.

Anderson, B., 1983/1991, *Imagined Communities: Reflections on the Origin and Spread of Nationalism,* London: Verso.

Anderson, L., 2011. 'Demystifying the Arab Spring: Parsing the Differences between Tunisia, Egypt, and Libya'. *Foreign Affairs* 90 (3), pp. 2–7.

Anderson, N., 2011, 'Major ISPs Agree to "Six Strikes" Copyright Enforcement Plan', *ArsTechnica,* http://arstechnica.com/tech-policy/news/2011/07/major-isps-agree-to-six-strikes-copyright-enforcement-plan.ars.

Appadurai, A., 1996, *Modernity at Large: Cultural Dimensions of Globalization,* Minneapolis: University of Minnesota Press.

Arendt, H., 1958, *The Human Condition,* Chicago: University of Chicago Press.

Arendt, H., 1977, *Between Past and Future,* New York: Penguin Books.

Arendt, H., 1996, *Love and Saint Augustine.* Ed. Scott J. Vecchiarelli and Judith Chelius Stark, Chicago: University of Chicago Press.

Aristotle, 1963, *Generation of Animals*. Introduction, text, trans. A. I. Peck, Loeb Classical Library. Cambridge: Harvard University Press.

Aristotle, 1999, *Nicomachean Ethics*, 2nd ed., Trans. Terence Irwin, Indianapolis: Hackett Publishing.

Arnett, J., 2000, *Emerging Adulthood: Prospects for the 21st Century*. New York: Cambridge: Oxford University Press.

Arnett, J., 2001, *Adolescence and Emerging Adulthood: A Cultural Approach*. Upper Saddle River, NJ: Prentice Hall.

Arntzenius, F., 2000, 'Are There Really Instantaneous Velocities?', *The Monist*, 83, 187–208.

Aronowitz, S., and Giroux, H., 2000, 'The Corporate University and the Politics of Education', *The Educational Forum*, 6:4, pp. 332–339.

Attran, S., 1987, 'Origin of the Species and Genus Concepts: An Anthropological Perspective', *Journal of the History of Biology*, 20:2, pp. 195–279.

Australia Unlimited, 2012, *Tyson Mowarrin-Digital Dreamings,* http://www.australiaunlimited.com/tags/term/tyson-mowarin.

Bacchi, C., 2009, *Analysing Policy: What's the Problem Represented To Be?*, Pearson Education. Frenchs Forest, Australia.

Bachelard, G., 1985, *The New Scientific Spirit*. Trans. A. Goldhammer, Boston: Beacon Press.

Bachelard, G., 2002, *The Formation of the Scientific Mind*. Trans. M. McAllester Jones, Clinamen, Bolton, 2002.

Bailey, C., 2006. 'What is Open Access?', in Jacobs, N., (ed.), *Open Access: Key Strategic, Technical and Economic Aspects*. Oxford: Chandos, pp. 13–26.

Baker, S., 2011, SOPA-ropa-dope, Skating on Stilts, http://www.skatingonstilts.com/skating-on-stilts/2011/12/the-sopa-rope-a-dope.htmlmber, December 14.

Bakhtin, M., 1941, *Rabelais and His World*, Bloomington: Indiana University Press.

Ball, S., and Olmedo, A., 2012, 'Care of the Self: Resistance and Subjectivity under Neoliberal Governmentalities', *Critical Studies in Education*, 54:1, pp. 85–89.

Banks, S., 2010, *Ethical Issues in Youth Work*. London: Routledge.

Baran, P., and Sweezy, P., 1966, *Monopoly Capital: An Essay on the American Economic and Social Order,* Monthly Review Press. New York.

Barber, B., 1984, *Strong Democracy: Participatory Politics for a New Age,* Berkeley: University of California Press.

Bartlett, R.H., 1993, *The Mabo Decision*, Butterworths, Sydney.

Barrionuevo, A., 2011, 'With Kiss-ins and Dances, Young Chileans Push for Reform'. *The New York Times*, 4 August.

Bartlett, R., 1993, 'The Proprietary Nature of Native Title', *Australian Property Law Journal*, 1, pp. 23–45.

Bastedo, H., 2012, 'They Don't Stand for Me: Generational Difference in Voter Motivation and the Importance of Symbolic Representation in Youth Voter Turnout', PhD thesis, University of Toronto.

Bear, A., 1970, 'Demonstrations and the Australian Press', *Politics*, 7:2, pp. 155–159.

Beck, U., 2000, *What Is Globalization?,* Cambridge: Polity Press.

Beck, U., 2002, *Individualization: Institutionalized individualism and Its Social and Political Consequences*, London: Sage.

Beck, U., and Beck-Gernsheim, E., 1996, 'Individualization and "Precarious Freedoms": Perspectives and Controversies of a Subject-Oriented Sociology', in Heelas, P., Lash, S., and Morris, P., (eds.), *Detraditionalization, Critical Reflections on Authority and Identity*, Oxfored, Blackwell.

Beck, U., and Beck-Gernsheim, E., 2002, *Individualisation*, London: Sage.

Beck U., and Beck-Gernsheim, E., 2009, 'Global Generations and the Trap of Methodological Nationalism for a Cosmopolitan Turn in the Sociology of Youth and Generation', *European Sociological Review*, 25:1, pp. 25–36. [doi://dx.doi.org/10.1093/esr/jcn032].

Beetham, D., 1974, *Max Weber and the Theory of Modern Politics*, London: Allen & Unwin.

Beetham, D., 1986, *Max Weber and the Theory of Modern Politics*, Cambridge: Polity.

Beetham, D., 1991a, *The Legitimation of Power*, Atlantic Highlands: Atlantic Press.

Beetham, D., 1991b, *The Legitimation of Power*, Oxford: Oxford University Press.

Beiser, F., (ed.), 2008, *The Cambridge Companion to Hegel and Nineteenth-Century Philosophy*, Cambridge: Cambridge University Press.

Beiser, F., 2005, *Hegel*, New York and London: Routledge.

Benhabib, S., 1994, 'Deliberative Rationality and Models of Democratic Legitimacy', *Constellations*, 1 (1), pp. 22–39.

Benhabib, S., 1996, 'Towards a Deliberative Model of Democratic Legitimacy', in Benhabib, S., (ed.), *Democracy and Difference: Contesting the Boundaries of the Political*, Princeton: Princeton University Press.

Benjamin, W., 1968, 'The Work of Art in the Age of Mechanical Reproduction', in *Illuminations*, New York: Schocken Books.

Benjamin, W., 1978, 'On the Mimetic Faculty', in *Reflections*, New York: Schocken Books, pp. 217–259.

Benkler, Y., 2006, *The Wealth of Networks: How Social Production Transforms Markets and Freedom*, New Haven: Yale University Press.

Benkler, Y., Roberts, H., Faris, R., Solow-Niederman, A., and Etling, B., 2013, *Social Mobilization and the Networked Public Sphere: Mapping the SOPA-PIPA Debate'*, The Berkman Center for Internet & Society Research Publication Series: http://cyber.law.harvard.edu/publications/2013/social_mobilization_and_the_networked_public_sphere.

Bennett, B., 1963, 'On the Youthfulness of Youth Cultures', *Social Research: An International Quarterly*, 30:3, pp. 319–342.

Bennett, S., Maton, K., and Kervin, L., 2008, 'The "Digital Natives" Debate: A Critical Review of the Evidence', *British Journal of Educational Technology*, 39:5, pp. 775–86. Available at http://tinyurl.com/ ycrklnq.

Berlant, L., 2011, *Cruel Optimism*, Durham: Duke University Press.

Berners–Lee T., 1996, 'The World Wide Web: Past, Present and Future', http://www.w3.org/People/Berners-Lee/1996/ppf.html.

Bernstein, A., 2103, 'Post-Soviet Body Politics: Crime and Punishment in the Pussy Riot Affair', *Somatosphere* 16 September, http://somatosphere.net/2013/09/post-soviet-body-politics-crime-and-punishment-in-the-pussy-riot-affair.html.

Bernstein, B., 1996, *Pedagogy, Symbolic Control and Identity*. London: Routledge.

Bertman, S., 1976, (ed.), *The Conflict of Generations in Greece and Rome*, Amsterdam: Gruner.

Bessant, J., 1995a, 'Government and the Never-never land of Adulthood', *Arena Magazine*, 19, pp. 27–29.

Bessant, J., 1995b, 'Consolidating an Industry and Prolonging Dependency: Professionals, Policies and Young People', *Australian Journal of Social Issues*, 30:3, pp. 249–274.

Bessant, J., and Watts, R., 2014, 'Cruel Optimism': A Southern Theory Perspective on the European Union's 'Youth Strategy', 2008–2012, *International Journal of Adolescence and Youth: Youth Policy in Austerity Europe*. Special issue, pp. 1–16. Link to this article http://dx.doi.org/10.1080/02673843.2013.833957.

Bessant, J., Hil, R., and Watts, R., 2005, *Discovering Risk: Social Research and Policy Making*, New York: Peter Lang.

Benkler, Y., 2006, *The Wealth of Networks How Social Production Transforms Markets and Freedom*, Yale University Press, New Haven and London, pp. 212–484.

Benkler, Y., Roberts, H., Faris, R., Solow-Niederman, Etling, B., 2013, *Social Mobilization and the Networked Public Sphere: Mapping the SOPA-PIPA Debate*, Berkman Centre, Harvard University, http://papers.ssrn.com/sol3/papers.cfm?abstract_id=2295953.

Bhabha, Homi K., 1996, 'Unsatisfied: Notes on Vernacular Cosmopolitanism', in Garcia-Moreno, L., and Pfeiffer, P. C., (eds.) *Text and Nation: Cross-Disciplinary Essays on Cultural and National Identities*. Columbia, SC: Camden House.

Bhaskar, R., 1978. *A Realist Theory of Science*, Hemel Hempstead: Harvester Wheatsheaf.

Bhaskhar, R., 1989. *The Possibility of Naturalism. A Philosophical Critique of the Contemporary Human Sciences*. Hemel Hempstead: Harvester Wheatsheaf.

Bilton. N., 2013, Disruptions: Digital Era redefining Etiquette, *New York Times*, 10 March http://bits.blogs.nytimes.com/2013/03/10/etiquette-redefined-in-the-digital-age/?_r=0.

Bimber, B. A., 1998, 'The Internet and Political Transformation: Populism, Community, and Accelerated Pluralis', *Polity* 31, pp. 133–160.

Bimber, B. A., 2012, 'Digital Media and Citizenship', in Simetko, H., and Scammell. M., (eds.), *Sage Handbook of Political Communication*, Thousand Oaks, CA: Sage.

Bimber B. A., and Davis, R., 2003, *Campaigning Online: The Internet in US Elections*, New York: Oxford University Press.

Blind, P., 2006, *Building Trust in Government: Review of Literature and Emerging Issues*, Global Forum On Reinventing Government Building Trust in Government, 26–29 June 2007, Vienna, Austria.

Bodin, P-A., 2009, *Language, Canonization and Holy Foolishness*. Stockholm: Stockholm University Press.

Bohmann, J., 1996, *Public Deliberation; Pluralism, Complexity and Democracy*, Cambridge: MIT Press.

Bolton, G., 1958, *John Forrest: His Life and Times,* Melbourne: Melbourne University Press.

Bolton, R., 2005, 'Habermas's Theory of Communicative Action and the Theory of Social Capital', *Meeting of Association of American Geographers*, Denver, CO, February.

Booz&Co, 2011, 'Angel Investors and Venture Capitalists Say They Will Stop Funding Some Internet Start-Up Business Models If Tough New Rules Are Enacted, Finds Booz & Company Study', http://www.booz.com/global/home/

press/article/49953717#sthash.c4Z9LtrA.dpuf   http://www.booz.com/global/home/press/article/49953717.

Bourdieu, P., 1977, *Outline of a Theory of Practice,* Cambridge: Cambridge University Press.

Bourdieu, P., 1998, *Practical Reason,* Cambridge: Polity Press.

Bourdieu, P., 2000, *Pascalian Meditations,* Cambridge: Polity Press.

Bourdieu, P., 1984, *Distinction: A Social Critique of the Judgement of Taste,* London: Routledge.

Bourdieu, P., 1990a, *Reproduction in Education, Society and Culture* (Theory, Culture and Society Series), London: Sage.

Bourdieu, P., 1990b, *The Logic of Practice,* Trans R. Nice, Stanford: Stanford University Press.

Bourdieu, P., 1993, '"Youth" Is Just a Word', in *Sociology in Question* London: Sage, pp. 94–102.

Bourdieu, P., 1996, *The Rules of Art.* Trans. Susan Emanuel. Cambridge: Polity Press.

Bourdieu, P., 1985, 'The Genesis of the Concepts of "habitus" and "_Eld"'. *Sociocriticism* 1:2.

Bourdieu P., and Passeron, J., 1977, *Reproduction in Education, Society and Culture,* Beverly Hills: Sage.

Bourdieu, P., and Wacquant, L. D. 1992, *An Invitation to Reflexive Sociology,* Cambridge: Polity Press.

Bourn, D., 2003, 'Global Perspectives in Youth Work', *Youth and Policy,* 80, pp. 6–21.

Bourn, D., 2008, 'Young People, Identity and Living in a Global Society', *Policy & Practice: A Development Education Review,* 7, pp. 48–61.

Boyd, D., 2008, 'Taken Out of Context: American Sociality in Networked Publics,' PhD thesis, University of California, Berkeley.

Boyd, D., 2012, 'The Politics of Real Names: Power, Context and Control in Networked Publics', *Communication and the ACM,* 55, 8, pp. 29–31. http://www.danah.org/papers/2012/CACM-RealNames.pdf.

Boyd, D., 2014, *It's Complicated: The Social Lives of Networked Teens,* New Haven: Yale University Press.

Brake, M., 1985. *Comparative Youth Culture: The Sociology of Youth Culture and Youth Subcultures in America, Britain and Canada,* New York, Routledge.

Brandom, R., 2002, *Tales of the Mighty Dead: Historical Essays in the Metaphysics of Intentionality,* Cambridge: Harvard University Press.

Brandom, R., 2009, *Reason in Philosophy: Animating Ideas,* Cambridge: Harvard University Press.

Brett J., and Moran, A., 2006, *Ordinary People's Politics: Australians Talk about Life, Politics and the Future of their Country,* Melbourne: Pluto Press.

Brooke, J., 2012, 'Analysis: Political Winter Descends on Russia', *Voice of America,* 23 October, http://www.voanews.com/content/analysis-political-winter-descends-on-russia/1531876.html.

Brookes, J., 2012, 'Lessig on How Money Corrupts Congress and How to Stop It', *Rolling Stone,* October 2012, http://www.rollingstone.com/politics/blogs/national-affairs/lawrence-lessig-on-how-money-corrupts-congress-and-how-to-stop-it-20111005.

Brown, P., Laugh Lauder and Ashton, D., 2010, *The Global Auction: The Broken Promises of Education, Jobs, and Incomes*, Oxford: Oxford University Press.

Brown, W., 2005, *Edgework: Critical Essays on Knowledge and Politics*. Princeton, NJ: Princeton University Press.

Burkitt, I., 1991, *Social Selves*, London: Sage.

Burkitt, I., 1997, 'The Situated Social Scientist: Reflexivity and Perspective in the Sociology of Knowledge', *Social Epistemology: A Journal of Knowledge, Culture and Policy*, 11:2, pp. 193–202.

Calhoun, C., 1992, (ed.), *Pierre Bourdieu: Critical Perspectives*, Chicago: University of Chicago Press.

Calhoun, C., 2002, 'Pierre Bourdieu in Context', paper presented at New York University, the University of Pennsylvania, and the New School for Social Research.

Carey, J., 2009, *A Cultural Approach to Communication: Communication as Culture*. New York: Routledge.

Carrington, K., 1993, *Offending Girls*, Sydney, Allen and Unwin.

Cass, B., and Brennan, D., 2002, 'Communities of Support or Communities of Surveillance and Enforcement in Welfare Reform Debates', *Australian Journal of Social Issues*, 37:3, pp. 247–262.

Castells, M., 1996, *The Rise of the Network Society*. Oxford: Blackwell.

Castoriadis, C., 1984a, *Crossroads in the Labyrinth*. Trans. Kate Soper and Martin H. Ryle, Cambridge: MIT Press.

Castoriadis, C., 1984b, 'The Imaginary: Creation in the Social-Historical Domain', in Castoriadis, C., 1997, *World in Fragments: Writings on Politics, Society, Psychoanalysis and the Imagination*. Trans. David Ames Curtis, Stanford: Stanford University Press, pp. 3–18.

Castoriadis, C., 1987, *The Imaginary Institution of Society*. Trans. Kathleen Blamey, Cambridge: Polity.

Castoriadis, C., 1991, *Philosophy, Politics, Autonomy: Essays in Political Philosophy*, Curtis, D. A., (ed.), New York, Oxford University Press.

Castoriadis, C., 1997, *The Imaginary Institution of Society [IIS]*. Trans. Kathleen Blamey, Cambridge: MIT Press.

Castoriadis, C., 1998, *The Castoriadis Reader*, Trans. and ed. David Ames Curtis, New York: Blackwell.

Chadwick A., 2006, *Internet Politics: States, Citizens, and New Communication Technologies*. New York: Oxford University Press.

Chambers, S., and Costain, A., 2000, (eds.), *Deliberation, Democracy and the Media*, Lanham, MD: Rowman & Littlefield.

Charlesworth, M., 1969, 'The Youth Revolution', *Meanjin Quarterly*, 3, pp. 391–397.

Chew, K., 2012, 'Russian Police Hunting Other Pussy Riot Members', 20 August, http://www.care2.com/causes/russian-police-hunting-other-pussy-riot-members.html.

Chomsky, N., 2012, *Occupy*. London, Penguin.

Chomsky, N., and McChesney, R., 2011, *Profit over People: Neoliberalism & Global Order*. OR: Seven Stories Press.

Circa, 2014, 'Pussy Riot Band Members Detained with 100 people at Moscow Protests', 25 February, Circa, http://cir.ca/news/pussy-riot-takes-on-putin.

Clark, E., 2004, *History, Theory, Text: Historians and the Linguistic Turn*, Cambridge: Harvard University Press.

Clarke, J., Hall, S., Jefferson T., Roberts B. (1976), Subcultures, Cultures and Class, in S. Hall and T. Jefferson (eds), *Resistance through Rituals: Youth Subcultures in Post-War Britain*, London: Hutchinson.

Cobb, M., 2006, *Generation*, London: Bloomsbury.

Cogin, J., 2012, 'Are Generational Differences in Work Values Fact or Fiction? Multi-country Evidence and Implications, *The International Journal of Human Resource Management*, 23:11, pp. 2268–2294.

Cohen, C., and Kahne, J., 2012, Participatory Politics: New Media and Youth Political Action, http://ypp.dmlcentral.net/sites/all/files/publications/YPP_Survey_Report_FULL.pdf.

Cohen, G., 1978, *Karl Marx's Theory of History: A Defence*, Princeton: Princeton University Press.

Cohen, J., 1996, 'Deliberation and Democratic Legitimacy', in Hamlin, A., and Pettit, P., (eds.), T*he Good Polity: Normative Analysis of the State*, Oxford: Blackwell, pp. 17–34.

Cohen, J., and Arato, A., 1992, *Civil Society and Political Theory*, Cambridge: MIT Press.

Cohn, D., 2013, 'More Young Adults Live with Their Parents', PEW Research Center, http://www.pewsocialtrends.org/2013/08/01/more-young-adults-live-with-their-parents/.

Coleman, J., 1961, *The Adolescent Society: The Social life of the Teenager and Its Impact on Education*, Glencoe, Free Press.

Coleman, S., and Gotze, J., 2001, *Bowling Together: Online Public Engagement in Policy Deliberation*, London: Hansard Society.

Coles, B., 1995, *Youth and Social Policy: Youth Citizenship and Young Careers*, London: UCL Press.

Commonwealth of Australia, 2010, *Australia to 2050: Future Challenges*, Canberra: Commonwealth of Australia.

Connell, R., 2013, 'The Neoliberal Cascade and Education: An Essay on the Market Agenda and Its Consequences', *Critical Studies in Education*, 54:2, pp. 99–112.

Connell, R., 1974, 'Patterns of Social and Political Opinion among Sydney Youth', *Australian Journal of Political History*, 20:3, pp. 177–185.

Connell, R., and Ashenden, D., 1982, *Making the Difference*, Sydney: Allen and Unwin.

Coupland, D., 1989, *Generation X*, New York: St. Martin's Press.

Coupland, D., 1991, *Generation Gap* First Recorded 1967; *generation x* is 1991, from book of that name; *generation y* attested by 1994.

Craig, G., 2007, 'Community Capacity-building: Something Old, Something New...?' *Critical Social Policy*, 27:3, pp. 335–359.

Cramer, B., 2013, 'The Two Internet Freedoms: Framing Victimhood for Political Gain', *International Journal of Communication*, 7, pp. 1074–1092.

Crick, B., 2005, *In Defence of Politics*, 5th ed., London: Continuum.

Critchley, S., 2012, *Infinitely Demanding: Ethics of Commitment, Politics of Resistance*, London: Verso.

Cruikshank, B., 1999, *The Will to Power: Democratic Citizens and Other Subjects*, Ithaca: Cornell University Press.

Crumpacker, M., and Crumpacker, J. M., 2007, 'Succession Planning and Generational Stereotypes: Should HR Consider Age-Based Values and Attitudes a Relevant Factor or a Passing Fad?', *Public Personnel Management*, 36, pp. 349–369.

d'Entrèves, M., 1994, *The Political Philosophy of Hannah Arendt*. London: Routledge.

Dahlberg, L., 2000, 'The Habermasian Public Sphere: A Specification of the Idealised Conditions of Democratic Communication', *Studies in Social and Political Thought*, www.sussex.ac.uk/cspt/documents/10–1a.pdf.

Dahlberg, L., 2001a, 'Computer-Mediated Communication – The Public Sphere: A Critical Analysis, http://jcmc.indiana.edu/vol1/issue1/dahlberg.html.

Dahlberg., L., 2001b, 'Extending the Public Sphere through Cyberspace: The Case of Minnesota E-Democracy', www.firstmonday.org/issues/issue6_3/dahlberg/index.html#note2.

Dahlgren, P., 2000, 'The Internet and the Democratization of Civic Culture', *Political Communication*, 17, pp. 335–340.

Dahlgren, P., 2005, 'The Internet, Public Spheres and Political Communication, *Political Communication*, 22, pp. 147–162.

Dahlgren, P., 2007, (ed.), *Young Citizens and New Media, Learning for Democratic Participation*, London: Routledge.

Dahlgren, P., 2009, *Media and Political Engagement: Citizens, Communication and Democracy*, Cambridge University Press.

Dahlgren, P., 2013, *The Political Web: Media Participation and Alternative Democracy*, Palgrave Macmillan.

Dardot, P., and, Laval, C., 2013, *The New Way of the World: On Neoliberal Society*, Trans. G. Elliott, London: Verso.

Davidoff, V., 2012, 'The Witch Hunt against Pussy Riot', *The Moscow Times*, 25 June, http://www.themoscowtimes.com/opinion/article/the-witch-hunt-against-pussy-riot/460968.html.

Davidson, A., 1994, 'Citizenship, Sovereignty and the Identity of the Nation-State', in James, P., (ed.), *Critical Politics: From the Personal to the Global*, Melbourne: Arena, pp. 111–125.

Davies, B. L., 2007, 'Warfare, State and Society on the Black Sea Steppe 1500–1700'.

Davis, M., 2007, 'Myths of the Generations: Baby Boomers, Z and Y', *Overland*, 187, pp. 4–14.

Dean, M., 1991, *The Constitution of Poverty: Towards a Genealogy of Liberal Governance*, London: Routledge.

Debord, G., 1967, *The Society of the Spectacle*. London: Black & Red.

Deger, J., 2006, *Shimmering Screens: Making Media in an Aboriginal Community*, Minneapolis: University of Minnesota Press.

Deleuze, G., 1990, *Expressionism in Philosophy: Spinoza*, Trans. Martin Joughin, New York: Zone Books.

Deleuze, G., 1991, *Empiricism and Subjectivity: An Essay on Hume's Theory of Human Nature*, Trans. Constantin Boundas, New York: Columbia University Press.

Deleuze, G., and Guattari, F., 1983, *Anti-Oedipus*, Minneapolis: University of Minnesota Press.

Deloitte Development, 2006, *Who Are the Millennials? A.K.A. Generation Y*, Tohmatsu: Deloitte Touche.

Dietz, R., and Moruzzi, S. 2009, (eds.), *Cuts and Clouds. Vagueness, Its Nature, and Its Logic,* Oxford: Oxford University Press.

Dodge, N., and Rosenfeld, E., 1995, (eds.), *From Gulag to Glasnost: Nonconformist Art from the Soviet Union.* New York: Thames and Hudson.

Dolby, N., and Rizvi, F., 2008, *Youth Moves: Identities and Education in Global Perspectives,* New York: Routledge.

Douglas, J., Ali Hortacsu, A., and Asis Martinez-Jerez, A., 2009, 'The Geography of Trade on eBay and Mercado Libre', *American Economic Journal: Microeconomics,* 1:1, pp. 53–74.

Dreyfus, H., 1990, *Being-in-the-world: A Commentary on Heidegger's Being and Time, Division I.* Cambridge: MIT Press.

Dryzek, J., 1990, *Deliberative Democracy,* Cambridge: Cambridge University Press.

Dryzek., J., 1996, *Democracy in Capitalist times: Ideals, Limits and Struggles,* New York: Oxford University Press.

Dugdale, S., 2012, (trans) 'Pussy Riot Testimonies Modern Poetry in Translation', http://www.mptmagazine.com/feature/pussy-riot-testimonies-59/.

Dumenil, G., and Levy, D., 2013, *The Crisis of Neoliberalism,* Cambridge: Harvard University Press.

Dumenil, G., and Levy, D., 2004, *Capital Resurgent: Roots of the Neoliberal Revolution,* Trans. D. Jeffers, Cambridge: Harvard University Press.

Dwyer, P., and Minnegal, M., 2010, 'Theorizing Social Change', *Journal of the Royal Anthropological Institute* 16, pp. 629–645.

Dyzenhaus, D., 1998, Introduction, in Dyzenhaus, D., (ed.), *Law as Politics: Carl Schmitt's Critique of Liberalism,* Durham: Duke University Press.

Dyzenhaus, D., 1997, *Legality and Legitimacy: Carl Schmitt, Hans Kelsen, and Hermann Heller in Weimar,* Oxford: Clarendon Press.

Eagleton, T., 2012, *Why Marx Was Right,* London: Verso.

Eisenstadt, S., 1956, *From Generation to Generation: Age Cohorts and Social Structure,* Glencoe, IL: Free Press.

Elder, M., 2012, Feminist Punk Band Pussy Riot Take Revolt to the Kremlin, *The Guardian,* http://www.guardian.co.uk/world/2012/feb/02/pussy-riot-protest-russia.

Elias, N., 1978, *What is Sociology?* Trans. S. Mennell and G. Morrissey, London: Hutchinson.

Elias, N., 1984, *The Civilising Process,* (2 vols.), Oxford: Blackwell.

Elliott, A., 2002, 'The Social Imaginary: A Critical Assessment of Castoriadis's Psychoanalytic Social Theory' *American Imago,* 59:2, pp. 141–170.

Elster, J., 1998, *Deliberative Democracy,* Cambridge: Cambridge University Press, epress.lib.uts.edu.au/ojs/index.php/mcs/article/viewArticle/824.

Entman, R. M., 1993, 'Framing: Towards Clarification of a Fractured Paradigm', *Journal of Communication,* 43:4, pp. 51–58.

Ereshefsky, M., 2008, 'Darwin's Solution to the Species Problem', *Synthese,* www.bristol.ac.uk/metaphysicsofscience/.../ereshefsky.pdf.

Espinel, V., Chopra, A., and Schmidt, H., 2012, 'Combating Online Piracy While Protecting an Open and Innovative Internet', 14 January, https://petitions.whitehouse.gov/response/combating-online-piracy-while-protecting-open-and-innovative-internet.

Euronews, 2012, (17 November), 'Merkel Provokes Putin over Pussy Riot Punishment', http://www.youtube.com/watch?v=3Pc3HSXM9VE.

Fanon, F., 1967, *Black Skins, White Masks*, New York: Grove.

Farrell, H., 2012, 'The Consequences of the Internet for Politics', *Annual Review of Political. Science*, 15, pp. 35–52.

Favret, R., 2013, 'Comment: Back to the Bad Old Days: President Putin's Hold on Free Speech in the Russian Federation', *Richmond Journal of Global Law and Business*, 12:2, http://rjglb.richmond.edu/wp-content/uploads/2013/07/12.2.2-Favret.pdf.

Feltham, O., 2004, 'Singularity Happening in Politics: The Aboriginal Tent Embassy, Canberra, 1972', *Communication and Cognition*, 37:1–2, pp. 1–14.

Ferejohn, M., 1991, *The Origins of Aristotelian Science*, New Haven: Yale University Press.

Feuer, L., 1968, *The Conflict of Generations*, New York: Basic Books.

Figes, O., 2014, *Revolutionary Russia, 1891–1991*, New York: Metropolitan Books.

Fish, S., 2009, 'God Talk, Part 2'. *The New York Times Online*. 17 May, http://fish.blogs.nytimes.com/2009/05/17/god-talk-part-2/>.

Fishkin, J., 1991, *Democracy and Deliberation*, New Haven: Yale University Press.

Flyvberg, B., 2001, *Making Social Science Matter: Why Social Inquiry Fails and How It Can Succeed Again*, Cambridge, Cambridge University Press.

Foucault M., 1979, *Discipline and Punish*, London: Penguin.

Foucault, M., 2008, *The Birth of Bio-politics: Lectures at the College de France, 1978–79*, London: Palgrave Macmillan.

Fowler, B., 1997, *Pierre Bourdieu and Cultural Theory: Critical Investigations*, London, California and New Delhi: Sage Publications.

France, A., 2008, *Understanding Youth in Late Modernity*, Berkshire: OUP.

Frances, A., 2009, 'A Warning Sign on the Road to DSM-V: Beware of Its Unintended Consequences' *Psychiatric Times*, http://www.psychiatrictimes.com/articles/warning-sign-road-dsm-v-beware-its-unintended-consequences?verify=0A.

Francis, M., 1996, 'Social Darwinism and the Construction of Institutionalised Racism in Australia', *Journal of Australian Studies*, 20: 50–51, pp. 90–105.

Fraser, N., 1990, 'Rethinking the Public Sphere: A Contribution to the Critique of Actually Existing Democracy', *Social Text*, 25/26, pp. 56–80.

Fraser, N., 1995, 'Politics, Culture and the Public Sphere: Toward a Postmodern Conception', in Nicholson, L., and Seidman, S., (eds.), *Social Postmodernism: Beyond Identity Politics*, Cambridge University Press, New York, pp. 287–314.

Freedom House, 2012, 'Freedom House Condemns Conviction of Pussy Riot in Russia', Freedom House, http://www.freedomhouse.org/report/freedom-world/freedom-world-2012.

Froomkin, M., 2004, 'Habermas@Discourse.Net: Toward a Critical Theory of Cyberspace', *Harvard Law Review*, 116, pp. 747–876.

Fry, R., 2013, 'A Rising Share of Young Adults Live in Their Parents' Home', PEW Research Center, http://www.pewsocialtrends.org/files/2013/07/SDT-millennials-living-with-parents-07-2013.pdf.

Fumerton, R., 1995, *Metaepistemology and Skepticism*, Lanham, MD: Rowman & Littlefield.

Furlong, A., and Cartmel, F. 2007, *Young People and Social Change*, 2nd ed., Buckingham: Open University Press/McGraw Hill.

Gaines, J., 2000, 'White Privilege and Looking Relations: Race and Gender in Feminist Film Theory', in Stam, R., and Miller, T., (eds.), *Film and Theory*, Malden: Blackwell.

Gardner, S. 2012, Wikimedia Foundation statement on 20 January, Event in Washington, *20 January, Wikimedia Foundation,* accessed 23 January.

Gare, A., 2002, Review of *Towards an Inclusive Democracy, Review of Radical Political Economics,* 34:1, 97–99.

Gasset, J., 1923/1961, *The Modern Theme,* New York: Harper.

Gelman, S. 2005, *The Essential Child: Origins of Essentialism in Everyday Thought.* New York: Oxford University Press.

Gerbaudo, P., 2012, *Tweets and the Streets: Social Media and Contemporary Activism,* London: Palgrave Macmillan.

Geuss, R., 2008, *Philosophy and Real Politics,* Princeton: Princeton University Press,.

Gillon, S., 2004, *Boomer Nation: The Largest and Richest Generation Ever, and How It Changed America,* New York: Free Press.

Gimmler, A., 2001, 'Deliberative Democracy, the Public Sphere and the Internet', *Philosophy and Social Criticism,* 27:4, pp. 21–39.

Giroux, H., 1997, *Channel Surfing: Racism, the Media, and the Destruction of Today's Youth,* New York: St. Martin's Press.

Glass, A., 2007, 'Understanding Generational Differences for Competitive Success', *Industrial and Commercial Training,* 39, pp. 98–103.

Gleick, J., 2011, *The Information: A History, a Theory and a Flood,* New York: Pantheon.

Glyn, A., 2006, *Capitalism Unleashed: Finance Globalisation and Welfare,* Oxford: Oxford University Press.

Goankar, D., 2002, 'Toward New Imaginaries: an Introduction', *Public Culture,* 14:1, pp. 1–19.

Goffman, E., 1974, *Frame Analysis: An Essay on the Organization of Experience.* Cambridge: Harvard University Press.

Goldman, E., 2011, 'Why I Oppose the Stop Online Piracy Act (SOPA)/E-Parasites Act', *Technology and Marketing Law Blog,* November 15, http://blog.ericgoldman.org/archives/2011/11/stop_online_pir.htm.

Gould, S. J., 1981, *The Mismeasurement of Man,* London: W.W. Norton.

Greenberg, G., 2013, *The Book of Woe,* New York: BlueRider Press.

Griffin, C., 2001, 'Imagining a New Narrative of Youth: Youth Research, the "New Europe" and Global Youth Culture', *Childhood,* 8:2, pp. 147–166.

Grossman, L., 1996, *The Electronic Republic: Reshaping Democracy in the Electronic Age,* New York: Penguin.

Gurman, D., 2009, 'Why Lakoff Still Matters: Framing the Debate on Copyright Law and Digital Publishing', *First Monday,* 14:6, http://journals.uic.edu/ojs/index.php/fm/article/view/2354/2210.

Gutternman, S., 2012, 'Putin Provokes Criticism with Anti-Semitism Charge', Reuters, 16 November, http://www.reuters.com/article/2012/11/16/entertainment-us-russia-germany-pussyrio-idUSBRE8AF1EW20121116.

Habermas J., 1992, *Postmetaphysical Thinking,* Trans. W. M. Hohengarten, Cambridge: MIT Press.

Habermas J., 1996, *Between Facts and Norms: Contributions to a Discourse Theory of Law and Democracy,* Trans. W. Rehg, Cambridge: MIT Press.

Habermas, J., 1991, *The Philosophical Discourse of Modernity: Twelve Lectures.* Cambridge: MIT Press.

Habermas, J., 1962/1994, *The Structural Transformation of the Public Sphere: An Inquiry into a Category of Bourgeois Society*, Trans. T. Burger, Cambridge: MIT Press.

Habermas, J., 1964, *Towards a Rational Society*, London: Heineman.

Habermas, J., 1968, *Towards a Rational Society*, London: Heineman.

Habermas, J., 1971, *Knowledge and Human Interests*. Boston: Beacon Press.

Habermas, J., 1972, *Knowledge and Human Interests*, London: Heineman.

Habermas, J., 1974, *Legitmation Crisis*, Boston: Beacon Press.

Habermas, J., 1984, *Reason and the Rationalisation of the Life World*, Boston: Beacon Press.

Habermas, J., 1984, *Reason and the Rationalization of Society, V1 of The Theory of Communicative Action*, Trans. T. McCarthy, Boston: Beacon Press.

Habermas, J., 1984, *The Theory of Communicative Action, V.1, Reason and Rationalisation of Society*, Boston: Beacon Press.

Habermas, J., 1987, 'Excursus on Cornelius Castoriadis: The Imaginary Institution'. In *The Philosophical Discourse of Modernity*. Trans. Frederick Lawrence, Cambridge: Polity, pp. 327–335.

Habermas, J., 1987, *Lifeworld and System: A Critique of Functionalist Reason, V.2 of The Theory of Communicative Action*, Trans. T. McCarthy, Boston: Beacon Press.

Habermas, J., 1987, *The Theory of Communicative Action: Lifeworld and System: A Critique of Functionalist Reason*, Vol. 2, Boston: Beacon Press.

Habermas, J., 1989, *Structural Transformation of the Public Sphere: An Inquiry into a Category of Bourgeois, Society*, Trans. T. Burger and F. Lawrence, Cambridge: MIT Press.

Habermas, J., 1989, *The Structural Transformation of the Public Sphere: An Inquiry into a Category of Bourgeois Society*, Trans T. Burger, Cambridge: MIT Press.

Habermas, J., 1991, 'The Public Sphere', in Muckerji, C., and Schudson, M., (eds.), *Rethinking Popular Culture: Contemporary Perspectives in Cultural Studies*, University of California Press, Berkeley.

Habermas, J., 1996, *Between Facts and Norms: Contributions to a Discourse Theory of Law and Democracy*, Cambridge: MIT Press.

Habermas, J., 2001, 'From Kant's Idea of "Pure Reason" to the Idealizing Presuppositions of Communicative action', in Rheg, J., and Bohmann, J., (eds.), *Pluralism and the Pragmatic Turn: The Transformation of Critical Theory*, Cambridge: MIT Press.

Habermas, J., 2009, *Between Naturalism and Religion*, Trans. Ciaran Cronin, Cambridge: Polity.

Hacking, I,. 2002, *Historical Ontology*, Harvard University Press, Cambridge.

Hall, R. E., 2002, *Digital Dealing: How e-Markets are Transforming the Economy*, New York: W. W. Norton.

Hall, S., 1999, 'The Question of Cultural Identity', in Hall, S., Held, D., and McGrew, A., (eds.), *Modernity and Its Futures*. Cambridge: Polity, pp. 274–316.

Hammarstrom, G., 2004, 'The Constructs of Generation and Cohort in Sociological Studies of Ageing: Theoretical Conceptualisations and Some Empirical Implications', in Oberg, M., (ed.), *Changing worlds and the Ageing Subject: Dimensions in the Study of Ageing Subject*, Ashgate, Aldershot.

Harre, R., 1970, *The Principles of Scientific Thinking*. London: Macmillan.

Harris, A., 2013, *GenXegesis: Essays on Alternative Youth*, The Popular Press New York.

Harris, J., 2013, 'Generation Y: Why Young Voters Are Backing the Conservatives', *The Guardian*, 26 June. http://www.theguardian.com/politics/2013/jun/26/generation-y-young-voters-backing-conservatives.

Harris, M., 2012, 'Is Occupy Wall Street a Youth Movement? *Student Activism*, http://studentactivism.net/2012/03/07/is-occupy-wall-street-a-youth-movement/.

Harris, W., 1994, *Heraclitus: The Complete Fragments: Translation and Commentary and The Greek text*, http://community.middlebury.edu/~harris/Philosophy/heraclitus.pdf.

Hartshorne, C., 1971, 'The Development of Process Philosophy', in Cousins, E., (ed.), *Process Theology*, Newman Press, New York.

Hartshorne, C., 1971, *Reality as Social Process*, Hafner, New York.

Harvey, D., 2003, *Young People in a Globalizing World*, World Youth Report, New York.

Harvey, D., 2005, *A Brief History of Neoliberalism*. Oxford University Press, Oxford.

Haslanger, S., 1989, 'Persistence Change and Explanation', *Philosophical Studies* 56: 1–28, 1989.

Hebdige, D., 1976, *Subculture: The Meaning of Style*. London: Methuen.

Heidegger, M., 1977, *The Question Concerning Technology and Other Essays*, Trans W. Lovitt, Harper and Row, New York.

Heidegger, M., 1996, *Being and Time*, Trans. J. Stambaugh, State University of New York Press, Albany.

Held, D., and McGrew, A (eds.) 2003., *The Global Transformations Reader: An Introduction to the Globalization Debate*, Cambridge: Polity.

Held, D., 1980, *Introduction to Critical Theory*. University of California Press, Berkeley.

Herman, A., 1997, *The Idea of Decline in Western History*, The Free Press, New York.

Hermant, A., 2012, 'Pussy Riot Members Found Guilty of Hooliganism', 18 August, http://www.abc.net.au/news/2012–08–17/pussy-riot-members-await-verdict/4207260.

Hey, J., 2001, *Genes, Categories and Species: The Evolutionary and Cognitive Causes of the Species Problem*, Oxford University Press, New York.

Hilton, M., McKay, J., Crowson, N., and Mouhot, J-F., 2010, '"The Big Society": Civic Participation and the State in Modern Britain', *History and Policy*, http://www.historyandpolicy.org/papers/policy-paper-103.html.

Hippocrates, 2000, *On Airs, Waters and Places*, Trans. F. Waters, The Internet Classics Archive, http://classics.mit.edu//Hippocrates/airwatpl.html.

Hoffman, M., and Jamal, A., 2012, 'The Youth and the Arab Spring: Cohort Differences and Similarities', *Middle East Law and Governance* 4, pp. 168–188.

Hofstadter, D., and Sander, E., 2013, *Surfaces and Essences: Analogy as the Fuel and Fire of Human Thought*, Basic Books, New York.

Hofweber, T., 2009, 'The Metaproblem of Change', *Nous*, 43:2, 286–314.

Homer, 2011, *The Iliad of Homer*, (trans) Lattimore, R., Chicago: University of Chicago, vi, pp. 146–150.

Hogan, Bell and Perez, 2008, 'Who Really are the First Baby Boomers?' Joint Statistical Meetings Proceedings, Social Statistics Section, American Statistical Association, Alexandria, VA, 1009–1016.

Howker, E., and Malik, S. 2013, *Jilted Generation: How Britain Has Bankrupted Its Youth*, Icon Books, London.

HuffPost Live, 2014, 'Yale Issued A "Corporate Apology" for Shutting Down Bluebook Website, Student Says', 29 January http://www.huffingtonpost.com/2014/01/29/yale-bluebook-plus_n_4688387.html.

Hulan, R., and Eigenbrod, R., 2008, (eds.), *Aboriginal Oral Traditions: Theory, Practice, Ethics*. Fernwood Publishing, Halifax.

Hume, D., 1961, *An Enquiry Concerning Human Understanding*, Anchor Books, New York.

Huxley, J., 1974. *Evolution: The Modern Synthesis*, Allen and Unwin, London.

Hyam, H., 1959, *Political Socialisation*, Free Press, New York.

Idov, M., 2012, 'Pussy Riot Prove the Only Professionals in Sight', *The Guardian*, 18 August, http://www.theguardian.com/commentisfree/2012/aug/17/pussy-riot-only-professionals-in-sight.

International Labour Organization (ILO), 2012, *Global Employment Trends for Youth 2012*, ILO, Geneva.

International Telecommunication Union (ITC), 2013, 'The World in 2013', ICT Data and Statistical Division, Telecommunication Development Bureau, ITC, Geneva http://www.itu.int/en/ITU-D/Statistics/Documents/facts/ICTFactsFigures2013.pdf.

James, P., 2006, *Globalism, Nationalism, Tribalism: Bringing Theory Back in*. London: Sage.

Jamieson, L., 2002, 'Theorising Identity, Nationality and Citizenship: Implications for European Citizenship Identity', *Sociologia*, 34:6, pp. 507–532.

Jangid, K., 2013, 'In Search of the New Historians: Fieldwork in the Holy Land: Voices from the Sylff Community', 19 November, http://www.tokyofoundation.org/sylff/12662.

Jay, M., 1994, *Downcast Eyes: The Denigration of Vision in Twentieth Century French Thought*, University of California Press, Berkeley.

Jefferies, S., 2010, A Rare Interview with Jürgen Habermas, *FT Magazine*, April, http://www.ft.com/cms/s/0/eda3bcd8-5327-11df-813e-00144feab49a.html#axzz1qqCbjklx accessed 15–12–2012.

Jeffs, T., and Smith, M., 1994, 'Young People, Youth Work and the New Authoritarianism'. *Youth and Policy*, (Autumn) pp. 17–32.

Jennings, M., and Niemi, R., 'The Transmission of Political Values from Parent to Child', *American Political Science Review*, 62:1, 169–184.

Johnson-Laird, P. N. 1983. *Mental Models*. Cambridge, MA: Harvard University Press.

Johnson, C., 1997. 'Anthropology and Sociology: From Mauss to Levi-Strauss'. *Modern and Contemporary France* 5, pp. 421–431.

Jones Y. L., 1980, *Great Expectations: America and the Baby Boom Generation*, Coward, McCann and Geoghegan, New York.

Jones, A., 2010, *Globalization: Key Thinkers*. Cambridge: Polity Press.

Jones, G., and Wallace, C., 1992, *Youth, Family and Citizenship*, Buckingham, OUP.

June, A. W., 2008, 'New School Faculty Senate Votes No Confidence in President Bob Kerrey', *Chronicle of Higher Education*, 10 December, http://chronicle.com/article/New-School-Faculty-Senate/42099.

Jung, C., 2008, *The Moral Force of Indigenous Politics: Critical Liberalism and the Zapatistas*, Cambridge University Press, New York.

J.Y., 2012, 'Pussy Riot's Final Statements, 14 August Aug 15th 2012, 11:29 by J.Y. | MOSCOW, http://www.economist.com/blogs/easternapproaches/2012/08/russian-politics-0 Russian politics.

Kahneman, D., 2003, 'Maps of Bounded Rationality: Psychology for Behavioral Economics'. *American Economic Review*, 93, pp. 1449–1475.

Kan, E., 2012, Pussy Riot: What Was Lost (and Ignored) in Translation', *The American Reader*, November, http://theamericanreader.com/pussy-riot-what-was-lost-and-ignored-in-translation.

Kattago, S., 2013, 'Why the World Matters: Hannah Arendt's Philosophy of New Beginnings', *The European Legacy: Toward New Paradigms*, 18:2, pp. 170–184.

Keane, J. 2009, *The Life and Death of Democracy*. United Kingdom: New York, W.W. Norton.

Keane, J., 1995, 'Structural Transformations of the Public Sphere', *Communications Review*, 1:1, pp. 1–22.

Keane, J., 2010, *Contradictions of the Welfare State*, MIT Press, Cambridge.

Keeter, S., 2006, 'Politics and the "DotNet" Generation', PEW Research Center, http://www.pewresearch.org/2006/05/30/politics-and-the-dotnet-generation.

Kelly, P, 1999, 'Wild and Tame Zones: Regulating the Transition of Youth at Risk', *Journal of Youth Studies*, 2:2, pp. 193–211.

Kelly, P., 2001, 'Youth at Risk: Processes of Individualisation and Responsibilisation in the Risk Society, *Discourse: Studies in the Cultural Politics of Education*, 22, pp. 23–33.

Kelly, P. 2006, 'The Entrepreneurial Self and "Youth-at-risk": Exploring the Horizons of Identity in the Twenty-First Century', *Journal of Youth Studies*, 9:1, pp. 17–32.

Kelly, P., 2009, *The March of Patriots*, Melbourne University Press, Melbourne.

Kelly, B., 2012, 'Structure: Why "Hacktivism" Can and Should Influence Cybersecurity Reform', *Boston University Law Review*, 92, pp. 1664–1711.

Kelly, P., 2013, *The Self as Enterprise: Foucault and the Spirit of 21st Century Capitalism*, Ashgate/Gower, Hampshire, England.

Kelly, P., and Harrison L., (2009), *Working in Jamie's Kitchen: Salvation, Passion and Young Workers*, Palgrave, London.

Kelly, S., *Forecasting Wealth in an Ageing Australia: An Approach Using Dynamics Microsimulation*, National Centre, for Social and Economic Modelling, University of Canberra, 2003, pp. 10–11.

Keniston, K., 1971. *Youth and Dissent: The Rise of a New Opposition*. Harcourt Brace Jovanovich, New York.

Kenny, A., 2012, *A New History Of Western Philosophy – In Four Parts*, Clarendon Press, Oxford.

Kirill cited in Smirnov, A., 22 April 2012 http://www.abc.net.au/news/2012-04-22/russians-pray-for-correction-of-anti-putin-punks/3965584.

Kirsch, I., 2012, *The Emperor's New Clothes, Exploding the Antidepressant myth*, Basic Books, New York.

Kleen, S., 2002, *Mathematical Logic*. Dover, New York.

Knatchpole, M., 2011, 'How Our Petition Beat Bank of America's Debit Card Fee', *The Guardian*, 3 November, http://www.theguardian.com/commentisfree/cifamerica/2011/nov/02/petition-bank-of-america-debit-card-fee.

Kogler, H., 2008, 'Reconceptualisng ReflexiveSociology: A Reply', *Social Epistemology: A Journal of Knowledge, Culture and Policy*, 11:2, pp. 223–250, http://www.tandfonline.com.ezproxy.lib.rmit.edu.au/doi/pdf/10.1080/02691729708578846.

Kogler, H., 1997, 'Alienation as Epistemological Source: Reflexivity and Social Background after Mannheim and Bourdieu', *Social Epistemology: A Journal of Knowledge, Culture and Policy*, 11:2, pp. 141–164.

Kohler, G., and Chaves, E., 2003, (eds.) *Globalisation: Critical Perspectives*, Hauppauge, New York.

Kryshtanovskaya, O., 2004, 'Mission Intrusion Is Complete', *Novay Gazeta*, http://2004.novayagazeta.ru/nomer/2004/63n/n63n-s43.shtml.

Kulik, I., 2012, 'Iskusstvo-sobytie' / 'An art event', *New Times*. 20 August, http://newtimes.ru/articles/detail/55949.

Kunda, Z., 1999, *Social Cognition: Making Sense of People*. Cambridge, MA: MIT Press.

Lacan, J., 1978, *The Four Fundamental Concepts of Psychoanalysis*, Trans. A. Sheridan, Norton, New York.

Lacroix, C., 2004, 'Images of Animated Others: The Orientalization of Disney's Cartoon Heroines from the Little Mermaid to the Hunchback of Notre Dame', *Popular Communication: The International Journal of Media and Culture*, 2:4, pp. 213–229.

Lakoff, G., 1999, *Moral Politics: How Conservatives and Liberals Think*, University of Chicago Press, Chicago.

Lakoff, G., 2 1973, 'Hedges: A Study in Meaning Criteria and the Logic of Fuzzy Concept', *Journal of Philosophical Logic*, 2, pp. 458–508.

Lakoff, G., 2004, *Don't Think of an Elephant*, Penguin, New York.

Lakoff, G., and Johnson, M., 1981, *Metaphors We Live By*, University of Chicago Press, Chicago.

Lancaster, L. C., and Stillman, D., 2002, *When Generations Collide: Who They Are. Why They Clash. How to Solve the Generational Puzzle at Work*. Collins Business, New York.

Langston, H., 2012, 'Meeting Pussy Riot', http://www.vice.com/read/A-Russian-Pussy-Riot.

Langston, H., 2012, http://www.vice.com/read/global-pussy-riot-day.

Langton, M., 2012, 'Lecture 1 – Changing the paradigm: Mining Companies, Native Title and Aboriginal Australians', Boyer Lectures ABC, Sydney, http://www.abc.net.au/radionational/programs/boyerlectures/boyers-ep1/4305610#transcript.

Laurence. Kotlikoff, 2004, *The Coming Generational Storm: What We Need to Know about America's Economic Future*, MIT, Massachusetts.

Leftwich, S., 2004, 'Thinking Politically: On the Politics of Politics', in Leftwich, S., (ed.), *What Is Politics?* Cambridge: Polity.

Lemley, M., Levine, D., and Post, D., 2011, 'Don't Break the Internet', *Stanford Law Review*. 34, pp. 34–38, http://www.stanfordlawreview.org/online/dont-break-internet.

Lessig, L., 1998, 'The Laws of Cyberspace', Taiwan Net Conference, http://www.lessig.org/content/articles/works/laws_cyberspace.pdf.

Lessig, L., 2004a. 'The Innovation Commons', in Stehr, Nico, (ed.), *The Governance of Knowledge*. New Brunswick, NJ: Transaction Publishers, pp. 227–239.

Lessig, L., 2004b. *Free Culture: The Nature and Future of Creativity*. New York: Penguin.

Lessig, L., 2005. 'Does Copyright Have Limits? *Eldred v Ashcroft* and Its Aftermath', *Queensland University of Technology Law and Justice Journal*, 5:2, pp. 219–230.

Lessig, L., 2006. 'Creative Economics', *Michigan State Law Review*, 2006:1, pp. 33–43.

Lessig, L., 2011, *Republic Lost: How Money Corrupts Congress – and a Plan to Stop It*, Twelve Hachette Book Company, New York.

Lessig, L., 1998, 'Domain Games: Internet Leaves the U.S. Nest', cited in Mills, E., *InfoWorld Daily News*, 13 October.

Lessig, L., 2011, 'Lawrence Lessig on How Money Corrupts Congress – and How to Stop It, cited in Brookes, J., 5 October, http://www.rollingstone.com/politics/blogs/national-affairs/lawrence-lessig-on-how-money-corrupts-congress-and-how-to-stop-it-20111005#ixzz2u7V1YObh.

Lessig L., 2012, 'After the Battle against SOPSA: What Next? *The Nation* 26 January 2012 http://www.thenation.com/article/165901/after-battle-against-sopa-whats-next#.

Levy, C., 2010, 'Microsoft Changes Policy over Russian Crackdown', *The New York Times*, http://www.nytimes.com/2010/09/14/world/europe/14raid.html.

Lippmann, W., 1922. *Public Opinion*. New York: Free Press.

Lizardo, O., 2009, 'The Cognitive Origins of Bourdieu's *habitus*', *Occasional Paper*, University of Arizona, Tucson.

Long, M., 2006, *The Flipside of Gen Y*, ACER–Monash University Centre for the Economics of Education and Training, Melbourne.

Lyons, T. J., and Tilling, M. V., 2004, 'Popular Youth Attitudes to Globalisation', *The Social Educator: Journal of The Social Educators Association of Australia*, 22:3, pp. 42–51.

Lyotard, J.-F. 1984, *The Postmodern Condition: A Report on Knowledge*, Manchester: Manchester University Press.

MacIntyre, A., 1977, 'Epistemological Crises, Dramatic Narrative, and the Philosophy of Science', *The Monist*, 49:2, pp. 55–71.

Mackenzie, G., and Labiner, J., 2002, *Opportunity Lost: The Decline of Trust and Confidence in Government after September 11*, Center for Public Service, Washington.

Mair, P., and van Biezen, I., 2001, 'Party Membership in Twenty European Democracies', *Party Politics*, Sage, London.

Makkreel, R., 1975, *Dilthey: the Philosopher of the Human Sciences*. Princeton University Press, Princeton, NJ.

Manen, M., van, 2007, 'Phenomenology of Practice', *Phenomenology and Practice*, 1:1, pp. 11–30.

Mannheim, K., 1986 (1925). *Conservatism*. London and New York: Routledge and Kegan Paul.

Mannheim, K., 1928 (1952) 'The Problem of Generations', in Mannheim, K., *Essays on the Sociology of Knowledge*. Ed. P. Kecskemeti, New York: Routledge and Kegan Paul.

Mannheim, K., 1936, *Ideology and Utopia*, Routledge, London.

Mannheim, K., 1940, *Man and Society in an Age of Reconstruction*, Routledge, London.

Mannheim K., 1952, *Essays on the Sociology of Knowledge*, Ed. and trans. Kecskenmeyi, P., 1952. London, Routledge and Kegan Pail.

Mannheim, K., (1955 [1936]). *Ideology and Utopia: An Introduction to the Sociology of Knowledge*. San Diego and New York: Harcourt.

Mannheim, K., 2011. 'The Problem of a Sociology of Knowledge', in Kurt H. Wolff (ed.), *From Karl Mannheim*, New Brunswick and London: Transaction Publishers, pp. 187–243.

Manning, J., 2011, *Membership of the 112th Congress: A Profile*, Congressional Research Service, 7–5700 www.crs.gov R41647http://www.senate.gov/reference/resources/pdf/R41647.pdf.

Manning, P., 1994, 'Fuzzy Description: Discovery and Invention in Sociology', *History of the Human Sciences*, 7:1, pp. 117–123.

Marcuse, H., 1967, *One Dimensional Man*, Sphere Books, London.

Marcuse, H., 1972, *Counterrevolution and Revolt*, Boston: Beacon Press.

Marcuse, H., and Neumann, F., 1944, 'Theories of Social Change', in Kellner, D., (ed.), *Technology, War and Fascism: Collected Papers of Herbert Marcuse*, Routledge, Abingdon, pp. 105–134.

Marks, G., 2009, 'Modernization Theory and Changes Over Time in the Reproduction of Socioeconomic Inequalities in Australia', *Social Forces* 88:2, pp. 917–944.

Marsh, D., O'Toole, T., and Jones, S., 2007, *Young People and Politics in the UK: Apathy or Alienation*, Palgrave Hampshire, Basingstoke.

Martin, A., 2011, 'Young People and Political Participation in Australia: Evidence from the ISSP', Australian Political Science Association Conference, Canberra.

Marx, K. and Engel s, F., 1848/1948, *The Communist Manifesto*, vol. 1, Progress Publishers, Moscow.

Marx, K., and Engels, F., 1848/1969, *The Communist Manifesto*, http://www.marxists.org/archive/marx/works/1848/communist-manifesto/ch01.htm#a1.

Marx, K., 1848/1969, *The Communist Manifesto*, Penguin, London.

Marx, K., 1859/1974. *Contribution to a Critique of Political Economy*, Penguin, London.

Mason, P., 2011, 'Twenty Reasons Why It's Kicking Off Everywhere', *BBC News Idle Scrawl Blog*, 5 February, http://www.bbc.co.uk/blogs/newsnight/paulmason/2011/02/twenty_reasons_why_its_kicking.html.

Maturana, H., and Varela, F., 1980, *Autopoeisis and Cognition: The Realization of the Living*, in Cohen, R., and Wartofsky M., (eds.), *Boston Studies in the Philosophy of Science* (42), D. Reidel, Dordrecht.

Mayer, H., 2012, 'Political Socialization Patterns in Younger and Older American Adolescents', hanskmeyer.com/research1/AGEPaperAEJ.docx.

Mayer, K. U. 2003, The Sociology of the Life Course and Life Span Psychology: Diverging or Converging Pathways?, in Staudinger, U. M. and Lindenberger, U. (eds.), *Understanding Human Development: Dialogues with Lifespan Psychology*. London: Kluwer Academic Publishers, pp. 463–481.

Mayer, S., 2013, 'The Size of a Song: Pussy Riot and the (People) Power of Poetry'. *Soundings* 54 147+. *Academic OneFile*.

McCaffrie, B, and Marsh, D. 2013, 'Beyond Mainstream Approaches to Political Participation: A Response to Aaron Martin', *Australian Journal of Political Science*, 48:1, pp. 112–117.

McCloskey, D., 1998, *The Rhetoric of Economics*, University of Wisconsin Press, Madison.

McDonald, K., 1999, *Struggles for Subjectivity: Identity, Action and Experience*, Cambridge, Cambridge University Press.

McGilchrist, I., 2011, *The Master and his Emissary*, Yale University Press, New Haven.

McGrew, A., and Held, D., 2007, *Globalization/Anti-Globalization Beyond the Great Divide*, 2nd ed., Cambridge, Polity Books.

McGuire, J., and Tuchanska, B., 2000, *Science Unfettered: A Philosophical Study in Sociohistorical Ontology*, Athens: Ohio University Press.

McLuhan, M., 1962, *The Gutenberg Galaxy: The Making of Typographic Man*, Routledge and Kegan, New York.

McMullin, J., Comeau, T., and Jovic, W., 2007, 'Generational Affinities and Discourses of Difference: A Case Study of Highly Skilled Information Technology Workers', *British Journal of Sociology*, 58, pp. 297–316.

McRobbie A., 1980, 'Settling Accounts with Subcultures: A Feminist Critique', *Screen Education*, 39, pp. 37–49.

McSherry, C., and Samuels, J., 2012, 'Thank you Internet! And the Fight Continues', Electronic Foundation, 18 January.

Medin, D. L., 1989. 'Concepts and Conceptual Structure'. *American Psychologist*, 44, pp. 1469–1481.

Melucci, A., 1988, 'Social Movements and the Democratisation of Everyday Life', in Keane, J. (ed.), *Civil Society and the State*, Verso, London.

Melucci, A., 1996, *Challenging Codes: Collective Action in the Information Age*, Cambridge: Cambridge University Press.

Michaels, E., 1988, 'Hollywood Iconography: A Warlpiri Reading', in Drummond, P., and Patterson, R., (eds.), *Television and Its Audience: International Research Perspectives*, British Film Institute, London, pp. 109–124.

Michaels, S., 2012, 'Anonymous Defaces Website of Court That Convicted Pussy Riot', *The Guardian*, http://www.guardian.co.uk/music/2012/aug/22/anonymous-website-court-pussy-riot.

Miles, S., 2000, *Youth Lifestyles in a Changing World*, Buckingham: Open University Press.

Miller, M., 2014, 'An Open Letter to the Yale Community from Dean Mary Miller', 20 January, http://yalecollege.yale.edu/content/open-letter-yale-community-dean-mary-miller.

Miller, N., 2014, 'Cossacks Attack Pussy Riot in Sochi with Whips and Pepper Spray', *The Age*, 20 February, http://www.smh.com.au/world/cossacks-at-tack-pussy-riot-in-sochi-with-whips-and-pepper-spray-20140220-hvd27.html#ixzz2xfmVrKe1 http://www.theage.com.au/world/cossacks-attack-pussy-riot-in-sochi-with-whips-and-pepper-spray-20140220-hvd27.html.

Mirovalev, M., 2012, 'Pussy Riot: Guide to All Six of Their Songs and How They Reflect Russia's Anti-Putin Uprising', *The Province*, August 18.

Mizen, P., 2005, *The Changing State of Youth*, Palgrave London.

Montell, G., 2006, 'The Art of the Bogus Rating', *The Chronicle of Higher Education*, https://chronicle.com/article/The-Art-of-the-Bogus-Rating/46887/.

Mortensen C., 2011, 'Change and Inconsistency', *Stanford Encyclopedia*, http://plato.stanford,edu/entries/change//.

Mortensen, C., 1985, 'The Limits of Change', *Australasian Journal of Philosophy*, 63, pp. 1–10.

Mouffe, C., 1998, 'Schmitt and Liberal Democracy', in Dyzenhaus, D., (ed.), *Law as Politics: Carl Schmitt's Critique of Liberalism* Duke University Press, Durham.

Mowarin, T., 2012, Digital Story Telling from Ngarluma Born People of the Pilbara Region of Western Australia, Tyson Mowarin, *X Media Lab.* http://www.xmedialab.com/news/2012/12/digital-indigenous-storytelling-from-the-ngarluma-born-people-of-the-pilaba.

Mowbray, M., 2005, 'Community Capacity Building or State Opportunism?' *Community Development Journal,* 40:3, pp. 255–264.

Moynihan, C., 2008, 'The Columbia and New School Sit-Ins, Compared', *The New York Times,* 19 December, http://cityroom.blogs.nytimes.com/2008/12/19/the-columbia-and-new-school-sit-ins-compared/?_php=true&_type=blogs&_r=0.

Muller, D. 2006, Fearless and Flexible: An Overview, Dusseldorp Skills Forum, NSW, <http://www.dsf.org.au/fearless.php>.

Muncie, J., 2008, 'The "Punitive" Turn in Juvenile Justice: Cultures of Control and Rights Compliance in Western Europe and the USA'. *Youth Justice,* 8:2, pp. 107–121.

Nash, L., 1979, 'Concepts of Existence: Greek Origins of Generational Thought', *Daedalus,* 107:4, pp. 1–29.

Navarro, Z., 2006, 'In Search of Cultural Interpretation of Power', *IDS Bulletin* 37:6, pp. 11–22.

Negri, A., 2003, *Time for Revolution.* Trans. by Matteo Mandarini, Continuum, New York.

Nemtsov, B., and Martynyuk, L., 2012, Жизнь раба на галерах (дворцы, яхты, автомобили, самолеты и другие аксессуары), http://www.putin-itogi.ru/rab-na-galerah.

Nemtsova, A., 2012, 'Pussy Riot Witch Hunt by Kremlin-Backed "Youth Movement"', 30September. http://www.thedailybeast.com/articles/2012/09/30/pussy-riot-witch-hunt-by-kremlin-backed-youth-movement.html.

Netburn, D., 2012, 'Wikipedia: SOPA Protest Led 8 Million to Look Up Reps in Congress', *Los Angeles Times,* 19 January.

Newman, L. S. 2009, 'Was Walter Lippmann Interested in Stereotyping? Public Opinion and Cognitive Social Psychology', *History of Psychology,* 12, pp. 7–18.

Newton-Small, J., 2013, 'Quietly, Pussy Riot Lobbies Washington, *Swampland Time',* 10 June. http://swampland.time.com/2013/06/10/quietly-pussy-riot-lobbies-washington/.

Niedenthal, P., and Cantor, N., 1984, 'Making Use of Social prototypes: From Fuzzy Categories to Firm Decisions', *Fuzzy Sets and Systems,* 14, pp: 5–27.

Nikitin, V., 2012, 'The Wrong Reasons to Back Pussy Riot', *New York Times,* 20 August, http://www.nytimes.com/2012/08/21/opinion/the-wrong-reasons-to-back-pussy-riot.html.

Ntumy, M., 1990, 'Essentialism and the Search for the Essence of Law', *Melanesian Law Journal,* 18, pp. 64.

Nussbaum, M., 2010, *Not for Profit: Why Democracy Needs the Humanities,* Princeton University Press, Princeton.

OECD, 2013, Unemployment Set to Remain High in OECD Countries through 2014 – Youth and Low-skilled Hit Hardest', http://www.oecd.org/employment/

unemployment-set-to-remain-high-in-oecd-countries-through-2014youth-and-low-skilled-hit-hardest.htm.

Offe, C., 1978, *Contradictions of the Welfare State*, Hutchinson, London.

Oleg-kozyrev.livejournal.com, 2011, December 28, http://oleg-kozyrev.live-journal.com/3926225.html.

Olive, N., 2007, *Enough Is Enough: A History of the Pilbara Mob*, Fremantle Press, Fremantle.

Ollman, B., *Dance of the Dialectic: Steps in Marx's Method*, University of Illinois Press, Chicago, IL.

Olson, K., 2006, *Reflexive Democracy: Political Equality and the Welfare State*, MIT Press Cambridge.

Olson, P., 2012, *We are Anonymous: Inside the Hacker World of LulzSec, Anonymous and the Global Cyberinsurgency*, Hachette Digital, New York.

Olsson, T., and Dahlgren, P., 2010, *Young People, ICYs and Democracy: Theories, Policies and Websites*, Nordicom, Gothenberg.

Ortega Y Gasset, J., 1961, [original Spanish 1923]), *The Modern Theme*. New York: Harper.

Ortis, I., Daniels, L., and Engilbertsdottir, S., (eds.), 2012, *Child Poverty and Inequality: New Perspectives*, UNICEF, Policy Division, New York.

Ortiz, I., and Cummins, M., 2012, *When the Global Crisis and Youth Bulge Collide: Double the Jobs Trouble for Youth*, UNICEF, Geneva.

Ostrowska, A. 2013, 'A Pussy is A Riot', 2 July, http://www.thefword.org.uk/reviews/2013/07/a_pussy_is_a_riot.

Owram, D., 1997, *Born at the Right Time*, Toronto: University of Toronto Press.

Palfrey, J., and Urs, G., 2008, *Born Digital: Understanding the First gGeneration of Digital Natives*, Basic Books, New York.

Palfrey, J., 2011, 'SOPA and Our 2010 Circumvention Study', http://jpalfrey.andover.edu/2011/12/22/sopa-and-our-2010-circumvention-study/.

Panitch, L., and Gindin, S., 2012, *The Making of Global Capitalism: The Political Economy of American Empire*. London: Verso.

Papacharissi, Z., (ed.), 2011, *A Networked Self: Identity, Community and Culture on Social Network Sites*, Routledge, New York.

Parker, K., 2012, 'The Boomerang Generation', PEW Research Center, http://www.pewsocialtrends.org/2012/03/15/the-boomerang-generation/.

Parkinson, J., 2003, 'Legitimacy Problems in Deliberative Democracy', *Political Studies*, 51:4, pp. 17–34.

Parsons, T., 1977. *Social Systems and the Evolution of Action Theory*, Free Press, New York.

Parsons, T., and Shils, E., 1951, *Towards a General Theory of Action*, Harvard University Press, Cambridge.

Parsons, T., 1951, *The Social System*, Free Press, Glencoe.

Parsons, T., 1954, 'Psychology and Sociology', in Gillin, J. (ed.), *For A Science of Social Man*, Macmillan, New York.

Parsons, T., 1970, 'On Building Social System theory: A Personal History', *Daedalus*, 99, pp. 826–881.

Pateman, C., 1988, *The Sexual Contract*, Cambridge: Polity.

Pavord, A., 2005, *The Naming of Names: The Search for Order in the World of Plant*, Bloomsbury, London.

Pearson, G., 1983, *Hooligans: A History of Respectable Fears*, Macmillan, London.

Pearson, N., 2005, 'Address by Noel Pearson to the National Reconciliation Planning Workshop', 30 May, NRPW, Canberra cyi.org.au/wp-content/.../Cape%2520York%2520Agenda%2520final.pdf.

Penny, L., 2011, 'Out with the Old Politics', in Hancox, D., (ed.), *Fightback: A Reader on the Winter of Protest*. London: Open Democracy, pp. 296–298.

Pettit, P., 1997, *Republicanism: A Theory of Freedom and Government*, Oxford University Press, Oxford.

Pew Research Center, 2010, 'Millennials: A Portrait of Generation Next', http://www.pewsocialtrends.org/2010/02/24/millennials-confident-connected-open-to-change/.

Pew Research, 2012, 'Millennials Will Benefit and Suffer Due to Their Hyperconnected Lives', http://www.pewinternet.org/files/oldmedia/Files/Reports/2012/PIP_Future_of_Internet_2012_Young_brains_PDF.pdf.

Pilcher, J., 1993, Mannheim's Sociology of Generations: An Undervalued Legacy, *British Journal of Sociology*, 45, pp. 481–499.

Pinkard, T., 1994, *Hegel's Phenomenology: The Sociality of Reason*, Cambridge University Press, Cambridge.

Pinkard, T., 2000, *Hegel: A Biography*, Cambridge University Press, Cambridge.

Pinker, S., 2007, *The Stuff of Thought: Language as a Window into Human Nature*, Viking, New York.

Pippin, R., 1989, *Hegel's Idealism: The Satisfactions of Self-Consciousness*, Cambridge University Press, Cambridge.

Pippin, R., 1997, *Idealism as Modernism: Hegelian Variations*, Cambridge University Press, Cambridge.

Pippin, R., 2008, *Hegel's Practical Philosophy: Rational Agency as Ethical Life*, Cambridge University Press, Cambridge.

Plato. 1956. *Phaedrus*. Trans. W. C. Helmbold and W. G. Rabinowitz, Indianapolis: Library of Liberal Arts-Bobbs.

Plucer-Sarno, A., 2008, (original blog), 'Eerie Orgy in the Biological Museum'. 29 February 29, New Action Art Group War, http://plucer.livejournal.com/55710.html.

Poole, C., 2010, Transcript of Chris Poole before the Honorable Thomas W. Phillips on April 22, 2010, In the United States District Court for the Eastern District of Tennessee. Northern Division, at Knoxville, Tennessee. CR 3–08–142, http://i.cdn.turner.com/dr/teg/tsg/release/sites/default/files/assets/poole-testimony.pdf.

Poster, M., 1997, 'Cyberdemocracy: Internet and the Public Sphere', in Porter, D., (ed.), *Internet Culture,* Routledge, London, pp. 201–218.

Pravda, 2012, Геростратова слава Pussy Riot 18 August, http://www.pravda.ru/politics/parties/other/18–08–2012/1125247-prgerostrat-0/

Prensky, M., 2001, 'Digital Natives, Digital Immigrants', *On the Horizon*, 9:5, http://www.marcprensky.com/writing/prensky%20-%20digital%20natives,%20digital%20immigrants%20-%20part1.pdf.

President of Russia website, 2013, 'Vladimir Putin Will Take Part in Russian Popular Front Conference', 28 March, http://eng.kremlin.ru/accreditation/5187.

Priest, G., 2006, *In Contradiction*, 2nd ed., Oxford University Press, Oxford.

Pusey, M., 1991, *Economic Rationalism in Canberra*, Cambridge University Press, Melbourne.

Pusey, P., 2007, 'The Changing Relationship between the Generations', *Youth Studies Australia*, 26:1, p.

Pussy Riot, n.d., http://freepussyriot.org/about.

Putin, V., 2012, 'Russia Today', 6 September, http://www.youtube.com/watch.

Putin, V., 2013a, 'Citizens of Russia, Members of the Council of Federation and the State Duma', 12 December, http://eng.kremlin.ru/transcripts/6402.

Putin, V., 2013b, News Conference of Vladimir Putin', 19 December, http://eng.kremlin.ru/news/6425.

Putin, V., 2013c, 'Meeting of the Valdai International Discussion Club', 19 September, http://eng.kremlin.ru/news/6007.

PwC, 2013, 'PwC's Next Generation: A Global Generational Study: Evolving Talent Strategy to Match the New Workforce Reality', PwC, USCLSB, London, http://www.pwc.com/en_GX/gx/hr-management-services/pdf/pwc-nextgen-study-2013.pdf].

Pyvis, D., 1991, 'The Exploitation of Youth: An Alternative History of Youth Policy in Australia', unpublished PhD thesis, Murdoch University.

Radcliffe-Brown, A. R., 1952, *Structure and Function in Primitive Society*, Free Press, Glencoe.

Radia, K., 2012, 'Anti-Putin Band Pussy Riot Found Guilty in Russian Court, Handed 2-Year Sentence', ABC news, 17 August, http://abcnews.go.com/International/anti-putin-band-pussy-riot-found-guilty-russian/story?id=17026471#.UC6 – BwQ_zA.

Rahn W., 2004. 'National Identities and the Future of Democracy, Part II: Globalization and the Decline of Civic Commitments'. Paper presented at the Conference on Democracy in the Twenty-First Century. University of Illinois, Chicago, pp. 24–26.

Rankin, S., and Bakes, J., 1996. *Big hArt: A Big Idea*, DEET, Canberra.

Rasmussen, M., Guo, X., Wang, Y., Lohmueller, K. E., and Rasmussen, S., et al., 2011, 'An Aboriginal Australian Genome Reveals Separate Human Dispersals into Asia', *Science*, 334:6052, pp. 94–98.

Rassmussen, T., 2007, 'Two Faces of the Public Sphere: The Significance of Internet Communication in Public Deliberation', *Nordicom Review*, 29:2, pp. 73–83.

Rawlinson, P., 2010, *From Fear to Fraternity: Economy and Modernity*, Cambridge: Polity.

Redding, P., 2007, *Analytic Philosophy and the Return of Hegelian Thought*, Cambridge University Press. Cambridge.

Rees, J., 2011, 'Student Revolts: Then and Now, in Bailey, M. and Freedman, D., (eds.), *The Assault on Universities: A Manifesto for Resistance*. London: Pluto Press, pp. 113–122.

Reeves, T.C., E., 2006, 'Do Generational Differences Matter in Instructional Design?', University of Georgia, EPIT, Athens : 294–310, http://itforum.coe.uga.edu/Paper104/ReevesITForumJan08.pdf.

Rescher N., 1982, *A Coherence Theory of Truth*, University Press of America, Lanham, MD.

Rescher, N., 1984, *The Limits of Science*, University of California Press, Berkeley and Los Angeles.

Rescher, N., 1996, *Process Metaphysics: An Introduction to Process Philosophy*, SUNY Press, Albany.

Rheingans, and Hollands, R., 2013, '"There Is No Alternative?": Challenging Dominant Understandings of Youth Politics in Late Modernity through a Case

Study of the 2010 UK Student Occupation Movement', *Journal of Youth Studies*, 16:4, pp. 546–564.

Rheingold, H., 2000, *The Virtual Community*: Homesteading on the Electronic Frontier, MIT Press. Cambridge.

Richards, R., 2010, *The Species Problem*, Cambridge University Press, Cambridge.

Richters, K., 2012, 'Pussy Riot, the Media and Church-State Relations in Russia Today', The University of Chicago, http://divinity.uchicago.edu/martyc-enter/publications/webforum/112012/Richters%20We   b%20Forum%20 November%202012.pdf.

Rigi, J., 2012, 'The Corrupt State of Exception and "Law and Disorder" in Russia: Putin in the Light of Agamben', *Social Analysis*, 56:3, pp. 69–88.

Roberts, S., 2010, 'Misrepresenting Choice Biographies? A Reply to Woodman', *Journal of Youth Studies*, 13:1, pp. 137–149. [doi://dx.doi.org/10.1080/ 13676260903233720]

Roggero, G., and Paolo Do, 2010, 'We Won't Pay for Your Crisis! Anomalous Wave, Living Knowledge, and the Common Institutions', *European Alternatives: Democracy, Equality, Culture Beyond the Nation State*, http://www.euroalter. com/2010/we-wont-pay-for-your-crisis.

Rorty, R., 1991, 'Wittgenstein, Heidegger, and the Reification of Language'. *Essays on Heidegger and Others*. Cambridge University Press, Cambridge.

Rosch, E., and Mervis, C. B., 1975, 'Family Resemblances: Studies in the Internal Structure of Categories'. *Cognitive Psychology*, 7, pp. 573–605.

Rosch, E., and Lloyd, B., 1978, (eds.), *Cognition and Categorization*, Lawrence Erlbaum, Hillsdale.

Rosch, E., Mervis, C., Grey, W., Johnson D., and Boyes-Braem, P., 1976, 'Basic Objects in Natural Categories', *Cognitive Psychology*, 8:1, pp. 382–439.

Rose, N., 1990, *Governing the Soul: The Shaping of the Private Self*. London: Penguin.

Runciman, D., 2014, *The Confidence Trap: A History of Democracy in Crisis from World War I to the Present*, Princeton University Press, Princeton.

Russian Legal Information Agency, 2012a, 'A Pussy Riot video Deemed Extremist, Banned in Russia', 29 November, http://www.rapsinews.com/judicial_ news/20121129/265581957.html.

Russian Legal Information Agency, 2012b, 'Text Coverage of Pussy Riot Video Extremism Trial.' Part 1, 14 November, http://www.rapsinews.com/judicial_ news/20121129/265576313.html.

Ryzik, M., 2013, 'Pussy Riot Takes Manhatten, Quietly', *New York Times*, 7 June http://www.nytimes.com/2013/06/08/arts/television/pussy-riot-takes-manhat-tan-quietly.html?pagewanted=all&_r=0.

Said, E., 1993, *Culture and Imperialism*, Pantheon Books, New York.

Samuel, A. S. 2004, 'Hacktivism and the Future of Political Participation', unpub-lished PhD dissertation, Harvard University, http://www.alexandrasamuel. com/dissertation/pdfs/Samuel-Hacktivism-entire.pdf.

Samutsevich, Y., 2012, 'Pussy Riot Closing Statements', n+1 Magazine, https:// nplusonemag.com/online-only/online-only/pussy-riot-closing-statements.

Samutsevich, Y., 2013, Baker, K., interviewer, 'Why Should We Be Afraid? Our Skype Session with Pussy Riot's Katia, Baker, K., interviewer, 18 July, http:// jezebel.com/why-should-we-be-afraid-our-skype-session-with-puss-816579294.

Schatzki, T., Knorr Cetina, K., and Savigny, E., 2001, (eds.), *The Practice Turn in Contemporary Theory*, Routledge, London.

Schedler, A., 1997, (ed.), *The End of Politics? Explorations into Modern Anti-Politics*, Macmillan, Houndmills.

Schmid, G., 2006, 'Social Risk Management through Transitional Labour Markets', *Socioeconomic Review*, 4:1, pp. 1–33.

Schmitt, C., 1993, *The Nomos of the Earth in the International Law of the Jus Publicum Europaeum*, Telos Press, St. Louis.

Schofield, P., 2006, *Utility and Democracy: The Political Thought of Jeremy Bentham*, Oxford University Press, Oxford.

Schooley, C., 2005, *Get Ready: The Millennials Are Coming! Changing Workforce*: Forrester Research, Cambridge.

Schroeder, S. R., 1970, 'Usage of Stereotypy as a Descriptive Term. *Psychological Record*, 20, pp. 337–342.

Schwartz-Weinstein, Z., 2013, *Not Your Academy: Occupation and the Futures of Student Struggles*, Columbia University Academic Commons, http://hdl.handle.net/10022/AC:P:21975.

Scott, B., Cooper, M., and Kinney, J., 2006, 'Why Consumers Demand Internet Freedom –Network Neutrality: Fact vs. Fiction', White Paper: Free Press, www.freepress.net/files/nn_fact_v_fiction_final.pdf.

Scruton, R., 1980, *Political Philosophy: Arguments for Conservatism*, Continuum.

Searle, J., 2004, *Mind: A Brief Introduction*, New York, Oxford University Press.

Searle, J., 1979, *Expression and Meaning: Studies in the Theory of Speech Acts*, Cambridge University Press, Cambridge.

Seibt, J., 2003, *Process Theories: Cross-Disciplinary Studies in Dynamic Categories*, Kluwer Academic, Dordrecht.

Seibt, J., 2012, 'Process Philosophy', *Stanford Encyclopedia of Philosophy*, http://plato.stanford.edu/entries/process-philosophy/.

Seiden, R., 2009, 'Parental Influences on the Political Ideologies of Young People', http://ase.tufts.edu/polsci/faculty/portney/studentSeiden.pdf.

Seidman, S., 1992, 'Postmodern Social Theory as Narrative with a Moral Intent', in Seidman, S. and Wagner, D., (eds.), *Postmodernism and Social Theory*, Blackwell, Cambridge, pp. 101–136.

Selwyn, N. (2004). 'Reconsidering Political and Popular Understandings of the Digital Divide', *New Media and Society*, 6:3, pp. 341–362.

Sen, A., 2002, 'Does Globalization Equal Westernization?', http://www.theglobalist.com/does-globalization-equal-westernization/.

Setterston, R., Furstenberg, J., and Rumbaut, R., 2005, *On the Frontier of Adulthood, Theory, Research and Public Policy*, Chicago, Chicago University Press.

Shalin, D., 2010, 'Liberal, Affect Control, and Emotionally Intelligent Democracy', *Journal of Human Rights*, 3:4, pp. 407–428.

Shuham, M., 2012, 'The Politics of a New Generation', *Harvard Political Review*, 8 August http://harvardpolitics.com/united-states/the-politics-of-a-new-generation/.

Simon, H. A., 1959, 'Theories of Decision-Making in Economics and Behavioral Science', *American Economic Review*, 49, pp. 253–283.

Simon, H. A. 1979, 'Rational Decision Making in Business Organizations', *American Economic Review*, 69, pp. 493–513.

Simon, H. A., 1985, 'Human Nature and Politics: The Dialogue of Psychology with Political Science', *American Political Science Review,* 79, pp. 293–304.

Simon, H., 1957, 'A Behavioral Model of Rational Choice', in *Models of Man, Social and Rational: Mathematical Essays on Rational Human Behavior in a Social Setting.* New York: Wiley.

Skocpol, T., 2003, *Diminishing Democracy – From Membership to Management in American Civic Life,* Harvard University Press, Cambridge.

Skop, Y., 2014, 'App Lets Tel Aviv University Students Rank Professors in Real Time', *Haaretz,* 15 March, http://www.haaretz.com/news/national/.premium-1.578836.

Smith, P., 2000, 'Station Camps: Legislation, Labour Relations and Rations on Pastoral Leases in the Kimberley Region, Western Australia', *Aboriginal History* 24, pp. 78–99.

Smithson, M., and Verkuellen, J., 2006, 'Internal Structure and Properties of a Fuzzy Set', in Smithson, M., and Verkuellen, J., (eds.), *Fuzzy set Theory,* Little Green Books, New York.

Smola, K., and Sutton, C., 2002, 'Generational Differences: Revisiting Generational Work Values for the New Millennium', *Journal of Organizational Behaviour,* 23:4, pp. 363–382.

Smyth, J., 2009, 'Critically Engaged Community Capacity Building and the "Community Organizing" Approach in Disadvantaged Contexts', *Critical Studies in Education,* 50: 1, pp. 9–22.

Solomon, C., and Palmieri, T., 2011. *Springtime: The New Student Rebellions.* Verso, London.

Sparling, R., 2012, 'Political Corruption and the Concept of Dependence in Republican Thought', *Political Theory,* 41: 30 6, pp. 18–47.

Spinosa, C., and Dreyfus, H., 1996, 'Two Kinds of Anti-essentialism and Their Consequence', *Critical Inquiry,* 22:4, pp. 735–763.

Spriggs, E., 2013, 'Rock Microbes Found in WA's Pilbara Could Be Earliest Signs of Life on Earth', ABC News, http://www.abc.net.au/news/2013–11–13/scientists-discover-earliest-signs-of-life-on-earth-in-pilbara/5088190.

Stanlis, P., 1993, *Edmund Burke: The Enlightenment and Revolution,* Transaction, New Brunswick.

Steeg Larson, B., and Tufte, 2003, 'Rituals in the Modern World: Applying the Concept of Ritual in Media Ethnography', in Kraidy, M., and Murphy, P., (eds.), *Global Media Studies: An Ethnographic Perspective,* Routledge, New York, pp. 90–106.

Steger, M., 2008, *The Rise of the Global Imaginary: Political Ideologies from the French Revolution to the Global War on Terror,* Oxford University Press, New York.

Steger, M., 2002, *Globalism: The New Market Ideology,* 3rd edition, Rowman and Littlefield, Oxford.

Steger, M., 2009, 'The Rise of the Global Imaginary and the Persistence of Ideology', *Global e: A Global Studies Journal,* http://global-ejournal.org/2009/07/30/the-rise-of-the-global-imaginary-and-the-persistence-of-ideology.

Steinholt, Y., 2013, 'Kitten Heresy: Lost Contexts of Pussy Riot's Punk Prayer', *Popular Music and Society,* 36:1, pp. 120–124.

Steinmetz, G., 2011, 'Bourdieu, Historicity, and Historical Sociology' *Cultural Sociology,* 11, pp. 45–61.

Stephan white and Olga Kryshtanovskaya, 2002, 'Generations and the Conversion of Power in Postcommunist Russia' (with Olga Kryshtanovskaya), *Perspectives in European Politics and Society* 3:2, pp. 229–242.

Stewart, K. D., and Bernhardt, P. C., 2010, 'Comparing Millennials to pre-1987 Students and with One Another', *North American Journal of Psychology*, 12, pp. 579–602.

Stiglitz, J., 2002, *Globalisation and Its Discontents*, W.W. Norton, New York.

Strasser H., 1977, *Functionalism and Social Change*, Research Memorandum No. 116, Institute for Advanced Studies, Vienna. www.ihs.ac.at/publications/ihsfo/fo116.pdf.

Strauss, W., and Howe, N., 2000, *Millennials Rising: The Next Great Generation*, Vintage, New York.

Strauss, W., and Howe, N., 1991, *Generations: The History of America's Future, 1584 to 2069*, Harper Perennial, New York.

Suber, P., 2008. 'A Bill to overturn the NIH Policy', *SPARC Open Access Newsletter*, No. 126 (October), http://www.earlham.edu/~peters/fos/newsletter/10-02-08.htm.

Such, E., Walker, O., and Walker, R., 2005, 'Anti-war Children: Representation of Youth Protests against the Second Iraq War in the British National Press. *Childhood*, 12, pp. 301–326.

Sukarieh M., and Tannock, S, 2011, 'The Positivity Imperative: A Critical Look at the "New" Youth Development Movement' *Journal of Youth Studies* 14:6, pp. 675–691.

Sukarieh, M., and Tannock, S., 2008, 'In the Best Interests of Youth or Neoliberalism? The World Bank and the New Global Youth Empowerment Project'. *Journal of Youth Studies* 11:3, pp. 301–312.

Sunstein, C., 2002, *Republic.com*. Princeton, NJ: Princeton University Press.

Sutter, J., 2010, '4Chan founder: Anonymous speech is endangered', *CNN SciTech Blog*, http://scitech.blogs.cnn.com/2010/02/12/4chan-founder-anonymous-speech-is-endangered/.

Sweezy, P., 1972, *Modern Capitalism and Other Essays*. New York: Monthly Review Press.

Syrova, M., cited in and translated by Voronina, O., Pussy Riot Steal the Stage in the Moscow Cathedral of Christ the Saviour: Punk Prayer on Trial Online and in Court. *Digital Icons: Studies in Russian, Eurasian and Central Europe New Media*, No. 9, pp. 73–74. http://www.digitalicons.org/issue09/olga-voronina/.

Tapscott, D., 1998. *Growing Up Digital: The Rise of the Net Generation*. New York: McGraw-Hill.

Tatto, M. T., 2007, 'International Comparisons and the Global Reform of Teaching', in Tatto, M. T., (ed.), *Reforming Teaching Globally*, pp. 7–18). Symposium Books, Oxford.

Taussig, M., 1993, *Mimesis and Alterity: A Particular History of the Senses*, Routledge, London.

Taylor, A., 2012, 'Here's What Russian Punk Band Pussy Riot Said at the Conclusion of Their Controversial Blasphemy Trial', *Business Insider*, 10 August, http://www.businessinsider.com/pussy-riot-trial-nadezhda-tolokonnikovas-closing-statement-2012-8.

Taylor, C., 1985, *Philosophy and the Human Sciences, Philosophical Papers 2*, Cambridge University Press, Cambridge.

Taylor, J., 2008, 'Whither March the Cohorts: The Validity of Generation Theory as a Determinant of the Sociocultural Values of Canadian Forces Personnel', CANADIAN FORCES COLLEGE – COLLÈGE DES FORCES CANADIENNES NSSP 10 – PESN10.

Theocharis, Y., 2011, 'Cuts, Tweets, Solidarity and Mobilisation: How the Internet Shaped the Student Occupations', *Parliamentary Affairs*, 65, pp. 162–194.

Thomas, M., 2011. *Deconstructing Digital Natives*. New York: Routledge.

Thrift, N., 2007, *Non-representational theory: Space, Politics, Affect*, Routledge, London.

Times staff, 2009, 'World's Most Influential Person Is...' *Time*, 27 April, http://content.time.com/time/arts/article/0,8599,1894028,00.html.

Tolokonnikova, N., 2014, Interview with Stephen Colbert, February www.tvguide.com/.../video-stephen-colbert-report-pussy-riot-interview.

Tolokonnikova, N., 2012a, 'Here's What Russian Punk Band Pussy Riot Said at the Conclusion of Their Controversial Blasphemy Trial, *Business Insider*, http://www.businessinsider.com/pussy-riot-trial-nadezhda-tolokonnikovas-closing-statement-2012–8.

Tolokonnikova, N., 2012b, (Shayevich, B) 'Pussy Riot Closing Statements', http://nplusonemag.com/pussy-riot-closing-statements.

Tomlinson, J., 1991, *Cultural Imperialism: A Critical Introduction* (illustrated, reprint ed.). Continuum International Publishing Group, London.

Toulmin, S., 1972, *Human Understanding*, (vol. 1), Oxford University Press, Oxford.

Toulmin, S., 1982, *The Return to Cosmology: Post Modern Science and the Theology of Nature*, University of California Press, Berkeley.

Toulmin. S., 1972, *Human Understanding: The Collective Use and Evolution of Concepts*, Oxford University Press, Oxford.

Touraine, A., 1981, *The Voice and the Eye: An Analysis of Social Movements*, Cambridge University Press, Cambridge.

Tribe, L., 2011, 'The Stop Online Piracy Act (SOPA) Violates the First Amendment', http://www.scribd.com/doc/75153093/Tribe-Legis-Memo-on-SOPA-12–6-11–1.

Turner, B.S., and Eyerman, R., 1998, 'Outline of a Theory of Generations', *European Journal of Social Theory*, 1:1, pp. 91–106.

Twenge, J. M., 2006. *Generation Me: Why Today's Young Americans Are More Confident, Assertive, Entitled – and More Miserable Than Ever Before*, Free Press, New York.

Twenge, J. M., and Foster, J. D., 2010, 'Birth Cohort Increases in Narcissistic Personality Traits among American College Students, 1982–2009'. *Social Psychological and Personality Science*, 1, 99–106.

Twenge, J., 2009, *The Narcissism Epidemic*, Free Press, New York.

Twenge, J., Campbell, W., and Freeman, A., 2012, 'Generational Differences in Young Adults' Life Goals, Concern for Others, and Civic Orientation, 1966–2009', *Personality Processes and Individual differences*, August, 1025–1045, http://www.apa.org/pubs/journals/releases/psp-102–5-1045.pdf.

United Nations (UN), 2013, 'UN Rights Expert Urges Russia to Ensure Independence of Judiciary, UN News Centre, http://www.un.org/apps/news/story.asp?NewsID=44771&Cr=judicial&Cr1=#.UivahxxrBb5.

United Nations, 2013, 'Intergenerational Solidarity and the Needs of Future Generations', Report of the Secretary-General, United Nations, http://sustaina-bledevelopment.un.org/content/documents/2006future.pdf.

US Census, 2010, *The Older Population: 2010: 2010 Census Briefs,* US Census Office, Washington, DC, http://www.census.gov/prod/cen2010/briefs/c2010br-09.pdf.

Valenzuela, S., Arriagade, A., and Scherman, A., 2012, 'The Social Media Basis of Youth Protest Behavior: The Case of Chile', *Journal of Communication,* 62, pp. 299–314.

Van Alstyne, M., and E. Brynjolfsson, 1996, 'Electronic Communities: Global Village or Cyberbalkans?', *Proceedings of the International Conference on Information Systems,* aisel.isworld.org/password.asp?Vpath=ICIS/1996&PDFpath=paper06.pdf.

Vandenberghe, F., 1999, '"The Real Is Relational": An Epistemological Analysis of Bourdieu's Generative Structuralism', *Sociological Theory,* 17:1, pp. 32–45.

Vietta, S., 2013, *A Theory of Global Civilization: Rationality and the Irrational as the Driving Forces of History,* Kindle Ebook.

Villa, D., 1996, *Arendt and Heidegger: The Fate of the Political.* Princeton University Press, Princeton, NJ.

Villa, D., 1999, *Politics, Philosophy, Terror: Essays on the Thought of Hannah Arendt.* Princeton University Press, Princeton, NJ.

von Gall, C., 2013, 'Failed for Now: Pussy Riot and the Rule of Law in Russia', Tran. from German by Christopher Findlay. *Russian Analytical Digest,* 122, pp. 2–5.

Voronina, O., 2013, 'Pussy Riot Steal the Stage in the Moscow Cathedral of Christ the Saviour: Punk Prayer on Trial Online and in Court', *Digital Icons: Studies in Russian, Eurasian and Central European New Media,* 9, pp. 69–85.

Vromen, A., 2011, 'Constructing Australian Youth Online: Empowered but Dutiful Citizens?' *Information, Communication and Society* 14, pp. 959–980.

Wacquant, L., 2005, *Pierre Bourdieu and Democratic Politics.* Cambridge: Polity.

Walker, M., 2014, 'Sites like "Rate My Professors" Earn Mixed Grades on Campus', *USA Today* College 4 February, http://www.usatodayeducate.com/staging/index.php/pulse/sites-like-rate-my-professors-earn-mixed-grades-on-campus.

Wall, J., and Anandini, D., 2011, 'Children's Political Representation: The Right to Make a Difference', *The International Journal of Children's Rights,* 19, pp. 595–612.

Walzer, M., 1994, *Thick and Thin: Moral Argument at Home and Abroad,* University of Notre Dame Press, Notre Dame.

Walzer, M., 1995, *Toward a Global Civil Society,* Berghahn Books, Providence.

Ward, H., 2012, 'Committing to the Future We Want: A High Commissioner for Future Generations at Rio+20, Discussion Paper.

Warschauer, M., 2004. *Technology and Social Inclusion: Rethinking the Digital Divide.* Cambridge: MIT Press.

Weber, M., 1978, *Economy and Society: An Outline of Interpretative Sociology,* (2 vols.) UCLA Press, Berkeley.

Weisman, J., 2012, 'After an Online Firestorm, Congress Shelves Antipiracy Bills', *New York Times.* 20 January.

Weiss, L., Thurton, E., and Mathews, J., 2005, 'How to Kill a Country: The US-Australia Free Trade Agreement', Evatt Foundation Paper, Sydney.

Western Australian Government, 2013, *Mineral and Petroleum Industry 2013 Review: Latest Statistics Release,* Department of Mines and Petroleum, Perth .http://www.dmp.wa.gov.au/1525.aspx.

Whispering Gums, 2014, 'Neomad: A Yijala Yala Project', 9 March, http://whisperinggums.com/2014/03/09/neomad-a-yijala-yala-project.

White, S., 2009, 'The Sovietization of Russian Politics', (with Olga Kryshtanovskaya), *Post-Soviet Affairs*, 25:4, pp. 283–309.

White, J., 2013, 'Thinking Generations', *The British Journal of Sociology*, 64:2, pp. 216–246.

Whitehead, A. N. 1929, *Process and Reality*, Macmillan, New York.

Willetts, D., 2011, *The Pinch – How Baby-Boomers Took Their Children's Future, and Why They Should Give it Back*, Atlantic Books, London.

Williams, E. C., 2009, 'We Are the Crisis', *Socialism and/or Barbarism* (blog), September 24, http://socialismandorbarbarism.blogspot.com/2009/09/we-are-crisis.html.

Williamson, J., Watts-Roy, D., and Kingston, J., 1999, (eds.) *The Generational Equity Debate*, Columbia University Press, New York.

Williamson, T., 2000, *Knowledge and Its Limits*, Oxford University Press, Oxford.

Winograd, M., and Hais, M. D., 2011, *Millennial Momentum: How a New Generation Is Remaking America*. Rutgers University Press, Piscataway.

Winterton, J. 2004. 'A Conceptual Model of Labour Turnover and Retention'. *Human Resource Development International*, 7:3, pp. 371–390.

Wittgenstein, L., 1953, *Philosophical Investigations*, Blackwell, Oxford.

Wolff, J., 2002, *Why Read Marx Today?* Oxford University Press, Oxford.

Woodman, D., 2013, 'Researching "Ordinary" Young People in a Changing World: The Sociology of Generations and the "Missing Middle" in Youth Research', *Sociological Research Online*, 18:1, p. 7, http://www.socresonline.org.uk/18/1/7.html.

Worth, S., and Adair, J., 1972, *Through Navajo Eyes*, Indiana University Press, Bloomington.

Wortham, J., 2012, 'A Political Coming of Age for The Tech Industry', *New York Times*. 17 January.

Wortham, J., 2012, 'Public Outcry over Anti-piracy Bills Began as Grassroots Grumbling', *New York Times*, 19 January,.

Xenos, M., and Foot, K., 2008, 'Not Your Father's Internet: The Generation Gap in Online Politics', in Bennett, L.W., (ed.), *Civic Life Online: Learning How Digital Media Can Engage Youth*. John D. and Catherine T. MacArthur Foundation Series on Digital Media and Learning. MIT Press, Cambridge.

Xuanming, Y., On the Unity of pluralistic Values, The Bases of Values in a Time of Change: Chinese and Western Studies, in Bunchua, K., Fangtong, xuanmeng, Wujin, Y., (eds), *The Bases of Values in a Time of Change: Chinese Philosophical Studies*, the Council for Research and Values, Washington. DC. XVI, p. 345.

Yeatman, A., 1994, 'Beyond Natural Rights: The Conditions of Universal Citizenship', in *Postmodern Revisings of the Political*, Routledge, New York.

Young-Bruehl, E., 2012, *Childism: Confronting Prejudice against Children*, Yale University Press, New Haven.

Young, I. M., 2000, *Inclusion and Democracy*, Oxford University Press, Oxford.

Zadeh, L., 1965, 'Fuzzy Sets and Systems Theory'. *Information and Control*, 8, pp. 338–353.

Zeichner, K., 2010, 'Competition, Economic Rationalization, Increased Surveillance, and Attacks on Diversity: Neo-liberalism and the Transformation of Teacher Education in the U.S.', *Teaching and Teacher Education*, 28:8, pp. 1544–1552.

Zemke, R., Raines, C., and Filipczak, B., 2000, *Generations at Work: Managing the Class of Veterans, Boomers, X-ers, and Nexters in Your Workplace.* Amacon, New York.

Žižek, S., 2012, 'The True Blasphemy', 7 August, http://chtodelat.wordpress. com/2012/08/07/the-true-blasphemy-slavoj-zizek-on-pussy-riot/.

Zizek, S., 2013, 'Dear Nadezhda, Nadezhda Tolokonnikova of Pussy Riot's Prison Letters to Slavoj Zizek', *The Guardian*, 16 November, http://www.theguardian. com/music/2013/nov/15/pussy-riot-nadezhda-tolokonnikova-slavoj-zizek.

Zody R., 1970, 'Generations and the Development of Political Behaviour', *Politics*, 5:1, pp. 18–29.

Zukin, C., Keeter, S., Andolina, Michael, X., and Jenkins, K., 2006, *A New Engagement? Political Participation, Civic Life, and the Changing American Citizen,* Oxford University Press.

Zuquete, J. P., 2011, 'Another World Is Possible? Utopia Revisited', *New Global Studies*, 5:2, pp. 1–19.

Index

316   *Index*

Foucault, M., 36, 100, 181, 202, 248
framing, 86, 94–95, 97, 211–212, 214,
   235, 243, 248–249, 251, 277–278
Fraser, N., 30, 31, 35, 49, 148, 262,
   267, 269
free market, neoliberal idea of
   freedom, ,46, 99–119 120–121,
   123, 126, *see* globalization
freedom, 7, 40, 44, 48, 61, 62–63, 77,
   81, 128, 130, 138, 159, 161, 164,
   172, 191, 205, 217, 225–226,
   253, 262–264, *see* Arendt;
   autonomy
   from coercion, 149, 180, 199, 201,
      214, 217, 261
   of expression, 2, 157, 158, 205,
      220, 227
   liberal notion, 150
   positive freedom, 81, 151, 203
   of speech, 1, 2, 6, 17, 21, 204, 206,
      213, 214
Freud, S., 46, 72, 78, 194, 272
Froomkin, M., 33
Fukuyama, F., 10, 37
functionalist, structural functionalist,
   45, 55, 64, 87, 88, 96, 98, 100,
   101
Furlong, A., and Cartmel R., 4, 7, 123
fuzzy categories, 16, 104, 105, 106,
   111, 118, 140, 142, 275

gate keepers, 32, 146, 149, 162
generation
   Gen X, Generation X, 82–84, 106,
      133, 134, 264
   Gen Y, 7, 82, 83–85, 101, 104–105,
      131, 133, 264
   gender, 31, 64, 109, 120, 157, 263,
      291
   generalizations, 97, 100, 109, 112,
      114, 135, *see* stereotypes
   generation baby boomers, 6, 82–83,
      103, 104, 109, 133
   generation, digital natives, 5, 7,
      14, 117
   generation gap, 85, 97
   generation, lost generation, 178
   generation, millenials, 7

generation, social category, concept
   of generation, 5, 7, 15–16, 49, 63,
   79, 81, 84, 87–135, 142–144, 264,
   273–275, *see* zeitgeist
generational change, 15, 51–81,
   82–108, 110, 222, 264, 273
generational conflict, 86, 94, 97
generational politics, 3, 5–7, 16–17,
   38, 49–50, 63, 71, 84–85, 97, 101,
   103, 137, 165–171, 177–181,
   188–189, 205, 210, 221–222, 236,
   241–242, 276
generational unit, 92, 93, 94, 111,
   135
generational units, antagonistic
   generational units, 84, 92, 111,
   see Mannheim
Gerbaudo, P., 223–224, 292
Geuss, R., 35, 113, 148
Giroux, H., 101, 186
global financial crisis, 2008, 133, 144,
   227
globalization, globalizing, 111–112,
   118–119, 126, 132, 135, 156,
   194, 253
Goffman, E., 127, 277
Gould, S. J., 137, 138
graduates, 22, 112, 120, 124,
   177–203, 223
graduates without a future, 112, 120,
   see unemployed
group think, 146, 191–192

Habermas, J., 11–15, 22–38, 49, 136,
   138, 141, 145–150, 181, 190,
   192–193, 195, 198–199, 209, 253,
   267, 269, 271–272
habitus, 61, 65–70, 80, 86, 108, 120,
   139, 144, 193, 223, 237
hackers, 207, 228, 302, *see* hacktivist
Hacking, I., 100, 106, 142
hacktivist, 1, 9, *see* hackers
Hall G. Stanley, 87
Hegel, G. F. W., 31 49, 54, 57–58, 67,
   139, 270, 273, 274, 284
hermeneutic, 91, 92–93, 253, 273
heteronomous, 40–41, 46, 73–75, 80,
   150–151
heuristic, 49, 136–152